4r 1983

By the same author

The Penguin Guide to
Sea Fishing in Britain and
Ireland

compiled by Ted Lamb

The Penguin Guide to Freshwater Fishing in Britain and Ireland

for coarse and game anglers

ALLEN LANE

ALLEN LANE
Penguin Books Ltd
536 King's Road
London SW10 0UH

First published 1983

British Library Cataloguing in Publication Data
Lamb, Ted
    The Penguin guide to freshwater fishing in
    Britain and Ireland.
    1. Fishing – Great Britain – History
    I. Title
    639'.21'09   SH255

    ISBN 0-7139-1572-2

Set in Monophoto Univers
Printed in Great Britain by
Richard Clay (The Chaucer Press) Ltd, Bungay, Suffolk

*To my wife Catherine, and
Zebedee and Octavia*

Contents

Acknowledgements

The author wishes to thank the many people who supplied information for this guide, not least the water authorities of England and Wales, the official tourism and fishery bodies in Northern and Southern Ireland, and the clubs throughout the British Isles who sent in much detailed and useful information. The many others who helped I cannot detail, but I hope a simple thank you will suffice.

Introduction

I wrote in the introduction to *The Penguin Book of Fishing* that we live in a group of islands well blessed with fishing waters of every description, and that luckily few anglers have to travel very far from home in search of good sport.

Nevertheless, there is a need for a comprehensive guide to angling waters. Variety of fishing experiences and contrasts of landscape draw the angler to seek enjoyment further afield, and family holidays take enthusiasts into unfamiliar territory which demands exploration with rod and line. Additionally all anglers, but beginners especially, will want to be well versed in the range of fishing that exists within the smaller compass of home.

This guide is designed to open the gate to many pleasurable experiences, from fishing in lush Southern English watermeadows to the remoter tarns and the tumbling rivers of the uplands, from quiet carp pools to huge reservoirs, the die-straight drains under broad skies of the Somerset and East Anglian flatlands, and the distinctive charm of gently curving canals.

To fulfil this purpose it has to be mindful that freshwater fishing is rule-bound, and that questions need to be answered about rod licences and the ownership of fishing rights in order to buy or ask for permission to fish.

The guide also needs to be aware that the travelling angler wants to see at a glance waters that can be fished with a day permit or a weekly permit, avoiding those which require more costly annual or season tickets, or full club membership.

Symbols used throughout this book, in the maps and in the text, mark these distinctions; a full list of the symbols and abbreviations is given on page 24 below.

On the question of costs, the guide cannot be specific. This is because they vary widely from place to place, and in any event they fluctuate considerably according to the vicissitudes of the economy. Figures given when going to press might be altogether different a week later. However, it is safe to say that the angler might have to pay a considerable amount for good salmon or sea-trout fishing – several hundred pounds for a week's fishing in exceptional areas – and somewhat less for trout angling. Coarse fishing is usually cheapest of all, but as with the other categories the cost can vary greatly according to the quality of the stock and the reputation of performance.

Salmon, sea-trout and trout fishing can be had for a few pounds a day – this charge by and large reflecting the quality of the water but in some instances remoteness and difficulty of access — while coarse fishing can vary from, say, 25p a day to fish a municipal pool to £2 and more to fish the highly regarded rivers of Hampshire and Dorset. And there are still some free fisheries.

The chapters which precede the Gazetteer explain how to seek and/or buy permission to fish; describe the regulations about close seasons and size limits; and give in full the Water Authorities' regulations and the details of the types of rod licences available for fishing in England, Wales, the Isle of Man and Northern Ireland. There are also notes on regulations regarding fishing in Eire and Scotland, where the picture is somewhat different.

An appendix gives addresses of angling organizations and clubs in the British Isles.

This freshwater guide for game and coarse fishermen complements *The Penguin Guide to Sea Fishing*, and all-rounders will find both books useful for planning their fishing.

Finally I would like to make a special appeal to anglers to respect the places in which they fish, to do nothing that will damage crops or harm livestock or wildlife, and to take all litter and discarded tackle home. The anglers who follow you will thank you for this.

Setting out to Fish

The following four checks should be made to cover legal requirements before setting out to fish any water.

1. Do I need a rod licence?

Almost invariably the answer is yes for all species in England, Wales, the Isle of Man and Northern Ireland, but in some fisheries the cost of a rod licence is incorporated in the permit price. This is particularly true of some water-authority-run reservoir trout fisheries. In the Gazetteer 'Rod licence incl.' denotes this. Some tidal stretches may also be outside water authority jurisdiction. No rod licences are needed to fish in Scotland, and no licence is needed for brown trout or coarse fish in Eire.

2. Do I need to pay for fishing?

It is necessary to check who owns the fishing rights of any water and seek or pay for permission to fish. Ownership and control usually falls into one of the following categories.

Free fishing
(N B. This means an appropriate rod licence must be bought beforehand, save for fishing in Scotland and fishing for brown trout and coarse fish in Eire, unless the water is out of authority jurisdiction.) These fisheries are rare in England and Wales now, but some still exist, particularly in towns or villages where public walks, towpaths and parks border a water. Some are limited to local anglers only. In Scotland, Eire and Northern Ireland, there is much free coarse and trout fishing and some free salmon and sea-trout fishing.

Farmer- or landowner-controlled
Some free fishing is for the asking, but, like the above category, it is becoming rare. It must never be assumed that a water which appears neglected can be fished without obtaining permission in advance, for you may break poaching and trespass laws.

Daily or weekly ticket fisheries

Private owners, clubs and associations, municipal authorities and water authorities are included in this category, which is the most important grouping from the visiting angler's point of view. With occasional exceptions a fee for fishing must be paid in advance.

Annual or seasonal subscription fisheries

Clubs and associations which offer an annual or seasonal permit but no daily or weekly openings make up most of this category, with some private concerns working on the same basis. Obviously this could prove expensive if only a short visit to the water in question is envisaged, but if you intend to fish it several times a year then the subscription makes good sense – the more you fish, the cheaper your fishing becomes.

Hotel fisheries

Some waterside hotels reserve local fishing rights for residents, and this is especially true of some good salmon beats. Occasionally the facilities are offered to anglers who are not guests at the hotel.

Private or restricted fisheries

These are club, syndicate or individually owned waters where there exist no chances for the freelance angler, or where long waiting lists make applications to join impractical. They are therefore outside the province of this guide, but are mentioned occasionally if they adjoin an accessible stretch to give some insight into the quality of fishing. Occasionally in this category members are allowed to give a guest access to the water. A personal approach to a member will be necessary.

3. Is a close season in force?

You cannot fish for certain species of fish when a close season, serving to protect spawning fish, is in force. There are national close seasons for England and Wales – salmon: 1 November–31 January; trout: 1 October– last day of February; coarse fish: 15 March–15 June (all dates inclusive) – but these serve only as guidelines and are varied by water authorities to suit fishing in their area; they may be further changed by clubs or fishery controllers (where this applies, details are given in the text).

In Northern and Southern Ireland and in Scotland, there are restrictions for game fishing only. Anglers are urged to study the next chapter for full details before setting out to fish.

4. Are there any other restrictions?

Fishery controllers may apply their own rules to their waters, such as fly fishing only, or even dry fly fishing only on many trout waters, and bans on certain baits, groundbait, and use of keepnets on coarse waters. These, where known, are noted in the text, but it is always advisable to check when you buy your permit if there are special restrictions.

Anglers are also warned that agricultural disease control may put waters out of bounds (as, say, in an outbreak of foot and mouth disease). Outbreaks of fish disease may also make emergency restrictions necessary.

Finding details

Rod licences, close seasons
The details of all water authority areas and the range of rod licences applicable to them are given in the next chapter, together with the close seasons operating in water-authority-controlled areas, Scotland, Ireland and the Isle of Man.

Rod licences are generally sold through tackle dealers in the area where they are operative, and in some cases through post offices and fishery agents. In all cases they may be bought direct from the authority concerned, enclosing a stamped, self-addressed envelope with the appropriate fee and full details of the licence required and the dates for which you want to be covered. An initial inquiry may be necessary to find what the licence currently costs.

Club changes in close seasons, where known, are given below in the individual entry concerned.

Permission or fee to fish
With free fisheries you need do little more than check that rights have not changed, buy the appropriate rod licence, and then fish. Similarly, permission granted by a farmer or landowner by word of mouth is quite satisfactory, although if a charge is made it might be wise to ask for a receipt. Again, a rod licence is necessary unless the landowner has a special dispensation to waive it.

For daily and weekly permits, written evidence should always be asked for and kept until you are clear of the fishery. Unless tickets are sold on the site (where known, this is mentioned in the guide), the angler must seek out the ticket seller or his agents and purchase the permit in advance of fishing. In many instances, particularly with clubs, local tackle shops will be the agents (this also applies to most annual or seasonal club memberships). Wherever possible, details of where to buy permits are given below; all clubs mentioned in the text are listed with addresses in the list of angling clubs and associations at the end of the book.

A telephone call to a hotel offering fishing will ascertain whether there are chances for non-guests. Even a hotel in which you plan to stay may have to limit the number of rods it can allow to fish its beat comfortably, so it is advisable to say that you wish to fish when you make a reservation.

Water Authorities and Regulations

This chapter includes the regulations for fishing in Scotland, the Isle of Man and Northern and Southern Ireland, but the water authorities of England and Wales are dealt with first, in alphabetical order.

Close seasons stipulated by the authorities are given, but it should be noted that there are sometimes circumstances where they do not apply or where they are altered, usually for enclosed still-water fisheries. Entries in the guide state this fact where it applies, while for all other entries it must be assumed that water authority close seasons, in the case of England and Wales, and other statutory close seasons in Scotland and Northern and Southern Ireland and the Isle of Man, are in force (in Southern Ireland, Scotland, and a few English and Welsh areas, e.g. the South-West Water Authority region, there is no coarse fish close season).

All dates given for close seasons are inclusive.

Most full rod licences are annual (i.e. running from 1 January to 31 December but excluding relevant close seasons), though some are seasonal, running from the end of the appropriate close season to its restart, and some are for the term of the fiscal year, 1 April–31 March.

Part-licences come in a variety of forms and all are mentioned below.

Fishing in England and Wales

Anglian Water Authority, Ambury Road, Huntingdon, Cambs. (Tel. Huntingdon 56181.)

Close seasons:

Salmon, sea-trout, rainbow trout and brown trout not in enclosed waters: 29 September–28/29 February.

Rainbow trout and brown trout in enclosed waters: 30 October–31 March.

Coarse fish (including eels): 15 March–15 June.

Rod licences:

The authority issues a blanket regional rod licence for fishing for all species and in all waters within its region, and it also offers divisional licences, for all species, covering groups of rivers, tributaries and lakes falling within its geographical catchment areas. A concessionary annual regional licence is available for men and women of pensionable age and juveniles aged twelve to fifteen. Children under twelve do not need a licence.

Divisional licences permit catching all species in the areas specified below – if you restrict your fishing to the division you need not pay more for the regional licence. Annual, seven-day, and annual concessionary divisional licences are available. The divisions are as follows:

1. Lincolnshire Division: The rivers Ancholme and Witham and their tributaries, all waters running into the sea between Whitton on the River Humber and the Witham estuary, and still waters within the catchment.

2. Welland and Nene Division: Rivers Glen, Welland and Nene and their tributaries, plus still waters in these catchments.

3. Great Ouse Division: Rivers Great Ouse, Babingley and Ingol with tributaries, the Heacham River and tributaries, plus still waters in catchment.

4. Norfolk and Suffolk Division: Rivers Yare, Wensum, Bure, Waveney, Orwell and Gipping with tributaries, waters running into the sea between Hunstanton and the Orwell estuary, plus still waters.

5. Essex Division: River Stour, Mar Dyke and tributaries, waters entering sea between the Thames and Stour estuaries, and still waters within the catchment.

Northumbrian Water Authority, Regent Centre, Gosforth, Newcastle on Tyne. (Tel. Gosforth 843151.)

Close seasons:

Salmon: 1 November–31 January.

Sea-trout: 1 November–2 April.

Brown trout, rivers and streams: 1 October–21 March.

Brown trout, lakes and reservoirs (subject to occasional alteration): 1 November–30 April.

Coarse fish (including eels): 15 March–15 June.

Rod licences:

Annual or fourteen-day licences are available for: (1) salmon, sea-trout, coarse fish and eels; (2) trout, excluding sea-trout, including coarse fish and eels.

An annual licence only is available for coarse fish (including eels).

Concessionary licences are available in all these categories for pensionable-age people and juveniles under sixteen years.

North-West Water Authority, New Town House, Buttermarket Street, Warrington, Cheshire. (Tel. Warrington 53999.)

Close seasons:

Salmon: 1 November–31 January, except in:

1. River Eden and all lakes and tributaries connected: 15 October–14 January.

2. Rivers Annas, Bleng, Esk, Mite, Irt, Calder and Ehen, and all tributaries and lakes connected: 1 November–31 March.

3. Rivers Derwent, Ellen, Waver and Wampool, tributaries and lakes connected: 1 November–14 February.

Sea-trout: In the rivers Annas, Bleng, Esk, Mite, Irt, Calder and Ehen: 1 November–30 April. Others: 16 October–30 April.

Brown trout, char (excluding rainbow trout): 1 October–14 March.

Coarse fish (excluding eels): 15 March–15 June.

Rod licences:

Salmon: Annual, part-year (from 1 June to end of season) and seven-day licences available. Part-year ticket covers fishing for all other species for whole year.

Sea-trout: Annual and seven-day licences.

Brown trout, rainbow trout, char and coarse fish (including eels): Annual and seven-day licences.

Concessionary licences in all categories for pensionable-age people, registered disabled and juniors aged fourteen to sixteen. Juveniles under fourteen need no licence.

Severn-Trent Water Authority, Abelson House, 2297 Coventry Road, Sheldon, Birmingham B26 3PR. (Tel. Birmingham (021) 743 4222.)

Close seasons:

Salmon: 1 October–1 February.

Sea-trout: 1 October–15 March.

Brown trout, Severn catchment: 16 October–17 March.

Brown trout, Trent catchment: 1 October–17 March.

Rainbow trout: In the rivers Derwent and Amber, including tributaries, upstream of confluence at Ambergate (excluding Wye from Blackwell Mill to Cressbrook Mill, and lakes formed by dams in these watercourses): 16 November–15 May. No close season elsewhere.

Coarse fish (excluding eels): 15 March–15 June.

Rod licences:

Salmon, Severn catchment: Annual and one-day (also entitles holder to fish for salmon in the Trent catchment and sea-trout, trout, coarse fish and eels in both Severn and Trent catchments).

Trout, coarse fish and eels (for both catchments – separate licences no longer exist): Annual and twenty-eight-day licences.

Reduced block licences for trout (excluding sea-trout), coarse fish and eels for parties of twenty or more persons available on application to the authority.

Concessionary licences for state pensioners, registered disabled, and juveniles aged twelve to sixteen available for Severn catchment salmon licence and annual trout, coarse fish and eels licence. Children under twelve need no licence.

Southern Water Authority, Guildbourne House, Chatsworth Road, Worthing, West Sussex. (Tel. Worthing 205252.)

Close seasons:

Salmon: 3 October–16 January.

Sea-trout: 1 November–30 April.

Brown trout, rainbow trout: 1 November–2 April.
Coarse fish (including eels): 15 March–15 June.

Rod licences:
Salmon (holder also covered for sea-trout, trout, coarse fish and eels): Annual, fourteen-day and one-day licences available.
Sea-trout, trout (covers for coarse fish and eels): Annual and fourteen-day licences available.
Coarse fish (including eels): Annual and fourteen-day licences.
Reduced annual licences are available to all juvenile anglers under sixteen to fish for sea-trout and trout (covering coarse fish), and to fish for coarse fish (including eels) alone. Coarse fishing is free for pensioners and registered disabled.
Rod licences cover one rod only, but one other rod may be used for a small additional charge.

South-West Water Authority, 3–5 Barnfield Road, Exeter, Devon. (Tel. Exeter 31666.)

Close seasons:
Salmon: Avon* river, 1 December–14 April; remainder of Avon district, 1 November–14 March; Axe, 1 November–14 March; Camel, 16 December–31 March; Plym, Yealm*, 16 December–31 March; remainder of Plym and Yealm district and Tamar and district, 15 October–28/29 February; Dart*, 17 September–31 January; Fowey, 16 December–31 March; Lyn, 1 November–31 January; Taw and Torridge, 1 October–28/29 February; Teign*, 1 October–31 January.
Sea-trout: Avon*, 1 October–14 April; Axe, 1 November–14 April; Camel, Fowey, 1 October–31 March; Tamar, Plym, 1 October–2 March; Teign, 13 October–14 March; other rivers, 1 October–14 March.
Brown trout: Rivers and streams, 1 October–14 March; enclosed waters, 13 October–14 March.
Rainbow trout: No close season.
Coarse fish: No close season.

Rod licences:
Salmon and sea-trout: Annual, week and day licences available (cover user for trout and coarse fishing).
Brown trout, rainbow trout: Annual, week and day licences (cover user for coarse fishing).
Coarse fish (including eels): Annual licence only.
Concessionary salmon annual, salmon day, trout annual and coarse fish annual licences available for old-age pensioners, juveniles aged ten to sixteen, full-time students under the age of eighteen, and registered disabled. Children under ten years need no licences.

---

* Rivers marked with an asterisk have been given temporary experimental close seasons, and the dates are liable to change.

Thames Water Authority, Reading Bridge House, Reading, Berks. (Tel. Reading 593333.)

Close seasons:
Salmon and trout, including rainbow trout in rivers: 1 October–31 March.
Rainbow trout in enclosed waters: No close season.
Coarse fish (including eels): 15 March–15 June. Eel fishing permitted in close season in tidal Thames below Thames Barrier.

Rod licences (N B. Applies to tidal Thames above line from Crowe Stone, Southend, to Yantlet Creek, Kent bank):
All fish, including eels: Annual (N B. valid 1 April–31 March) and fifteen-day licences available.
Concessionary licences (annual only) for juveniles twelve to fifteen years inclusive, old-age pensioners and registered disabled. No licence needed by children under twelve years.

Welsh Water Authority, Cambrian Way, Brecon, Powys. (Tel. Brecon 3181.)
In this large administrative area the authority has created seven divisions in which close seasons show some variance.

Divisions and their close seasons:

Dee and Clwyd Division:
Salmon: Dee and tributaries, 18 October–25 January; Clwyd and tributaries, 18 October–19 March.
Sea-trout: 18 October–19 March.
Brown trout: Rivers, 1 October–2 March; still waters except Lake Bala, 18 October–19 March; Lake Bala, 15 August–14 January.
Rainbow trout: Rivers, 1 October–2 March; still waters, no close season.
Coarse fish: 15 March–15 June.
Eels: No close season this division.

Gower Division:
Salmon: 18 October–19 March.
Sea-trout: 18 October–19 March.
Brown trout: Rivers, 1 October–2 March; still waters, 18 October–19 March.
Rainbow trout: Rivers, 1 October–2 March; still waters, no close season.
Coarse fish (including eels): 15 March–15 June.

Gwynedd Division:
Salmon: 18 October–19 March.
Sea-trout: 18 October–19 March.
Brown trout: Rivers, 1 October–2 March; lakes, 18 October–19 March, except Trawsfynydd Lake, 1 September–28/29 February.

Rainbow trout: Rivers, 1 October–2 March; still waters, no close season.
Coarse fish and eels: No close season this division.

Taff Division:
 Salmon: 18 October–19 March.
 Sea-trout: 18 October–19 March.
 Brown trout: Rivers, 1 October–2 March, except River Taff between entry
of Afon Hydfron and sea, 1 September–31 January; lakes, 18 October–19
March.
 Rainbow trout: Rivers, 1 October–2 March; lakes, no close season.
 Coarse fish (including eels): 15 March–15 June.

Usk Division:
 Salmon: 18 October–25 January.
 Sea-trout: 18 October–19 March.
 Brown trout: Rivers, 1 October–2 March; lakes, 18 October–19 March.
 Rainbow trout: Rivers, 1 October–2 March; lakes, no close season.
 Coarse fish (including eels): 15 March–15 June, except eels only in Usk
below George Street, Newport, no close season.

West Wales Division:
 Salmon: 18 October–19 March.
 Sea-trout: 18 October–19 March.
 Brown trout: Rivers, 1 October–2 March, except River Rheidol between
Penybont Bridge and sea and River Ystwyth between Gosen Bridge and
sea, 1 September–31 January; lakes, 18 October–19 March.
 Rainbow trout: Rivers, 1 October–2 March; lakes, no close season.
 Coarse fish (including eels): 15 March–15 June.

Wye Division:
 Salmon: Main river and tributaries above Llanwrthwl Bridge, 26 October–
25 January; below bridge, main river and tributaries, 18 October–25
January.
 Sea-trout: 18 October–19 March.
 Brown trout: Rivers, 1 October–2 March; lakes, 18 October–19 March.
 Rainbow trout: Rivers, 1 October–2 March; lakes, no close season.
 Coarse fish: 15 March–15 June.
 Eels: No close season in this division.

Rod licences:
 Faced with the administrative difficulty of issuing licences for a wide
range of game fishing in a huge area, the authority has classified rivers
according to quality of fishing, with separate charges for good, moderate
and less productive waters.
 These used to be on the alphabetical scale A–E, but since 1980 the B-
class rivers have been amalgamated with those of class C, making the scale
A, C, D, E.
 Since the charges reflect the quality of salmon and sea-trout fishing, the
full list of rivers and their classifications appears below. As an example of

the relative charges for each class, in 1980 a season permit for salmon and sea-trout on class A water cost £37.25; class C, £18.65; class D, £12.40; and class E, £9.80 (N B. some rivers fall in more than one classification).

Class A: River Wye below Llanwrthwl Bridge (see also class C).

Class C: Conwy, main river between Conwy Falls and Dolgarrog (see also class D); Dee, main river below River Alwen junction (see also class D); Dovey, main river (see class D); Teifi, main river below Lampeter Bridge; Towy, main river below Brianne Dam (see class D); Cothi, main river below Aberbranddu Falls; Usk, entire main river; Wye, main river above Llanwrthwl Bridge (see class A).

Class D: Aeron, entire main river; Alwen, entire main river; East Cleddau, entire main river; West Cleddau, entire main river; Clwyd, entire main river; Conwy (see class C); Lledr, entire main river; Llugwy, main river below Swallow Falls; Dee, between Bala Sluices and Alwen confluence (and excluding class C water); Dwyfawr, entire main river; Dwyryd, main river below Rhydysarn; Dovey tributary Twymyn, entire main river; Dulas North, entire main river; Dulas South, entire main river; Cleifon, entire main river; Dysynni, main river below Bont Abergynolwyn; Eden, main river below Bont Dolgefeilau; Elwy, entire main river; Glaslyn, entire main river including Llynnoedd Dinas and Gwynant; Gwyrfai, entire main river; Llyfni, entire main river; Loughor, entire main river; Mawddach, entire main river; Neath, main river below confluence with River Mellte; Nevern, entire main river; Ogmore, main river below confluence of main Ogwr Fawr and Ogwr Fach; Ogwen, entire main river; Rheidol, main river below Cyfarllwyd Falls; Seiont, entire main river including Llynnoedd Padarn and Peris; Taff, entire main river; Towy (except class C water); Gwili, entire main river; Wnion, entire main river; Ystwyth, main river below Llanafan Bridge.

Class E: All rivers, tributaries and streams not named in the above classes.

(N B. Licences cover for all water classes below the main choice, but not for classes above.)

Salmon and sea-trout: Season, week and day licences available for all classes (also cover users for trout and coarse fishing).

Brown trout, rainbow trout and char: Season, week and day licences. These cover the whole WWA area and also entitle holders to fish for coarse fish and eels.

Coarse fish (including eels): Season, week and day licences available.

Annual permits only (for all classifications and groups of species) are available at concessionary prices for old-age pensioners and juveniles under sixteen years.

Wessex Water Authority, PO Box 9, King Square, Bridgwater, Somerset. (Tel. Bridgwater 57333.)

Close seasons:
    Salmon: Rivers Frome (Dorset) and Piddle in Avon and Dorset division, 1 October–28/29 February; all other waters, 1 October–31 January.
    Sea-trout: 1 November–14 April.

Brown trout, rainbow trout: Rivers, 16 October–31 March, except Avon (Hampshire) above Bickton Mill with tributaries (excluding Nadder above road bridge at Barford St Martin), 16 October–14 April; lakes and reservoirs, 16 October–23 March (no close season for enclosed waters stocked exclusively with rainbow trout).

Coarse fish: 15 March–15 June.

Rod licences:

Salmon: Annual, weekly or daily licences (cover users for sea-trout, trout and coarse fishing).

Sea-trout, brown trout, rainbow trout: Annual, weekly or daily licences (cover coarse fishing).

Coarse fish (including eels): Annual, weekly or daily.

Concessionary half-price licences for all species, groups and periods available for juveniles aged eleven to sixteen, persons of pensionable age and registered disabled people. Children under eleven years need no licence.

Yorkshire Water Authority, West Riding House, 67 Albion Street, Leeds LS1 5AA. (Tel. Leeds 448201.)

Close seasons:

Salmon and sea-trout: 1 November–5 April.

Trout: 1 October–24 March.

Coarse fish: 28 February–31 May.

Rod licences:

All species, entire region: Season and seven-day licences available.

All species, waters excluding Whitby Esk and tributaries and streams north of the Esk: Season and seven-day licences (the exclusion of the Esk reduces the cost against the general licence).

Concessionary licences available to pensioners, disabled people and children aged ten to thirteen inclusive. Children under ten years need no licence.

Fishing in the Isle of Man

Fishing in the island is controlled by the Isle of Man Board of Agriculture and Fisheries, Government Offices, Douglas, IoM. (Tel. Douglas 3995.)

Close seasons:

Salmon: 1 November–9 March.

Trout: 1 October–9 March.

No specific close seasons are laid down for sea-trout or coarse fish, but it is assumed sea-trout are classed with brown trout. Coarse times are at the discretion of the fishery controller.

Rod licences:

All freshwater species: Season and fourteen-day licences available.

Concessionary licences, season and fourteen-day, available for children under thirteen years.

Fishing in Scotland

Fishing in Scotland differs from fishing in England and Wales in that there are no rod licences as such. Instead permission must be obtained from the controller or riparian owner of the fishery concerned, which usually means paying an appropriate fee in the case of salmon and sea-trout fishing. Some trout fishing and most coarse fishing is free, but permission must still be sought from the controller or riparian owner, who has complete discretion over allowing anybody to fish.

Close seasons:

There are close seasons for salmon, sea-trout, and brown trout (none for rainbow trout, but the controller can make his own restrictions), and none for coarse fish.

Salmon, sea-trout: Differing statutory close seasons apply to individual rivers, and these are given in the guide entries as open period – i.e. the time during which fishing is allowed. Controllers may shorten these open periods at their discretion but they cannot lengthen them; where altered open periods are known to be in force, the guide notes them. N B. No person may fish for salmon or sea-trout *anywhere in Scotland* on a Sunday.

Brown trout: Statutory close season for the whole of Scotland is 7 October–14 March. While there is no statutory rule against fishing on Sunday for trout, a ban is quite often applied. Again, where this information is supplied, it is given in the guide. Where no specified close season is given for trout and it is assumed that the statutory close season applies, it is still advisable to check that the water is open before your trip.

There are no statutory close seasons for either rainbow trout or coarse fish, but again, controllers may impose their own limits; where such information has been given, it appears in the guide. The same caveat on Sunday fishing for brown trout applies to rainbow trout and coarse fishing.

Any trip to Scotland should be preceded by a call or letter to the fishery concerned to ensure that the water is open for fishing. The entries in this guide are subject to change by fishery controllers, and it is better to be safe than make a fruitless trip.

Fishing in Northern Ireland

Close seasons and rod licences in Northern Ireland are controlled by two bodies, the Fisheries Conservancy Board, 21 Church Street, Portadown, Co. Armagh, and the Foyle Fisheries Commission, 8 Victoria Road, Londonderry. The relevant details are given with individual entries in the guide.

Close seasons, Fisheries Conservancy Board area:

Salmon, sea-trout, brown trout: Lough Erne system, including River Erne, 16 October–28/29 February; Lough Melvin, 16 October–31 January; River Bush, 1 October–28/29 February; all other waters, 1 November–28/29 February.

Rainbow trout: No close season in specially designated rainbow trout fisheries.

Coarse fish: No close season.

Close seasons, Foyle Fisheries Commission area:

Salmon, sea-trout, brown trout: Rivers Foyle and Finn, 16 September–13 March; all other waters, 21 October–31 March.

Coarse fish: No close season.

Rod licences, Conservancy Board:

Salmon, sea-trout, trout: Annual and fifteen-day licences available (cover users for coarse fishing).

Coarse fish: Annual and fifteen-day licences.

Rod licences, Foyle Fisheries Commission area:

Salmon, sea-trout, trout: Season and seven-day licences available.

Coarse fish: No rod licence required.

Fishing in Southern Ireland

For administrative purposes the control of Irish fisheries has been delegated to seven Regional Fishery Boards (see page 229 below).

There is no close season for coarse fish in Southern Ireland.

Rod licences:

Salmon, sea-trout: Combined state licence needed. Season, twenty-one-day and seven-day licences are available covering all Southern Ireland, and season licences at a reduced cost are available to fish within an individual district. In addition, part-season licences from July to the season's end are available to fish the whole of Southern Ireland or individual fishery districts. If there is any difficulty in obtaining licences, which are sold in many tackle shops, contact the Central Fishery Authority, Earl's Island, Galway.

Brown trout: No licence needed, but in some areas, if methods are used which could catch salmon or sea-trout (e.g. spinning), then the cover of a game licence will be needed.

Coarse fish: No licence needed.

N B. Anglers are warned to be especially wary of taking their own bait to Ireland, where the Agriculture Ministry is anxious about importing plant, animal and fish diseases. The effect of this has sometimes seen worms, maggots and so on confiscated on arrival. As a general rule, it is wise to arrange in advance of your trip for bait to be supplied in the Republic (see page 229 below).

Symbols and Abbreviations used in the Gazetteer

It has been decided to use relatively few symbols in the Gazetteer so that the information does not become confusing and lead to constant reference to the key. One special symbol, ●, denoting a day-ticket still water offering fly fishing for trout, makes an easy reference for this popular and expanding branch of the sport.

The unbracketed symbols represent the types of fish the angler will find in a water, and those in brackets are abbreviations of other information:

T	Trout
ST	Sea-trout
S	Salmon
C	Coarse fish
●	Day-ticket fly-only still trout water
(DT)	Day ticket
(WT)	Weekly ticket
(Adv.)	Tickets/permission to be obtained in advance of fishing
(B)	Boat(s) or punt(s)
(MB)	Motor boat(s)
(L)	Number of rods per beat limited; thus 'L–5' = 5 rods only
(Rod licence incl.)	No extra rod licence required
yds	yards
m	mile(s)
WA	Water Authority

GAZETTEER

One

English Rivers
(including canals and land drains)

English rivers have been classified under the water authorities which control them to save constant reference to these bodies and to avoid a huge and unwieldy list of all English waters under one heading. With rivers, a county-by-county guide will not suffice, since in many instances the waters concerned cross one or more county boundaries, and under such an arrangement references would be repeated again and again. If the reader is unsure about which water authority controls the water he is interested in, the index will enable him to find it quickly.

Anglian Water Authority Rivers

The Anglian Water Authority controls a huge area, bordered in the north, at the Humber, by the Yorkshire Water Authority's area; in the west by the administrative area of the Severn–Trent Water Authority and in the south by the Thames Water Authority boundary.

The principal waters in this region are the easterly-flowing rivers draining the heart of England, with the exception of the Trent. To make administration easier and in order to offer the angler a cheaper rod licence to fish in parts only of this big area, the authority has created five divisions. The Lincolnshire Division consists of the rivers Ancholme and Witham and their tributaries, and all waters running into the sea between Whitton, on the Humber, and the Witham estuary.

The Welland and Nene Division covers the rivers Glen, Welland and Nene and their tributaries, and the Great Ouse Division covers the rivers Great Ouse, Babingley and Ingol with tributaries, plus the Heacham River. Into the above areas fall all the great land drainage systems of the Fens.

The fourth Anglian division is the Norfolk and Suffolk Rivers Division, which among other waters covers the great angling rivers of the Broads. Principal waters are the rivers Yare, Wensum, Bure, Waveney, Orwell and Gipping with tributaries, and waters running into the sea between Hunstanton and the Orwell estuary.

Finally there is the Essex Division, covering the River Stour, Mar Dyke and tributaries, and waters entering the sea between the Thames and Stour estuaries.

The Anglian Water Authority area as a whole is noted mainly for its superb coarse fisheries, many of the rivers lending themselves admirably to match fishing. There are some trout-only waters, mostly preserved, but the enthusiast will find trout in many rivers. While sea-trout enter many estuaries, they do not occur anywhere in sufficient numbers to make fishing for them worthwhile.

Ancholme

Much canalized in its lower reaches, where angling has improved enormously in recent years, the Ancholme runs through North Lincolnshire to join the Humber at Ferriby Sluice. Much of the upper river neglected and still not of much account.

Roach and bream predominate.

Ferriby Sluice, Lincs. 18 m to Brigg.

C (DT bank or Scunthorpe and Dist. AA).

Tributaries: East Drain, Rolands Drain.
Lincolnshire Rivers Division.

Ant
Rises Antingham, but main fisheries below Honing, after which it runs into Barton Broad and then on into Bure. Best stretches Irstead to Bure. A shallow water, much affected in summer by boats.

A noted bream river, also pike to 20 lb. Match records top 60 lb.

How Hill, Norfolk. ½ m below How Hill.
C (Free fishing).

Ludham, Norfolk. Ludham Bridge to Ant Mouth, left bank.
C (DT from tackle shops in area or Norwich AA, Adv.).

Wayford Bridge, Norfolk. Honing Lock to Bure except where access prevented.
C (Free fishing part of bank at Wayford and from boats to junction with Bure. M B Barton Broad).
Tributary of Bure system.
Norfolk and Suffolk Rivers Division.

Babingley River
Small river entering Ouse below King's Lynn. Private, no access for visiting anglers.

Bain
Rises Ludford and flows through Horncastle and Coningsby to Witham by Dogsdyke.
Mostly coarse, some trout upper reaches.

Coningsby, Lincs.
C (Some free water).
Tributary of Witham system.
Lincolnshire Rivers Division.

Bargate Drain (Maud Foster Drain)
Part of West Fen drainage system running from Cowbridge, north of Boston, to Witham outfall below Boston.

A good coarse water, especially for bream, with lengths suitable for matches.

Boston, Lincs. Right bank, entire water.

C (DT Boston AA or tackle shops, Adv.).
Lincolnshire Rivers Division.

Barling's Eau
Small water joining Witham at Branston Ferry.

Fair fishing for chub, dace, bream and some roach.

Branston Ferry, Lincs.
C (DT Lincoln and Dist. AA, Witham Joint Anglers Federation).
Tributary of Witham system.
Lincolnshire Rivers Division.

Bellwater Drain
Part of Boston drains system, branching from East Fen Catchwater near Stickney and running through Thorpe Fen to the Steeping River (permits as Bargate Drain, above).
Lincolnshire Rivers Division.

Bevill's Leam
Drain running from Tebbit's Bridge to Twenty-Foot River at Angle Bridge.

Excellent coarse water, especially for bream and roach. Suitable for match fishing.

Ponders Bridge, Cambs. Ponders Bridge to Twenty-Foot.
C (DT on bank or Adv. Anglian Water Authority).
Welland and Nene Rivers Division.

Billinghay Skirth
Drain running from North Kyme through Billinghay to Witham above Tattershall Bridge.

Good bream fishery, especially when Witham is high. Big pike.

Tattershall Bridge, Lincs. 3½ m above junction with Witham.
C (DT Adv. tackle shops or Witham Joint Anglers Federation).
Tributary of Witham system.
Lincolnshire Rivers Division.

Blackwater (Suffolk)
Rises near Bocking and runs through Maldon and on to North Sea. An excellent coarse fishery offering roach, bream and dace, but unfortunately associations control the entire river and there are no

day-ticket opportunities for visitors. Details of membership possibilities from club secretaries, Maldon A S, Braintree and Bocking A S, Kelvedon and District A A.

Tributaries: Can, Chelmer, Chelmer Navigation.

Box
Rises near Great Waldingfield and flows through Boxford to the Suffolk Stour.

Good trout water, mostly strictly preserved.

Stoke by Nayland, Essex ¾ m.

T fly only (D T Adv. Essex Rivers Division, Anglian Water Authority, 129 Springfield Road, Chelmsford. L–3 rods, usually heavily booked in advance).

Tributary of Suffolk Stour.

Branston Delph
Short drain running from east of Heighington to Witham near Branston Island.

Good coarse fishing.

Branston Booths, Lincs. 4 m Branston to Sincil Drain, Lincoln.

C (D T Adv. tackle shops or Witham Joint Anglers Federation and associate clubs).

Tributary of Witham system.

Lincolnshire Rivers Division.

Brant
Rises near Stragglethorpe and runs north to Witham near Auborn. Not a noted fishery, mostly private.

Broads Rivers
The main Broads rivers are entered under individual headings. See rivers Ant, Bure, Candle Dyke, River Chet, New Cut, rivers Thurne, Waveney and Wensum, Womack Water, River Yare.

Bure
In its lower reaches, one of the major waters of the Broads. The river rises in North Norfolk near Melton Constable, where it is a normal stream offering coarse and trout fishing. Most of this is private. Below Coltishall, the river becomes navigable and there is much free fishing for roach to 2 lb and big bream, especially at Coltishall itself and Horning and Wroxham. The latter two places offer extremely good winter fishing, and the river here also offers good pike. Below Acle the river becomes extremely strong and deep, and the tidal influence is a deterrent to the novice, although there are fish for the taking. The winter angler will also find good sport in the branching backwaters and boatyards of the lower river, where much of the fishing is free provided permission is sought.

Coltishall, Norfolk. Coltishall Common to Stokesby except where access is prohibited.

C (Free fishing).

Horning Ferry, Norfolk. ½ m to Woodbastwick.

C (Free fishing).

St Benet's Abbey, Norfolk. 2 m Ant mouth to Thurne mouth.

C (D T Adv. tackle shops in area or Norwich and Dist. A A).

South Walsham, Norfolk. Nearly 4 m Ant mouth to beyond Upton Dyke, including Upton Dyke and Fleet Dyke.

C (Free fishing).

Stokesby, Norfolk. Stokesby to sea.

C (Free fishing).

Bure tributaries: Ant, Candle Dyke, Thurne, Womack Water.

Norfolk and Suffolk Rivers Division.

Burwell Lode
Land drain running from Burwell to the River Cam at Upware.

Roach and bream, controlled by Cambridge Fish Preservation Society.

Burwell, Cambs. 4 m Burwell to junction with Cam, Upware.

C (D T Adv. from The Garage, 40 Causeway, Burwell, or T. Parsons, 24 The Avenue, Burwell).

Tributary of Great Ouse system.

Great Ouse Rivers Division.

Cam
The river rises near Letchworth and flows through Cambridge to join the Ouse at Stretham.

With some sections dredged and others shallow, it offers the angler a variety of conditions. Holds excellent bream stocks, which have led to some good match results, besides good roach and other coarse species.

Cambridge, Cambs. 5 m Edgware down to Fish and Duck Hotel.
C (DT Adv. Cambridge Albion AS).

Cambridge, Cambs. Grantchester Meadows.
C (Free fishing).

Clayhithe, Cambs. ¾ m Clayhithe Fishery.
C (DT Adv. Great Ouse Fishery Consultative Association).

Milton, Cambs. 2 m left bank Chesterton to Clayhithe.
C (DT Adv. keeper at Baits Bite Lock; T. Franklin, barber, High Street, Chesterton; tackle shop, 4 Ferry Lane, Chesterton, or Cambridge tackle shops).
Tributary of Great Ouse system.
Great Ouse Rivers Division.

Can

A tributary of the Suffolk Blackwater running through Chelmsford.
Fair coarse fishing.

Chelmsford, Essex. Sections of river bordering Central Park and Admiral's Park.
C (Free fishing).
Tributary of Blackwater (Suffolk) system.
Essex Rivers Division.

Candle Dyke

Connects the Thurne with Hickling Broad.
Huge shoals of bream often concentrated in this water.

Martham, Norfolk. Boat only access to bank fishing.
C (Free fishing). B, MB available Martham and Hickling).
Tributary of Bure system.
Norfolk and Suffolk Rivers Division.

Castle Dyke Drain

Part of the Boston drains system, it starts near New York and runs to join the Witham upstream of Boston.

Occasionally produces good catches of bream.

New York, Lincs. 8 m to Anton's Gowt.
C (DT tackle shops locally, Adv., or Boston AA).
Lincolnshire Rivers Division.

Chater

Rises near Halstead, Leicestershire, and runs to join Welland near North Luffenham. A fair coarse water but association-controlled, with no known openings for visitors.
Tributary of Welland system.
Welland and Nene Rivers Division.

Chelmer

One of the tributaries of the Suffolk Blackwater at Chelmsford.
Offers fair coarse fishing with some trout.

Chelmsford, Essex. Downstream of Victoria Road, Chelmsford, to junction of Can, also between 5th and 7th avenue, Broomfield Road.
C (Free fishing).

Hartford Mill, Essex. Small area near mill.
T, fly only (DT one angler at any time, so advance booking essential – Anglian Water Authority, 129 Springfield Road, Chelmsford).
Tributary of Blackwater (Suffolk).
Essex Rivers Division.

Chelmer Navigation

Largely canalized water offering good coarse fishing.

Chelmsford, Essex. Brown's Wharf to Sandford Mill Bridge, Stoneham's Lock to Rickett's Lock and from Beeleigh Lock to Hall Bridge, Heybridge.
C (DT Adv. from lock-keepers).

Sandford, Essex. 2 m from third lock, Sandford, to fifth lock, Stonehead.
C (DT Adv. from keeper, Myrtle Cottage).
Tributary of Blackwater (Suffolk) system.
Essex Rivers Division.

Chet
Rises near East Poringland and runs 10 m through Loddon to join the Yare above Reedham.

A good coarse fishery when in trim.

Loddon, Norfolk, 3 m left bank between Loddon and the Yare.
C (Free fishing).
Tributary of Yare system.
Norfolk and Suffolk Rivers Division.

Cock Bank Drain
Runs from Angle Bridge near Whittlesey, Cambs, to the old course of the River Nene at Flood's Ferry.

Good roach and bream fishing.

Whittlesey, Cambs. 2½ m of right bank from Angle Bridge.
C (D T on bank or Adv. Whittlesey A A).
Welland and Nene Rivers Division.

Colne (Essex)
Rises near Haverhill and runs to North Sea near Colchester.

Fair coarse fishing, but no known opportunities for visitors. Season tickets available from Colchester A P S, Colchester Piscatorial Society and Colnes A S.
Essex Rivers Division.

Coronation Channel
An excellent coarse water off the main Welland, although much is reserved for match fishing.

Predominantly roach and bream.

Spalding, Lincs. 2½ m between Cowbit Road and Marsh Road sluices.
C (D T tackle shop, Spalding, Adv., or Anglian Water Authority, North Street, Oundle).
Tributary of Welland system.
Welland and Nene Rivers Division.

Counter Drain
Starts near River Glen south of Bourne and follows river to Pinchbeck Common, then going on to Vernatt's Drain at Pode Hole.

Fair coarse fishery offering roach and bream.

Spalding, Lincs. Entire drain.
C (D T Adv. tackle shop, Hawthorn Bank, Spalding, or Spalding A A).
Welland and Nene Rivers Division.

Counterwash Drain
Not to be confused with Counter Drain (above) to north. Starts at Earith, running to Welches Dam.

A good coarse fishery offering mainly roach and bream.

Earith, Cambs. 3 m between Black Sluice and Sutton Gault.
C (D T Adv. Great Ouse Fishery Consultative Association).

Welches Dam, Cambs. Just over mile to Forprey's Farm, both banks.
C (D T Adv. Great Ouse Fishery Consultative Association).
Great Ouse Rivers Division.

Cut-Off Channel
Links the River Lark near Bury St Edmunds with the Relief Channel near Denver Sluice, and is one of the most recently constructed Fen drains. Fishing restricted in some parts through difficult banks.

Developing as a fine coarse fishery offering bream and roach, especially at Relief Channel end. Zander also caught, with big pike from time to time.

Hilgay, Norfolk. 5 m from Wissington Bridge to Relief Channel.
C (D T Adv. Bridge Stores, or tackle shops Downham Market and King's Lynn, or Anglian Water Authority, Great Ouse House, Clarendon Road, Cambridge).
Great Ouse Rivers Division.

Deben
Rises near Debenham and flows 30 m to sea at Felixstowe Ferry.

Fair coarse fishery.

Wickham Market, Suffolk. 2 m town bridge to Glevering Bridge.
C (D T Adv. Rod and Gun Shop, Woodbridge).
Essex Rivers Division.

Delph
Drain running from Welches Dam to Hundred-Foot Drain near Welney, partly parallel with Old Bedford River.

Roach, bream, pike and zander.

Manea, Cambs. 5 m Welches Dam to Stokes Bridge.

C (D T on bank, or Adv. Manea A C).

Welney, Norfolk. ½ m upstream Welney Bridge.

C (D T on bank).

Welney, Norfolk. 4 m Welney Bridge to Welmore Lake Sluice.

C (D T Adv. Three Holes Post Office, or F. Clarke, Bridge House, Welney).

Great Ouse Rivers Division.

East Drain

Drain running to Ferriby Sluice.

Fair coarse fishery offering roach, bream, some tench and pike.

Ferriby, Lincs. 1 m Horkstow Bridge to Ferriby Sluice.

C (D T on bank).

Tributary of Ancholme system.

Lincolnshire Rivers Division.

East Fen Catchwater

Starts at Little Steeping and runs to Sibsey Trader above Northlands Bridge.

Offers mainly roach and bream and is reserved for pleasure anglers only.

Stickford, Lincs. 6 m Stickford to Cherry Corner.

C (D T Adv. tackle shops, Boston, or Boston A A).

Lincolnshire Rivers Division.

Eye Brook

Drains Eyebrook Reservoir and joins Welland just below Caldecott.

Private trout fishing.

Tributary of Welland system.

Welland and Nene Rivers Division.

Fodder Dike

Runs from the Hobhole dyke through East Leake to Marfleet Bridge. One of the Boston system of drains, reserved for pleasure anglers only.

Offers mainly roach and bream.

Midville, Lincs. 4 m to Eastville, right bank.

C (D T Adv. tackle shops, Boston, or Boston A A).

Lincolnshire Rivers Division.

Folly River

With Car Dyke forms part of Roman canal joining Nene and Witham. The Folly is coverted to a drain and links Car Dyke to the Welland near Peakirk.

Roach, bream, some chub and dace.

Peakirk, Cambs. 2 m from Peakirk to Welland.

C (D T local tackle shops, or Anglian Water Authority, North Street, Oundle – both Adv.).

Tributary of Welland system.

Welland and Nene Rivers Division.

Forty-Foot Drain (or Ramsey Forty-Foot or Vermuden's Drain)

Begins at Ramsey and runs to north-east of Chatteris, entering Old Bedford River at Welches Dam.

Good, if shallow, coarse fishery with bream, roach, tench and pike. Has good match lengths but usually space for pleasure anglers. Stretches weedy in summer.

Chatteris, Cambs. 4½ m between Puddock Bridge and Horseway Sluice.

C (D T on bank or Adv. tackle shops in area).

Ramsey, Cambs. Nearly 3 m Puddock Bridge to Wells Bridge, road bank.

C (D T on bank or Adv. tackle shops in area).

Great Ouse Rivers Division.

Foss Dyke

Roman navigation channel joining Witham at Brayford Pool, Lincoln, with Trent at Torksey Lock.

Fair coarse fishing, mainly roach, bream and good pike from time to time.

Saxilby, Lincs. Entire water, access one bank only.

C (D T Adv. tackle shops or Witham Joint Anglers and associated clubs).

Tributary of Witham system.

Lincolnshire Rivers Division.

Frith Bank Drain

One of the Boston drains reserved for pleasure anglers, running from Cowbridge to Newham Drain near Frith Bank.

Louth Canal

Runs from Louth to North Sea below Tetney Lock.

Fishing worthwhile below Thoresby Bridge, where roach and bream are the main species.

Thoresby Bridge, Lincs. 5 m to Tetney.
C (D T Adv. tackle shops in area, or Witham Joint Anglers Federation).

Lud

Small river rising at Louth running into Louth Canal below town.

Stocked with trout in recent years. Access difficult in many parts as far as canal.

T (Free fishing where accessible).
Lincolnshire Rivers Division.

Martin Delph (Timberland Delph)

Starts south of Martin and joins the Witham below Kirkstead.

Good coarse fishing with roach and bream predominant, especially when Witham is high.

Timberland, Lincs. $2\frac{1}{2}$ m upstream from junction with Witham.
C (D T Adv. from tackle shops in area or from Witham Joint Anglers Federation and associate clubs).
Tributary of Witham system.
Lincolnshire Rivers Division.

Maxey Cut

A flood-relief branch of the Welland starting just below Tallington, and crossing Peterborough–Deeping road to re-enter river below Deeping St James and the Several Fishery.

Fair fishing for bream and roach, some chub.

Peakirk, Cambs. $5\frac{1}{2}$ m Peakirk to Tallington.
C (D T Adv. tackle shops in area or Anglian Water Authority, North Street, Oundle).
Tributary of Welland system.
Welland and Nene Rivers Division.

Medlam Drain

The northern branch of West Fen Drain in the Boston drains system centred on Cowbridge.

Roach and bream; reserved for pleasure anglers. Level can be low from autumn onwards.

Revesby, Lincs. 6 m running south to junction with West Fen.
C (D T Adv. tackle shops in area or Boston AA).
Lincolnshire Rivers Division.

Middle Level

Large drain and a famed match water (weights to 70 lb), running between St Germans and Three Holes. The water splits at Outwell on the Wisbech–Downham road with an aqueduct section known as the High Level and the other section as the Low Level.

Predominantly bream and roach, with excellent winter pike fishing.

Downham Market, Norfolk. 10 m between Three Holes and St Germans.
C (D T Adv. from R. Groom, 13 Sluice Road, St Germans, or Post Office, Three Holes).
Great Ouse Rivers Division.

Morton's Leam

Drain running beside Nene, entering main river at Guyhirn. Begins at Old Fletton, Peterborough.

Roach, bream and some tench.

Whittlesey, Cambs. 12 m between Guyhirn and Peterborough.
C (D T Adv. tackle shops in area or Anglian Water Authority, North Street, Oundle).
Welland and Nene Rivers Division.

Nar

Springs near Litcham, Norfolk, and runs through Narborough to join Great Ouse above King's Lynn.

An excellent coarse fishery holding some very big bream. The river above Wormgay is private fishing.

Wormgay, Norfolk. 5 m of right bank below Wormgay to junction with Ouse.
C (D T Adv. tackle shops, King's Lynn).
Tributary of Great Ouse system.
Great Ouse Rivers Division.

Nene

One of the most important rivers of the Midlands from an angling point of view, rising near Daventry and flowing through Northampton, Wellingborough, Oundle and Peterborough, below which there is a long tidal section before the river enters the Wash.

The river offers a variety of forms above Peterborough, with straights, pools and streamy sections, while below the town lies the famous North Bank section, straight and wide and a superbly even match location.

The roach and bream fishing is good throughout, while many sections hold good chub. The water also holds carp, largely in the area near and below the Peterborough power station (see Peterborough Cut). Although the warm water which attracts these fish has been reduced by the power station in recent years, many carp are still taken in both the cut and the main river.

The largest carp ever taken in a river, a mirror of 34 lb 8 oz, came from the Peterborough Cut in 1965.

Barbel have been introduced to the water and are occasionally caught. The river is much affected by bleak shoals in the summer.

Billing, Northants. ½ m left bank at Billing Bridge, including part of Billing Aquadrome grounds.
C (D T Adv. Northampton tackle shops). (N B. Part of fishery in aquadrome grounds closed between 1 Nov. and 16 June.)

Nassington, Northants. 4 m from below Yarwell to a point upstream of Elton, except parts marked on map from Leicester tackle dealers.
C (D T on bank or from Leicester tackle dealers).

Northampton, Northants. 6 m from Northampton to Doddington.
C (D T on bank or Northampton tackle shops).

Oundle, Northants. 2½ m both banks from Thrapston road bridge to Peterborough road bridge.
C (D T on bank or Oundle tackle shop; also Riverside Hotel, Oundle).

Peterborough, Cambs. 20 m from Wansford to Dog in a Doublet sluice (south bank).
C (D T Adv. from Peterborough tackle shops, and for Wansford, Stibbington and Water Newton sections from C. Howes, 63 Church Lane, Stibbington).

Peterborough, Cambs. 4 m from Fitzwilliam Bridge to Dog in a Doublet sluice, road side (north bank).
C (D T Adv. lock-keeper, Dog in a Doublet, or Peterborough tackle shops, or Anglian Water Authority, North Street, Oundle).

Wansford, Cambs. 2 m from Wansford to Water Newton, right bank.
C (D T Adv. Sibson Fisheries, New Lane, Stibbington).

Warmington, Northants. From Old Mill to main river.
C (D T Adv. C. Day, 9 Croyland Road, Walton, Peterborough).

Yarwell Mill, Northants. ¾ m downstream of mill, left bank.
C (D T Adv. ticket office at mill. M B).
Tributaries of Nene: Old River Nene, Peterborough Cut.
Welland and Nene Rivers Division. (N B. Old River Nene is in Great Ouse Rivers Division.)

New Cut

Channel linking the Waveney at St Olaves with Yare at Reedham.

An excellent fast-running summer fishery offering good roach and bream.

Reedham, Norfolk. Entire water.
C (Free fishing).
Tributary of Waveney system.
Norfolk and Suffolk Rivers Division.

Newham Drain

Part of the Boston Drains system joining West Fen downstream of Bunkers Hill with Frith Bank drain.

Offers roach and bream, reserved for pleasure anglers.

Cowbridge, Lincs. All water.
C (D T Adv. tackle shops Boston or Boston A A).
Lincolnshire Rivers Division.

North Delph
Runs parallel with north bank of Witham
from Lincoln to Bardney.
   Roach, bream, but not highly rated.
Lincoln, Lincs. All right bank.
   C (DT Adv. Lincoln tackle shops or
   Witham Joint Anglers Federation).
   Tributary of Witham system.
   Lincolnshire Rivers Division.

North Drove
Drain running from east of Baston, Lincs,
to Vernatt's Drain at Pode Hole.
   Roach and bream predominate.
Spalding, Lincs. Entire water.
   C (DT Adv. Spalding tackle shop.
   L–20).
   Welland and Nene Rivers Division.

North Level Drain
Starts near Parson Grove and runs to
tidal Nene below Tydd Gote.
   A much improved fishery offering
roach and some very big bream.
Tydd Gote, Cambs. From pumping
   station to Church Lane Bridge, Tydd
   St Giles.
   C (DT on bank or from Crown and
   Mitre, Tydd St Giles; Five Bells, Tydd
   St Mary; or Woolpack, Tydd Gote).
   Welland and Nene Rivers Division.

Old Bedford River
Starts at Earith, Cambs, and runs north
to Welches Dam and on to Great Ouse
below Denver Sluice, parallel with
Counter Drain and River Delph.
   An excellent roach and bream fishery,
also holding pike (best tops 29 lb) and
occasional big zander.
Earith, Cambs. 4 m from Earith to
   Welches Dam.
   C (DT Adv. Cambridge Albion A S).
Manea, Cambs. ½ m from Ship Inn to
   pumping station.
   C (DT Adv. Ship Inn).
Purl's Bridge, Cambs. 4½ m from Purl's
   Bridge to Welney Hotel.
   C (DT Adv. F. Clarke, Bridge House,
   Welney, or Post Office, Three Holes).
Salter's Lode, Norfolk. 3 m from Double
   Lift Mill to Old Bedford Sluice.
   C (DT Adv. as Purl's Bridge, above).

Welney, Cambs. 1 m from Welney Hotel
   to Welney Bridge.
   C (DT Adv. Great Ouse Fishery
   Consultative Association).
   Great Ouse Rivers Division.

Old River Nene
The former course of the River Nene
during flood-prevention work in the
eighteenth century. The water starts at
the Twenty-Foot drain at Ramsey St
Mary and runs through Benwick, March
and Upwell, joining Well Creek at
Outwell.
   Excellent coarse fishery with roach
and bream predominating.
Forty Foot Bridge, Cambs. 1½ m from
   Bodsey Road Bridge to Halfpenny Toll
   Bridge, Benwick.
   C (DT on bank).
Ramsey St Mary, Cambs. 2 m from
   Exhibition Bridge to old footbridge.
   C (DT on bank or from tackle shop,
   Ramsey St Mary).
   Great Ouse Rivers Division.

Old West River
Section of the Great Ouse system be-
tween Earith and junction of River Cam
near Stretham.
   Good coarse water.
Stretham, Cambs. 1½ m upstream of
   Stretham, right bank.
   C (DT Adv. Cambridge Albion A S).
   Part of Great Ouse system.
   Great Ouse Rivers Division.

Ouzel
Rises in Bedfordshire and joins Great
Ouse near Milton Keynes.
   Mostly association water, with few
openings for visitors.
   Tributary of Great Ouse System.
   Great Ouse Rivers Division.

Peterborough Cut (Electricity Cut)
Short canalized outfall from Peterborough power station, accessible from
path at main town bridge over
Nene. Although only about ¾ m to its
junction with the Nene, the Cut has
produced many big carp, whose growth
is encouraged by the warm water from

the power station. The station now operates at a lower level, but fine carp are still caught, with roach and bream. Often much weeded in summer, when bleak can be a nuisance.
Peterborough, Cambs. Entire water.
   C (D T on bank or from Peterborough tackle shops).
   Tributary of Nene.
   Welland and Nene Rivers Division.

Popham's Eau
A popular match water of West Norfolk, running from Old River Nene to Sixteen-Foot and Middle Level at Three Holes, then running on as a largely unfishable dyke to Nordelph.
   Mainly roach and bream, with some tench, pike and perch.
Three Holes, Norfolk. 4 m from Three Holes to Old River Nene.
   C (D T Adv. from R. Groom, 13 Sluice Road, St Germans, or Post Office, Three Holes).
   Great Ouse Rivers Division.

Pulver Drain
Small channel off Relief Channel, Norfolk.
   Good bream and roach, especially noted for big catches of bream in early season near junction with Channel.
St Germans, Norfolk. ¾ m from near main rail line to Relief Channel, right bank.
   C (Free fishing).
   Great Ouse Rivers Division.

Reach Lode
Links Reach Village with Burwell Lode.
   Fair roach and bream fishing.
Burwell, Cambs. 4 m Reach to Burwell Lode.
   C (D T Adv. The Garage, 40 Causeway, Burwell, or K. Peacock, General Stores, Reach).
   Tributary of Great Ouse system.
   Great Ouse Rivers Division.

Relief Channel
This huge flood-relief drain runs through West Norfolk from the Great Ouse at Denver Sluice to St Germans, near King's Lynn, where it rejoins the main river.

Deep and very wide, it holds good shoals of roach and bream of excellent size and quality, although the water is so vast that the visitor needs local advice on where to find fish.
   Also noted for its zander stocks, which since their introduction have spread and thrived so much that they pose a threat to native fish stocks, and culling has had to be introduced in latter years. From this introduction zander are spreading throughout the linked drainage system. The zander run to 15 lb, and the water also holds big pike. Shoals of large perch occasionally concentrate near the road bridges. Match catches of 70 lb and over have been taken on this water.
Downham Market, Norfolk. 11 m entire water.
   C (D T Adv. from shops, public houses and cafés near bridges and from tackle shops in Downham Market and King's Lynn).
   Great Ouse Rivers Division.

Rolands Drain
Short Fen drain running into Ancholme north of Brigg.
   Fair roach and bream fishing.
Ferriby, Lincs. 1 m Horkstow Bridge to Ferriby Sluice.
   C (D T on bank).
   Tributary of Ancholme system.
   Lincolnshire Rivers Division.

Sibsey Trader (Stonebridge Drain)
A popular match drain running from Cowbridge to the two branching Catchwater Drains in the Boston system.
   Good roach and bream fishing, but match bookings can rule out weekend pleasure fishing. Match catches of more than 50 lb taken.
Cowbridge, Lincs. Entire drain.
   C (D T Adv. tackle shops in area or Boston A A).
   Lincolnshire Rivers Division.

Sincil Dyke (South Delph)
Runs parallel with Witham from Lincoln to join main river near Branston Island.

Fair fishing for bream and roach, with some tench.

Lincoln, Lincs. 6 m Lincoln to Bardney Lock, left bank.

C (DT Adv. Lincoln tackle shops or Witham Joint Anglers Federation).

Tributary of Witham system.

Lincolnshire Rivers Division.

Sixteen-Foot River

A well-known Fen drain linking the Forty-Foot near Chatteris, Cambs, to the Middle Level at Three Holes.

Offers bream, roach, tench and perch. Pike to 30 lb.

Stonea, Cambs. 9 m from Cotton's Corner.

C (DT Adv. R. Groom, 13 Sluice Road, St Germans, or Post Office, Three Holes).

Great Ouse Rivers Division.

Slea

Rises near Sleaford and flows east to South Kyme, where it changes name to Kyme Eau or Sleaford Cut.

This upper section used to offer good chub fishing, but is lately affected by abstraction and little rated.

Tributary of Witham system.

Lincolnshire Rivers Division.

South Drove Drain

Starts on Deeping Common and runs north to Vernatt's Drain at Pode Hole.

Fair coarse fishing.

Spalding, Lincs. Entire water.

C (DT Adv. D. Ball, tackle shop, Hawthorn Bank, Spalding, or Spalding FC. L-20).

Welland and Nene Rivers Division.

South Forty-Foot

Major Fen drain running from Guthram Gowt, near Bourne, Lincs, north to Swineshead, where it turns to join Witham estuary at Boston.

A noted fishery and an especially good match water – the record is near 100 lb for a six-hour match. Although small at the Bourne end, the drain widens along its course.

Bream and roach are the main species,

although big tench and perch have been taken, with pike to 30 lb.

Swineshead, Lincs. 34 m Guthram Gowt to Boston.

C (DT Adv. tackle shops and pubs and cafés near water in Boston, Hubbert's Bridge, Wyberton, Swineshead and Donington).

Lincolnshire Rivers Division.

South Holland Drain

Starts near River Welland at Peak Hill near Cowbit and runs east to tidal Nene near Sutton Bridge.

A long, extremely good coarse fishery, although controlled by Holbeach AA, with no openings for visitors save for local open matches.

Welland and Nene Rivers Division.

Steeping

Rises in Lincolnshire Wolds north of Spilsby and runs through Wainfleet to sea at Gibraltar Point nature reserve. At Thorpe Culvert the river is linked to the Steeping Relief Channel.

Both river and channel offer good coarse fishing, with roach and bream the main species.

Wainfleet, Lincs. 10 m entire river plus relief channel.

C (DT Adv. Witham Joint Anglers Federation).

Lincolnshire Rivers Division.

Stour (Suffolk)

Rises near Haverhill and from Wixford on forms the border between Suffolk and Essex, entering the sea at Manningtree. After Sudbury it enters Constable country, running through Dedham and Flatford Mill.

A fine river, with good stocks of all coarse species except barbel, occasional trout and some sea-trout in lower stretches. It is worth mentioning that Colchester APS has water at Nayland, Wormingford, Wiston, Boxted, Stratford St Mary, Little Horkesley, Flatford and Langham, while the London Anglers' Association has rights at Clare, Foxearth, Glemsford, Great Horkesley, Bures, Nayland, Henny, Lamarsh, Pitmore Lock, Middleton and Sudbury.

Bures, Suffolk. 1 m above London AA notice board on right bank upstream of Bures.

C (DT on bank).

Bures, Suffolk. 1½ m Bures to Lamarsh.

C (DT on bank).

Cattawade, Suffolk. 2 m Cattawade Barrage to sea.

C, ST (Free fishing).

Dedham, Essex. Flour mill section.

C (DT Adv. Clovers Ltd, Flour Mills, Dedham).

Flatford Mill, Essex. Flatford Mill to Judas Gap.

C (DT from keeper).

Flatford Mill, Essex. Elm Park, Hornchurch and Dist. AA stretch marked on boards above Flatford Mill.

C (DT from keeper).

Great Henny, Suffolk. 300 yds opposite Swan Inn, right bank, and Great Cornard AC water on left bank.

C (DT Adv. Henny Swan public house, Great Henny).

Sudbury, Suffolk. 6 m between Sudbury and Throught.

C (DT on bank or from tackle shops in area).

Tributary: Box.

Essex Rivers Division.

Thurne

Rises near West Somerton and flows 5 m through Martham Broad (private) to Martham, Potter Heigham and the Bure.

Holds good stocks of coarse fish throughout the year, with big roach and rudd (specimens of more than 3 lb taken), but especially noted for big winter catches of roach and bream when shoals move in off the shallower Broads. Has produced pike to 35 lb. Martham and Potter Heigham best for bank access, but boats available.

Bastwick, Norfolk. 3½ m Repp's Staithe to Martham Broad, left bank.

C (Free fishing).

Cold Harbour, Norfolk. 1 m from stile to River Bure.

C (DT from keeper, tackle shops in area, or Norwich and Dist. AA).

Potter Heigham, Norfolk. 4½ m Martham Broad to Cold Harbour, in-

cluding 2 m Candle Dyke and Womack Water.

C (Free fishing).

Tributary of Bure system.

Norfolk and Suffolk Rivers Division.

Till (Lincs.)

Rises near Gainsborough and flows south to Foss Dyke at Odder.

A good coarse fishery, with the best fishing at Broxholme. Roach and bream predominate.

Broxholme, Lincs. 1 m Broxholme Bridge to Odder Bridge, left bank.

C (DT Adv. Bridge Garage, Dunham Bridge).

Odder, Lincs. ½ m of right bank below Odder Bridge.

C (DT Adv. Good's Farm, Odder).

Tributary of Witham system.

Lincolnshire Rivers Division.

Tove

Stream joining Great Ouse near Stony Stratford.

Fair coarse fishing, but mostly controlled by local associations, with no openings for visitors.

Stony Stratford, Bucks. Short section in Cosgrove Lodge Park.

C (DT Adv. ticket office in park entrance).

Tributary of Great Ouse system.

Great Ouse Rivers Division.

Twenty-Foot River

Runs from Angle Bridge, near Whittlesey, Cambs, to Goosetree Farm, and skirts north of March to join Old River Nene.

A very good drain fishery offering roach, bream, tench and pike. Match records show catches to 57 lb, and a pike of 29 lb was caught in 1973.

Whittlesey, Cambs. 4½ m Angle Corner to Goosetree.

C (DT from keeper).

Welland and Nene Rivers Division.

Vernatt's Drain

Runs from Pode Hole north-east to Welland near Surfleet.

A good drain fishery offering roach, bream, rudd, tench and perch, with some pike. Match records boast an 81 lb catch for six hours, a 4 lb 8½ oz perch (1956) and a 3 lb 4 oz rudd (1955).

Spalding, Lincs. Entire water.

C (DT Adv. from keeper, J. Moore, Kiro, Station Road, Surfleet, or tackle shop, Hawthorn Bank, Spalding).

Welland and Nene Rivers Division.

Waveney

Rises near Diss, Norfolk, and runs through Scole to Geldeston Lock, below which it is tidal.

The upper river holds good mixed coarse stock, with big roach, dace and chub. Huge shoals of big bream are a feature of the tidal river, where match catches of more than 100 lb have been recorded. A sea-trout of 8½ lb was caught in the tidal river in 1920, but in recent years not many have been seen.

Aldeby, Norfolk. ¾ m left bank at Aldeby.

C (Free fishing).

Bungay, Suffolk. 1¾ m Bungay to Outney Common, right bank.

C (DT Adv. Suffolk County Amalgamated AA).

Earsham, Norfolk. 2½ m total in separated sections of left bank above and below Earsham Mill.

C (Free fishing).

Geldeston, Norfolk. Four sections of right bank above lock and water from lock to sea, except where access prohibited.

C (Free fishing).

Gillingham, Suffolk. ¾ m upstream of Beccles, right bank, and 1½ m of left bank downstream of Beccles Bridge.

C (Free fishing).

Needham, Norfolk. Two short stretches on right bank above Needham Mill and left bank below mill.

C (Free fishing).

Wainford, Norfolk. 250 yds above Wainford Mill.

C (Free fishing).

Worlingham, Suffolk. 170 yds, right bank.

C (Free fishing).

Tributary: New Cut.

Norfolk and Suffolk Rivers Division.

Welland

This very popular East Midlands water rises near Market Harborough, Leicestershire, and runs as a fairly streamy river, stocked with trout in parts, to its main coarse sections below Market Deeping, where the course has been straightened and widened into a flood-relief channel which makes a fine match stretch.

Besides trout the upper river holds splendid coarse fish, especially chub, roach and dace, while barbel have established themselves in the Several Fisheries area around the Deepings. The Several and the lower canalized reach hold big bream shoals, and match weights of 50 lb and more are taken. In this section it is sometimes hard to find space at weekends.

Barrowden, Northants. 3 m Barrowden to Tixover Church, right bank.

C (DT Adv. Stamford Welland AA).

Collyweston, Northants. 3½ m from Collyweston to Ketton Pile Bridge.

C (DT Adv. Stamford Welland AA).

Market Deeping, Lincs. 6½ m Several Fishery to Kennulph's Stone, Welland High Bank.

C (DT on bank at weekends only, or from keeper Mon.–Fri., 15 Bridge Street, Deeping St James, and tackle shop, Church Street, Deeping St James, Mon.–Fri. only).

Spalding, Lincs. 10 m from Kennulph's Stone to Spalding.

C (DT Adv. tackle shops, Spalding or Crowland, or Golden Ball public house, Spalding, or Anglian Water Authority, North Street, Oundle).

Stamford, Lincs. 3 m from Ketton Pile Bridge to Broadend Bridge near Stamford.

C (DT Adv. Stamford Welland AA).

Stamford, Lincs. Just over 1 m Stamford Town Bridge and Broadend Bridge, left bank.

C (Free fishing).

Tallington, Lincs. 1 m Uffington Bridge to one field above Tallington.

C (DT Adv. Stamford Welland AA).

Uffington, Lincs. 4 m Hudd's Mill to Uffington Bridge, right bank.

C (DT Adv. Stamford Welland AA).
Tributaries of Welland: Chater,
Coronation Channel, Eye Brook, Folly
River, Glen, Maxey Cut.
Welland and Nene Rivers Division.

Wensum

Famed for its remarkable roach, the
Wensum rises above Raynham and runs
through Fakenham and on to Norwich,
where there is a very good tidal section,
brought about by clearing up pollution.

During 1976 two roach of 3 lb 2 oz
were taken from the river, which also
boasts big dace and chub and some
extremely big trout. The tidal section,
largely free fishing, holds big shoals of
roach, with match catches of 30 lb and
more.

Bintree Mill, Norfolk. 1 m right bank and
½ m left bank between disused rail
bridge to near mill.
C (Free fishing).

East Dereham, Norfolk. ¾ m, including
rights to fish three local lakes.
C, T (DT Adv. from keeper, house
beside fishery).

Fakenham, Norfolk. More than ½ m
from Kersley Mill upstream, right bank.
C, T (Free fishing).

Fakenham, Norfolk. ½ m right bank
below Sculthorpe Mill to Grogg's Mill,
and 1½ m downstream from Dewing
and Kersley Mill.
C, T (DT Adv. tackle shop, Norwich
Street, Fakenham. Trout fly only).

Great Ryburgh, Norfolk. 2½ m Great
Ryburgh to Guist.
T, fly only (Free fishing).

Norwich, Norfolk. Newmills Yard down to
junction with Yare, unless access prohibited, mainly on left bank roadsides.
C (Free fishing).

Taverham, Norfolk. Section beside
Taverham Gravel Pits (permit also
covers pits).
C (DT Adv. keeper on site).
Tributary of Yare system.
Norfolk and Suffolk Rivers Division.

West Fen Catchwater

The north-west branch of the northern
end of the Sibsey Trader, which runs

south of East Kirby and Revesby to meet
the heads of Medlam Drain and Newham
Drain.

This part of the Boston drains system
is reserved for pleasure anglers, offering
roach and dace. It has produced good
pike in latter years.

East Kirkby, Lincs. 5 m to Cherry Corner.
C (DT Adv. tackle shops in area or
Boston AA).
Lincolnshire Rivers Division.

West Fen Drain

Not to be confused with the West Fen
Catchwater (above). It runs north from
Cowbridge to meet the southern end of
the Medlam Drain, turning north-west to
cross Newham Drain and run almost to
the Witham at Chapel Hill.

The lower section near Cowbridge is a
noted match water, with roach and
bream, which are often big, and some
tench. Most of the northern section is
reserved for pleasure fishing. Pumping
can reduce the levels considerably from
October onwards.

Cowbridge, Lincs. 5 m Dalton's Bridge
to Cowbridge.
C (DT Adv. tackle shops in area or
Boston AA).
Lincolnshire Rivers Division.

Whittlesey Dyke

Short dyke linking King's Dyke and Cock
Bank.

A fair coarse fishery offering some
roach, bream, tench and perch.

Whittlesey, Cambs. 1½ m Whittlesey
Sluice to Angle Corner, left bank.
C (DT on bank).
Welland and Nene Rivers Division.

Wissey

Rises in West Norfolk and runs through
Whittington, Stoke Ferry and Hilgay to
join the Ouse near Ten Mile Bank rail
bridge.

The upper river, a series of linked
pools, holds big trout and is strictly preserved. Lower, the river holds very good
roach and other coarse fish, while occasional trout are still taken.

Hilgay, Norfolk. 4 m Dereham Belt to
Ouse.

C (DT Adv. bailiff's house, Hilgay Bridge).

Southery, Cambs. 1½ m of left bank, Five Mile House Farm, Stoke Fen Ferry on Southery to Wereham road.

C (DT on bank).

Stoke Ferry, Norfolk. ½ m above and below ferry.

C (DT Adv. bailiff's house, Hilgay Bridge).

Tributary of Great Ouse system.

Great Ouse Rivers Division.

Witham

Famed for its lower section match lengths, the Witham rises near Grantham and meanders as a small country river through Claypole and Bassingham before running into the large Brayford Pool in the heart of Lincoln. Below here it has been the subject of successive widening programmes and alters character entirely, becoming slow and deep.

Between Lincoln and Boston week-end matches cover most of the water, although there are reserved stretches for individual anglers. The most popular lengths, though, such as the Kirkstead road stretch, are best during the week. The upper river is a fine mixed coarse fishery, while below Lincoln bream predominate and there are some huge shoals with many very large fish. However, because of the intensity of match fishing, the water has a reputation of being extremely hard fishing for extremely shy fish. Five-hour match records have topped 70 lb, and the records also boast a roach of 3½ lb and a bream of 9 lb 3 oz.

Bassingham, Lincs. Upper river, Bassingham to Auborn, ¾ m of right bank.

C (DT Adv. Sheffield and Dist. AA).

Boston, Lincs. 31 m from Stamp End Lock, Lincoln, to Grand Sluice, Boston, except for sections posted on markers.

C (DT Adv. tackle shops in Boston, Kirkstead, Lincoln, or Witham Joint Anglers Federation).

Chapel Hill, Lincs. ½ m of right bank

from below Jimmy's Hill to Smallwood's Caravan Park club-house.

C (DT Adv. from ticket office, Smallwood's Caravan Park).

Claypole, Lincs. Upper river, 1½ m.

C (DT Adv. F. Allen, Oddhouse Farm, Claypole).

Doddington, Lincs. Upper river, 1 m of right-hand bank downstream of bridge.

C (DT Adv. New Inn, Newark AC).

Kirkstead, Lincs. See Boston (above).

Lincoln, Lincs. See Boston (above).

Long Bennington, Notts. Upper river, 1 m right bank downstream of Long Bennington Bridge.

C (DT on bank).

Martindales, Lincs. Short length on Schoolhouse bend, right bank, below junction of Martin Delph.

C (DT on bank).

South Hykeham, Lincs. 4 m on towpaths from River Brant junction down to Brayford Pool, Lincoln.

C (DT Adv. tackle shops, Lincoln).

Tattershall, Lincs. 300 yds of right bank upstream from Pick's Farm Fence, Sandholes.

C (DT on bank).

Tributaries of Witham: Bain (Lincs.), Barling's Eau, Billinghay Skirth, Branston Delph, Brant, Foss Dyke, Kyme Eau, Martin Delph, North Delph, Sincil Dyke, Slea, Till (Lincs.), Timberland Delph.

Lincolnshire Rivers Division.

Womack Water

A backwater of the Thurne, navigable to Ludham.

Weed cutting makes several stretches fishable on this secluded water offering good bream and roach fishing.

Ludham, Norfolk.

C (DT Adv. from keeper at Womack Holidays, Womack Woods, Ludham. B, MB available).

Tributary of Bure system.

Norfolk and Suffolk Rivers Division.

Yare

Rises in West Norfolk and flows 20 m to

Norwich, increasing in width and depth on its way to Yarmouth. Above the tidal length chub are encountered as well as large roach and bream, while the extreme upper reaches are mostly private, holding coarse fish and some trout.

Tides are strong in the lower section and would give difficulty to the novice. Fish stocks are good, however, although the average size is generally smaller.

Bawburgh, Norfolk. 6½ m Bawburgh Road Bridge to ¾ m below Earlham Road Bridge, right bank.
C (Free fishing).

Buckenham Ferry, Norfolk. Ferry to Cantley, Rockland, Claxton and Langley.
C (Free fishing).

Easton, Norfolk. Short stretch.
C (Free fishing).

Norwich, Norfolk. Trowse Mill to sea, except where access prohibited.
C (Free fishing).

Postwick, Norfolk. 600 yds opposite Surlingham Ferry.
C (Free fishing).

Trowse, Norfolk. ¾ m from Wensum to Trowse Church, right bank.
C (D T Adv. Norwich and Dist. A A).

Tributaries of Yare: Chet, Wensum.

Norfolk and Suffolk Rivers Division.

Northumbrian Water Authority Rivers

While not covering such a vast range of waters as the Anglian Water Authority, the Northumbrian Water Authority controls two large watersheds, those of the Tyne and Wear and their tributaries in Northumberland and Durham.

This is principally a game fishing area, but there are some openings for coarse fishing, such as the middle stretches of the Tyne and some of its tributaries.

Both the major waters have suffered in the past from pollution, which has hampered runs of salmon and sea-trout, but happily there is now a concerted effort to clean up the lower reaches and sport is improving noticeably.

Aln

Rises in the Cheviots to flow east through Whittingham and Alnwick to the North Sea at Alnmouth.

Mainly a trout river, with major re-stocking in some areas. There are runs of sea-trout, with occasional salmon.

Alnwick, Northumb. 4 m Denwick Bridge to Alnmouth Bridge, excluding grounds of Lesbury House.
T, ST, S (D T, WT, Adv. R. Murray Sports Ltd, 2 Narrow Gate, Alnwick, or R. Jobson & Sons, Tower Show Rooms, Alnwick. Fly only except between Lesbury footbridge and Duchess's Bridge. Seasons: T, 22 Mar.–30 Sept.; S, 1 Feb.–31 Oct.; S T, 3 Apr.–31 Oct. No Sunday fishing).

Blyth (Northumbria)

Rises near Throckington in mid-Northumberland and runs 20 m to the sea at Blyth.

Has suffered greatly from pollution but is recovering well after extensive re-stocking. The main species are trout and grayling, but there are some coarse fish, notably roach.

Bedlington, Northumb. 3 m Stannington to Bedlington.
C, T (D T Adv. bona fide visitors only, Bedlington and Blagdon A A).

Coquet

Best-known of the North-East's salmon rivers, the Coquet rises in the Cheviots and runs to the North Sea at Warkworth.

The fishing is excellent but access for visitors is restricted, with much water held by Northumbrian Anglers Federation, who offer membership to local anglers only.

Rothbury, Northumb. 6 m Hepple to Healey, except where access prohibited.
T, S (D T Adv. tackle shop, Rothbury).

Thropton, Northumb.
T, S (D T Adv. Rothbury and Thropton A C, Sandaig, Hillside, Rothbury).

Weldon Bridge, Northumb.
T, S (D T Adv. Anglers Arms, Weldon Bridge, Morpeth, Northumb).

Derwent (Durham)

A fine trout and grayling river, rising on Nookton Fell, where it feeds Derwent Reservoir, and running on to Shotley Bridge and the Tyne.

Access for visitors limited.

Winlaton Mill, Tyne and Wear. 5 m Winlaton Mill to Lintz Ford.

T and grayling (DT Adv. Axwell Park and Derwent Valley AA, 5 Naylor Avenue, Winlaton Mill, Blaydon, Tyne and Wear).

Tributary of Tyne system.

East Allen

Rises in Pennines on border of Durham and Northumberland and runs through Sinderhope and Allendale Town and on to junction with West Allen stream and South Tyne near Bardon Mill.

Fair trout fishing.

Allendale, Northumb. 8 m as detailed on permit.

T (Fortnight ticket only, from Allendale Post Office. Adv. Fly only).

Tributary of Tyne system.

North Tyne

The northern branch of the Tyne, rising in Kielder Forest to flow south-east through Falstone and Bellingham, joining South Tyne above Hexham.

Upper reaches hold trout, but lower there are coarse fish, especially roach, and the occasional salmon.

Chollerford, Northumb. 1½ m left bank.

C, T (DT Adv. George Hotel, Chollerford).

Falstone, Northumb. ¾ m Falstone Rectory to Mouseyhaugh.

T, S (DT Adv. Black Cock Inn, Falstone, or Falstone FC, G. W. Robson, 3 Mousey Lough, Falstone, Hexham).

Part of Tyne system.

Rede

Rises in west Cheviots and runs south through Otterburn to join the Tyne at Redesmouth.

Mostly trout with occasional salmon in autumn.

Otterburn, Northumb. 3½ m Mill Bridge to Meadow Haugh.

C, T, some S (DT Adv. Otterburn Towers Hotel, Otterburn).

Tributary of Tyne system.

South Tyne

Rising on Alston Moor, Cumbria, the South Tyne runs through Alston and then east through Haydon Bridge to join the North Tyne at Hexham.

Mainly a trout water, with occasional sea-trout and salmon, especially late in the season. Mostly private with a few openings for visitors.

Alston, Cumbria. 7 m as described on permit.

T, ST, S (DT, WT Adv. from D. Middleton, ironmonger, High Market Place, Alston, except Tues. afternoons and Sunday. No visitors' permits after 30 Sept.).

Haltwhistle, Northumb. 7 m Featherstone to Bardon Wood.

T, ST, S (WT Adv. Greggs Sports Shop, Main Street, Haltwhistle).

Haydon Bridge, Northumb. South Tyne AC waters.

T, ST, S (WT Adv. J. O. Moore, 24 Strothers Close, Haydon Bridge. No visitors' permits after August).

Part of Tyne system.

Tees

Rises high on Cross Fell in the Pennines and flows through Teesdale to Middleton-in-Teesdale, Barnard Castle and on into Durham Lowlands, running south of Darlington and into Teesside estuary.

The upper river is streamy, holding trout and grayling, and then it drops through High Force falls above Middleton. Below Piercebridge, coarse fish start to be encountered, with good stocks of chub and dace right down to Middlesbrough, where pollution begins to take a hold.

Barnard Castle, Durham. Between Stone Bridge and Thorngate Bridge.

C, T (Free fishing).

Croft, N Yorks. 5½ m downstream from Croft Road Bridge to Ring Field, left bank, and Dalton Rail Bridge down to Rockliffe Scar.

T, C (D T Adv. by arrangement with Thornaby A A, secretary A. G. Butler, 5 Melsonby Grove, Hartburn Grange, Stockton-on-Tees).

Croft, N Yorks. 5 m Croft to Darlington.

T, C (D T Adv. Thornaby A A; see entry immediately above).

Middleton-in-Teesdale, Durham. 7 m Broken Way to ford below Newbiggin and Newbiggin footbridge to Cauldron Snout, left bank.

T (D T Adv. Raby Estate Office, Middleton-in-Teesdale. Fly only, season 22 Mar.–30 Sept.).

Middleton-in-Teesdale, Durham. Stretch on right bank.

T (D T Adv. Cleveland Arms, Middleton, or J. A. Turnbull, estate agents, 152 Front Street, Chester-le-Street. Fly only to 1 June, season 22 Mar.–30 Sept.).

Neasham, Durham. Left bank opposite Neasham village green.

C (Free fishing).

Yarm, Cleveland. 7 m from 1 m above Yarm to Leven mouth, left bank, and 3 m right bank at Yarm.

C (D T Adv. F. and K. Flynn, 12 Vard Terrace, Stockton. L–12.)

Tyne

Formed by the junction of the North Tyne and South Tyne at Hexham, the Tyne flows east to Newcastle and the sea.

The largest river in Northumberland, it has suffered greatly from pollution, but an improvement programme is having a marked effect on salmon and sea-trout runs. The river also holds a head of coarse fish, especially roach, which occur in the middle and upper reaches and some tributaries. Trout are also taken throughout the river, but mostly in the middle and upper stretches.

Access for visitors is difficult, with the Northumbrian Anglers Federation restricting membership to local anglers.

Hexham, Northumb. 1 m from old Border Counties Bridge on right bank.

T, S (D T Adv. Tynedale District Council, Prospect House, Hexham. Fly only).

Tributaries: Derwent (Durham), East Allen, North Tyne, South Tyne, Rede.

Wansbeck

Rises in west of Northumberland and runs through Morpeth to Seaton.

Holds mainly trout; no known access for visitors.

Wear

Rises near Burnhope Seat on the Durham–Cumbria border, running into Burnhope Reservoir and then through Stanhope and Wolsingham in Weardale to Bishop Auckland and finally Sunderland.

This is another of the North-East waters that have been badly affected by industrial pollution in the past, and where a concerted effort is being made to restore runs of migratory fish. Of these the sea-trout runs have improved enormously, while salmon are making a comeback. The trout fishing is good.

Durham, Durham. Left bank from Milburngate Bridge to sewage works, and right bank from below ice rink to Kepier Priory Farm.

T, S (Free fishing).

Stanhope, Durham. 2 m Stonebridge to Kemp Laws.

T, ST (D T Adv. ticket office. L–10).

Stanhope, Durham. 3½ m from ½ m upstream of Hagg Bridge, Eastgate, to Stanhope, right bank.

T, ST, S (D T Adv. Phoenix Hotel, Stanhope. Fly only to 1 July).

Westgate, Durham. 5 m Westgate to Cowshill.

T (D T Adv. St John's Chapel Inn, Westgate, or Upper Weardale A A. No Sunday fishing).

Willington, Durham. 4 m above and below Willington.

T, ST (D T Adv. tackle shop, 80 High Street, Willington).

Witton-le-Wear, Durham. 1 m between A68 bridge and Home Farm, Witton Castle Estate.

T, ST, S (D T Adv. from T. Marshall, The Cottage, Witton-le-Wear, or The

Estate Office, Lambton Park, Chester-le-Street. Fly only).

North-West Water Authority Rivers

The area's rivers offer a fine range of fishing for coarse and game anglers, some lying in the popular Lake District, where many anglers seek holidays.

Besides this there are some excellent canals, and the native anglers of the region have brought canal fishing to a fine art.

Aira Beck
A small trout stream which runs through Dockray and Aira Force to Ullswater.

Fair fishing, especially in spring and early summer.

Ullswater, Cumb. National Trust land.

T (Free fishing).

Bolton and Bury Canal
This short waterway runs between Bury and Bolton.

Good mixed coarse fishing.

Bury, Greater Manchester. Towpath bank.

C (D T Adv. tackle shops in Bury).

Brathay
Rises on Bow Fell and runs 9 m through Great Langdale to Lake Windermere.

Holds trout and coarse fish, with trout fishing fair in spring and early summer.

Ambleside, Westmld. 2 m of right bank from Jiffy Knots to lake.

T, C (D T Adv. tackle shops in area).

Bridgewater Canal
Stretches from Leigh to Salford, Western Manchester, Preston Brook and the junction of the Trent and Mersey Canal, and then joins the Mersey at Runcorn.

Most parts of this lengthy water hold fair stocks of coarse fish, including some large carp. However, the fishing is not consistent throughout, with some parts poor, and the well-fished lengths have fish which are shy and need a fine approach. Much match fishing on summer weekends. Warrington A A, who own the fishing on a large stretch, offer open season membership but no day tickets.

Leigh, Greater Manchester. Towpath for 2 m from Leigh Town Bridge to Plank Lane Bridge.

C (D T on bank or from tackle shops, Leigh).

Leigh, Greater Manchester. 5 m of towpath from Leigh Town Bridge to Worsley motorway bridge.

C (D T on bank or from tackle shops, Leigh).

Leigh, Greater Manchester. Towpath Dover Lock Bridge to Plank Lane, Leigh.

C (D T on bank).

Runcorn, Cheshire. 6 m from Turnover Bridge, Preston Brook, to Runcorn.

C (D T on bank or from Runcorn tackle shop, or W. Durr, Footbridge Cottage, Canal Street, Runcorn).

Sale, Greater Manchester. 6 m from Broadheath Bridge, Sale, to Leigh.

C (D T on bank or from tackle shops in area).

Brock
Small tributary of Wyre system.

No known openings for visitors.

Calder (Cumbria)
Rises on Kenniside Fells south-west of Ennerdale Water and joins sea near mouth of River Ehen.

A fine game water, especially for large salmon. Unhappily there are no known openings for visiting anglers.

Calder (Lancs)
After rising near Burnley the Calder flows through industrial Lancashire.

It has suffered from pollution, some of which it eventually introduces to the River Ribble, but there is fair trout and coarse fishing in some lengths.

Great Harewood, Lancs. $\frac{1}{2}$ m left bank upstream of Cock Bridge, Martholme Estate.

C, T (D T on bank or from Northern A A).

Tributary of the Ribble.

Calder Brook
Runs off Calder Fell to join the Wyre near
Catterall.
No known openings for visitors.

Clough
Rises at Garsdale Head on the Cumbria
border and flows through Garsdale to
join the Dee at Sedbergh.
Good trout fishing, with some sea-
trout and salmon.
Sedbergh, Cumb. Stretches near
Sedbergh.
T (WT Adv. tackle shop, Sedbergh).
Tributary of the Lune system.

Cocker
Rises on Borrowdale Hause and runs
through Buttermere, Crummock Water
and the Lorton Valley to the Derwent at
Cockermouth.
Trout, sea-trout and salmon, but no
known openings for visitors.
Tributary of Derwent (Cumb.) system.

Crake
Runs 4 m from southern end of
Coniston Water to the Leven estuary at
Greenodd.
A fair game water with some coarse
fish.
Lowick, Lancs. Short stretch near
Lowick Mill Farm.
T, S, ST, C (DT Adv. Lowick Mill
Farm, Lowick Bridge. L–3).
Tributary of Leven system.

Dane
Rises near Cat and Fiddle Pass west of
Buxton at the edge of the Peak District
and runs through Danebridge,
Congleton, Holmes Chapel and
Middlewich to join the Weaver near
Hartford.
Mainly trout fishing in upper reaches,
with coarse fish appearing in the middle
and lower reaches. The river is improving
immensely after periods of neglect. Trout
fishing opportunities are limited.
Bostock, Cheshire. $2\frac{1}{2}$ m from
Middlewich to Davenham.
T (DT Adv. tackle shops in
Middlewich and Winsford).

Byley, Cheshire. 3 m right bank below
M6 bridge to Byley Bridge, and from
Byley Bridge to Pochins Bridge.
C (DT on bank Mon.–Fri. only).
Middlewich, Cheshire. 1 m Pochins
Bridge to Croxton Weir.
C (DT on bank).

Dee
Rises on Cragg Hill and flows to join the
Lune below Sedbergh.
Offers excellent game fishing, but
most water strictly preserved.
Sedbergh, Cumb. 3 m.
T (WT Adv. tackle shop, Sedbergh).
Tributary of Lune system.

Derwent (Cumbria)
Rises on Scafell Pike and runs through
Derwentwater then Bassenthwaite Lake
to Cockermouth and sea at Workington.
Noted for salmon and sea-trout, with
some early fish. Best season July–Sept.
The river also offers good trout fishing
and some coarse fishing, mainly perch
and pike.
Cockermouth, Cumb. Egremont Estate
water.
T, ST, S (DT Adv. Egremont Estate
Co., The Castle, Cockermouth).
Cockermouth, Cumb. Town waters in
War Memorial Gardens from Derwent
Bridge to Harris Mill Bridge, left bank
at High Sand Lane and Lower Sand
Lane, and from junction with Cocker
to area of pylon.
T, ST, S (WT Adv. Town Hall,
Cockermouth).
Keswick, Cumb. $1\frac{1}{2}$ m stretch at
Keswick.
T, S (DT Adv. tackle shop, Station
Street, Keswick. Trout open season
20 Mar.–14 Sept.; salmon, 2 Apr.–
31 Oct.).
Tributaries: Cocker, Greta.

Eamont
A fine game fishery linking the Eden with
Ullswater, but unhappily there are no
known openings for visitors.

Eden (Cumbria)
Rises near Kirkby Stephen and runs 70 m
through Appleby and Armathwaite.

The Eden is noted among other things for producing the largest salmon caught in England, a 60 lb fish taken by L. Bridger (fly) in 1888. The spring fishing is especially good, starting in January. Summer fish start in June, but the main runs are in July. Sea-trout are best from June to Oct. Besides the migratory fish the trout fishing is good, and coarse fish are appearing in ever-increasing numbers, with the lower reaches around Carlisle gaining fame as a match water. Match records top 60 lb. Big chub and dace are present in most of the lower river, while grayling occur throughout.

There are considerable restrictions on fishing for coarse species in the river, and anglers are advised to take note of them.

Appleby, Cumb. 11 m Bolton to Sandford.
  C, grayling (D T Adv. 1 Oct.–31 Jan. only, tackle shop, Market Place, Appleby).

Appleby, Cumb. 11 m Eden and tributaries.
  T (Residents only, Tufton Arms, Market Square, Boroughgate. Fly only).

Armathwaite, Cumb. Stretch in area.
  T, ST, S, C (Residents only, Red Lion, Armathwaite).

Armathwaite, Cumb. 1½ m at Armathwaite, left bank.
  T, S (Residents only, Duke Head Inn, Armathwaite. Fly only).

Carlisle, Cumb. 7 m at Carlisle.
  T, S (D T Adv. tackle shops, Carlisle. Fishery open 15 Jan.–14 Oct. only).

Carlisle, Cumb. 6 m from M6 motorway bridge to rail bridge west of Carlisle.
  C (D T Adv. tackle shop, Grove Lane, Carlisle, or Border Coarse A C. Fishery only open between 15 Oct. and 16 Jan. and strictly prohibited on other dates).

Kirkby Stephen, Cumb. 2¼ m total at Outhgill, White Bracken and Stenkrith.
  T (D T Adv. Thornaby A A. Fly only).

Lazonby, Cumb. Four beats in area.
  T, S (Residents only, Bracken Bank Lodge, Lazonby. B available. Fly only).

Warwick-on-Eden, Cumb. Warwick Hall waters.
  T, S (D T Adv. Crown Hotel, Wetheral, or owner, Mrs Elwes, Warwick Hall, Carlisle. B available).
  Tributaries: Eamont, Goldrill, Hartsop, Irthing.

Ehen

Runs from the western end of Ennerdale Water through Egremont and Beckermet to the sea close to the Calder estuary.

The river offers fine trout fishing through most of its 12 m length, and salmon and sea-trout, some of which can be large. The best time for salmon is May, and the sea-trout runs are best from June to Sept. Some coarse fish.

Cleator Moor, Cumb. Most of water below Ennerdale Water.
  T, ST, S, C (D T Adv. Post Office, Wath Brow, Cleator Moor, or Wath Brow and Ennerdale A A. Fishery open 20 Mar.–31 Oct.).

Ellen

Rises on Uldale Fells and runs to Solway Firth at Maryport.

An improving river offering good salmon and sea-trout, plus fair trout fishing. Migratory fish best mid-July to end of Sept.

Aspatria, Cumb. 7 m from Ellenhall Bridge to Harvey Brow.
  T, ST, S (WT Adv. only to anglers living outside 30 m radius of Aspatria, from The Colour Shop, Outgang Road, Aspatria).

Esk (Cumbria)

Rises on Scafell Pike and runs to sea at Ravenglass.

Good runs of salmon and sea-trout from July, with excellent trout fishing in spring and early summer. Few openings for visitors.

Ravenglass, Cumb. ½ m from Esk Bridge to Eskdale Estate.
  T, S (D T Adv. Pennington Arms Hotel, Ravenglass).

Gilpin

Joins the River Kent just before it reaches Morecambe Bay.

Principally a game river, noted for late salmon run and some good sea-trout fishing. Mainly preserved, but worth inquiries at farms.

Lythe Valley, Cumb. Short stretch on Bell's Land near Windermere.

T, S T (D T Adv. Northern A A).

Tributary of Kent system.

Gleaston Beck

Runs from the Furness Peninsula to Morecambe Bay near Gleaston.

Fair trout fishing.

Gleaston, Cumb. 2 m from Gleaston to mouth.

T (D T Adv. Furness Fishing Association. The fishery opens on 1 Apr.).

Goldrill

Small stream linking Brothers Water with Ullswater.

Fair trout fishing, especially early in season, near junction with Ullswater.

Ullswater, Cumb. National Trust land.

T (Free fishing).

Greta

Formed by the union of Glendaramakin Beck and St John's Beck and flows 4 m to Keswick and the Derwent.

Offers good trout and salmon.

Keswick, Cumb. ½ m of right bank as detailed on permit.

T, S (D T Adv. tackle shop, Station Road, Keswick. Trout season 20 Mar.–14 Sept.; salmon, 2 Apr.–31 Oct.).

Tributary of Derwent (Cumbria) system.

Grizedale Beck

Rises in Grizedale Forest and runs through Satterthwaite to Rusland Pool and the Leven at Haverthwaite.

Fair trout fishing.

Satterthwaite, Lancs. 2 m from Home Farm, Grizedale, to Force Bridge.

T (D T Adv. ticket office).

Tributary of Leven system.

Hartsop

Small tributary of Eden (Cumbria) system.

Fair trout fishing.

Patterdale, Cumb.

T (Free fishing).

Hodder

Runs through the Forest of Bowland to join the Ribble above the mouth of the Calder.

One of the best-known game fishing tributaries of the Ribble, it offers fine salmon and sea-trout fishing, good trout fishing and some coarse fish. Most of the water, though, is strictly preserved, and the best bets for game fishing are hotel stretches. It is worth approaching some game fisheries for permission to seek coarse fish.

Bashall Eaves, Lancs. 600 yds left bank from bridge.

T, S (Residents only, Hodder Bridge Hotel).

Whitewell, Lancs. 5 m stretch at Whitewell.

T, S (Residents only, Whitewell Hotel. Fly only).

Tributary of Ribble system.

Huddersfield Narrow

This waterway helps to form the link between the Calder and Hebble Navigation with the Ashton Canal near Manchester.

Coarse fishing, mainly good but patchy (see also Yorkshire Water Authority area rivers and canals).

Greenfield, Greater Manchester. 1½ m from Lock 24 at Saddleworth to Greenfield.

C (D T on bank, from tackle shops in area, or from Oldham and Dist. Amalgamated A A).

Oldham, Lancs. 3 m from Ward Lane, Diggle, to Hartshead Power Station Road, excluding Wool Lane to Calf Lane Bridge.

C (D T on bank or from tackle shops, Oldham).

Irt

Drains Wastwater into estuary of Mite and Cumbrian Esk at Ravenglass.

Although short, the Irt is noted for its big sea-trout, which run over 15 lb.

These and the salmon, which can be prolific, run from June, although July onwards is generally rated best. The trout fishing is good. Most of the water is strictly preserved but there is some hotel water.

Holmbrook, Cumb. 3½ m from The Willows to Meadow Pool.

T, ST, S (Residents only, Lutwidge Arms Hotel, Holmbrook. Seasons for water, trout, 20 Mar.–15 Sept.; sea-trout, 1 May–31 Oct.; salmon, 1 Apr.–31 Oct.).

Irthing

Rises on the border of Northumberland and flows to join the Eden near Carlisle.

Most of the river's game fishing is strictly preserved, but there are op-portunities for trout and coarse fishing.

Brampton, Cumb. Sections as described on permit, also part of River Gelt.

T, C (DT Adv. Sports Shop, Front Street, Brampton).

Brampton, Cumb. Stretches in area.

T (DT Adv. Sports Shop, Front Street, Brampton. Fishing open to end of season, fly only to 1 Aug.).

Tributary of Eden (Cumbria) system.

Kent

Rises to the south of High Street and runs through Kentmere, Staveley and Kendal to Morecambe Bay.

A fine game river, it offers some spring salmon, especially below Kendal, al-though the middle and upper stretches fish best from June to Oct. The trout fishing is also good. Most of the water is privately controlled.

Kendal, Cumb. Kendal Town Water.

T, ST, S (Free fishing).

Kendal, Cumb. 2 m from Low Levens to estuary.

T, S (DT Adv. Low Levens' Farm, Sampool Lane, Kendal).

Kendal, Cumb. 8 m Burneside to Sedgwick.

T, S (DT Adv. tackle shop, Kendal. Not issued in Sept. and Oct.).

Staveley, Cumb. 5 m from Kentmere to Staveley.

T (DT Adv. Staveley newsagents. B available).

Tributaries: Gilpin, Mint, Sprint.

Kirkby Pool

In spite of the name, a river running near Kirkby and Barrow-in-Furness.

Small trout, some sea-trout and coarse fish.

Kirkby, Cumb. Stretch between Reeks Bridge and sea.

T, ST, C (DT Adv. Furness Fishing Association. Trout season opens 1 Apr. L–3).

Lancaster Canal

Runs from Stainton in the north some 70 m south through Carnforth, Lancaster and Garstang to Preston.

Good mixed coarse fishing, with formerly patchy stretches restocked as part of a research programme of Salford University. Nearly all the water is con-trolled by the Northern Anglers' Association, including the Glasson arm linking the canal to the Lune estuary.

Preston, Lancs. Approx. 57 m of towpath from Stainton to Preston.

C (DT on bank).

Lake District Rivers

See Aira Beck, Brathay, Calder (Cumbria), Cocker, Crake, Derwent (Cumbria), Ehen, Esk (Cumbria), Gilpin, Goldrill, Greta, Grizedale Beck, Irt, Kent, Leven, Mint, Rothay, Sprint, Trout Beck, Ulverston Canal.

Leeds and Liverpool Canal

The famous waterway joining Leeds with Liverpool, crossing the Pennine range through Shipley, Skipton, Gargrave, Burnley, Blackburn, Chorley and Wigan.

The fishing is variable, depending on the extent of restocking, but there are some notable stretches boasting roach over 1 lb, with many other coarse fish. The water is very popular for weekend matches. Most of the Yorkshire end of the canal is controlled by the Leeds and Liverpool Canal AA; in Lancashire,

Liverpool and District AA, Wigan and District AA and the Northern Anglers' Association hold water. See also Yorkshire Water Authority area rivers.

Chorley, Lancs. 24 m from Chorley to Halsall, near Ormskirk, including Haigh Canal.

C (DT on bank).

Halsall, Lancs. 18 m from Halsall to Liverpool.

C (DT Adv. Liverpool and Dist. AA).

Leven

Runs from Windermere through Newby Bridge to Morecambe Bay at Greenodd.

An excellent game river holding good trout and some coarse fish besides. However, it is strictly preserved for most of its length, although coarse fishing inquiries can be worthwhile.

Newby Bridge, Cumb. 300 yds stretch.

T (DT Adv. Swan Hotel, Newby Bridge).

Windermere, Cumb. Area around lake outfall.

C, T (Free fishing).

Tributaries: Crake, Grizedale Beck.

Lune

One of the best-known of the North-West game rivers, the Lune rises at Ravenstonedale, near Ash Fell, and runs south to Tebay, Kirkby Lonsdale, Hornby, Caton and Halton before entering a long estuary at Lancaster.

Besides salmon and sea-trout, which show best in the later half of the season, the Lune holds very big trout (record 8½ lb) and fine stocks of coarse fish, notably roach, dace and chub.

Caton, Lancs. 2 m upstream from Caton.

T, ST, S (DT Adv. tackle shop, 6 Moor Lane, Lancaster).

Caton, Lancs. 5 m from Hornby to Caton.

T, S (DT Adv. Mon.–Fri. only, tackle shop, 6 Moor Lane, Lancaster, or Curwen, Greenup Cottage, Hornby. No Sunday fishing, fly only at certain times as shown on permit. L–12).

Halton, Lancs. Halton fishery above Halton Weir.

C (DT Adv. tackle shop, 6 Moor Lane, Lancaster, or Station Hotel, Caton).

Halton, Lancs. Halton fishery above and below Halton Weir.

ST, S (DT Adv. tackle shop, 6 Moor Lane, Lancaster, or Station Hotel, Caton. Rods limited depending on section.)

Kirkby Lonsdale, Cumb. 2 m in area.

T, ST, S (Mon.–Fri. permit, Adv., no DT, tackle shop, Kirkby Lonsdale. Fishery open 1 Feb.–31 Oct.).

Lancaster, Lancs. Skerton Fishery, Beaumont Beck to Scaleford.

C, ST, S (DT Adv. tackle shop, 6 Moor Lane, Lancaster, or Station Hotel, Caton. Rod limit depending on section for S, ST).

Sedbergh, Cumb. 3 m near Sedbergh.

T, ST, S (WT Adv. tackle shop, Sedbergh).

Tebay, Cumb. 9 m from Gaisgill to Lowgill.

T, ST, S (WT Residents only Junction Hotel, Tebay, or George Hotel, Orton).

Whittington, Lancs. 400 yds of right bank at Whittington.

T, S (DT Adv. H. G. Mackereth, Whittington Farm).

Tributaries: Clough, Dee, Greta, Rawthey, Wenning.

Macclesfield Canal

The former cotton and coal route between Marple, Cheshire, and Kidsgrove, Staffs.

The water used to have a reputation for large roach and big pike, and although big fish are rare these days, stocks on the whole are good and re-stocking is building up some sections. Staffordshire AA, open for season membership, has sections on the canal.

Macclesfield, Cheshire. 9 m of left bank from Buxton Road, Macclesfield, to Robin Hood, Congleton.

C (DT on bank or from tackle shops in area).

Scholar Green, Staffs. 3½ m from Watery Lane Aqueduct to Hall Green Lock, towpath.

C (DT on bank or from J. Triwer, 650 Cinderhill Lane, Kent Green, Staffs).

Mersey
Perhaps the most polluted piece of water in Britain, although efforts are being made to improve water quality. Most of the river and the Goyt, which links the system to the main tributary, the Tame, are of little interest to anglers. Occasional pockets of fish are discovered from time to time near clean water outlets, which encourage the hope that fishing might flourish in the future.
Tributary: Tame.

Mint
Joins the Kent just above Kendal in the Lake District.
Offers fair trouting, although the fish are generally small, and the occasional salmon and sea-trout. Upstream farms are worth an inquiry for fishing permission.
Kendal, Cumb. 1 m from Laverick Bridge to Kent.
T, S (D T Adv. tackle shop, Kendal, or Kent A A).
Tributary of Kent system.

Peak Forest Canal
Runs from Whaley Bridge, Derbyshire, through Marple to Ashton Canal near Ashton-under-Lyne.
The section between Marple and Whaley Bridge is much polluted but improving with restocking. The best section is below Marple Lock.
Hyde, Cheshire. 4 m of towpath from Woodley Long Tunnel to Ashton Junction.
C (D T on bank or from tackle shop, Market Street, Hyde. Free permits for disabled anglers and pensioners by application to Hyde Federation of Anglers).
Whaley Bridge, Derbys. 6 m Whaley Bridge to Woodley.
C (D T on bank).

Rawthey
Joins the Lune near Sedbergh.
Fair trout fishing, some salmon.
Sedbergh, Cumb. 6 m near Sedbergh.
T, S (WT Adv. tackle shop, Sedbergh).
Tributary of Lune system.

Ribble
Rises at Cam Fell on the Yorkshire Moors and flows through Ribblesdale and then to Clitheroe and Preston to enter a long estuary.
Lower reaches offer coarse fish, while salmon and sea-trout are best in the middle reaches. The upper river offers good trout fishing, but is mostly private. Fish caught in the Ribble include a trout of more than 13 lb; chub, 8 lb; pike, 20 lb; and roach, 2 lb 9 oz.
Alston, Lancs. 4 m right bank from Stubbins Wood to Red Scar Wood.
C (D T on bank or from Ribble and Wyre F A).
Clitheroe, Lancs. 600 yds near hotel.
T, ST, S (D T Adv. Roefield Hotel, Edisford).
Clitheroe, Lancs. Stretch at Mitton Hall Farm, including part of Calder.
C, T, ST, S (D T Adv. Mitton Hall Farm, Great Mitton. Fly only in parts for game fish, L–14 rods only for game fish, 4 fly only, 12 for coarse fish in Calder).
Cuerdale, Lancs. Samlesbury School to Ribbleside Farm.
C (D T on bank or from Ribble and Wyre F A).
Great Mitton, W Yorks. Mitton Fishery from Mitton Bridge to Calder Foot.
C, T, ST, S (D T Adv. Mrs M. M. Haynes, Mitton Hall Farm, Great Mitton. L–10 rods from Mitton Bridge to Mitton Wood, 10 from Mitton Wood to Calder Foot).
Long Preston, N Yorks. Low Bridge to wood.
C, T, ST, S (D T Adv. ticket office on site).
Preston, Lancs. 2½ m from Darwen junction, including part of Darwen, to Liverpool Road Bridge, left bank.
C mainly (Free fishing).
Ribchester, Lancs. 1 m right bank upstream of Ribchester Bridge.
C (D T Adv. from farm on notice-board at bridge).
Ribchester, Lancs. 300 yds left bank downstream of Ribchester Bridge.
C (Free fishing).
Samlesbury, Lancs. Left bank

Samlesbury Church to Bezza Brook.
C (DT on bank or from Ribble and
Wyre FA).
Samlesbury, Lancs. Daisy Hill Farm to
Lower House Farm.
C (DT on bank or from Northern AA).
Settle, N Yorks. 4½ m.
T, S (DT Adv. Royal Oak, Settle. Fly
only, trout open season 1 Apr.–31
Oct.).
Tributaries: Calder (Lancs.), Hodder.

Rochdale Canal

Runs from the Calder and Hebble
Navigation at Sowerby Bridge, Yorks, to
the Bridgewater Canal at Manchester.

Contains quality coarse fish, but generally recognized as a problem fishery
because of the clarity of the water, which
demands a careful approach.
Middleton, Greater Manchester. 5 m of
towpath from Slattocks Bridge to
Manchester boundary.
C (DT on bank or from tackle shops in
area).
Rochdale, Lancs. From locks 36 to 49
and 51 to 55.
C (DT Adv. tackle shops in area).

Rothay

Formed from tributary streams above
Grasmere, the Rothay runs through
Rydal Water to empty out in Windermere
at the northern tip of the lake.

Mostly trout fishing, with some pike
and perch near Windermere.
Ambleside, Cumb. 5 m from Grasmere to
Ambleside.
C, T (DT Adv. tackle shops in
Ambleside, Bowness and
Windermere).

Shropshire Union Canal

This 150-mile system offers good coarse
fishing in the section which falls within
the North-West Water Authority area.
Clubs holding rights, some of them
offering day tickets, are Shropshire
Unions Canal AA, Hazeldine AA, Izaak
Walton (Staffs) AA, Provincial AA and
Whitmore Reans AA. (See also Severn-
Trent Water Authority rivers and canals,
and Welsh rivers and canals.)

Sprint

Joins the Kent above the junction with
the Mint.

Trout numerous but small, with sea-
trout and salmon from August onwards.
Farms upstream worthy of inquiries for
fishing.
Kendal, Cumb. 800 yds from Manchester
Water Pipe to Kent.
T, S (DT Adv. tackle shop, Kendal).
Tributary of Kent.

Tame

The Tame suffered greatly in the past
from pollution, but efforts are being
made to clean the water up, especially
by the Border Anglers and Naturalists,
part of Oldham and District AA.

Trout and grayling have been intro-
duced experimentally in some sections.
Greenfield, Greater Manchester. Water at
Alexandra Mill.
T (DT Adv. Border Anglers and
Naturalists. L–4).
Tributary of Mersey system.

Tarnbrook Wyre

One of the headstreams forming the
Wyre. Worth inquiries from landowners.
Tributary of Wyre system.

Trent and Mersey Canal

The Potteries canal, inspired in part by
Josiah Wedgwood, starting at Preston
Bridge Tunnel on the Bridgewater Canal
and running through Middlewich and
Stoke-on-Trent to join the Coventry
Canal at Fradley Junction, and on to
Trent at Burton-on-Trent.

The water can be patchy, but there is
a good section between Colwich Lock
and Wolseley Bridge, where results
are excellent. Clubs holding water on
the canal, some offering day tickets,
are Cheshire AA, Derby AA, Derby
Railway Institute FC, Fenton and District AS, North Staffs AA, and Stoke
City and District AA. The North-West
Water Authority area covers the canal
from Kidsgrove northwards; to the
south it falls in the Severn-Trent
Water Authority (q.v.) Trent Rivers
Division.

Avon (Warwickshire)
Famous as Shakespeare's river, the Warwickshire Avon rises in the east of the county, sweeping around Coventry and passing through Warwick, Stratford, Evesham and Pershore before joining the Severn at Tewkesbury.

It is an excellent coarse river, holding all main species, including barbel. It boasts roach of 2 lb 11 oz and a chub of 6 lb in records, and the match record tops 60 lb. This river hosted the World Championships at Luddington in 1981, with excellent results despite flood conditions.

Much of the water is controlled by associations, particularly Birmingham AA, which holds extensive fishing rights. Other associations are Worcester and District UAA, Royal Leamington Spa AA, and Rugby Federation of Anglers.
Cleeve Prior, Hereford and Worcs. Three fields from lane at Cleve Prior, left bank.
C (Free fishing).
Eckington, Hereford and Worcs. 7 m from Bredon to Eckington, plus stretch at Birlingham.
C (DT Adv. Bell Inn, Eckington; Mr Stayt, Boon Street, Eckington, or Cheltenham FC).
Evesham, Hereford and Worcs. 1 m from Boat Lane to rail bridge.
C (DT Adv. café, Hampton Ferry, Boat Lane, Evesham).
Pershore, Hereford and Worcs. 3½ m upstream and downstream of Pershore, from boats only.
C (Free fishing).
Pershore, Hereford and Worcs. ½ m above and below entry of Piddle Brook, right bank.
C (Free fishing).
Stratford-upon-Avon, Warwicks. 1½ m from Stratford towards Warwick and 2 m in Evesham direction.
C, T (DT on bank or from Captain A. E. Heath, 3 Garrick Way, Evesham Road, Stratford-upon-Avon).
Tewkesbury, Glos. 1½ m from Nealings Mill to Lower Lode.
C (DT on bank).

Warwick, Warwicks. ½ m at St Nicholas Park, right bank.
C (DT Adv. Amenities Officer, 10 Newbold Terrace, Leamington Spa).
Wood Norton, Hereford and Worcs. 1½ m of right bank.
C (DT Adv. tackle shop, 2 Severnside South, Bewdley).
Tributary of Severn system.
Severn Rivers Division.

Bandspinner Drain
Starts near Hatfield, Yorks, and then follows the Sheffield and South Yorkshire canal from Thorne almost to Keadby, where it enters Black Drain in the Keadby Drain system.
Fair to good coarse fishing, with roach, bream and some tench.
Crowle, Lincs. 1 m from Crowle.
C (DT Adv. Friendship Hotel, Keadby).
Trent Rivers Division.

Banwy
Rises in Welsh mountains and runs to join the Vyrnwy near Heniarth.
Trout, grayling, coarse fish and some salmon. Birmingham AA holds water on this river.
Llanerfyl, Powys. 2 m left bank and ½ m right bank above and below road bridge.
C (DT on bank, tackle shops Chester, or Northern AA).
Llanerfyl, Powys. 1½ m at Llanerfyl and Rhydarwydd.
C, T, S (DT Adv. Liverpool and Dist. AA).
Tributary of Severn system.
Severn Rivers Division.

Beeston Canal
Also known as Beeston Cut, this short waterway runs from Beeston Lock into Nottingham and back into the Trent at Meadow Lane lock.
Fair coarse fishing with some good roach.
Lenton, Notts. Lenton Chains junction to Beeston Lock.
C (DT on bank).
Trent Rivers Division.

Berk
Small stream which runs through Berkeley Vale to enter Severn estuary.

Trout and some coarse fish. Inquiries from local landowners may be worthwhile.

Severn Rivers Division.

Birmingham Canal
Starts at Worcester Bar in the heart of Birmingham and runs through Smethwick, West Bromwich, Tipton and Wolverhampton to join the Staffs.–Worcester Canal at Aldersley Junction.

Very patchy, with some pockets of coarse fish.

Wolverhampton, Staffs. Alma Street, Heath Town, to Wards Bridge, Wednesfield.
C (DT Adv. Whitmore Reans CAA).
Trent Rivers Division.

Birmingham–Fazeley Canal
Another of the waterways starting in the heart of Birmingham, the Birmingham–Fazeley runs under Spaghetti Junction, links with the Coventry Canal at Fazely Junction, and runs on to the Trent and Mersey Canal at Huddlesford.

Again, a patchy water, although there are fish in the heart of industrial development and local anglers sometimes catch quite good bags. Most of the water is run by Birmingham AA, which offers only season cards.

Fazeley, Staffs. 1 m of towpath from Tamworth to Fazeley.
C (DT on bank).
Trent Rivers Division.

Black Drain (Keadby Drains)
The three Keadby Drains, sometimes known simply as the Three Drains, run alongside one another from Pilfrey Bridge to Keadby (the other drains in the system being the Engine Drain and the Middle Drain).

They are excellent coarse fisheries, holding roach, bream and some tench and carp. Best fished in summer and autumn.

Keadby, Humberside. 1 m on all three drains.

C (DT Adv. Post Office, Keadby, or from Sheffield and Dist. AA).
Trent Rivers Division.

Blythe
A much improved tributary of the Tame which offers trout and coarse fishing, though most of it is association-controlled.

Meriden, Warwicks. 3 m in Packington Estates Fisheries.
T, C (DT Adv. ticket office or Packington Fisheries, Broadwater, Maxstoke Lane, Meriden. Fly only on trout section, L–14 rods for trout, 40 for coarse fishing. Trout season 18 Mar.–15 Oct.; coarse, 16 June–14 Mar.).
Trent Rivers Division.

Bradford
Joins the Lathkill near Bakewell.

Trout fishing, mostly preserved.

Youlgrave, Derbys. Stretch from Alport to Youlgrave.
T (DT Adv. Estate Office, Haddon Hall, near Bakewell. Fly only, L–2 rods. Trout season 1 Apr.–30 Sept. No Sunday fishing).
Trent Rivers Division.

Cain
Tributary joining the River Vyrnwy near Llansantffraid.

Holds trout and some coarse fish, mostly preserved.

Llanfyllin, Powys. 400 yds near hotel.
T (Residents only, Llanfyllin Bodfach Hall Hotel).

Llansantffraid, Powys. Road bridge to footbridge, left bank.
C, T (DT Adv. Lion Hotel, Llansantffraid).
Tributary of Severn system.
Severn Rivers Division.

Camlad
Small Severn tributary joining near Forden.

Trout and coarse fish.

Forden, Powys. 2 m of right bank Stalloe Road Bridge to Gaer Road Bridge.
T, C (DT Adv. Bond's or Millington's

tackle shops, Welshpool. Fly only).
Severn Rivers Division.

Char (Little Avon)
Rises on the Cotswold edge and skirts
Charfield to join the Severn estuary near
Berkeley.
Trout, some coarse fish.
Charfield, Avon. 5 m from Charfield to
Severn.
C, T (D T Adv. Charfield Motel).
Severn Rivers Division.

Chesterfield–Stockwith Canal
Runs from Chesterfield to the Trent at
West Stockwith.
At one time a patchy water, but re-
stocking has improved the quality of
coarse fishing immensely, especially
from Worksop to the Trent. Associations
holding water are Sheffield and District
A A, Retford A A, and Worksop A A A.
East Retford, Notts. 6½ m from West
Retford Bridge to Church Lane,
Clayworth.
C (D T on bank).
Gringley on the Hill, Notts. 8 m from
Drakeholes to Stockwith Basin.
C (D T Adv. Sheffield and Dist. A A).
Trent Rivers Division.

Churnet
Streams from Tittesworth Reservoir and
Rudyard Lake meet to form the Churnet,
which then runs through Leek to join the
Dove.
Offers trout and some coarse fish. Hit
by pollution in the past, but improving in
latter years.
Leek, Staffs. 3 m of right bank from
Macclesfield Road to Leek Brook.
C, T (D T Adv. to bona fide visitors
only, Leek and Moorlands F C).
Tributary of Trent system.
Trent Rivers Division.

Coventry Canal
Runs north from Coventry to meet the
Oxford Canal at Hawkesbury Junction
and on to Birmingham–Fazeley Canal at
Fazeley Junction.
Fairly good coarse fishing, though
patchy. Coventry A A has major holding.

Coventry, W Mids. 21 m from Bull's Head
Bridge, Polesworth, to Coventry.
C (D T on bank or from tackle shops in
area).
Tamworth, Staffs. 6 m from Fazeley to
Polesworth.
C (D T on bank).
Trent Rivers Division.

Cranfleet Canal
Cut joining the Trent below the Erewash
Canal.
Fair coarse fishing.
Long Eaton, Derbys. 150 yds of left bank
from Erewash Canal to bridge.
C (D T on bank or from tackle shop,
Long Eaton).

Derwent (Derbyshire)
Perhaps the most important tributary of
the Trent for anglers, the Derwent rises
in the Peak District, feeding a series of
reservoirs, including Ladybower. It runs
on to Belper, passing through some of
the prettiest country in the Midlands,
finally joining the Trent at Milne.
The upper river holds trout and grayling,
and much of the fishing is preserved.
Lower, coarse fish become evident, although a head of trout is maintained
throughout. Ticket fishing is easier to
come by on the lower reaches.
Clubs and associations holding water
include Derby Railway Institute F C,
Belper A C, and Chesterfield A A. Derby-
shire County Council A C has coarse
fishing only from Borrowash to Wilne.
Derby, Derbys. 3 m from Five Arches rail
bridge to Darley Abbey Weir.
C, T (D T from keeper).
Derby, Derbys. 5 m from Darley Weir to
Borrowash.
C, T (D T Adv. tackle shops, Derby).
Duffield, Derbys. 2½ m Milford Bridge
to Little Eaton.
C, T (D T Adv. tackle shops in area,
Bridge Inn, Duffield, or Derby A F).
Matlock Bath, Derbys. 100 yds right
bank from bridge to park.
C, T (D T Adv. Midland Hotel, Matlock
Bath).
Rowsley, Derbys. 2 m from Rowsley
Bridge to Duke's Seat.

T (Residents only, Peacock Hotel, Rowsley. Fly only).

Rowsley, Derbys. 1 m rail bridge to Primrose Bridge.

T (Residents only, Grouse and Claret Hotel, Rowsley. Fly only).

Whatstandwell, Derbys. 150 yds left bank from bridge to foundry.

C, T (D T Adv. Derwent Hotel, Whatstandwell).

Tributary of Trent system.

Trent Rivers Division.

Devon

Rises at Knipton and runs north to the Trent near Newark.

Restocking has created a good coarse fishery.

Hawton, Notts. 1 m upstream of bridge and 1½ m below.

C (D T Adv. Ransome, Hoffman and Pollard A C).

Newark, Notts. 1 m from Springhouse public house to Newark Dyke.

C (Free fishing).

Tributary of Trent system.

Trent Rivers Division.

Dove

The river beloved of Izaak Walton and his friend Charles Cotton. It rises in the Peak District and flows through Dovedale.

The trout and grayling fishing is fair, though not of the quality Walton would have found. Most of the fishing is preserved, and hotel waters are the only known access.

Hartington, Derbys. Stretch of left bank at Hartington.

T (Residents only, Charles Cotton Hotel, Hartington. Fly only).

Thorpe Cloud, Derbys. 2 m from Staffs border to Black Rock.

T (Residents only, Izaak Walton Hotel, Thorpe, Dovedale. Fly only).

Tributary of Trent system.

Trent Rivers Division.

Ecclesbourne

Rises near Wirksworth and runs to the Derbyshire Derwent near Derby.

Fair trout fishing, mostly preserved.

Turnditch, Derbys. ½ m stretch.

T (D T Adv. tackle shops, Derby. L–6. Fly only).

Tributary of Trent system.

Trent Rivers Division.

Engine Drain (Keadby Drains)

See Black Drain.

Erewash Canal

A coal waterway from Langley Mill, Derbys, to Trent Lock on the Trent at Long Eaton.

This water has been much improved by restocking and is now a fair coarse fishery.

Cotmanhay, Derbys. Shipley Lock to Stenson's Lock.

C (D T Adv. tackle shop, Cotmanhay Road, Ilkeston, or Bridge Inn, Cotmanhay).

Langley Mill, Derbys. 2½ m Shipley Lock to Langley Mill.

C (D T on bank).

Long Eaton, Derbys. 2 m of left bank from Long Eaton Lock to Trent Lock.

C (D T on bank or from tackle shop, Long Eaton).

Long Eaton, Derbys. 2 m from Sandiacre Lock to Long Eaton Lock.

C (D T Adv. Bridge Tackle, Derby Road, Long Eaton).

Trowell, Derbys. Barker's Lock to Whitehouse Lock.

C (D T on bank or from Horse and Groom public house, Ilkeston).

Trent Rivers Division.

Eye

A tributary of the Wreake rising at Saltby and joining the main river above Melton Mowbray.

Fair coarse fishing.

Melton Mowbray, Leics. Stretch of left bank from Wyfordby to Melton.

C (D T on bank or from Leicester tackle shops).

Tributary of Trent system.

Trent Rivers Division.

Grand Union Canal

Part of the main line of this great waterway falls in the Severn-Trent catchment, as does the Leicester Branch and the

Welford Arm (see also Anglian Water Authority and Thames Water Authority areas).

Most of the canal holds good stocks of the main coarse species, with occasional big carp. Associations holding water include Birmingham AA, Calpac, Coventry AA, London AA, Luton AC, Royal Leamington Spa AA, Leicester AS, Leicester and District ASA (both on Leicester Branch), Rugby Federation of Anglers (Leicester Branch), and Coventry AA (Welford Arm).

Braunston, Leics (Leicester Branch). From north end of Braunston Tunnel to Oxford Canal junction.
C (DT on bank or from tackle shops in area).

Husband's Bosworth, Leics (Leicester Branch). Mowsley Road Bridge to point near Honeypot Lane.
C (DT on bank).

Knowle, W Mids. 3 m, bridges 71–78 inclusive.
C (DT on bank or from keeper, D. Harris, The Cottage, Kixley Lane, Knowle).

Lapworth, Warwicks. Bridges 64–67.
C (DT on bank).

Leamington Spa, Warwicks. 12 m Warwick to Napton.
C (DT from keeper).

Leicester, Leics (Leicester Branch). 6 m Blaby to Leicester.
C (DT on bank).

North Kilworth, Leics (Leicester Branch). From south end of Bosworth Tunnel to Bridge 37, South Kilworth, including Welford Arm.
C (DT on bank or from tackle shops in area).

Wigston, Leics (Leicester Branch). 8 m Glen Parva Bridge to Saddington Tunnel.
C (DT on bank or from tackle shops in area).
Trent Rivers Division.

Grantham Canal
Formerly a waterway linking Grantham and Nottingham, the canal has fallen into disuse and stretches are no longer fishable through heavy weeding. The stretch between Knipton and Nottingham falls in the Severn-Trent Water Authority area, the rest in the Anglian Water Authority (q.v.) Lincolnshire Rivers Division. Nottingham AA holds stretch for members only.
Trent Rivers Division.

Greet
Small tributary of Trent which runs through Southwell.
Private trout fishing.
Trent Rivers Division.

Idle
Formed by a meeting of streams to the south of Retford, the Idle runs a shallow course to the Trent at Idlestop.

A fine coarse fishery, despite being difficult fishing. Restocking is making amends for past pollution.

Everton, Notts. $4\frac{1}{2}$ m of right bank from Newington to Gringley-on-the-Hill.
C (DT Adv. tackle shops Rotherham or Rotherham UAF).

Haxey, Humbs. Right bank for $\frac{1}{2}$ m above and below Gate Inn Bridge.
C (DT Adv. Gate Inn).

Haxey, Humbs. 4 m from Langholme to Trent.
C (DT Adv. Gate Inn, Haxey, or Sheffield and Dist. AA).

Idlestop, Notts. Just over mile of left bank at Idlestop.
C (DT Adv. Park Drain Hotel, Idlestop).

Mattersey, Notts. Three stretches of right bank below Mattersey main road.
C (DT Adv. Barley Mow Hotel, Mattersey).

Misson, Notts. 1 m of left bank from ferry downstream.
C (DT Adv. White Horse public house, Misson).

Newington, Notts. Stretch of left bank downstream of Green Lane.
C (DT Adv. Ship Inn, Newington).

West Stockwith, Notts. Right bank from the Soss, Misterton, to Trent.
C (DT Adv. White Hart public house, West Stockwith).
Tributary of Trent system.
Trent Rivers Division.

Keadby Drains
See Black Drain.

Leadon
Rises to the north of Ledbury and joins the Severn opposite Gloucester.

Trout and coarse fish, including barbel, but no known opportunities for visiting anglers.

Severn Rivers Division.

Leam
The Leam rises near Daventry and runs through Leamington Spa to join the Warwickshire Avon at Warwick.

Like the Avon, a good coarse fishery.

Leamington Spa, Warwicks. Stretches at Newbold Comyn, Victoria Park, Edmondscote and Mill Gardens.

C (D T on bank or from Amenities Officer, 10 Newbold Terrace, Leamington Spa. Newbold Comyn, L–40; Victoria Park, L–20; Edmondscote, L–20; Mill Gardens, L–20).

Tributary of Severn system.

Severn Rivers Division.

Loughborough Canal
Built to bypass a part of the Soar between Barrow-on-Soar and Loughborough.

Fair coarse fishing.

Loughborough, Leics. $2\frac{1}{2}$ m from Barrow to Loughborough.

C (D T Adv. tackle shops in Barrow and Loughborough).

Trent Rivers Division.

Manifold
Runs through the Manifold Valley, the Derbyshire beauty spot, to join the Dove.

Trout and grayling mainly.

Longnor, Derbys. 7 m stretch.

T (Residents only Crewe and Harpur Hotel, Longnor. Fly only).

Tributary of Trent system.

Trent Rivers Division.

Mann (Maun)
One of the rivers forming the Idle. Apparently fishless through pollution.

Mease
A good coarse fishery with chub to 6 lb recorded, the Mease runs to join the Trent above Burton.

No known ticket opportunities for visitors.

Trent Rivers Division.

Meece
Rises in North Staffs and runs through Millmeece to join the Sow near Great Bridgeford.

Fair coarse fishing.

Millmeece, Staffs. Stretch at Badnall Wharf.

C (D T Adv. Whitmore Reans C A A).

Tributary of Trent system.

Trent Rivers Division.

Meese
Rises near Newport, Salop, and flows to join the Tern just above its junction with the Roden.

Holds trout and some coarse fish.

Caynton, Salop. 2 m of right bank below Caynton Mill.

C (D T Adv. Whitmore Reans C A A).

Tributary of Severn system.

Severn Rivers Division.

Middle Drain (Keadby Drains)
See Black Drain.

Moira Canal
See Ashby Canal.

Mule
A trout stream rising near Newtown and flowing north to the Severn at Abermule.

Abermule, Powys. 4 m from Abermule to Kerry.

T (D T Adv. tackle shop, Newtown. Fly only).

Tributary of Severn system.

Severn Rivers Division.

Newark Dyke
Breaks from the Trent at Staythorpe, Notts, and runs through Newark to rejoin the Trent at Crankley Point.

Excellent roach fishing (especially

Shropshire Union Canal

Part of this 150-mile system falls in the Severn-Trent Water Authority region, the rest being in the North-West Water Authority catchment and the Welsh Water Authority region (q.v.).

Holds good stocks of roach, perch and bream (especially near Ellesmere Port), with some pike, tench and carp.

Abermule, Powys (Montgomery Branch). 2½ m from Bridge 142 to Bridge 148.
C (D T Adv. Cammell Laird Sports Club angling section).

High Onn, Staffs. Bridge 25, High Onn, to Bridge 23, Cowley.
C (D T Adv. tackle shop, Stafford, or Izaak Walton, Staffs., A A. Coarse season 16 June–30 Sept.).

Welshpool, Powys. Right bank from below lock to Gallows Tree.
C (D T Adv. Bond's or Millington's tackle shops, Welshpool, Green Dragon public house, Buttington, or Westwood Park Hotel, Welshpool).

Wolverhampton, W Mids. 3 m from Autherley Junction to Wheaton Aston lock.
C (D T on bank or from keeper, Waterways Board Junction Office, Autherley).

Wolverhampton, W Mids. Pendeford Bridge 4 to Broomhall Bridge 16.
C (D T Adv. Whitmore Reans C A A).
Severn Rivers Division.

Snow Sewer

Short branch of Warping Drain, which was unaffected by 1976 pollution. Well stocked.

Idlestop, Notts. 1 m near Park Drain Hotel.
C (D T Adv. Park Drain Hotel or Mrs Wilson, Beech Cottage, Main Street, Owston Ferry).
Trent Rivers Division.

Soar

Rises to the south of Leicester to flow through the town and on to Loughborough and the Trent near Kegworth.

The Soar has suffered greatly from pollution in the past, but concerted efforts to clean it up and restock it are paying off. A popular match water at weekends.

Barrow-upon-Soar, Leics. 3 m of left bank from Mountsorrel to Barrow.
C (D T Adv. from keeper, E. Lewin, 15 High Street, Barrow-upon-Soar. L–60).

Kegworth, Leics. Right bank from road bridge to first lock.
C (D T on bank or from tackle shop, Long Eaton).

Kegworth, Leics. From Nottingham A A board below Kegworth Bridge to Kingston Dyke, left bank.
C (D T on bank).

Kegworth, Leics. 2 m from Kegworth Flood Lock to Ratcliffe Lock, including Ratcliffe Deep.
C (D T Adv. tackle shop, Long Eaton, or Anchor Inn, Kegworth).

Leicester, Leics. Abbey Park water.
C (Free fishing).

Loughborough, Leics. 10 m from Barrow Locks to Sutton Bonington.
C (D T Adv. tackle shops in area or from Rose and Crown Inn, Ashby de la Zouch).

Mountsorrel, Leics. Point above Rothley Brook to Thackholme Deeps, except as marked.
C (D T on bank or from Leicester tackle shops).

Quorndon, Leics. Stretch within Proctor's Pleasure Park.
C (D T Adv. ticket machine at entrance).

Ratcliffe-on-Soar, Leics. 1 m of left bank from Soar mouth upstream.
C (D T Adv. on Sundays, L–2 rods when matches being fished; tickets on bank on weekdays or from Granville A C).

Redhill Lock, Leics. From Lock to Trent.
C (D T Adv. Redhill Lock keeper).
Tributary of Trent system.
Trent Rivers Division.

Sow

Flows through Stafford to join the Trent above Rugeley.

Fair coarse fishing with occasional trout. Izaak Walton, Staffs., AA holds some water.

Great Bridgeford, Staffs. 1 m at Great Bridgeford and at Worstan Hall.

C (DT Adv. Whitmore Reans CAA).

Stafford, Staffs. Water at and around Stafford.

C (DT Adv. tackle shop, Stafford, or from Izaak Walton, Staffs, AA).

Stafford, Staffs. Part of left bank upstream of town.

C (Free fishing).

Stafford, Staffs. 6 m near Great Bridgeford to Brancote.

C (DT Adv. tackle shop, Stafford).

Tributary of Trent system.

Trent Rivers Division.

Sowe

Much polluted tributary of the Warwickshire Avon, generally considered to be worthless until improved.

Severn Rivers Division.

Staffs. and Worcs. Canal

Extension of Trent and Mersey Canal built to link the Mersey and Severn. Runs from Great Haywood Junction near Stafford to Kidderminster and on to Stourport.

An improving coarse water, which is being heavily restocked in parts. Birmingham AA, Izaak Walton, Staffs., AA, Provincial AA and Whitmore Reans CAA hold water.

Coven, Staffs. Cross Green Bridge to Slade Heath Bridge.

C (DT from keeper or Goodyear AC).

Gailey, Staffs. Gravelly Way Bridge to Gailey Road Bridge.

C (DT Adv. Whitmore Reans CAA).

Penkridge, Staffs. $4\frac{1}{2}$ m from Boat Inn, Penkridge, to Bridge 94.

C (DT Adv. Whitmore Reans CAA).

Sharshill, Staffs. Bridges 74–75.

C (Fishing for bona fide visitors by arrangement with Essington WMC Angling Section).

Stafford, Staffs. 5 m from bridge to Milford Aqueduct.

C (DT Adv. tackle shop, Stafford).

Wolverhampton, W Mids. Wightwick Locks to Botterham Locks.

C (DT Adv. from Whitmore Reans CAA).

Severn Rivers Division.

Stour (Warwickshire)

Rises near Long Compton and runs through Shipston-on-Stour to the Warwickshire Avon below Stratford.

Good coarse fishing, especially for chub, dace and bream, with some trout. No known ticket access, but water is held by Birmingham AA, which has open season membership.

Severn Rivers Division

Stour (Worcestershire)

Rises near Dudley and flows to the Severn at Stourport.

Suffers a great deal from pollution, and fishing is not considered worthwhile.

Severn Rivers Division.

Stratford-on-Avon Canal

Links Stratford with the Worcs and Birmingham Canal at King's Norton.

Birmingham AA has large holdings along the 24-mile waterway, but there are no known ticket openings. Besides main coarse species the canal holds carp.

Severn Rivers Division bridges 24–25 and 27 to Stratford.

Trent Rivers Division bridges 25–27, and Lifford to bridge 24.

Tame

Rises near Walsall and runs through Birmingham, where pollution has all but finished it off. At the time of going to press some restocking is in progress.

Trent Rivers Division.

Tame Valley Canal

Part of the Birmingham Navigations (see Rushall Canal).

Contains some pockets of fish, but not generally considered a worthwhile proposition.

Trent Rivers Division.

Tanat

Rises in Wales and flows to the Vyrnwy near Llanymynech.

Holds trout, grayling, chub, dace and some salmon.

Llangedwyn, Clwyd. Stretch of left bank.

C, T, S (DT Adv. Green Inn, Llangedwyn. Fly only during trout season).

Llansantffraid, Powys. Stretch near hotel.

C, T, S (DT Adv. Bryn Tanat Hall Hotel, Llansantffraid).

Llan-y-Blodwel, Salop. 1 m stretch near inn.

T (DT Adv. Horse Shoe Inn, Llan-y-Blodwel. L–4, fly only).

Tributary of Severn system.

Severn Rivers Division.

Teme

Rises above Felindre and runs through Leintwardine and Tenbury Wells to the Severn below Worcester.

Holds trout, coarse fish and some salmon, but there are no known ticket openings.

Severn Rivers Division.

Tern

Tributary of the Severn, running mostly along the Staffs–Shropshire border.

Coarse fish and some trout.

Marsh Green, Salop. Isombridge Farm land.

C, T (DT Adv. Whitmore Reans CAA).

Severn Rivers Division.

Torne

Rises near Maltby in Yorkshire and flows to the Trent at Keadby.

A river improving from restocking and offering good roach fishing, with other species.

Keadby, Lincs. 9 m from Keadby to Acomb Bar Bridge.

C (DT Adv. Cross Keys public house, Wroot).

Tributary of Trent system.

Trent Rivers Division.

Trent

The main artery of a huge river system, the Trent rises in the heart of the Potteries and flows to Rugeley, Burton-on-Trent, Nottingham, Newark and the Humber. Below Cromwell Lock, down river of Newark, the river is tidal.

The history of the Trent is a modern success story in the battle against pollution. In the days before massive pollution entered from the Potteries and the Peak District and the industrial towns of the lower reaches, it was, like the Thames, a salmon river and boasted among other attractions a fine head of big barbel. With the Peak pollution much reduced, and that from the Potteries diminishing, the river staggered back from a mediocre coarse fishery to one of the best Midlands venues. It now boasts a fine head of roach and chub, while barbel seem to be growing in numbers, and carp are obviously thriving, with two fish over 30 lb recorded. In latter years, too, salmon have been sighted in the lower river, some of which were hooked on rod and line. It is in the lower tidal part of the river that the biggest improvement has taken place. Match records now top 50 lb. After the monumental effort taken to clean the river, clubs along the length and the Water Authority are stopping at nothing to continue the work, and there is hope that the whole river can be returned to its pre-industrial glory.

Clubs holding water on the Trent include Birmingham AA, Coventry AA, Nottingham AA, Derby AA, Doncaster AA, Lincoln AA, Swadlincote AA, Goole and District AA, Slaithwaite AA, Hull and District AA and Chesterfield AA.

Attenborough, Notts. 1 m left bank Barton Ferry to Beeston.

C (DT on bank. No visitors Sundays because of match bookings).

Barton, Notts. Right bank from Barton Ferry to Island.

C (DT on bank. No visitors Sundays because of match bookings).

Besthorpe, Notts. 1 m right bank from Besthorpe Gravel Pits to first fence downstream.

C (DT on bank).

Bleasby, Notts. Stretch of left bank from Bleasby to Hazelford.

C (DT on bank or from Star and Garter public house, Bleasby).

Burton Joyce, Notts. 4 m of left bank from one field below Radcliffe Viaduct to Gunthorpe Bridge.

C (DT on bank).

Chilwell, Notts. From second clappergate above Mitchell's Boating Station to sixth clappergate below weir, left bank.

C (DT on bank).

Clifton, Notts. 500 yds of right bank from behind church to weir.

C (DT on bank).

Collingham, Notts. 5 m of right bank from Cromwell Weir to Besthorpe Wharf.

C (DT on bank. L–200).

Colwick Park, Notts. ¾ m marked by Water Authority boards at Colwick, plus Trent Loop above weir, left bank.

C (DT Adv. tackle shop, E. Kirk, Carlton Road, Nottingham, or Netherfield Pets and Gardens, Netherfield, Nottingham).

Cottam, Notts. 1 m of left bank from below Torksey Bridge.

C (DT Adv. Sheffield and Dist. AA).

Cromwell, Notts. ¾ m of left bank from Ness Farm to Cromwell Lock.

C (DT Adv. from Ness Farm).

Cromwell, Notts. 1 m of left bank from one field below weir to wharf opposite Jolly Bargeman.

C (DT Adv. Sheffield and Dist. AA).

Dunham, Notts. 2 m of right bank at Dunham Bridge.

C (DT Adv. tackle shop, Rotherham; Bridge Garage, Dunham Bridge; or Rotherham and Dist. UAF).

Dunham Bridge, Notts. 1 m left bank down from Dunham Bridge to Rampton Island.

C (DT Adv. Bridge Garage, Dunham Bridge).

Dunham Bridge, Notts. ¾ m left bank upstream of Dunham Bridge.

C (DT Adv. Bridge Garage, Dunham Bridge, or G. Beaumont, The Green, Dunham Bridge).

Farndon, Notts. ¾ m left bank from Farndon Ferry to junction of Newark Dyke.

C (DT Adv. S. Clark, 11 Avebury Close, Clifton, or from Britannia Inn).

Fiskerton, Notts. ½ m of left bank from Hazelford Lock downstream.

C (DT Adv. Bromley Arms, Fiskerton).

Fledborough, Notts. ⅜ m of left bank from Fledborough downstream.

C (DT Adv. Sheffield and Dist. AA).

Flintham, Notts. 1¾ m right bank from Hazelford, Nabb's Island, upstream.

C (DT on bank).

Girton, Notts. 1 m right bank from Girton upstream.

C (DT Adv. Sheffield and Dist. AA).

Gunthorpe, Notts. ¾ m left bank below Gunthorpe Lock.

C (DT on bank).

Hallowell, Notts. 2¾ m right bank from Holme Pierrepoint to Stoke Weir.

C (DT on bank).

Hazelford, Notts. 300 yds left bank from second clappergate above Star and Garter to clappergate below.

C (DT Adv. Star and Garter, Hazelford).

Hazelford, Notts. 500 yds from weir upstream, left bank.

C (DT on bank).

High Marnham, Notts. ¾ m of left bank from Bromley Arms to first fence downstream.

C (DT on bank).

Holme, Notts. 2½ m of right bank from Winthorpe Lake down to Cromwell Lock.

C (DT on bank or from keeper, K. F. Brumpton, Church Cottage, Holme, near Newark).

Holme Pierrepoint, Notts. 1½ m of right bank, Holme Pierrepoint Country Park.

C (DT Adv. Ranger's Post in park. L–50).

Hoveringham, Notts. 1½ m left bank from Dover Beck to second meadow below Elm Tree Inn.

C (DT Adv. Elm Tree Inn, Hoveringham).

Kelham, Notts. ½ m of left bank upstream of Kelham Bridge.

C (DT Adv. Notts County Council, Kelham Hall, Newark).

Kettlethorpe, Lincs. ¾ m of right bank downstream of Laughterton.

C (DT Adv. tackle shop, Rotherham; Bridge Garage, Dunham Bridge; or from Rotherham UAF).

Long Eaton, Derbys. Left bank from Soar Mouth to Leisure Waters.

C (DT Adv. Trent Lock Café).

Long Eaton, Derbys. Left bank from spinney to Sawley Bridge.

C (DT on bank or from Harrington Arms public house, Sawley, near Long Eaton).

Long Eaton, Derbys. 2 m of left bank from Thrumpton Ferry to junction with Erewash.

C (DT on bank or from tackle shop, Long Eaton).

Newton Solney, Staffs. 300 yds of right bank from Trent Lane downstream.

C (Free fishing for local anglers only).

North Muskham, Notts. Footit's Marsh, left bank for ½ m.

C (DT Adv. Crown Inn, North Muskham).

North Muskham, Notts. ¾ m of left bank to Ness Farm.

C (DT on bank).

North Muskham, Notts. ¾ m of left bank above Newcastle Arms.

C (DT Adv. Newcastle Arms public house, North Muskham).

Nottingham, Notts. Victoria Embankment from Trent Bridge to Wilford Bridge.

C (Free fishing).

Rolleston, Notts. 2 m of left bank from Fiskerton to Farndon.

C (DT Adv. from Watson's tackle shop, Oak Street, Nottingham; R. Dibble, 40 Belvedere Street, Mansfield, or Post Office, Rolleston).

Sawley, Derbys. 200 yds of right bank at Trent Lock.

C (DT on bank).

Sawley, Derbys. Right bank from Leisure Sport fishery to Soar Mouth.

C (DT Adv. tackle shop, Long Eaton, or café, Trent Lock).

Shardlow, Derbys. 3 m from point above

Derwent's entry to end-of-fishery boards.

C (DT Adv. Crown Inn, Shardlow).

Shelford, Notts. 2½ m of right bank from Stoke Weir to Old Gunthorpe Bridge remains, plus small sections below old bridge buttress.

C (DT on bank).

South Clifton, Notts. 6½ m of right bank from South Clifton to Besthorpe.

C (DT from keeper at North and South Clifton or Sheffield Amalgamated AS).

Sutton-on-Trent, Notts. Nearly 3 m of left bank from Holes Mill to Girton Stakes.

C (DT Adv. from keeper, G. W. Richardson, 1 Middleholme Lane, Sutton).

Torksey, Notts. ½ m of right bank in the Trent Arm.

C (DT Adv. Sheffield and Dist. AA).

Whitmore Grove, Notts. ¾ m upstream from Causeway Dyke.

C (DT Adv. Star and Garter public house, Hazelford).

Willington, Derbys. 10 m from Willington to Swarkestone.

C (DT Adv. Rising Sun public house, Willington, or tackle shop, Crewe and Harpur, Swarkestone).

Winthorpe, Notts. ½ m of right bank at Winthorpe.

C (DT Adv. from keeper, Mrs I. Potter, Winthorpe Rail Crossing).

Winthorpe, Notts. Right bank for 1½ m from opposite Crankley Point to Winthorpe Rail Crossing.

C (DT on bank).

Winthorpe, Notts. ¾ m from Winthorpe Rail Crossing to Winthorpe Lake, right bank.

C (DT on bank or from keeper, K. F. Brumpton, Church Cottage, Holme, near Newark).

Tributaries of the Trent system: Amber, Anker, Blythe, Bradford, Churnet, Derwent (Derbyshire), Devon, Dove, Ecclesbourne, Eye, Greet, Idle, Loughborough Canal, Manifold, Mann, Mease, Newark Dyke, Penk, Poulter, Ryton, Sence, Snow Sewer, Soar, Sow, Tame, Torne, Warping

Drain, Whiston Brook, Wreake, Wye (Derbyshire).
Trent Rivers Division.

Trent and Mersey Canal
Fair coarse fishing (see description under North-West Water Authority area).
Cheddleton, Staffs (Caldon Branch). 6 m from Cheddleton road bridge to Frogall Basin.
C (D T Adv. by arrangement with Leek and Moorlands F C, for bona fide visitors only).
Trent Rivers Division.

Vyrnwy
Runs from Lake Vyrnwy in the north of Powys through Dolanog and Myfod to join the Severn near Llandrinio.
An important Severn tributary for Midland anglers, offering excellent coarse fishing, with some sea-trout and salmon. A club match in 1973 yielded the record-winning weight of 101 lb 5 oz. Associations holding water include Birmingham A A, Coventry A A and Warrington A A.
Llansantffraid, Powys. 1 m of left bank at Colfryn Farm.
C, T, S (DT Adv. tackle shops, Liverpool, or from Liverpool and Dist. A A).
Llansantffraid, Powys. 2 m of right bank at Llansantffraid and Houghton.
C, T, S (D T Adv. Liverpool and Dist. A A).
Llanwddyn, Powys. 3 m of right bank from weir below Dam Pool.
C, ST, T, S (D T Adv. Lake Vyrnwy Hotel, Llanwddyn).
Llanymynech, Salop. 1½ m of left bank from Pentre Farm to A483 road bridge and stretch of left bank below bridge.
C, T (D T on bank, tackle shop, Chester, or Northern A A).
Llanymynech, Salop. 1 m of left bank from Great Dyffrydd.
C, T, S (D T Adv. Bond's or Millington's tackle shop, Welshpool).
Maesbrook, Salop. Stretch of left bank at Maesbrook.

C, T (D T on bank, tackle shop, Chester, or Northern A A).
Severn Rivers Division.

Walsall Canal
Part of the Birmingham Canal Navigations system.
Not regarded as anything of a fishery at present.
Trent Rivers Division.

Warping Drain
Starts near Idlestop and runs to the Trent at Owston Ferry.
The water was hit by pollution in the 1970s, but restocking has restored its worth as a coarse fishery.
Owston Ferry, Notts. From below Park Drain Hotel to Trent.
C (D T Adv. Park Drain Hotel, Idlestop, or Mrs Wilson, Beech Cottage, Main Street, Owston Ferry).
Trent Rivers Division.

Whiston Brook
Rises near Wheaton Aston and joins the River Penk near Whiston, Staffs.
Holds some coarse fish.
Penkridge, Staffs. Left bank, Preston Mill Farm to Penk.
C (D T Adv. Whitmore Reans C A A).
Tributary of Trent system.
Trent Rivers Division.

Wreake
Rises on Leicestershire border to join Soar downstream of Leicester.
Improving coarse fishery.
Melton Mowbray, Leics. Stretches at Asfordby, Frisby, Hoby and Melton, described on Leicester A S map from Leicester tackle shops.
C (D T on bank or from Leicester tackle shops).
Tributary of Trent system.
Trent Rivers Division.

Wye (Derbyshire)
Said to be one of only two waters in England where rainbow trout breed naturally, the Derbyshire Wye rises near Buxton and runs through Bakewell to join the Derbyshire Derwent at Rowsley.
It also contains brown trout and gray-

ling, and the rainbows are under the protection of the trout close season for the water.

Bakewell, Derbys. 5½ m Ashford to Rowsley.

T (Residents, The Rutland Arms, The Square, Bakewell, and The Peacock, Rowsley. Dry fly only, season 16 May–15 Nov.).

Baslow, Derbys. 4½ m from Cressbrook Mill to Ashford Marble Works.

T plus grayling (Residents, The Cavendish, Baslow. Trout fishing fly only).

Tributary of Trent system.

Trent Rivers Division.

Wyreley and Essington Canal

Part of the Birmingham Canal Navigations system.

Its fishing worth is doubtful.

Trent Rivers Division.

Southern Water Authority Rivers

This water authority's area, which includes the Isle of Wight, covers the relatively short south-flowing waters occurring south of the downs, below the Thames watershed, and the Medway, relatively long and easterly-flowing.

To the west the area is bordered by the famed Avon of Hampshire, within the Wessex Water Authority borders, but it does boast famous waters of its own such as the Test. One of the great escape areas from the fairly close metropolis, but more people rush through in search of beaches and to meet ferries than stop to sample the fishing.

Adur

Rises near Horsham, flowing to the Channel at Shoreham.

Like many waters of the area it has a long tidal reach which adds mullet and bass to the stocks of coarse fish. Sea-trout are also encountered. Much of the river is association-controlled.

Dial Post, W Sussex. Short stretch from Tenchford to the first weir.

C (DT Adv. tackle shops, Worthing and Hove, or from Swallows Farm, Dial Post).

Steyning, W Sussex. 3 m from Beeding Bridge to Streatham Bridge.

C (DT Adv. tackle shop, Steyning).

Arun

Rises in the north of Sussex to run through Pulborough and Arundel to the Channel at Littlehampton.

A good coarse fishery, with bass and mullet in summer in the long estuary. Some sea-trout are also taken.

Amberley, W Sussex. 2 m from Amberley downstream.

C (DT Adv. café, Amberley Bridge).

Arundel, W Sussex. 2½ m South Stoke Bridge to Arundel Bridge.

C, ST (DT Adv. tackle shop, Arundel).

Arundel, W Sussex. Right bank between Arundel and Ford rail bridge.

C, ST (Free with obligatory ticket from Area Engineer, Southern Water Authority, River Road, Arundel).

Bury, W Sussex. 2 m of right bank from Houghton Bridge to Bury Ferry.

C (DT Adv. tackle shops, Worthing and Hove, or Houghton Bridge Tea Rooms in summer only).

Littlehampton, W Sussex. 5 m Arundel Bridge to Littlehampton.

C, ST (Free fishing).

Pulborough, W Sussex. Just over mile from fence below Swan Bridge to sluice above Greatham Bridge.

C (WT Adv. Leisure Sport, RMC House, High Street, Feltham, Middx).

Pulborough, W Sussex. 4 m from Stopham Bridge to Greatham Bridge.

C (DT Adv. from keeper).

Pulborough, W Sussex. 1½ m from Stopham to Swan.

C (DT Adv. newsagent's shop, Swan Corner, Pulborough).

Wisborough Green, W Sussex. 3 m of right bank from Orford Farm entry to Wisborough Green.

C (DT Adv. Crawley AS).

Tributaries of Arun: Kird, West Rother.

Batley Stream (Bartley Stream)

Small tributary of the Teise.

Coarse fish and trout.

Tunbridge Wells, Kent. Stretch from Lamberhurst to Bells Yew.

C (D T Adv. weekdays from The Forge Garage, Little Bayham, or by post from Estate Office, Little Bayham, Lamberhurst. Fishery closed 30 Oct.–31 Mar.).

Tributary of Medway system.

Beaulieu

A short game river rising in the New Forest and flowing through Beaulieu to the Solent opposite Cowes.

Best-known for its sea-trout and trout, the river also has some coarse fish. The fishery is largely preserved in the upper reaches.

Buckler's Hard, Hants. 8 m of right bank from Bailey's Hard to mouth of river.

S T, T, C (D T Adv. from ticket office. L–20).

Beult

Rises to west of Ashford and runs to the Medway at Yalding.

An excellent coarse water with big chub, but there are no known ticket opportunities for visitors.

Tributary of Medway system.

Brede

Rises near Sedlescombe and runs to Rye, where it meets the Rother.

Coarse fish and some trout.

Rye, E Sussex. Short stretch from Rye to riverside pillbox.

C (D T Adv. tackle shop, Rye).

Tributary of Rother (Sussex and Kent).

Chichester Canal

A 4-mile waterway connecting the town of Chichester with Chichester Harbour near Birdham.

Roach, rudd, bream and perch, and some tench and carp.

Chichester, W Sussex. Most of towpath.

C (D T Adv. Daughtry's tackle shop, The Hornet, Chichester, or Dunnaway's Stores, Hunston).

Cray

The main tributary of the River Darent.

Fair coarse fishing for most species.

Crayford, Kent. Stretch at Five Arches.

C (Free fishing).

North Cray, Kent. Five Arches to Old Mill, Bexley.

C (Free fishing).

Tributary of Darent.

Cuckmere

Rises on the Weald and runs to the Channel between Beachy Head and Seaford.

It holds trout and coarse fish, with some sea-trout. The upper reaches are mostly preserved.

Alfriston, E Sussex. 3½ m Alfriston to Compleat Angler F C fishery border.

C (D T Adv. tackle shop, 22 Pevensey Road, Eastbourne).

Alfriston, E Sussex. Alfriston Lock to sea.

S T plus bass and mullet (Free fishing).

Darent

Rises near Westerham and runs to the Thames estuary near Dartford.

The upper reaches hold trout and are preserved, while the lower reaches offer coarse fishing with some trout.

Dartford, Kent. 2½ m Brookland's Lake to Dartford Creek (includes fishing in lake).

C (D T Adv. Dartford A P S).

Tributary: Cray.

Eden (Kent)

Runs through Edenbridge and Penshurst to join the Medway near Tonbridge.

Offers trout and coarse fishing, but most of the river is preserved, with some access through associations.

Penshurst, Kent. Stretch of right bank at Salman's Farm.

T, C (D T Adv. Salman's Farm. Trout fly only 1 Apr.–15 June).

Tributary of Medway system.

Itchen

Rating among the most exclusive, and perhaps most expensive, chalk stream fisheries in England, the Itchen has fame in past writings and present-day results. It rises near Alresford and runs through

Winchester and then Southampton to Southampton Water.

Most of the fishing is strictly private, and the limited ticket water may be booked well ahead or subject to a waiting list. Some season rods are let by the Test and Itchen Fishing Association Ltd, and can cost up to £800. Again, a long waiting list applies (contact may be made through the secretary, Mrs M. F. Baring, Well House, Malshanger, Basingstoke, Hants). Besides the famous trout there are runs of sea-trout and salmon.

Southampton, Hants. 1 m of left bank from Woodmill to Mansbridge.
C (Free fishing).

Swaythling, Hants. Stretch of left bank downstream from Swaythling Weir.
C, T, S (Free fishing).

Winchester, Hants. 1½ m in area.
T (DT Adv. The Rod Box, 52 St George's Street, Winchester. Fly only. L–5).

Winchester, Hants. Between City Mill and Wharf Mill.
C, T (Free fishing).

Kird

Rises near Northchapel and runs through Kirdford to the Arun near Wisborough Green.
Coarse fish, some sea-trout.

Wisborough Green, W Sussex. 1 m of left bank from Orfold Farm Weir.
C (DT Adv. Crawley AS).
Tributary of Arun.

Little Stour

A chalk stream tributary of the Kent Stour.

The upper reaches hold trout and are mostly preserved, with coarse fish in reaches close to the Stour.

Pluck's Gutter, Kent. 3 m stretch upstream from Pluck's Gutter.
C (DT on bank or from Dog and Duck Inn, Pluck's Gutter).
Tributary of Stour (Kent).

Lymington River (New Forest Streams)

The New Forest Streams feed the Lymington River, which runs from near New Park to Lymington and the Channel.

While the Lymington River itself is preserved by associations, the streams hold trout, and many may be fished on day tickets.

Lyndhurst, Hants. New Forest streams.
T (DT Adv. Lyndhurst Camp Site; Lymington tackle shop, or from Forestry Commission, The Queen's House, Lyndhurst. Fly only). (NB. No rod licence needed to fish these streams.)

Medway

From its source at Forest Row, the Medway runs through Tonbridge and Maidstone to the Thames Estuary below Rochester.

Some parts of the upper river above Tonbridge are stocked with trout, but below the town the coarse fishing is good, with roach and bream predominating. There is also much match fishing, especially at weekends, with the record for a six-hour match topping 60 lb. Other records include a carp of 23½ lb, a chub of 7 lb 9 oz, a perch of 5 lb 4 oz, and two roach of 2 lb 7 oz each.

Maidstone, Kent. 3 m of towpath from Barming Bridge to Maidstone, and 2 m from Maidstone to Aylesford Lock.
C (Free fishing).

Tonbridge, Kent. Blackfriars Meadow.
C (DT on bank).

Tonbridge, Kent. Town Lock to Eldridge Lock, left bank.
C (DT on bank).

Wateringbury, Kent. 1 m of towpath.
C (DT Adv. Riverside Café, Wateringbury).

Yalding, Kent. 200 yds of towpath upstream of Yalding Sluices.
C (Free fishing).

Yalding, Kent. 3½ m of towpath from point below East Lock downstream.
C (DT on bank, weekdays only).

Yalding, Kent. ½ m of right bank upstream of Yalding Bridge.
C (DT on bank).

Yalding, Kent. 5 m of towpath from Yalding to below Barming Bridge, except length at Wateringbury.
C (D T Adv. Maidstone Victory A and M PS).
Tributaries of Medway: Batley Stream (Bartley Stream), Beult, Eden (Kent), Teise.

Meon

Flows from East Meon to the Solent near Fareham.
Offers trout and sea-trout, with most of the fishing preserved.
Fareham, Hants. 1½ m from Titchfield to Segensworth.
ST, T (D T Adv. tackle shop, 55 Portland Street, Fareham. Fly only. Fishery open 1 June–30 Sept. only. L–4).

Ouse (Sussex)

Rises near Horsham and runs through Lewes to the Channel at Newhaven.
The Ouse holds trout and coarse fish, with sea-trout from June to Aug. mainly. No known ticket opportunities for visitors, but some Sussex associations hold stretches and offer seasonal membership.
Tributary: Uck.

Pevensey Haven Level

Part of the Pevensey Levels drainage system, entering the Channel near Pevensey.
Coarse fish, including carp.
Pevensey, E. Sussex. 1½ m from Pevensey to Chilley Bridge, left bank. C (D T Adv. tackle shop, 22 Pevensey Road, Eastbourne).

Romney Five Waterings Sewer

Part of the Romney Marsh drainage system.
Good general coarse fishing, with some big bream shoals. Rye and District A S, which offers day tickets, holds water on this and other drains in the area.
East Guldeford, Kent. 1½ m from Rye to White Kemp Sewer.
C (D T Adv. tackle shop, Rye).

Snargate, Kent. 2 m from Appledore to Snargate.
C (D T Adv. tackle shop, Rye).

Romney High Knock Channel

Part of the Romney system (see immediately above).
Iden, E Sussex. 1½ m from Royal Military Canal up.
C (D T Adv. tackle shop, Rye).

Romney New Knock Sewer

See Romney Five Waterings Sewer (above).
Iden, E Sussex. Iden to River Rother.
C (D T Adv. tackle shop, Rye).

Romney Reading St Sewer

See Romney Five Waterings Sewer.
Stone, Kent. 3 m from Ferry Inn, Stone, to Appledore.
C (D T Adv. tackle shop, Rye).

Romney White Kemp Sewer

See Romney Five Waterings Sewer.
Bluehouse, Kent. 1½ m from Bluehouse to New Romney.
C (D T Adv. tackle shop, Rye).
East Guldeford, Kent. 1½ m from Rye to East Guldeford.
C (D T Adv. tackle shop, Rye).

Rother (Sussex and Kent)

Rises at Rotherfield, Sussex, and flows through Bodiam and Newenden to estuary.
Trout and coarse fish in upper reaches, with most coarse fish in lower reaches, plus some sea-trout, which are said to be on the increase. The estuary holds mullet and bass in the summer.
Bodiam, E Sussex. 3 m at village.
C, T (D T Adv. at Bodiam Stores on weekdays and on bank at weekends, provided water not booked for a match).
Iden Bridge, Kent. 1 m of right bank from Iden Bridge downstream to Scot's Float.
C (Free fishing).
Newenden, Kent. 12 m from Robertsbridge to Iden, except 3 m stretch at Bodiam.

C (DT Adv. B. Hart, Riverside
Cottages, Newenden).
Rye, E Sussex. 2½ m from Rye to
Wittersham.
C (DT Adv. tackle shop, Rye, or
Bedford Arms public house, Rye).
Tributaries of Rother: Brede,
Tillingham.

Royal Military Canal
Built during the Napoleonic Wars as a
strategic defence, the water runs across
the north border of Romney Marsh and
forms part of the drainage system.
A fine coarse fishery, holding a good
head of bream and some carp, but can
be heavily booked for weekend matches.
Mainly a summer water, with the levels
lowered in winter.
West Hythe, Kent. Entire water, 37 m.
C (DT Adv. tackle shops in West
Hythe, Ruckinge, Warehorne and
Appledore, and at Light Railway
Restaurant, Hythe).

Stour (Kent)
Having some of the quality of a chalk
stream on its course through the North
Downs, the Kentish Stour rises near
Ashford and runs to Canterbury and then
the Channel by Sandwich.
Offers mixed fishing for trout and
coarse fish, with some sea-trout. Below
Canterbury, coarse fish are much more
prevalent.
Canterbury, Kent. Section within city
boundary except Municipal Gardens,
left bank.
C (Free fishing).
Canterbury, Kent. 4 m from Grove Ferry
to Plucks Gutter.
C (DT on bank or from Canterbury and
Dist. AA).
Sandwich, Kent. 1 m from Vigo Sluice to
Minster Road.
C (Free fishing).
Tributary: Little Stour.

Teise
Rises on the Weald and flows through
Lamberhurst and Goudhurst to the
Medway at Yalding.
The river is mostly preserved, with

trout in the upper reaches and coarse fish
and trout lower down. London AA holds
water, but there are no known day ticket
opportunities.
Tributary of Medway system.

Test
Perhaps one of the most famous chalk
streams in the world, the Test rises near
Overton and flows through Whitchurch
and Romsey to Totton on Southampton
Water.
Its trout are legendary, with the brown
trout record topping 15 lb. Its fisheries
are for the most part highly exclusive,
with openings subject to long waiting
lists, and can be very expensive. Water
is owned by the Test and Itchen Fishing
Association Ltd (for details see the
entry for the River Itchen above).
Besides its trout, the river holds big
grayling and has a run of salmon below
Romsey. Anglers should note that the
limited openings below are also booked
well ahead, and there may be a waiting
list.
Romsey, Hants. 400 yds at Memorial
Park, Romsey.
C, T, S (DT Adv. Test Valley Dist.
Council, Duttons Road, Romsey.
L–2).
Stockbridge, Hants. 300 yds of left bank
near hotel.
T (DT Adv. Greyhound Hotel,
Stockbridge. Fly only; trout season
open 1 May–31 Oct.).

Tillingham
Runs roughly parallel with the Brede
stream from Broad Oak to link with the
Rother at Rye.
Mainly coarse fishing.
Rye, E Sussex. 3½ m from Rye to
Hundred House Lane (and also water
on the Brede).
C (DT Adv. tackle shop, Rye, or from
Rye and Dist. AS).
Tributary of Rother (Sussex and
Kent).

Uck
Rises on the Weald and runs to join the
Ouse (Sussex) below Uckfield.
No known openings for visitors.

Wallers Haven Level
One of the drains on the Levels to the east of Hailsham, the other being Pevensey Haven.
Fair coarse fishing, including tench, bream and carp.
Pevensey, E Sussex. 4 m from Boreham Street to Norman's Bay.
C (D T Adv. tackle shop, 22 Pevensey Road, Eastbourne).

West Rother
A West Sussex river joining the Arun at Stopham.
It has had barbel introduced at Coultershaw Mill, which appear to be thriving; otherwise it has a good head of coarse fish, some trout, and occasional sea-trout.
Fittleworth, W Sussex. 2 m from Fittleworth Bridge to Stopham.
C (D T Adv. General Store, Fittleworth, Mon.–Fri. only, or from Chichester A S).
Midhurst, W Sussex. 1½ m of right bank from North Mill to upstream boundary board.
C (D T Adv. tackle shop, West Street, Midhurst).
Petworth, W Sussex. 4½ m overall, stretch from Coultershaw Mill to Fittleworth on left bank and part of both banks downstream of Fittleworth.
C (D T Adv. tackle shop, Petworth, or Red Lion Inn, Petworth, or Petworth A C).
Tributary of Arun.

Yar (Isle of Wight)
Rises near middle of island and runs to sea at Bembridge.
Trout in upper reaches, with coarse fish lower down.
Alverstone, IoW. From Alverstone upstream to Burnt House.
C (D T Adv. from island tackle shops or Isle of Wight F A A).
Brading, IoW. 1 m of right bank from Yarbridge to Brading.
C (D T Adv. island tackle shops or Isle of Wight F A A).

South-West Water Authority Rivers

Although perhaps most famed for its coastal scenery, the region covered by the South-West Water Authority (formed from the old Devon and Cornwall water boards) has a rugged beauty of its own inland, where clear, rapid brooks rise in spectacular moorland. In these upper reaches even the tiniest streams hold trout, although most of them do not grow beyond a few ounces. Lower, migratory game fish are much in evidence, and the sea-trout fishing can be wonderful, especially late on in a summer evening. Although there is not a great deal of coarse fishing on offer, one or two rivers do hold sizeable populations in their lower reaches, and there is the added attraction that the Authority has abolished the close season for coarse fish. Bass, mullet and flounders also enter the estuary stretches of many of the West's rivers.

Allen
Like the Camel, which it joins near Wadebridge, the Allen holds salmon, sea-trout and trout, with the late runs of migratory fish best. The trout fishing is fair.
Wadebridge, Cornwall. 1 m stretch.
T, ST, S (D T or WT Adv. Appleton & Craig, Wadebridge. Fishery open 1 Apr.–30 Nov. L–4).
Tributary of Camel.

Avon (Devon)
Rises on Dartmoor and flows 20 m to south Devon coast at Bantham.
An excellent sea-trout river, with some salmon. The trout fishing is fair.
South Brent, Devon. 14½ m South Brent to Aveton Gifford.
S, ST, T (WT, also fortnight, month, from post offices at Loddiswell and Diptford; D. M. Blake, Fore Street, Totnes, or Molyneaux Sports, Fore Street, Kingsbridge. Fly only, except after 1 Oct., when spinning permitted for salmon below Silverbridge).

South Brent, Devon. 1000 yds stretch.
ST, T (DT, also WT, fortnight and
month, from Mrs J. Theobald, Little
Aish Riding Stables, South Brent).

Axe (Devon)

Rises inside Dorset and runs through
Axminster to the Channel at Seaton.

Offers fine sea-trout fishing, salmon
and trout, with some coarse fish, notably
roach to large size, in the lower reaches.
Axminster, Devon. 600 yds stretch.
S, ST, T (DT, also WT if beats not
taken by guests, from Mrs A. E. Jones,
George Hotel, Axminster. L–4).
Longbridge, Devon. 800-yd stretch at
farm.
S, ST, T (by arrangement with owner,
Mr Summerhayes, Ulcombe Farm,
Upottery, near Honiton, Devon).

Barle

Rises on Exmoor and runs through the
Barle valley to join the Exe below
Dulverton.

Offers good salmon and trout fishing.
Dulverton, Somt. Stretches on Exe and
Barle.
S, T (DT Adv. Exmoor Forest Hotel,
Simonsbath, Somt).
Dulverton, Somt. Water on Exe and
Barle.
S, T and grayling (DT if not taken by
guests from Caernarvon Arms Hotel,
Dulverton, Somt).
Winsford, Somt. 4½ m of water on Exe
and Barle.
S, T (DT Adv. Tarr Steps Hotel,
Winsford, Somt).
Tributary of Exe.

Bovey

Rises on Dartmoor and runs south-east
to join the Teign below Bovey Tracey.

Holds trout, sea-trout and some
salmon.
Bovey Tracey, Devon. Water on Bovey
and Teign.
T, ST, S (DT Adv. tackle shop, Queen
Street, Newton Abbot, or Lower Teign
Fishing Association, Market Street,
Newton Abbot).
Tributary of Teign.

Bray

North Devon river entering the Mole, a
tributary of the Taw which joins the main
river below South Molton.

Trout, sea-trout and salmon, with a
spring main run of the latter.
Brayford, Devon. 1 m in area.
T (DT Adv. Mr and Mrs C. Hartnoll,
Little Bray House, Brayford,
Barnstaple).
South Molton, Devon. Water on Bray
and Taw.
ST, T (DT Adv. The Gun and Sports
Centre, 130 East Street, South
Molton).
South Molton, Devon. Water on Bray
and Taw.
ST, T (DT Adv. Poltimore Arms, North
Molton).
Tributary of Taw system.

Bude Canal

Canalized section of the rivers Stratt and
Neet flowing into Bude and out into
Bude Bay.

Coarse fish, including tench and carp,
with some flounders.
Bude, Cornwall. Entire water.
C (DT on bank or from tackle shops,
Bude).

Camel

Rising above Camelford, the Camel
flows to Wadebridge and into the long
estuary on which Padstow stands.

It is one of Cornwall's best-known
game rivers, with salmon running
throughout the season. However, there
is a notable run of grilse in July and Aug.
if water conditions are right, and a big
late run of salmon from Sept. through to
Dec. The trout, though numerous, are
mainly small, and sea-trout move
throughout the year. The estuary is a
noted bass water.
Bodmin, Cornwall. 12 m from Fenteroon
Bridge to Polbrock Bridge.
T, ST, S (DT Adv. except in Dec. from
A. Cowl, Camel Valley Cottage,
Dunmere, Bodmin. L–10).
Wadebridge, Cornwall. 3 m stretch plus
length of tidal river.

T, ST, S (D T Adv. Appleton & Craig, Wadebridge. Fishery open 1 Apr.–30 Nov. L–4).

Tributary: Allen.

Carey

Rises east of Holsworthy and joins the Tamar near Launceston.

Fair trout fishing.

Launceston, Cornwall. ½ m of right bank from Carey Foot to Heal Bridge.

T (D T or W T Adv. tackle shop, Launceston. Fly only, fishery open 1 Mar.–30 Sept.).

Tributary of Tamar.

Constantine Brook

A trout stream rising near Constantine and flowing to meet the Helford River.

Constantine, Cornwall. Most of water.

T (Mostly free, but essential to obtain permission from farmers).

Creedy

Rises above Crediton and flows beside the A377 road to join the Exe above Exeter.

Holds trout and some coarse fish in the lower reaches.

Cowley Bridge, Devon. 150 yds from Cowley Bridge, right bank.

C (W T Adv. tackle shops, Exeter).

Crediton, Devon. Water on Creedy, also Exe and Yeo.

T (by arrangement with members of Crediton Fly Fishing Club; inquiries to G. Eccles, James Combe, Alexandra Close, Crediton).

Tributary of Exe system.

Culm

Rises near Otterhead and flows through Culmstock and Cullompton to the Exe above the mouth of the Creedy, making it the Exe's longest tributary.

Offers fair trouting, with some coarse fish in the lower reaches.

Hemyock, Devon. 4 m in area.

T (D T or W T Adv. from The Bakery, Hemyock, or Upper Culm Fishing Association, H. M. Saunders, Sunset, Clayhiddon, Devon. Fly only, no Sunday fishing).

Stoke Canon, Devon. Stretches of both banks above and left bank below A396 road bridge.

C (W T Adv. tackle shops, Exeter).

Uffculme, Devon. 1½ m from Uffculme to Fivefords.

T (D T Adv. from Parsonage Farm House, Uffculme. Fly only; fishery open 15 Apr.–15 Sept. L–10).

Tributary of Exe system.

Dart

Formed at the junction of the East Dart and West Dart at Dartmeet, the river runs through Buckfastleigh and Totnes to Dartmouth.

Salmon fishing begins in the spring in the lower reaches, and the runs reach the upper river at around Sept. The main sea-trout runs are from July to Sept. The trout fishing is fair, with occasional big fish.

Ashburton, Devon. 1 m of right bank.

S (D T Adv. Holne Chase Hotel, near Ashburton. Fly only).

Buckfastleigh, Devon. Stretch of left bank.

S, ST, T (D T Adv. The Sports Shop, Fore Street, Buckfastleigh).

Buckfastleigh, Devon. ½ m from Dartbridge to Weir.

T, ST, S (D T Adv. Dart Bridge Guest House, Buckfastleigh. Fishery open 14 Feb.–30 Sept.).

Hexworthy, Devon. 1 m of right bank.

S, T (D T Adv. Forest Inn, Hexworthy).

Princetown, Devon. Most of East and West Dart.

T, ST, S (D T Adv. tackle shop, Newton Abbot, post offices at Princetown and Postbridge, or Forest Inn, Hexworthy. Fly only. Trout open season 1 Mar.–30 Sept.; salmon, 14 Feb.–15 Sept.).

Totnes, Devon. 6 m of left bank from Totnes to Buckfastleigh.

T, ST, S (D T Adv. tackle shop, Totnes. Fly only. No Sunday fishing).

Totnes, Devon. Stretch of left bank at Totnes.

S T, S (Residents only, Seymour Hotel, Bridgetown. M B available).

Tributaries: East Dart, West Dart, Swincombe, Walla Brook.

East Dart
Rises on Cut Hill and runs to join West Dart at Dartmeet (see River Dart above, Princetown entry).

Exe
Rises north-west of Exford and runs a long course south through Bampton, Tiverton and Exeter to large estuary at Exmouth.

Mostly game fishing in the middle and upper reaches, but the lower stretches, particularly at and around Exeter, are becoming increasingly popular as a coarse fishery. Among other species the river now holds a head of bream, with some carp. Grayling are present in the middle and upper river. Salmon run through from May to Sept., with good summer sea-trout fishing.

Bickleigh, Devon. Short stretch from Bickleigh Bridge downstream.
T, S (DT Adv. Fisherman's Cot Hotel, Bickleigh. Trout fly only. Ghillie available).

Dulverton, Somt. 5½ m in area including water on Barle.
S, T (DT Adv. Caernarvon Arms Hotel, Dulverton. Trout season open 15 Mar.–31 Oct.; salmon, 15 Feb.–31 Oct. Ghillie available).

Dulverton, Somt. 3 m of right bank from Chilly Bridge to Barlyngy Farm.
T, S (DT Adv. Lamb Hotel, Dulverton. Fly only).

Exeter, Devon. Countess Wear Fishery above and below weir.
C, T, ST, S (WT Adv. Bridge Café, Countess Wear, or tackle shops, Exeter).

Exeter, Devon. 500 yds towards Cowley Bridge from Stoke Cannon Bridge.
S, T, C (DT Adv. tackle shops, Exeter).

Exwick, Devon. ½ m Exwick Mill Race to rail bridge, right bank.
C (WT Adv. tackle shops, Exeter).

Oakham Barton, Devon. ½ m of left bank between rail bridges.
C (WT Adv. tackle shops, Exeter).

Stoke Woods, Devon. 500 yds left bank between Cowley Bridge and Stoke Cannon.
C, T, ST, S (WT Adv. tackle shops, Exeter).

Thorverton, Devon. 2½ m stretch.
C, T, S (DT Adv. T. Mortimer, High Banks, Latchmore, Thorverton. Trout fly only).

Tiverton, Devon. 2 m from Washfield to Head Weir.
T, S (DT Adv. Hartnoll Country House Hotel. Fly only, trout season 16 Mar.–30 Sept.; salmon, 14 Feb.–30 Sept. No close season for rainbow trout).

Winsford, Somt. 1 m through village.
T (DT Adv. Royal Oak Inn, Winsford. Fly only).
Tributaries of Exe: Barle, Creedy, Culm, Haddeo.

Exeter Canal
Also known as the Exeter Ship Canal, this 6½-mile canal links Exeter with the navigable roads of the estuary and holds mixed coarse species including big bream and some carp. Flounders are also taken.

Exeter, Devon. 4½ m from Turf Hotel to Double Lock Hotel.
C (WT Adv. tackle shops, Exeter, or Bridge Café, Countess Wear).

Fal
Rises near Roche and flows to long estuary at Falmouth.
Trout, with a run of sea-trout best in May.

Falmouth, Cornwall. Stretches in area.
T, ST (Some free fishing, for which permission must be sought in advance from landowners).

Fowey
Rises near Brown Willy, the highest point on Bodmin Moor, and runs east around Liskeard to its estuary at Lostwithiel.
Salmon, with a late run into December, and extremely good sea-trout fishing from late April. Good trouting.

Bodmin, Cornwall. ½ m at A38 road bridge.
T, ST, S (DT Adv. A. Cowl, Camel

Valley Cottage, Dunmere, Bodmin. Fishery open 1 Apr.–14 Dec.).

Dobwalls, Cornwall. Four stretches in area.

T, S T, S (D T Adv. to 15 Oct. only from Post Office, Rilla Mill, Callington; Botterell's, Fore Street, Liskeard; W. S. Buckingham, 40 Fore Street, Callington; P. Gardner, Southgate Street, Launceston, or Liskeard and Dist. A C. Parts of fishery fly only).

Lanhydrock, Cornwall. 2 m in area.

S T, S (D T Adv. Lanhydrock A A, The National Trust, The Estate Office, Lanhydrock Park, Bodmin).

Lostwithiel, Cornwall. From upstream of Restormel Manor to town bridge.

S, S T, T (W T Adv. tackle shops, Bodmin, St Austell, or F G Motors, Quay Street, Lostwithiel; Messrs Penhaligon, 15 Queen Street, Lostwithiel, or Lostwithiel F A. Salmon season open 1 Apr.–15 Dec.; sea-trout, 1 Apr.–30 Sept.; trout, 16 Mar.–30 Sept.).

Lostwithiel, Cornwall. Town Bridge to sea.

T, S T, S (Free fishing).

Grand Western Canal

Runs from Tiverton through Sampford Peverell to Burlescombe.

Although it has suffered from some leakages through bank failure, parts of the canal, especially at Sampford Peverell, hold good stocks of roach, perch, tench and pike. Elsewhere, stretches are shallow and weeded, with a few deeper sections holding fish.

Tiverton, Devon. 10 m of towpath to Burlescombe.

C (D T Adv. Devon County Council offices, Exeter, tackle shop, Tiverton, or Sampford Peverell Post Office).

Haddeo

Runs off Haddon Hill to join the Exe below Dulverton.

Trout and occasional salmon.

Dulverton, Somt. 3½ m from Hartford to Weir Bridge.

T, S (D T Adv. Lamb Hotel, Dulverton. Fly only).

Tributary of Exe.

Harbourne

Small river rising on lower Dartmoor to run into estuary of Dart at Tuckenhay.

Salmon, sea-trout and fair trout fishing.

Harberton, Devon. 1 m at Harberton.

T, S T, S (D T Adv. tackle shop, Totnes. Fly only).

Kensey

Runs through Launceston, Cornwall, to join the Tamar.

Fair trout fishing.

Launceston, Cornwall. 1½ m stretch through Launceston.

T (D T and W T Adv. tackle shop, Launceston. Fly only. Fishery open 1 Mar.–30 Sept.).

Tributary of Tamar.

Lew

Rises to east of Okehampton and joins the Torridge near Hatherleigh.

Trout, with some sea-trout and salmon.

Hatherleigh, Devon. Stretch in area.

T, some S T, S (D T Adv. Simon and John Gawesworth, A P G A I, the West of England School of Game Angling, Caynton House, Torrington).

Tributary of Torridge system.

Little Dart

Tributary of the Taw running into the main river just below Eggesford.

Offers trout, sea-trout and some salmon.

Chulmleigh, Devon. Stretch in area.

T, S T, S (D T or evening permit Adv. Fox and Hounds Hotel, Eggesford. Salmon fly only June–Sept.).

Looe (**East** and **West**)

Both short rivers meet at the same estuary just above Looe.

Trout, with runs of sea-trout beginning in late April or May.

Looe, Cornwall. Two reaches of East Looe, as defined on guide issued with ticket.

T, S T (D T Adv. to 15 Oct. only from tackle shops in Launceston, Callington and Liskeard; Post Office at Rilla Mill,

Callington, or from Liskeard and Dist. AC).

Looe, Cornwall. From Moorswater, Liskeard, to Terrace Crossing, Looe, on West Looe.

T, ST (DT as East Looe, above).

Lyn (**East** and **West**)

The East Lyn rises in Exmoor Forest to run through Lynmouth, and is joined by the West Lyn, both being spate waters associated with the flood disaster in the 1950s.

They hold trout and have good runs of salmon and sea-trout depending on spates. Salmon best from July onwards. Most of the West Lyn is preserved, although farmers may offer some access.

Brendon, Devon. 200 yds right bank above Rockford.

T, S (DT Adv. Stagg Hunters Inn, Brendon. Fly only).

Lynmouth, Devon. 3½ m Lynmouth to Rockford Bridge.

S, T (DT Adv. from Post Office, Lynmouth, or J. Lyon & Co., iron-monger, Porlock. Fishery open 1 Feb.–31 Oct.).

Lynher

Rises on Bodmin and flows to meet the Tamar estuary.

Salmon run early, from the end of Mar. if conditions are favourable, with the main run usually in early summer. The Lynher also has good runs of sea-trout, with the largest fish coming early. Fair stocks of trout, although these are generally small.

Callington, Cornwall. Several stretches in area, detailed on map available with permit.

T, ST, S (DT Adv. to 15 Oct. only from Post Office at Rilla Mill, Callington, tackle shops in Callington, Launceston and Liskeard, or from Liskeard and Dist. AC).

Meavy

Rises near Princetown and feeds Burrator Reservoir, then continues to Shaugh Prior to meet the Plym.

Offers salmon, occasionally early, and sea-trout, but not beyond the reservoir dam. Fair trouting.

Burrator, Devon. Several stretches from reservoir down.

T, ST, S (DT Adv. Barkells tackle shop, 15 Duke Street, Tavistock. Trout and sea-trout fly only on this water).

Tributary of Plym.

Menalhyl

Small Cornish water rising near St Colomb Major and running through the Mawgan Valley.

Fair trout fishing.

St Mawgan, Cornwall. 2 m from Mawgan Porth to St Mawgan.

T (DT Adv. Merrymoor public house, Mawgan Porth, or from St Mawgan AC. No Sunday fishing on parts of water).

Mole (Devon)

Tributary of Taw joining the main river below the junction of the Little Dart.

Some salmon spring and early summer, with fair fishing for trout and sea-trout.

South Molton, Devon. ¾ m stretch.

T, ST (DT Adv. South Molton AC, I. T. S. Binding, 40 Perklands, South Molton, or the Gun and Sports Centre, 130 East Street, South Molton. Fly only).

South Molton, Devon. 1¼ m in area.

T, ST (DT Adv. Thompsons, 6 The Square, South Molton).

South Molton, Devon. 200 yds beat.

S, ST, T (DT Adv. A. W. Youings, Garramarsh, Queen's Nympton, South Molton).

Tributary of Taw system.

Okement

Rises on Dartmoor to flow north through Okehampton to join the Torridge near Hatherleigh.

Mainly trout.

Okehampton, Devon. 1¾ m of left bank.

T (DT Adv. Hill Barton Farm, Okehampton).

Tributary of Torridge.

Otter

Rises in north-east Devon and flows through Honiton and Ottery St Mary to estuary at Budleigh Salterton.

Trout, with some sea-trout. Mullet fishing in the estuary is good in summer.

Budleigh Salterton, Devon. 1½ m down from Clamour Bridge.

T, ST (Free fishing from 1 Apr.–30 Sept. only).

Ottery St Mary, Devon. 1000 yds from Gosford Bridge.

T (DT Adv. if all permits not taken by residents from Venn Ottery Barton Guest House, Venn Ottery, Ottery St Mary. Fly only).

Weston, Devon. 5 m stretch.

T (DT or WT Adv. Deer Park Hotel, Weston, Honiton. Fly only).

Weston, Devon. 1¼ m.

T (DT Adv. if not taken by residents from Combe House Hotel, Gittisham, near Honiton).

Weston, Devon. 600 yds stretch.

T (DT Adv. C. P. May, Bridge House, Weston, Honiton. Fly only).

Ottery

Small river joining the Tamar above Launceston.

Fair trout fishing.

Launceston, Cornwall. 1½ m upstream from Yeolm Bridge on left bank.

T (DT Adv. tackle shop, Launceston. Fly only).

Tributary of Tamar system.

Plym

Rises on Dartmoor and runs south to long estuary at Plymouth.

Attracts sea-trout and salmon, some of which can be early. Fair trout fishing.

Plymouth, Devon. Stretch in area.

T, ST, S (DT Adv. for bona fide visitors from D K Sports, 204 Exeter Street, Plymouth. L–2).

Sheepstor, Devon. Right bank from Sheepstor parish boundary to Blacka Brook, both banks from Blacka Brook to Bickleigh Bridge.

T, ST, S (DT, WT Adv. tackle shop, 15 Duke Street, Tavistock. Trout and sea-trout fly only).

Tributary: Meavy.

Polperro Brook

Small stream running from above the village, through which it is culverted to harbour.

Holds small trout.

Polperro, Cornwall. Whole water.

T (Free fishing).

St Allen

Small water which rises at Zelah, near Truro.

Holds small trout.

Truro, Cornwall. Entire water.

T (Free fishing, provided permission sought from landowners).

Seaton

Small river rising above Hessenford and running into the sea at the west end of Seaton beach.

Mainly small trout but occasional bigger fish, with sea-trout when estuary bar permits run and very occasional salmon. Many parts are much overgrown.

Hessenford, Cornwall. Right bank from end of gardens below Hessenford Bridge to just above Keveral Mill, right bank.

T (DT Adv. to 15 Oct. only from Post Office, Rilla Mill, Callington, tackle shops in Callington, Launceston, and Liskeard, or from Liskeard and Dist. AC).

Seaton, Cornwall. Right bank for 1 m above Seaton.

T, some ST (DT Adv. B. G. Wilson, The Bruff, Rilla Mill, Callington).

Swincombe

Small Dartmoor water running into the West Dart near Princetown.

Fair trout, with occasional sea-trout.

Princetown, Devon. All water.

T, ST (DT Adv. tackle shop, Newton Abbot, Forest Inn at Hexworthy, post offices at Princetown and Postbridge. Fly only. Trout season open 1 Mar.–30 Sept.).

Tributary of Dart system.

Tamar

Rises in the north of Cornwall and feeds

the Upper and Lower Tamar reservoirs before forming the boundary between Devon and Cornwall down to its estuary at Plymouth.

A major game river, the beautiful Tamar has a salmon run in late spring and early summer, with good sea-trout fishing from June to September. The trout fishing is fair throughout, with some coarse fish in the Tavistock area.

Bridgerule, Devon. Parts of Kilkhampton, Whitstone and North Tamerton reaches.

T (D T Adv. tackle shops, Bude and Holsworthy. Fly only).

Launceston, Cornwall. 5 m Launceston to Boynton.

T, ST S (DT, WT Adv. tackle shop, Launceston. Salmon season open 1 Mar.–14 Oct.; trout, 15 Mar.–30 Sept.).

Lifton, Devon. About 20 m of Tamar and tributary streams.

T, ST, S (D T Adv. Arundell Arms Hotel, Lifton. Trout and sea-trout fly only. Ghillie available, also tuition. Salmon season open 1 Mar.–14 Oct.; sea-trout, 3 Mar.–30 Sept.; trout, 16 Mar.–30 Sept.).

Tavistock, Devon. Stretch in area.

T, S (D T Adv. Bedford Hotel, Tavistock. Fly only).

Tributaries of Tamar: Carey, Kensey, Ottery.

Tavy

Rises on Dartmoor and runs south through Tavistock to the Tamar estuary below Maristow.

An excellent game river, offering salmon, sea-trout and fair trout fishing. Some coarse fish in lower reaches.

Calstock, Cornwall. 3½ m stretch.

T, S (D T Adv. Danescombe Valley Hotel, Calstock. Trout fly only).

Tavistock, Devon. Stretches at Double Waters 3½ m extent.

T, ST, S (DT, WT Adv. tackle shops in Tavistock and Plymouth. Trout fly only. Salmon season open 1 Mar.–14 Oct.; sea-trout, 3 Mar.–14 Oct.; trout, 16 Mar.–30 Sept.).

Tributary: Walkham.

Taw

Runs north off Dartmoor to Eggesford and then to Umberleigh and Barnstaple, where it is tidal.

A good game water, offering salmon from Mar. to May and sea-trout from July on. The trout fishing is fair and there are coarse fish in the lower reaches, with roach to 2 lb. Mullet fishing is good in the tidal water during the summer, and it also holds flounders, mainly in Dec. and Jan.

Barnstaple, Devon. Point below Newbridge to sea.

ST, S (Free fishing).

Barnstaple, Devon. ½ m stretch.

T, S, ST, C (D T Adv. The Rod Room, Boutport Street, Barnstaple).

Colleton, Devon. 7½ m Hawkridge to Colleton.

T, S (D T Adv. Fox and Hounds Hotel, Eggesford, Chulmleigh).

Lapford, Devon. Right bank for 1¾ m from Nymet Bridge.

T, S (D T Adv. from Mr Yates, Gemini, Lanham Lane, Winchester, Hants, or Mr Sawkins, 4 Victoria Lawn, Barnstaple).

Newbridge, Devon. Right bank from Newbridge down to first stile, and 1 m of left bank from bridge to tidal water.

T, ST, S (D T Adv. tackle shops, Barnstaple and Bideford. Trout fishing fly only).

Umberleigh, Devon. 3½ m stretch.

T, ST, S (D T Adv. if not booked from Rising Sun Hotel, Umberleigh. Fly only after mid-Apr. Salmon season open 1 Mar.–30 Sept.; trout and sea-trout, 15 May–30 Sept.).

Tributaries of Taw: Bray, Little Dart, Mole (Devon), Yeo (Devon).

Teign

Drains off Dartmoor to a long estuary beginning at Newton Abbot.

Another early West Country game river, with runs of salmon and sea-trout starting in April. Also offers fair trout fishing, while the estuary fishes for bass and mullet in the summer and flounders in Dec. and Jan. – often large fish.

Chagford, Devon. 12 m from Chagford to Dunsford.

T, S, ST (DT Adv. Bowdens tackle shop, Chagford, or from Angler's Rest public house, Fingle Bridge, Drewsteignton. Open season for trout 15 Mar.–30 Sept.; sea-trout, 15 Mar.– 12 Oct.; salmon, 1 Dec.–31 July).

Newton Abbot, Devon. 3 beats totalling 15 m from Newton Abbot to Sowton Weir, Dunsford.

T, ST, S (DT Adv. Lower Teign Fishing Association, or Percy Hodge, tacklist, Queen Street, Newton Abbot. L–3 rods per beat).

Tributary: Bovey.

Tiddy

Runs from Marymeet, Cornwall, through Tideford to Tamar estuarial complex.

Mainly trout, with sea-trout running as far as Tideford in the tidal river.

Tideford, Cornwall. Entire water.

T, ST (Free fishing, provided permission sought from landowners).

Torridge

Rises inland from Clovelly and runs to Sheepwash, then on to Torrington and tidal water stretching to Bideford.

Best runs of salmon in late spring, with sea-trout from July onwards. Fair trout fishing. Bass, mullet and flounders in the tidal reaches.

Beaford, Devon. Right bank for 1½ m below Beaford.

T, ST, S (DT Adv. Group Captain P. Norton-Smith, Little Warham, Beaford, Winkleigh, Devon. Fishery open 1 Mar.–30 Sept.).

Holsworthy, Devon. 4 m at Woodford Bridge Hotel, Milton Damerel.

T (DT Adv. Woodford Bridge Hotel, Milton Damerel).

Sheepwash, Devon. 10 m from Sheepwash to Torrington.

T, S (DT Adv. Half Moon Inn, Sheepwash. Fishery open as Beaford, above).

Torrington, Devon. 7 beats totalling 5 m from Blinsham to Torrington.

T, ST, S (DT Adv. C. R. Rowe, The Holt, Appledore, Devon. Fly only on some beats. L–5).

Tributaries: Lew, Okement.

Walkham

Rises on Dartmoor to meet the River Tavy below Tavistock.

Salmon, sea-trout and trout, with evening sea-trout fishing best from July on.

Walkhampton, Devon. Stretches in area.

T, ST, S (DT, WT Adv. tackle shop, 15 Duke Street, Tavistock. Trout and sea-trout fly only).

Tributary of Tavy.

Walla Brook

Short tributary of East Dart above Dartmeet, joining at Babeny.

Trout, some salmon.

T, S (DT Adv. tackle shop, Newton Abbot, Forest Inn, Hexworthy, or post offices at Princetown and Postbridge. Salmon season open 14 Feb.–15 Sept.; trout, 1 Mar.–30 Sept.).

Tributary of Dart system.

West Dart

Joins East Dart at Dartmeet to form River Dart (see River Dart above, Princetown entry).

Yeo (Devon)

Two Taw tributaries bear this name, the biggest being this one which rises in the west of Exmoor, running south-west to Barnstaple and the Taw estuary. It offers trout and some sea-trout.

The other Yeo is a small tributary of the Mole which eventually joins the Taw, again offering similar fishing (inquiries to tackle shop, South Molton).

Barnstaple, Devon. 2 m of right bank from Raleigh Weir to second wood.

T, ST (DT Adv. tackle shops, Barnstaple and Bideford).

Tributary of Taw system.

Thames Water Authority Rivers

The Thames itself makes up the major part of this authority's area, stretching eastwards from the edges of the Wessex Water Authority and Severn-Trent Water Authority areas. It offers a variety of fishing, from excellent chalk-stream trouting to mixed and coarse fisheries in lush lowland country. However, the Thames system contains no migratory game fish because of the past neglect of the lower Thames. The situation is improving, with fish being taken right down to the city. If efforts continue to make the water cleaner, sea-trout and salmon may be re-planted at some future date – certainly, pre-industrial London enjoyed the occasional sight of a leaping salmon. In the waters near London there is a good deal of pressure on fishing space at week-ends.

Basingstoke Canal
Runs from Basingstoke through Aldershot to Woking.

Fair coarse fishing, with roach, rudd, some tench, carp, perch and pike.
Basingstoke, Hants. 17 m Greywell to Farnborough.
C (D T Adv. tackle shop, Basingstoke).
Odiham, Hants. 2 m Odiham to North Wanborough.
C (D T on bank or from Greaves tackle shop, Odiham High Street).

Cherwell
Rises north-east of Banbury to run south through Heyford to Oxford and the Thames.

Good fishing, especially for roach, chub and dace right into Oxford.
Banbury, Oxon. 5 m from Cropredy to Banbury and 12 m from Nell Bridge to Bletchingdon.
C (DT Adv. The Suitcase tacklist, Church Lane, Banbury, or Banbury and Dist. A A).
Bicester, Oxon. Stretch in area as defined on permit.
C, some T (WT Adv. Wilkins, James Street, Oxford, and other tacklists in area).
Tributary of Thames system.

Chess
This Buckinghamshire stream, a tributary of the Colne, shares with the Derbyshire Wye the distinction of being a place where rainbow trout breed naturally.

Most of the water is preserved trout fishing, with no known openings for visiting anglers.
Tributary of Thames system.

Coln
Rises on the Cotswolds and runs through Bibury, where there is a big trout hatchery, to the Thames at Lechlade.

A chalk stream well stocked with big trout and some grayling, it is mostly preserved, with some hotel water.
Bibury, Glos. 250 yds stretch near hotel.
T (D T Adv. Swan Hotel, Bibury. Fly only. L–3).
Fairford, Glos. 1½ m stretch.
T, grayling (D T Adv. Bull Hotel, Market Place, Fairford. Fly only).
Fairford, Glos. Stretch near inn.
T, grayling (D T Adv. Bull Hotel, Market Place, Fairford. Fly only).
Tributary of Thames system.

Colne
Runs from near Rickmansworth through Uxbridge and West Drayton to Staines.

Stocked with trout in upper reaches. Fair coarse fishing in middle and lower river, mostly preserved.
Uxbridge, Middx. Section on Uxbridge Moor.
C (Free fishing).
Tributary of Thames system.

Evenlode
Rises in the Cotswolds and runs through Long Hanborough to the Thames below Eynsham.

Trout in upper reaches, mixed fishing in middle and lower reaches. Mostly preserved, with no known openings for visiting anglers.
Tributary of Thames system.

Gade
Small river entering the Colne.

Holds some trout and coarse fish.

Watford, Herts. Section within
Cassiobury Park.
C (Free fishing).
Tributary of Thames system.

Grand Union Canal

Part of this enormous waterway falls
within the Thames Water Authority area
(see also entries under Anglian Water
Authority and Severn-Trent Water
Authority areas).

Good coarse fishing, with roach, rudd,
perch, pike, tench and some carp.

Aylesbury, Bucks. Aylesbury arm of
canal from Aylesbury to Aston
Clinton.
C (DT on bank except Sundays when
matches booked).

Croxley Green, Herts. 3 m from Lock 78
to Lock 80.
C (DT on bank. Avoid strictly private
water Lock 75 to Lock 78).

Osterley, Greater London. 18 m from
Osterley to Paddington.
C (DT on bank).

Rickmansworth, Herts. 5½ m from
Lock 81 to Lock 87.
C (DT on bank).

Slough, Bucks. 8 m from Slough to West
Drayton.
C (DT on bank).

Tring, Herts. 14 m from Tring to King's
Langley.
C (DT on bank).

Uxbridge, Greater London. 4 m Denham
Lock to West Drayton.
C (DT on bank).

Kennet

One of the best-known Thames tributaries, the Kennet rises in the Wiltshire
Downs near Yatesbury, above Marl-
borough, and runs through Hungerford
and Newbury to the Thames at Reading.

In its upper reaches, where stretches
are inclined to disappear in dry weather,
it is a superb chalk stream offering trout
and big coarse fish, especially chub. It
holds trout for most of its length, with
coarse fish becoming more prevalent the
lower down you travel. Many parts also
hold barbel, some of them big. Among

the fine fish this river has produced are a
trout of 10 lb 12 oz, a 3 lb 2½ oz roach,
a dace of 1 lb 3 oz, a chub of 7 lb 4 oz
and a barbel of more than 14 lb. Much
of the water is preserved by associations.

Aldermaston, Berks. ½ m stretch at Mill
Pools.
C (DT Adv. The Old Mill,
Aldermaston).

Newbury, Berks. ¾ m stretch from upstream to downstream lock.
C (DT Adv. White House public
house, Newbury. No Sunday fishing).

Reading, Berks. Towpath for 1 m from
Duke Street Bridge to River Thames.
C (Free fishing).
Tributary of Thames system.

Kennet and Avon Canal

Much work is being done at present to
reopen this waterway, which once linked
the Thames with the Bristol Avon
through the Kennet Valley and the Vale
of Pewsey. Part of it falls within the
Wessex Water Authority area (q.v.).

Outside some of the disused stretches,
where heavy weeding makes fishing
impractical, the canal is a fine coarse
fishery which, besides the usual still
water coarse fish, also contains chub,
dace and barbel in parts. Bream to 10 lb,
tench to 6 lb, roach of 2 lb and over, big
pike and some carp also feature. Some
stretches are preserved, with no openings for visitors.

Aldermaston, Berks. 500 yds of left bank
from Aldermaston.
C (DT on bank).

Sulhampstead, Berks. ¾ m of towpath,
also stretch of Kennet.
C (DT on bank or from Mrs A. Bartlett,
Canal Cottage, Sulhampstead).

Thatcham, Berks. 2 m of towpath, including rights to fish canalside lakes.
C (DT Adv. tackle shops in area).

Lee

This river and the Dove were much written about by Walton and Cotton, although it is now much altered from
the point of view of fishing quality and

scenery. The river rises near Luton, flowing through Hertfordshire to Tottenham and on to the Thames.

These lower reaches are polluted, although fish are taken as far down as Tottenham. The river above Hertford is mostly preserved, but there are many chances to fish the middle reaches. The fair stocks of coarse fish are said to be steadily improving, and the water is popular for matches and pleasure fishing alike at weekends.

Broxbourne, Herts. 4½ m Crown Fishery from Dobb's Weir Lock down to Crown Meadow.
C (D T on bank).

Hertford, Herts. 2 m towpath from Hertford Basin to Hertford Lock.
C (Free fishing).

Hoddesdon, Herts. Upstream of Dobb's Weir Lock, including weirpool, and towpath for 1 m.
C (D T on bank).

Hoddesdon, Herts. From point above Dobb's Weir down to Dobb's Weir Lock, towpath, and part of right bank from Dobb's Weir Road down to Lock.
C (D T on bank).

Ponders End, Greater London. Stretches in area unless prohibited.
C (Free fishing).

Tottenham, Greater London. To Ponders End.
C (Free fishing).

Ware, Herts. Towpath for 2 m from Ware Lock to Hertford.
C (Free fishing).

Wormley, Herts. Sections above and below King's Weir. N B. Old River Lee King's Weir fishery for London A A members only.
C (D T on bank).

Lee tributaries: Lee Flood-Relief Channel, Lee Navigation, Rib, Stort.

Lee Flood-Relief Channel

Channel between Waltham Abbey and Fishers Green, built to take flood pressure off main river.

Maintained as a fishery by the Water Authority, who restock when necessary.

Main species are roach, chub, bream and pike.

Waltham Abbey, Essex. Water Authority stretches.
C (D T Adv. from Thames Water, Lee Division, The Grange, Crossbrook Street, Waltham Cross, Herts, or P. & B. Hall, tacklists, 44 Highbridge Street, Waltham Abbey, Essex).
Tributary of Lee system.

Lee Navigation

Canalized section linking with the Thames at Barking Creek.
Fair coarse fishing.

Cheshunt, Herts. 15 m from Aqueduct Lock to Thames, except for small sections marked.
C (Free fishing).

Loddon

Rises in Berkshire and runs through Shinfield, Winnersh and Twyford to the Thames near Wargrave.

Mainly coarse fish, with some barbel, also some trout.

Stratfield Saye, Berks. Stratfield Saye Estate water.
C (D T Adv. Stratfield Saye Estate office).

Twyford, Berks. From below road bridge on A321 to ford, including permission to fish lake alongside and part of St Patrick's Stream.
C (W T Adv. tackle shops in area or Leisure Sport, R M C House, High Street, Feltham, Middx).

Winnersh, Berks. 1½ m to boundary notices from Sindlesham Mill.
C (D T on bank or from Waterside, Mill Lane, Winnersh. No Sunday fishing if booked for matches).
Tributary of Thames system.

Mole (Surrey)

Rises near Betchworth and runs through Dorking, Leatherhead, Cobham and Esher to Thames at East Molesey.

Some trout but mostly chub, roach, dace and a few barbel. No known openings for visiting anglers.
Tributary of Thames system.

Oxford Canal

Strikes north from Oxford through Banbury to join with Grand Union for short distance from Napton to Braunston, then parts to run to Coventry Canal at Hawkesbury. Above Fenny Compton the canal falls within the Severn-Trent Water Authority area (q.v.).

The Oxford end of the canal undoubtedly has the best coarse fishing, with all main species, including carp. In this area Banbury and District AA and London AA hold water.

Banbury, Oxon. 5 m from Cropredy to Banbury and 8 m from Nellbridge to Lower Heyford.
C (DT Adv. The Suitcase tacklists, Church Lane, Banbury, or Banbury and Dist. AA).

Banbury, Oxon. Bridge 160 above Banbury to Bridge 187.
C (DT on bank or from tackle shops in area).

Bletchingdon, Oxon. Heyford Bridge (No. 206) to Bridge 228 at Kidlington Green Lock.
C (DT on bank or from tackle shops in area).

Claydon, Oxon. 3½ m Claydon to Fenny Compton.
C (DT on bank. NB. Severn-Trent or Thames Water Authority rod licences valid in this water).

Wolvercote, Oxon. 5 m from Oxford to Kidlington.
C (DT from keeper or Waltonian Tackle, Observatory Street, Oxford).

Ray (Bucks)

Rises to the south of Buckingham and feeds into the River Cherwell at Islip.
Coarse fish, with some trout.

Bicester, Oxon. Stretch in area as described on permit.
C, T (WT Adv. tackle shops in area).
Tributary of Thames system.

Ray (Wilts)

Rises near Swindon and runs a few miles to the Thames.
Holds coarse fish from a point below power station cooling towers at Blunsden, Swindon, and said to be improving after past pollution.

Blunsden, Wilts. From above Blunsden to Thames.
C (WT Adv. South Cerney AC).
Tributary of Thames system.

Rib

Rises near Collier's End and runs to join the Lee above Ware.
Coarse fish and some trout, although most water is preserved.

Ware, Herts. 1000 yds left bank from pumphouse to footbridge.
C (WT Adv. Leisure Sport, RMC House, High Street, Feltham, Middx).
Tributary of Lee system.

Roding

Rises to the west of Great Dunmow and runs south to the Thames estuary near Beckton.

Polluted in lower reaches, but the upper river, which has a narrow, fast course, offers fair coarse fishing, with chub, roach and dace.

Buckhurst, Essex. Buckhurst Hill Bridge to Loughton Bridge, Cascades rail bridge to Redbridge, plus section at Woodford.
C (Free fishing).

Passingford Bridge, Essex. Stretch of left bank downstream from bridge.
C (DT on bank).

Passingford Bridge, Essex. 1 m left bank upstream from bridge.
C (DT from keeper at lodge at bridge).

Stapleford Abbot, Essex. Left bank from Mill House down to Arnold's Farm.
C (DT Adv. Arnold's Farm, Stapleford Abbot).
Tributary of Thames system.

St Patrick's Stream

This short piece of water links the Thames and Loddon below Sonning.
Fair coarse fishing.

Twyford, Berks. 1500 yds St Patrick's Bridge to Loddon Drive Bridge.
C (WT Adv. Leisure Sport, RMC House, High Street, Feltham, Middx).
Tributary of Thames system.

Stort
Rises near Clavering and runs through
Bishop's Stortford and Harlow to join the
Lee below Roydon.

Fair coarse fishing.

Harlow, Essex. Stretches above and
below Burnt Mill Lock.
C (D T on bank).

Harlow, Essex. 2 m of left bank from
Parndon Mill to Harlow Mill.
C (D T Adv. ticket office, Harlow Town
Hall).

Roydon, Essex. 1½ m Roydon Mill to
Lower Lock.
C (D T from keeper, Lock House, Brick
Lock).

Sawbridgeworth, Herts. 3½ m Ted-
nambury to Feake's Lock.
C (D T on bank).

Spellbrook, Essex. Left bank of Stort
Navigation below Spellbrook Lock.
C (D T on bank to local residents
only).
Tributary of Lee system.

Thame
Rises near Aylesbury and runs south-
west through town of same name to the
Thames at Dorchester.

Good coarse fishing, mainly roach,
chub and dace with some bream.
Birmingham A A, Oxford Waltonian A S
and Leighton Buzzard A C hold water.

Shabbington, Oxon. 1 m of bank on
Shabbington Island.
C (D T Adv. Old Fisherman's Inn,
Shabbington).
Tributary of Thames system.

Thames
Anglers have a special affection for
London's river, although those who live
in the capital are not all familiar with its
upper course in the Cotswolds. From its
source just off the Tetbury–Cirencester
road, the infant river swells to a chalk
stream offering good trouting and some
fine coarse fish. Moving on to Lechlade
it becomes a much broader river, for
which it pays the penalty of carrying
summer boat traffic. However, the fish
stocks are excellent, and on through
Oxford and down to Reading and then

London and finally the tidal water, the
quality of fishing is maintained. The river
used to be different from others in Britain
in that no rod licence was needed to fish
it. Since 1976, after the formation of the
Thames Water Authority, rod licences
have been necessary.

All the British coarse species are rep-
resented in varying quantities throughout the course; in the upper reaches
grayling have been introduced; further
down, the roach, dace and chub are large
and present in quantities, with barbel an
added attraction. Rudd, too, make an
appearance in the slower lower reaches,
together with big shoals of bream (although some shoals of this fish occur up
to Lechlade and beyond). The many
backwaters of the river also offer the
same sort of fishing. Thames weirs for
most of its length also hold trout, usually
big fish. The species not found are migratory trout and salmon, unable to pene-
trate the polluted estuary. But the picture
is changing here, with a concerted effort
under way to clean up the legacy of the
past. Coarse fish have even been taken
in the parts of the river running by the
city, and it might eventually be possible
to replant sea-trout and salmon.

The weirs of the Thames mentioned
above may be fished on a Water
Authority permit obtainable from the
Thames Water Authority (Finance
A D M), Nugent House, Vastern Road,
Reading, Berks, while all the fishing
below the City Stone at Staines is free to
rod licence holders.

Clubs holding water on the Thames
include Birmingham A A, Coventry A A,
Dorchester A A, London A A, Oxford and
District A A, Oxford Alliance, and Radcot
A A. Some of these and other clubs offer
ticket fishing besides seasonal membership.

Abingdon, Oxon. 3 m Nuneham rail
bridge to Culham footbridge.
C (D T Adv. Abingdon Town Council,
Stratton Lodge, Bath Street,
Abingdon. B, M B available).

Abingdon, Oxon. From point below
Sandford Lock to Radley old boathouse.

C (WT and fortnight visitors' permits from Oxford A and P S, or Abingdon Angling and Restocking Association, Adv.).

Bablock Hythe, Oxon. 1½ m of left bank from Chequers Inn downstream.
C (D T Adv. Chequers Inn, Bablock Hythe).

Bablock Hythe, Oxon. 2½ m of right bank from Bablock Hythe to Pinkhill.
C (WT and fortnight visitors' permits from Oxford A and P S, Adv.).

Bourne End, Berks. 1¼ m from opposite Wootton's Boatyard to Bourne End.
C (D T on bank).

Buscot, Berks. Stretches above and below lock.
C (D T on bank).

Clifton Hampden, Oxon. 1½ m left bank from Clifton Hampden Bridge down to Clifton Hampden Lock, plus 1 m on backwater above lock.
C (WT, fortnight visitors' permits from Oxford A and P S or Clifton Hampden P S, Adv.).

Clifton Hampden, Oxon. From third meadow below Clifton Hampden Bridge, right bank, 1½ m downstream.
C (D T Adv. Oxford A A).

Cookham, Berks. 1 m Slogrove Island to Bray Lock.
C (D T Adv. tackle shop, High Street, Maidenhead).

Cookham, Berks. ½ m from My Lady Ferry to Slogrove Island, right bank.
C (Free fishing).

Dorchester, Oxon. 1 m of left bank from notice-board to Ferry Garden.
C (D T on bank or from Cricketers Arms public house, Warborough).

Dorchester, Oxon. 2 m from Day's Lock to below Thame mouth, left bank.
C (D T Adv. Dorchester A A).

Eaton Hastings, Oxon. 3 m stretch.
C (D T Adv. Anchor Inn, Eaton Hastings).

Eton, Berks. Left bank meadow from relief road bridge to Cuckoo Bridge.
C (D T on bank).

Eton Wick, Berks. 1 m of left bank from

Boveney Church to Cuckoo Bridge, excluding lock.
C (D T on bank).

Eynsham, Oxon. Right bank stretch from Pinkhill down to Eynsham.
C (WT and fortnight visitors' permits from Oxford A and P S, Adv.).

Hannington, Wilts. 1½ m stretch Kempsford to Radpool.
C (by prior arrangement with Haydon Street W M C A C).

Henley-on-Thames, Oxon. 2½ m of right bank from Henley Bridge to below Temple Island.
C (D T on bank).

Hurley Lock, Berks. Stretches of right bank above and below lock.
C (D T on bank).

Inglesham, Wilts. 3 m Radpool to Inglesham.
C, T (by prior arrangement with Haydon Street W M C A C).

Lechlade, Glos. 2 m of right bank from Round House, Inglesham, to Trout Inn.
C (D T on bank or from Trout Inn, Lechlade, or Lechlade tacklists).

Lechlade, Glos. 2½ m right bank from St John's Lock to Round House.
C (D T on bank, from Trout Inn, Lechlade, or Lechlade tacklists).

Maidenhead, Berks. Last garden at Dorney, left bank, to Boveney Lock.
C (D T Adv. tackle shop, High Street, Maidenhead).

Maidenhead, Berks. Left bank stretch at Sounding Arches, The Wall, Maidenhead.
C (Free fishing).

Maidenhead, Berks. 1 m of right bank from above Boulter's Lock to Maidenhead Bridge.
C (Free fishing).

Marlow, Bucks. 200 yds left bank below Marlow Bridge.
C (Free fishing).

Newbridge, Oxon. 2½ m stretch of right bank.
C (D T Adv. Maybush Inn, Newbridge).

Newbridge, Oxon. ½ m stretch from Newbridge.
C (D T Adv. Rose Revived public house, Newbridge).

Northmoor, Oxon. Left bank for 3 meadows from Northmoor Lock.
C (WT and fortnight visitors' permits from Oxford A and P S, Adv.).

Oxford, Oxon. Godstow Lock to Port Meadow and stretches on to Osney Bridge, Sandford and Kennington.
C (D T Adv. Oxford A A).

Pangbourne, Berks. ½ m upstream of weir.
C (Free fishing).

Pangbourne, Berks. 1 m of right bank from Whitchurch Bridge down, and right bank on Child-Beale Trust Land.
C (Free fishing).

Radcot, Oxon. 4 m Grafton Lock to Richens Brook.
C (D T Adv. Swan Hotel, Radcot Bridge, or Radcot A P C).

Reading, Berks. 3 m Thames-side Promenade to King's Meadow.
C (D T Adv. tackle shops, Reading).

Runnymede, Surrey. 1¼ m of right bank downstream from Bell Weir.
C (Free fishing).

Rushey Weir, Oxon. 2 m of left bank from Radcot Lock down to weir.
C (D T Adv. Clanfield A C).

Shillingford, Oxon. From 2 meadows below Shillingford Bridge nearly to Benson Weir.
C (D T Adv. Crown Square Garage, Benson).

Sonning, Berks. 2½ m of right bank from Kennet mouth to Sonning Bridge, also stretch from power station to lock.
C (Free fishing).

Sonning, Berks. 1 m of left bank upstream from Sonning Bridge.
C (D T on bank).

Staines, Surrey. From City Stone below Staines Bridge (includes Chertsey, Chiswick, Hampton Court, Kew, Kingston, Laleham, Molesey, Richmond, Shepperton, Sunbury, Teddington, Twickenham and Walton-on-Thames).
C (Free fishing).

Tadpole Bridge, Oxon. 2 m from road bridge to Tenfoot Bridge.
C (D T Adv. Trout Inn, Tadpole Bridge).

Tilehurst, Reading, Berks. 2 m of right bank from Roebuck Inn to Reading Thames-side Promenade.
C (Free fishing).

Wallingford, Oxon. 3 m Benson Weir to Wallingford Bridge and 1 m stretch below Bow Bridge, both right bank.
C (D T Adv. tackle shop, Wallingford, or Wallingford Jolly Anglers A C).

Wallingford, Oxon. ½ m of left bank downstream from Wallingford Bridge.
C (D T Adv. tackle shop, Wallingford).

Wallingford, Oxon. 3 m from Cholsey to Benson.
C (D T Adv. tackle shop, Wallingford. B, M B available.)

Windsor, Berks. Royal Meadow, ½ m stretch of left bank from first back-water down to Windsor road bridge and Windsor Bridge down to Albert Bridge, Home Park.
C (Free fishing).

Windsor, Berks. Romney Island and right bank on meadow by island, from boatyard to Black Potts Bridge.
C (D T on bank).

Windsor, Berks. ½ m of left bank from Cuckoo Bridge to first backwater above Windsor road bridge.
C (D T on bank).

Wolvercote, Oxon. 1 m from Godstow Bridge to King's Lock.
C (D T Adv. Waltonian Tackle, Observatory Street, Oxford. L–10).

Tributaries of the Thames: Cherwell, Chess, Coln, Colne, Evenlode, Gade, Kennet, Loddon, Mole (Surrey), Ray (Bucks), Ray (Wilts), Roding, St Patrick's Stream, Thame, Wey, Wey Navigation, Windrush.

Wey

One of the longer Thames tributaries, the Wey rises near Alton and runs through the North Downs to Farnham and on to Guildford and Woking, joining the Thames at Weybridge.

Upper reaches stocked with trout and preserved, with coarse fish in middle and lower reaches. Ticket opportunities are limited.

Addlestone, Surrey. Wey Manor Farm
Fishery.
  C (WT Adv. Leisure Sport, RMC
  House, High Street, Feltham, Middx).
  Tributary of Thames system.

Wey Navigation

Canalized boat channel through
Weybridge to Ripley.
Fair coarse fishing.
Weybridge, Surrey. 9 m left bank from
  Weybridge to Ripley.
  C (DT on bank).
  Tributary of Thames system.

Windrush

Rises like the Thames in the Cotswolds
and runs through Burford and Witney to
the Thames.
  Most of the upper reaches are strictly
preserved trout fisheries, with coarse fish
of good quality from the middle reaches
down. Excellent chub, roach and dace,
with some big trout, but openings for
visitors limited.
Burford, Oxon. 2 m as detailed on map
  at Royal Oak.
  C, T (DT Adv. Royal Oak public house,
  Witney Street, Burford).
Newbridge, Oxon. 1 m stretch of left
  bank.
  C (DT Adv. Rose Revived public
  house, Newbridge).
  Tributary of Thames system.

Wessex Water Authority Rivers

This authority's area offers, among other
attractions, the famed game and coarse
river, the Hampshire Avon. Other South
Coast waters in the area are just as attractive, while in the north is the Bristol
Avon system and, to the south of this,
the Somerset flatlands and their excep-
tionally good drain fisheries. The area
covers part of the Kennet and Avon
Canal and the Bridgwater–Taunton
canal, both offering splendid coarse
fishing.

Allen (Dorset)

Rises near Wimborne St Giles and runs

through Wimborne Minster to join the
Dorset Stour at Wimborne.
  An attractive chalk stream, mostly pre-
served, offering trout fishing throughout,
with coarse fish in the middle and lower
reaches.
Wimborne, Dorset. $2\frac{1}{2}$ m downstream
  from Bull Inn.
  C, T (DT Adv. Bull Inn, Wimborne).
Wimborne Minster, Dorset. $4\frac{1}{2}$ m
  Cricket Mill to Brockington.
  T (Residents only (L–3) WT, fly only,
  Horton Inn, Wimborne Minster).
Wimborne St. Giles, Dorset. Shaftesbury
  Estate water.
  T (Occasional rods only, Shaftesbury
  Estate Office, Wimborne St Giles).
  Tributary of Stour (Dorset).

Aller Moor Relief Channel

Fairly recent drain cutting through land
between Othery and Langport, part of it
running beside King's Sedgemoor Drain.
  Now holds fair stocks of bream, roach,
rudd and some tench.
Langport, Somt. Entire water.
  C (DT Adv. tackle shops in
  Bridgwater, Langport and Highbridge).

Avon (Bristol)

Forms from two headwaters rising above
Tetbury and Sherston and amalgamating
at Malmesbury and then runs through
Chippenham, Melksham, Bradford-on-
Avon, Bath, and on into Bristol with its
docks complex and the tidal water running to the Severn estuary through the
Avon Gorge.
  Most of the upper river is strictly preserved trout fishing, although coarse fish
are present in varying numbers for much
of its course. From Chippenham down-
wards coarse fish are more prevalent,
with quality roach, dace and chub, and
perch and pike in some parts. Barbel
have been introduced in the Avoncliffe
and Limpley Stoke areas and are now
thriving, while the population of bream
in the lower river from Bath down is increasing. The Bristol docks have bene-
fited greatly from a clean-up operation
and now support quite good stocks of

roach and bream. The fact that the river is cleaner altogether is illustrated by the odd catches of sea-trout in the past few seasons, with some being taken beyond Bath. As far down as Keynsham there is always a chance of trout and when taken these are usually big.

Unhappily for the visitor most of the clubs on the Avon do not offer day tickets, and the best way to fish the river is to join a club. Seasonal membership tickets are sold through many of the tackle shops in the area. Many of the smaller clubs holding Avon water belong to the Bristol and District Amalgamated A C or to the Bristol and West of England Anglers' Federation. Other clubs: Bath A A, Bathampton A A, Bradford-on-Avon A A, Calne A A, Keynsham A A and Ushers A A.

Bath, Avon. Stretches of towpath.
C (Free fishing).

Chippenham, Wilts. 3½ m Chippenham to Kellaways road bridge.
C (D T Adv. tackle shop, Chippenham).

Hanham, Avon. Old towpath, Hanham Weir.
C (Free fishing).

Harbour and docks, Bristol, Avon.
C (Inquiries Baltic Wharf Leisure Centre, Baltic Wharf, Bristol).
Bristol Avon tributaries: By Brook, Chew, Frome (Somt), Frome (Bristol), Semington Brook.

Avon (Hampshire)
Rises above Amesbury and runs through Salisbury, Downton, Fordingbridge and Ringwood to Christchurch and the sea.

Perhaps one of the most famous fishing rivers in England, it boasts some staggeringly big fish in its record, although at the present there is worry that the overall quality of fishing has declined through a number of factors. Not least of these is the neglect of the carriers which once laced the watermeadows along its banks, a factor now being remedied by their restoration. That aside, the fishing in most parts can still be regarded as excellent. The coarse fish records speak

for this: chub, 7 lb 8 oz; dace, 1 lb 2 oz; perch, 8 lb; pike, 37 lb 8 oz; roach, 3 lb 10 oz; and, last but not least, a 13 lb 12 oz barbel. This last fish is actually topped by a monster barbel of 17 lb 14 oz caught by a salmon angler, and one of 16 lb 1 oz which was foulhooked in 1960. The Avon is also a game river, with a run of salmon, usually big fish (record 49 lb), sea-trout in the lower reaches, and big trout (records: brown, 20 lb 8 oz; rainbow, 10 lb 12 oz).

Much of the river above Salisbury is preserved trout water, with coarse fish becoming more and more prevalent in the middle and lower reaches. Here, though, the river suffers from heavy weeding in summer. The fishing culminates at Christchurch in the famous Royalty stretch, which has produced most of the big barbel besides being a prime sea-trout fishery. Associations holding water include Ringwood and District A A, Salisbury and District A C and London A A.

Amesbury, Wilts. 2 m stretch.
T (D T Adv. from keeper, R. Poule, 4 Avonstoke Close, Amesbury. Fly only, season open 14 Apr.–14 Oct.).

Braemore, Hants. 3 m from below Burgate to Braemore.
C, T, S (D T Adv. Bat and Ball Hotel, Braemore, 8 a.m.–10 p.m.).

Braemore, Hants. 3½ m from bridge below Bat and Ball Hotel.
C, T (D T Adv. Bat and Ball Hotel, Braemore).

Charford, Hants. 1 m of left bank from Downton to Charford.
C, T, S (D T Adv. tackle shop, Downton).

Christchurch, Dorset. Royalty Fishery, from Alderbush to town bridge.
C, S T, S (D T for S, S T Adv. The Bailiff, Avon Buildings, Christchurch. Advance bookings: The Manager, West Hampshire Water Co., Mill Road, Christchurch. D T for C, Adv. tackle shop, Christchurch).

Christchurch, Dorset. 12 m from Christchurch to Ringwood.
C (D T Adv. tackle shops, Christchurch

and Ringwood, or from Christchurch A C).

Downton, Wilts. 1¼ m of left bank plus island.
C, T, S (D T Adv. Bull Hotel, Downton. L–20. B available).

Fordingbridge, Hants. 1 m of right bank from Burgate towards Fordingbridge.
C, T, S (D T Adv. Burgate Manor Farm, Burgate).

Fordingbridge, Hants. Stretch at Albany Hotel.
C, T, ST (Residents only, Albany Hotel, Fordingbridge).

Fordingbridge, Hants. Stretch on Hunter's Island.
C (D T Adv. Hunter's tackle shop, Fordingbridge).

Godshill, Hants. Water abutting Godshill Holiday Centre.
C (D T Adv. ticket office, Godshill Holiday Centre).

Ibsley Bridge, Hants. 3 m Upper Somerly Water.
C (D T Adv. Lt-Col. S. H. Crow, Bailiff's Cottage, opposite bridge. Personal applications only 9 a.m.–10 a.m., 1 Aug.–30 Sept. only).

Kingston, Hants. 3 m on left bank upstream from Kingston (Bisterne Fishery).
C (D T Adv. from keeper, J. Knight, Riverside Cottages, Kingston).

Ringwood, Hants. From Avon Causeway to first fishing hut enclosure downstream.
C (Residents only, New Queen Hotel, Avon, near Christchurch).

Ringwood, Hants. 3 m Several Fishery upstream from Ringwood.
C, T, ST (D T on bank or N. Ward, Avon Dairy Farm, The Bridges, Ringwood).

Ringwood, Hants. 2 m Somerley Estate water.
C (D T Adv. tackle shop, Bridge Street, Ringwood, or Christchurch A C. Season open 16 June–31 Jan.).

Salisbury, Wilts. Length in city.
C, T, S (D T Adv. Salisbury District Council, Bourne Hill, Salisbury).

Salisbury, Wilts. 3 m from Salisbury to Stratford.

C, T (D T Adv. tackle shop, Castle Street, Salisbury).

Winkton, Dorset. ½ m Winkton Fishery from Lower Sopley to Winkton Weir.
C (D T Adv. Davis Tackle, Christchurch, or the Fisherman's Haunt Hotel, Winkton. Season 1 July–31 Jan. L–25).
Tributaries: Nadder, Wylye.

Axe (Somerset)
Rises near Wells in the Mendips to run to the Bristol Channel at Brean.
Upper reaches mainly preserved trout fishing, with coarse fish in middle and lower reaches.

Rackley, Somt. 16 m from Lympsham Coal Wharf to Clewer.
C (D T Adv. tackle shops, Bristol, Bridgwater, Clevedon, Highbridge and Weston).
Tributaries: Cheddar Yeo, Crooked River.

Bridgwater and Taunton Canal
Links the River Parrett at Bridgwater with the Tone near Taunton.
Provides good coarse fishing, with large shoals of bream and big roach and rudd. There are also some tench and carp.

Bridgwater, Somt. 7½ m towpath from Durston to Bridgwater.
C (D T Adv. tackle shops, Bridgwater, Langport and Highbridge).

Taunton, Somt. 5 m Taunton to Durston.
C (D T Adv. Bridge Sports, Taunton, or St Quintin Hotel, Caravan and Camping Park, Taunton).

Brue
Rises above Bruton in the Mendips and runs to West Lydford, where it becomes incorporated in the drainage system of the Somerset flatlands and has been straightened, widened and deepened.
Holds good stocks of coarse fish, especially bream.

Glastonbury, Somt. 13 m from West Lydford to Westhay.
C (WT Adv. tackle shops, Street or Glastonbury).

Highbridge, Somt. 8 m from Highbridge
nearly to Burtle.
C (D T Adv. tackle shop, Highbridge).

By Brook
Formed from Broadmead Brook and
Burton Stream above Castle Combe and
runs to join the Bristol Avon near
Bathford.
Mainly preserved trout fishing, but
holds good coarse fish. Produced area
record dace of 14 oz 4 dr.
Castle Combe, Wilts. ½ m stretch in
Manor House Hotel grounds.
T (D T Adv. Manor House Hotel,
Castle Combe. Fly only. Season open
1 Apr.–30 Sept.).
Tributary of Avon (Bristol).

Cheddar Yeo
Runs from Cheddar Gorge, running
through Cheddar to cross the lowland
moors and join the Axe.
Preserved trout fishing down to
Cheddar, with fair stocks of coarse fish
on the moor.
Rackley, Somt. ½ m from Rackley to
Axe.
C (D T Adv. tackle shops, Bridgwater,
Bristol, Clevedon, Highbridge and
Weston).
Tributary of Axe (Somt).

Chew
Rises near Chewton Mendip and feeds
Chew Valley Lake, then runs through
Chew Magna and Compton Dando to
meet Avon at Keynsham.
Trout throughout, but the middle and
lower reaches hold good coarse fish. No
known openings for visiting anglers;
season association membership (see
Bristol Avon) is the best approach.
Tributary of Avon (Bristol).

Cripps
Links the River Brue with the Huntspill
near Gold Corner Bridge.
Good coarse fishing, especially bream.
Can be weedy in summer but fishes well
when the rivers hold a lot of water in
winter.
Bridgwater, Somt. Entire water.

C (D T Adv. tackle shops, Bridgwater,
Langport and Highbridge).

Crooked River (Lox Yeo)
Small tributary of the Axe running
through Loxton.
Mainly coarse fish.
Loxton, Somt. 1 m stretch.
C (D T Adv. tackle shops, Bridgwater,
Bristol, Clevedon, Highbridge and
Weston).
Tributary of Axe (Somt).

Eighteen-Foot Rhyne
Drains moorland to the north of the
King's Sedgemoor Drain into the main
channel.
Coarse fish, mainly bream and roach.
Greinton, Somt. 1½ m Walton to King's
Sedgemoor.
C (D T Adv. tackle shops, Bridgwater,
Langport and Highbridge).

Frome (Bristol)
Rises at Dodington and flows through
Winterbourne to be culverted to Bristol
Docks.
Has suffered greatly from pollution in
the past but is said to be improving, with
coarse fish in lower reaches and some
trout water above Winterbourne. No
known openings for visiting anglers;
association membership offers the best
chances.
Tributary of Avon (Bristol) system.

Frome (Dorset)
Rises to the east of Beaminster and runs
through Dorchester to the sea at Poole
Harbour.
A fine chalk stream game fishery, it has
produced the biggest sea-trout recorded
in England – 22 lb 8 oz. Also has a run of
salmon and good trout fishing, with
coarse fish in middle and lower reaches.
Mostly preserved.
Wareham, Dorset. 2 m South Bridge to
Poole Harbour.
C, S (Free fishing, provided permission
sought from landowner).
Wool, Dorset. 1½ m of left bank above
and below Wool Bridge.
ST, S (D T Adv. Woolbridge Manor

Hotel, Wool. Fishery open 1 Mar.–30 Sept.).

Frome (Somerset)

Drains from the chalk around Warminster to run to Frome and on to the Avon (Bristol) at Freshford.

Trout throughout, with increasing coarse fish from Frome onwards. Most of the river is preserved by associations, and season membership gives the best access.

Frome, Somt. 8 m from Lower Marston to Shawford.

C, T (DT Adv. tackle shop, Frome. Trout fly only).

Tributary of Avon (Bristol).

Horner Water

Small river running through the National Trust Holnicote Estate near Porlock.

Fair trout fishing.

Porlock, Somt. 4 m.

T (DT Adv. tackle shop, High Street, Porlock. Fly only).

Huntspill

Excavated during the last war, this is an important part of the Somerset drainage system and holds excellent stocks of coarse fish. A popular match water, it has been the venue of the National Championships. A 1973 match produced a record catch of 74 lb 6 oz, with the first ten anglers weighing in a total of 511 lb 8 oz. Roach and bream predominate.

Bridgwater, Somt. 3½ m from Gold Corner to Sloway Bridge.

C (DT Adv. tackle shops, Bridgwater, Langport and Highbridge).

Kenn (New Blind Yeo)

Fairly recent cutting to the north of the Congresbury Yeo near Clevedon.

The river has produced some very good roach, many in the 2 lb class, with perch, bream and a few tench. Hit by pollution in the Somerset floods of 1981, when salt swept into lower reaches, but hopefully improving.

Clevedon, Avon. Most of water.

C (DT Adv. tackle shops, Clevedon, Weston and Highbridge).

Kennet and Avon Canal

See entry in Thames Water Authority area. Much of the canal near Bath is shallow and weeded and in need of dredging. Here access is restricted, with associations preserving water. Access for visitors is better in Wiltshire, where the water offers excellent coarse fishing, with roach, bream, tench, rudd, some carp, perch and pike.

Devizes, Wilts. 15 m from Semington road bridge to Ladies Bridge, Wilcot.

C (DT Adv. Barge Inn, Seend; Barge Inn, Honeystreet; tackle shop, Devizes, or Devizes AA).

Pewsey, Wilts. 3 m from Milk House Water to Wilcot.

C (DT Adv. tackle shop, Pewsey, or Miss Butler, 15 The Crescent, Pewsey).

King's Sedgemoor Drain

Like the Huntspill, one of the main waters of the Somerset drainage systems, and remarkable for its fine match catches, especially record results in the National Championships (76 lb 9 oz).

Something of a problem water in summer, when weed can be a nuisance. The fishery declined in recent years but is now considered to be climbing back to its old form.

Bridgwater, Somt. Entire water.

C (DT Adv. tackle shops, Bridgwater, Highbridge and Langport).

Langacre Rhyne

Runs water off moorland to the south of King's Sedgemoor into the main drain. Fishing similar to main drain.

Langport, Somt. 1 m from main drain to Othery.

C (DT Adv. tackle shops, Bridgwater, Highbridge and Langport).

Lydden

Rises near Buckland Newton and runs through Lydlinch to the Dorset Stour above Sturminster Newton.

Trout fishing, mostly preserved, with some coarse fish.

Stalbridge, Dorset. 2½ m of left bank from near Lydden to Stour.

C, T (D T Adv. tackle shop, Stalbridge, or Stalbridge Arms, Stalbridge). Tributary of Stour (Dorset).

Nadder

Rises near Tisbury and runs to join the Wylye at Wilton.

Holds trout, grayling and good coarse fish, especially roach, with occasional salmon.

Salisbury, Wilts. Stretch in city.
C, T (D T Adv. Salisbury District Council, Bourne Hill, Salisbury).
Salisbury, Wilts. 2½ m Lower Bemerton to Salisbury.
C, T (D T Adv. The Boathouse, Castle Street, Salisbury).
Salisbury, Wilts. 2 m stretch at Harnham.
T, S (D T Adv. The Boathouse, Castle Street, Salisbury. Fly only. L–10).
Tributary of Avon (Hants.) system.

North Drain

Drains moorland to the north of the River Brue.

Fair stocks of bream, roach, rudd and perch.

Bridgwater, Somt. 1½ m from Brue.
C (D T Adv. tackle shops, Bridgwater, Highbridge and Langport).
Mark, Somt. 1½ m from pumping station.
C (D T Adv. tackle shops in area).

Parrett

Rises near Crewkerne and runs through Langport and on to Bristol Channel below Taunton.

The river holds some trout in the upper reaches, but is mostly noted for its coarse fish.

Langport, Somt. 6 m Thorney to Oath.
C (D T Adv. tackle shop, Parrett Close, Langport).
South Petherton, Somt. 8 m Thorney Mill to Bow Bridge.
C (D T Adv. tackle shops in area or Half Moon Hotel, Stoke-sub-Hamdon).
Tributaries: Tone, Yeo (Somerset).

Semington Brook

Rises near Devizes and joins the Bristol Avon near Holt.

Fair trout fishing and coarse fish.
Trowbridge, Wilts. Stretch from Pineckley Bridge to sewage works.
T, C (D T Adv. Lavington A C).
Tributary of Avon (Bristol).

South Drain
(Old Glastonbury Canal)

Runs from Edington to the Huntspill at Gold Corner.

Water has been extensively restocked and offers carp in addition to roach, bream, tench and perch.

Bridgwater, Somt. 6 m from Edington to Glastonbury.
C (D T Adv. tackle shops, Bridgwater, Highbridge and Langport).
Highbridge, Somt. 2 m Gold Corner to Edington.
C (D T Adv. tackle shop, Church Street, Highbridge).

Stour (Dorset)

Rises in the Wiltshire Downs near Stourton and runs through Stalbridge, Blandford and Wimborne to a joint estuary with the Hampshire Avon.

Like the Avon it has a reputation for fine coarse fish and also offers sea-trout and salmon, some of them large. The salmon record stands at 48 lb, and the best trout weighed 9 lb. Of the coarse fish, most have come from the famous Throop Fishery: barbel, 13 lb 14 oz; chub, 8 lb 8 oz; roach, 3 lb 8 oz; and pike, 39 lb 7 oz. A bigger barbel, 16 lb 4 oz, was taken on a spinner by a game angler during the close season in 1961. Most sea-trout are taken in the lower stretches; they and the salmon begin to run mainly from July onwards.

Blandford, Dorset. 8 m of left bank from Durweston Bridge to Crawford Bridge, Spetisbury.
C (D T Adv. tackle shop, Blandford).
Bournemouth, Dorset. 1 m of right bank from Brecon Close to Shelley Lodge.
C (Free fishing).
Canford Bridge, Dorset. Fishing from boats only.
C, T (D T Adv. Newman's Boatyard, Canford Bridge).

Christchurch, Dorset. 1½ m Christ-church to Ilford Bridge.
C (D T Adv. tackle shop, Barrack Road, Christchurch).

Corfe Mullen, Dorset. ½ m of left bank plus island.
C, T, S (D T Adv. The Old Mill Hotel, Corfe Mullen. B available).

Durweston, Dorset. 3 m from corner of Preshaw Wood, right bank, to Durweston road bridge.
C (D T Adv. from Post Office, Durweston, or Durweston A S. L–10).

Gillingham, Dorset. 6 m Huntingford to Fifehead Magdalen plus 1 m at Fontmell Parva.
C, ST, S (D T Adv. tackle shop, Gillingham).

Holdenhurst, Dorset. Throop Fishery, 5½ m from Martin's Pool to Oak Tree Pool.
C, ST, S (D T Adv. E. Leah, South Lodge, Holdenhurst, or (coarse fishing only) Taylor's Tackle, Christchurch).

Little Canford, Dorset. From below Canford School to Iron Bridge below Manor Farm.
C (D T Adv. Manor Farm, Little Canford).

Northbourne, Dorset. Right bank from just below West Parley Bridge to cara-van park.
C, T (Free fishing).

Stalbridge, Dorset. 5½ m of right bank from Cale Bridge to King's Mill.
C, T (D T Adv. tackle shop, Stalbridge, or from Stalbridge Arms).

Sturminster Newton, Dorset. 7 m in area.
C (D T Adv. tackle shop, Sturminster Newton, or from White Hart, Sturminster Newton).
Tributaries: Allen (Dorset), Lydden.

Tone
Headwater runs into Clatworthy Reservoir, after which the river runs a 20-mile course on to Taunton, below which it widens and deepens before joining the Parrett.
Holds trout, grayling and coarse fish, which predominate in the lower reaches.

Taunton, Somt. Stretches from Taunton to Atherly.
C (D T Adv. Bridge Sports, Taunton).

Taunton, Somt. Left bank downstream of French Weir for 300 yds.
C (Free fishing).

Wellington, Somt. 2 m from Wellington to Harpford Farm.
C, T (D T Adv. Wellington A A).

Wellisford, Somt. 12 m Wellisford to Taunton.
T (D T Adv. tackle shops in area).
Tributary of Parrett system.

West Sedgemoor Main Drain
Drains the area to the south of the Par-rett, which it joins near Stathe.
Stocked with carp in addition to main coarse species.

Stathe, Somt. 1½ m Stathe to Pinkham.
C (D T Adv. Bridge Sports, Taunton).

Wylye
Rises near Kilmington and flows, part underground, through the Wylye Valley to join the Avon (Hants).
Trout and grayling, strictly preserved, with no known openings for visiting anglers.
Tributary of Avon (Hants.).

Yeo (Congresbury)
Runs, like the New Blind Yeo, to the Bristol Channel near Clevedon, after feeding Blagdon Reservoir.
Preserved trout water down to Wrington, where coarse fish start to take over.

Congresbury, Somt. West of Congres-bury to motorway bridge.
C (D T Adv. tackle shops in area).

Yeo (Somerset)
Rises to the south of Yeovil to feed Sherborne Lake, from which it runs to Yeovil and on to join the Parrett near Langport.
Trout in the upper reaches, with good coarse fishing in middle and lower reaches.

Ilchester, Somt. 5 m from River Cam to Beary Corner.
C (D T Adv. tackle shop, The Square,

Ilchester, or Ilchester and Dist. AA).

Yeovil, Somt. 7½ m from below town to Sherborne.

T, C (DT Adv. Hagas Fishing Centre, Silver Street, Yeovil).

Tributary of Parrett system.

Yorkshire Water Authority Rivers

This authority's area is dominated by the great Yorkshire Ouse system, stretching from the foothills of the Pennine Range to its estuary at Goole. The fishing ranges from moorland trouting to chalk-stream conditions, with some excellent coarse fishing and one or two black spots of pollution.

Besides its river fishing, the area also offers many stretches of canal.

Aire

Rises at Aire Head near Malham and runs through Airedale to Skipton, Keighley and Saltaire to Leeds. Pollution at Leeds makes fishing impractical down to the Aire's junction with the Ouse near Airmyn.

The upper reaches offer trout and grayling, with more and more coarse fish the lower you travel. Bradford City AA, Bradford No. 1 AA and Leeds AS A hold water.

Bingley, W Yorks. 1½ m Bingley to Saltaire.

T, C (DT Adv. tackle shops in area or Bingley A C. Open 1 Apr.–27 Feb.).

Cononley, N. Yorks. 6½ m at Cononley, Kildwick and Steeton.

C, T (DT Adv. tackle shops, Bradford, or C. Summerskill, 15 Cragg View, Cononley).

Keighley, W. Yorks. 9 m Kildwick to Bingley.

C (DT Adv. tackle shops, Bingley, Bradford, Keighley, Steeton and Utley).

Shipley, W. Yorks. 2 m Shipley to Bingley.

C, T (DT Adv. Boathouse, Victoria Road, Saltaire).

Skipton, N. Yorks. 3½ m Carleton to Skipton.

C, T (DT Adv. Skipton AA. No Sunday fishing in summer).

Skipton, N. Yorks. 2 m from above Carlton to Snaigill.

C, T (DT Adv. Skipton AA).

Stockbridge, S. Yorks. 2 m of left bank from Keighley Golf Course to Silsden Playing Fields.

C, T (DT Adv. tackle shops, Leeds. Fishery open 1 Apr.–27 Feb.).

Tributary of Ouse (Yorks) system.

Bain (Yorks.)

Runs from Cragdale Moor into Semerwater Lake and then on to the Ure at Bainbridge.

Trout and some coarse fish, mostly preserved.

Bainbridge, N. Yorks. 1 m from outfall as marked.

T (DT Adv. Rose and Crown, Bainbridge. No Sunday day tickets).

Tributary of Ouse (Yorks.) system.

Beverley and Barmston Drain

Runs 12 m from Hempholme, E Yorks, to Hull.

Rated best as a winter coarse fishery; the water is clear and often weedy in summer.

Hull, Humbs. Entire 12 m to Hempholme.

C (Free fishing).

Calder (Yorks.)

A river which has suffered greatly from pollution, although great efforts are being made to restore fishing, particularly by Bradford No. 1 AA from Brighouse to Sowerby Bridge. No known openings for visiting anglers. The river feeds the Aire.

Tributary of Ouse (Yorks.) system.

Calder-Hebble Navigation

Built to link the West Riding with the Rochdale Canal, running from Castleford to Wakefield and Sowerby Bridge. Polluted to Huddersfield but restored upstream.

No known openings for visiting anglers.

Cod Beck

Rises to the north-east of Thirsk and runs to join the River Swale near Topcliffe. Holds trout and coarse fish.

Topcliffe, N. Yorks. 1½ m right bank above and below Richmond Farm.

C, T (D T Adv. Moss's tackle shop, Thirsk).

Tributary of Ouse (Yorks.) system.

Costa Beck

Tributary of the Derwent.

Trout and grayling, mostly preserved.

Kirby Misperton, N. Yorks. 3 m from Flamingo Zoo downstream.

T and grayling (D T Adv. Caravan Site, Kirby Misperton. Fishery open 1 Apr.–27 Feb.).

Tributary of Ouse (Yorks.) system.

Cover

Rises at Cover Head, Great Whernside, and runs through Coverdale to the Ure near Middleham.

Trout, grayling.

East Witton, N. Yorks. Ure to Hall's Bridge.

T (D T Adv. Coverbridge Inn, Middleham, or Estate Office, East Witton Estate, Leyburn).

Tributary of Ouse (Yorks.) system.

Dearne

Runs through the Yorkshire coalfield, where it picks up much pollution, and is probably barren.

Derwent (Yorks.)

Rises in the Cleveland National Park on the North Yorkshire Moors and runs by Malton and through Stamford Bridge to the Ouse near Barmby on the Marsh.

Trout and some grayling down to the junction of the Rye, near Malton, where coarse fish begin to be seen. Most of the upper river is preserved. Barbel are another attraction of the lower river.

Bubwith, Humbs. 4 m of left bank from Bubwith to Ellerton.

T, C (D T Adv. White Swan, Bubwith, or Boot and Shoe, Ellerton. Fishery open all year).

Elvington, N. Yorks. 1½ m right bank downstream from Elvington Bridge.

T, C (D T Adv. keeper, Tom Ashton, Sutton-on-Derwent. Fishery open 1 Apr.–27 Feb.).

Hackness, N. Yorks. 8 m through Forge Valley.

T (Residents only, Hackness Grange Country Hotel. Fly only).

Hackness, N. Yorks. 12 m West Ayton to Langdale End.

T (D T Adv. tackle shop, Eastborough, Scarborough; Hackness Grange Country Hotel or Everley Hotel, Hackness. Fly only, no Sunday fishing. Fishery open 1 Apr.–30 Sept.).

Stamford Bridge, Humbs. 4 m of right bank from Stamford Bridge to Kexby Bridge.

C (D T Adv. Post Office, Stamford Bridge. Fishery open 1 June–27 Feb.).

Stamford Bridge, Humbs. ½ m on left bank downstream from Stamford Bridge.

C (D T Adv. Post Office, Stamford Bridge. Fishery open 1 June–27 Feb.).

Sutton-on-Derwent, N Yorks. 4 m on left bank from above Elvington Bridge to 2½ m below Sutton Dam.

C, T (D T Adv. from keeper, Tom Ashton, Sutton-on-Derwent. Fishery open 1 Apr.–27 Feb.).

Yedlingham, N. Yorks. 3 m, stretches from Foulbridge to 2 m below Yedlingham Bridge.

C, T (D T Adv. Providence Inn, Yedlingham. Fishery open 1 Apr.–27 Feb.).

Tributary of Ouse (Yorks.) system.

Don

Running through industrial country past Doncaster to Goole, the Don is said to be among the most polluted pieces of water in Britain. Efforts to restore it recently have not met with noticeable success.

Tributary of Ouse (Yorks.) system.

Dove

Tributary of the Rye.

Preserved trout and grayling fishing.

Driffield Canal (Driffield Beck)
Despite its name, a fine chalk stream offering trout and grayling. Feeds into the Hull at Struncheonhill Lock.

Brigham. Humbs. From point below Snakeholme Lock to junction of Frodlingham Beck.

T, C (Free fishing).

Tributary of Hull system.

Esk (Yorks.)
The only salmon river in Yorkshire, thanks to work by the former Yorkshire Water Board and later by the Yorkshire Water Authority. Rises on Westerdale Moor and runs through Grosmont and Sleights to Whitby. The river also has a run of sea-trout and good brown trout.

Whitby, N. Yorks. From Sleights to pier end at Whitby, except from Ruswarp Weir to downstream side of Ruswarp road bridge.

T, ST, S (DT Adv. tackle shop, Haggersgate, Whitby).

Foss
Rises near Foston and runs through Strensall to the Ouse at York.

Mostly coarse fishing, with some good pike on record.

Earswick, N. Yorks. Part of right bank.

C (Free fishing).

Tributary of Ouse (Yorks.) system.

Foulness River
Rises north of Market Weighton and runs to join Market Weighton Canal near Newport.

Shallow and streamy, offering good roach fishing with some bream.

Market Weighton, Humbs. Entire water.

C (Free fishing).

Frodingham Beck
Another of the chalk streams feeding the Hull system and offering trout and coarse fish.

Frodingham, Humbs. Frodingham Bridge to Hempholme Lock.

C (Free fishing).

Tributary of Hull system.

Holderness Drain
Drains parts of E. Yorks into the Humber at Marfleet.

A shallow water influenced by tides in the Humber, with fair stocks of roach and bream.

Hull, Humbs. Wawne to Hull.

C (Free fishing).

Huddersfield Narrow
One of the connections between Yorkshire and Lancashire. The Narrow links the Calder and Hebble Navigation with the Ashton Canal near Manchester.

Fair coarse fishing.

Huddersfield, W. Yorks. 7 m from Lock 4, Longroyd Bridge, to Stanage Tunnel End, Marsden.

C (DT Adv. tackle shop, Chapel Hill, Huddersfield, or Albion Inn, Longroyd Bridge).

Hull
Starts at Struncheonhill Lock and runs south from Hempholme through Hull to the Humber.

Fair coarse fishing and has produced some big pike.

Beverley, Humbs. Beverley to Hempholme Lock.

C (Free fishing).

Tributaries: Driffield Canal, Frodingham Beck, Leven Canal.

Keyingham Level (Stone Creek)
Small E. Yorks. land drain running into Humber.

Mainly winter flounder fishing, with a few coarse fish.

Hull, Humbs. Entire water.

C (Free fishing).

Laver
Short stream joining the Ure at Ripon.

Mainly trout.

Ripon, N. Yorks. 2 m Birkby Nab to Rustic Bridge, Ripon.

T (DT Adv. Hodgsons, Ripon. Fly only, 1 Apr.–30 Sept.).

Tributary of Ouse (Yorks.) system.

Leeds and Liverpool Canal

Links the north end of the Aire and Calder Navigation at Leeds with Liverpool over the Pennines; the longest single canal in Britain. It runs via Shipley, Skipton and Gargrave into Lancashire, where part of it is known as the Haigh Canal.

Offers carp in addition to good general coarse fishing, and is a popular match water.

Skipton, N. Yorks. 36 m Leeds to Bank Newton.

C (D T Adv. tackle shops in area).

Leven Canal

Links Leven with the River Hull near Aike.

Good roach fishing, with some bream and pike.

Leven, Humbs. Entire water, 6 m.

C (D T Adv. Everett's tackle shop, Beverley).

Market Weighton Canal

Runs from Market Weighton to Newport and the Humber at Broomfleet Lock.

Although it has suffered a decline in recent years, restocking is restoring the canal's fishing to its former glory – it was once rated the best canal fishing in Yorkshire.

Holds silver as well as bronze bream, and roach, dace and pike.

Market Weighton, Humbs. 6 m Broomfleet Lock to Sod House Lock.

C (Free fishing).

New Junction Canal

Short waterway linking the Aire and Calder Navigation near Cowick to the Sheffield and South Yorkshire Canal near Doncaster.

Fair coarse fishing, though patchy in recent times.

Sykehouse, S. Yorks. Most of water.

C (D T Adv. lock house, Sykehouse).

Nidd

Rises in the Pennines at Great Whernside and flows through Pateley Bridge and Nidderdale to the Ouse near Nun Monkton.

Fine trout and grayling fishing in the upper reaches, with coarse fish, including barbel, lower down towards Ouse. Most of the upper reaches private fishing.

Knaresborough, N. Yorks. ¾ m of right bank from Grimbald Bridge to Birkham Wood.

T, C (D T Adv. tackle shop, Knaresborough).

Knaresborough, N. Yorks. Right bank stretch between town bridges.

C (D T Adv. tackle shop, Knaresborough).

Skip Bridge, N. Yorks. ¾ m of right bank from Wilstrop rail bridge to Skip Bridge.

C (D T Adv. Skip Bridge Garage. Fishery open 1 June–27 Feb.).

Tockwith, N. Yorks. 1 m of right bank from Fleet Beck down to notice-board above weir.

C (D T Adv. Crown Inn, Kirk Hammerton. Fishery open 1 June–27 Feb.).

Tributary of Ouse (Yorks.) system.

Ouse (Yorks.)

The Ouse proper begins at a point near the meeting of the rivers Ure and Swale, and the entry of the Ouseburn Beck is generally thought to mark its birth. It runs to York and on to the Humber, collecting a vast array of tributaries.

While it holds trout, some of them big, the Ouse is best rated as a coarse fishery offering roach, dace and chub, with big barbel and some large shoals of bream (some big fish).

Acaster, N. Yorks. Stretch of right bank below Acaster Weir, with marked gaps.

C (D T Adv. Post Office, Acaster).

Fulford, N. Yorks. 1½ m of left bank from moorings below Fulford pumping station to Naburn sewage works.

C (D T Adv. Hoe's Bakery, Main Street, Fulford. Fishery open 1 June–27 Feb.).

Low Dunsforth, N. Yorks. 4 m of right bank from Holbech Drain to Morgan's Drain.

C (D T Adv. Anchor Inn, Dunsforth. Fishery open 1 June–27 Feb.).

Nether Poppleton, N. Yorks. 3 m of right bank from rail bridge downstream.

C (DT Adv. Leeds Amalgamated A S. Fishery open 1 June–27 Feb.).

Newton-on-Ouse, N. Yorks. More than 6 m from lodge gates, Newton, to Clifton Ings except gap at Bushey Close, left bank.
C (DT Adv. tackle shops, York. Fishery open 1 June–27 Feb.).

Newton-on-Ouse, N. Yorks. ¾ m of left bank upstream of River Kyle.
C (DT Adv. Fotherby's Garage, Newton-on-Ouse. Fishery open 1 June–27 Feb.).

Ouseburn, N. Yorks. 3 m of right bank upstream from Aldwark Bridge.
C (DT Adv. Anchor Inn, Dunsforth. Fishery open 1 June–27 Feb.).

Widdington, N. Yorks. ¾ m on right bank from weir fish pass to opposite Kyle mouth.
C (DT Adv. tackle shops, York. Fishery open 1 June–27 Feb.).

York, N. Yorks. 1½ m within city bounds.
C (Free fishing).
Tributaries of the Ouse (Yorks.): Aire, Bain (Yorks.), Calder, Cod Beck, Costa Beck, Cover, Dearne, Derwent (Yorks.), Don, Dove (Yorks.), Foss, Laver, Nidd, Pickering Beck, Riccal, Ripon Canal, Rivelin, Rother (Derbys.), Rye, Seph, Seven, Swale, Ure, Wharfe, Wiske.

Partington Haven
Small land drain running into Humber.
Flounder fishing main sport, with a few coarse fish.
Hull, Humbs. Whole water.
C (Free fishing).

Pickering Beck
Small chalk-stream tributary of the Costa Beck, which runs into the Yorkshire Derwent.
Mainly trout, private fishing.
Tributary of Ouse (Yorks.) system.

Pocklington Canal
Runs from Pocklington 13 m to River Derwent at East Cottingwith.
Offers coarse fish, including tench, which can be large, and good pike. Stocks good.

Pocklington, Humbs. Entire water.
C (DT Adv. College Arms, Bielby, or Wellington Oak, Pocklington; also Brocklebanks Garage, Melbourne, or Rossmere Garage on B1228).

Riccal
Rises on the North Yorkshire Moors and runs to the Rye near Harome.
Trout and some coarse fish.
Nunnington, N. Yorks. Nunnington Estate water.
T, C (DT Adv. Estate Office, Nunnington Hall. Fishery open 1 Apr.–30 Sept.).
Tributary of Ouse (Yorks.) system.

Ripon Canal
Short waterway linking the Ouse with the Ure near Ripon.
Coarse fish and some trout.
Ripon, N. Yorks. Towpath, entire water.
C, T (DT, WT, Adv. B. Wain, 82 Bondgate, Ripon, or from Brewers Arms, Bondgate Green, Ripon).

Rivelin
Tributary of the Loxley joining at Malin Bridge in Sheffield.
Has been badly overgrown and neglected, but efforts are under way to restore it as a trout fishery.
Tributary of Ouse (Yorks.) system.

Rother (Derbys.)
Rises to the south of Chesterfield and joins the River Don at Rotherham. Too polluted to support fish.
Tributary of Ouse (Yorks.) system.

Rye
Rises in the Cleveland Hills at Ryehead and runs through Helmsley and Nunnington to the Derwent (Yorks.) near Wykeham.
Mostly trout and grayling above Nunnington, with coarse fish in the deeper and slower stretches below Nunnington. Hull and District A A, York and District Amalgamation and Leeds A S A hold water.
Hawnby, N. Yorks. 4 m Arden Hall to Shaken Bridge.

T (DT Adv. Hawnby Hotel, Hawnby. Fly only).

Nunnington, N. Yorks. 1½ m Nunnington Fishery Top Water.

T (DT Adv. Estate Office, Nunnington Hall. Fly only. Season open 1 Apr.–30 Sept. L–4).

Nunnington, N. Yorks. 1 m from below Ford Mill to Ness.

T, C (DT Adv. Estate Office, Nunnington Hall. Season open 1 Apr.–30 Sept. L–25).

Tributary of Ouse (Yorks.) system.

Seph

Rises in the Cleveland Hills and runs beside the B1257 road to the River Rye near Hawnby.

Trout and grayling.

Hawnby, N. Yorks. 6 m of right bank from Malkin Bower to Shaken Bridge.

T (DT Adv. Hawnby Hotel, Hawnby. Fly only).

Tributary of Ouse (Yorks.) system.

Seven

Rye tributary draining from the North Yorkshire Moors.

Trout and grayling, mostly preserved, with no known openings for visitors.

Tributary of Ouse (Yorks.) system.

Sheffield and South Yorkshire Navigation

Built to carry Sheffield traffic to the Humber through the Trent at Keadby.

Has suffered greatly from pollution, but restocking is said to be having some good effect.

Skeffling Drain

E. Yorks land drain running into Humber.

Winter flounder fishing is main sport, with a few coarse fish.

Hull, Humbs. Entire water.

C (Free fishing).

Swale

An excellent Yorkshire fishery, rising above Keld and running through Swaledale to Muker, Richmond, then on through Catterick, Topcliffe and Cundall to the Ure below Boroughbridge.

Trout in the upper reaches, but the river is justifiably famed for the coarse fish, particularly barbel, chub and roach, of the middle and lower reaches. Match records top 59 lb, with barbel to 10 lb, chub to 7 lb, roach to 2 lb 4 oz, trout to more than 5 lb. Bradford clubs, Leeds ASA and Thornaby AA hold water.

Baldersby, N. Yorks. 1 m of right bank downstream from gas pipe bridge.

C, T (DT Adv. Moss's tackle shop, Thirsk).

Catterick, N. Yorks. Stretch upstream of Catterick Bridge and 1 m of right bank from A1 bridge to notice-board.

C, T (DT Adv. Thornaby AA).

Catterick, N. Yorks. 1 m right bank near hotel.

C (DT Adv. Bridge House Hotel, Catterick).

Grinton, N. Yorks. 5½ m right bank from upstream of Grinton Bridge to Isles Bridge.

T (DT Adv. Thornaby AA).

Maundby, N. Yorks. 3 m of left bank upstream from Maundby.

C (DT Adv. Buck Inn, Maundby. Fishery open 1 June–27 Feb.).

Morton-on-Swale, N. Yorks. 4 m Morton Bridge to Far Fairholme.

C, T (DT Adv. keeper, J. Grainger, Morton-on-Swale. Fishery open 1 May–31 Dec.).

Pickhill, N. Yorks. Two meadows at New Leys Farm.

C, T (DT Adv. Thornaby AA).

Reeth, N. Yorks. 1½ m near hotel.

T (Residents only, Black Bull Hotel, Reeth).

Richmond, N. Yorks. 18 m from Marske to Great Langton.

C, T (DT Adv. tackle shop, Richmond, or Richmond and Dist. AS). L–10 rods between 1 Oct.–28 Feb. No limit below Richmond 1 June–30 Sept.).

Skipton-on-Swale, N. Yorks. ½ m on right bank above Skipton Bridge and stretches below.

C, T (DT Adv. Moss's tackle shop, Thirsk).

Topcliffe, N. Yorks. From 1 m above Topcliffe Weir to ½ m below.

C, T (D T Adv. Black Bull public house, Topcliffe. Fishery open 1 Apr.–27 Feb.).
Tributary of Ouse (Yorks.) system.

Ure

Rises on Lunds Fell to run through Hawes, Aysgarth and Middleham, then on to Ripon and Boroughbridge to join the Swale at Swale Nab.

Mainly a trout river above Aysgarth but, like the Swale, it holds superb stocks of coarse fish, with big shoals of chub, roach to 3 lb, and shoals of bream (some big fish) in the lower reaches. The river has produced a dace of 1 lb 4 oz and a trout of 8 lb 4 oz.

Aysgarth, N. Yorks. $\frac{1}{2}$ m of left bank near Woodhall.
T (D T Adv. Skipton A A).

Aysgarth, N. Yorks. 300 yds stretch of right bank from Aysgarth falls.
T, C (D T Adv. Palmer Flatt Hotel, Aysgarth).

Bainbridge, N. Yorks. 6 m in area.
T and grayling (D T Adv. keeper, C. Peacock, Countersett, Semerwater Lake; or Rose and Crown Hotel, Bainbridge. Fishery open for trout, 1 Apr.–30 Sept.; grayling, 1 June–28 Feb. No Sunday fishing).

Boroughbridge, N. Yorks. $\frac{3}{4}$ m of left bank from Boroughbridge to Milby Nab End.
C, T (D T Adv. tackle shops, Harrogate and Knaresborough, or Three Horse Shoes public house, Boroughbridge).

Boroughbridge, N. Yorks. $1\frac{1}{2}$ m of right bank from Cricket Field one field below town bridge to Hall Arm Lane.
C (D T Adv. Post Office, Boroughbridge).

Boroughbridge, N. Yorks. 1 m downstream from Westwick Weir.
C (D T Adv. Skelton Lodge, Newby Hall Estate Office, Skelton-on-Ure, near Ripon).

Boroughbridge, N. Yorks. 1 m Ellenthorpe Hall Fishery, left bank from 3 fields below lock.
C (D T Adv. Ellenthorpe Hall Farm).

East Witton, N. Yorks. $1\frac{1}{2}$ m right bank from Ushaw Bridge to Harker Beck.

C, T (D T Adv. Blue Lion, East Witton. Fly only L–2).

Hawes, N. Yorks. 8 m from Moorcock Inn to Borwins.
T, grayling (W T Adv. Hawes A A).

Kilgrimbridge, N Yorks. Over 1 m on left bank upstream of village.
T, C, (D T Adv. Thornaby A A).

Middleham, N. Yorks. Over 1 m of right bank from below Iron Bridge.
T, C (D T Adv. Old Horn Inn, Spennithorne. Fishery open 1 Apr.–27 Feb.).

Ripon, N. Yorks. 1 m of right bank from Sykewood to old Military Bridge.
T, C (D T Adv. Hodgsons Tackle, Ripon. Fly only 1 Apr.–31 May. L–2).

Ripon, N Yorks. 7 m from Ure Bank Caravan Site to Newby Hall.
C, T (W T Adv. B, Wain, 82 Bondgate, Ripon, or Brewers Arms, Bondgate Green, Ripon).

Roecliffe, N. Yorks. 500 yds right bank Harrisons Farm Fishery.
C (D T Adv. Harrisons Farm).

Spennithorne, N. Yorks. Left bank 1 m above and 1 m below Beggar's Mouth.
C, T (D T Adv. Old Horn Inn, Spennithorne. Open 1 Apr.–27 Feb.).

Ullshaw Bridge, N. Yorks. 1 m of left bank above bridge.
C, T (D T Adv. Old Horn Inn, Spennithorne. Open 1 Apr.–27 Feb.).
Tributary of Ouse (Yorks.) system.

Wharfe

Another famed Yorkshire coarse fishery, although it also offers fine trouting, especially in the upper reaches. Rising on Cam Fell, it runs through Kettlewell and Threshfield and into Wharfedale. It passes through Bolton Abbey, Ilkley, Otley, Boston Spa and Wetherby to join the Ouse near Tadcaster.

Coarse fish are most concentrated below Otley, but the lower part of the river near Tadcaster has suffered in the past through pollution and a continuing effort is being made to restore it.

Appletreewick, N. Yorks. $\frac{1}{2}$ m of left bank from dry wall to wood.
T, C (D T Adv. New Inn, Appletreewick).

Bolton Abbey, N. Yorks. 3 m from Bolton Bridge to Barden Bridge.

T, grayling (DT Adv. Estate Office, Bolton Abbey, on weekdays, and cottage next to Hole in Wall public house in village. Fly only. Fishery open for trout, Apr.–30 Sept.; grayling, 15 June–31 Dec.).

Boston Spa, W. Yorks. 3 m from Gasworks to Newton Kyme.

C, T (DT Adv. Spa Baths, Boston Spa).

Boston Spa, W. Yorks. ½ m from road bridge to Green Gate, right bank.

C, T (DT Adv. Spa Baths, Boston Spa).

Buckden, N. Yorks. Right bank, ½ m above bridge and 1½ m below.

T, C (DT Adv. keeper, Mrs Lambert, Buckden. Fishery open 1 Apr.–30 Sept.).

Buckden, N. Yorks. 3½ m stretch.

T (DT Adv. Buck Inn, Buckden, or Langstroth Services Ltd, Greenfield, Buckden. Fly only. B available).

Burnsall, N. Yorks. 6 m from Grassington to Barden.

T, grayling (DT Adv. tackle shop, Skipton; Red Lion Hotel or Fell Hotel, Burnsall. Fly only, for trout. Fishery open 1 June–30 Sept. for trout; grayling, 1 Nov.–31 Jan.).

Grassington, N. Yorks. 2¼ m in area.

T, grayling (DT Adv. Devonshire Arms, Grassington, or Grassington Post Office. Trout fly only. Fishery open for trout, 1 Apr.–30 Sept.; grayling, 1 Oct.–28 Feb. No Sunday fishing).

Ilkley, W. Yorks. 1½ m from Old Packhorse Bridge to Benrhydding stepping stones.

C, T (DT Adv. Cree's Pet Stores, Ilkley, or Runnymede News Agency, Iklley).

Pool-in-Wharfedale, W. Yorks. 5 m from River Washburn to Castley Beck.

T (DT Adv. from The Stores, Hanson Coyle, Pool. Fishery open 1 Apr.–31 Oct.).

Ryther, N. Yorks. 2 m right bank Ryther to Button Hill.

C (DT Adv. Ulleskelf Arms, Ulleskelf. Fishery open 1 June–27 Feb.).

Ryther, N. Yorks. 3 fields on right bank from Mucky Lane.

C (DT Adv. Ulleskelf Arms, Ulleskelf).

Tadcaster, N. Yorks. 2 m at Tadcaster.

C (DT on bank, from Webb's, Kirkgate, Tadcaster, or Britannia Inn, Tadcaster).

Tadcaster, N. Yorks. 1½ m of left bank from Salmon Pool up to sewage outfall.

C (DT Adv. tackle shops, Leeds, or from Britannia Inn, Tadcaster. Fishery open 1 June–27 Feb.).

Ulleskelf, N. Yorks. 3 m of right bank from Salmon Pool, Tadcaster, to Ship Inn, Ulleskelf.

C (DT Adv. tackle shops, Leeds, or Ulleskelf Arms, Ulleskelf. Fishery open 1 June–27 Feb.).

Wetherby, W. Yorks. 2 m from Collingham to Wetherby.

C, T (DT Adv. Sports and Leisure shop, Wetherby; George and Dragon, Wetherby, or Old Star Filling Station, Collingham).

Tributary of Ouse (Yorks.) system.

Wiske

Rises in N. Yorks and runs past Northallerton to the Swale below Kirby Wiske.

Trout, with coarse fish in lower reaches. Association membership offers best chance of fishing.

Tributary of Ouse (Yorks.) system.

Two

English Still Waters (by county)

England offers a wealth of still water fishing, although day ticket water is becoming increasingly hard to find. The guide does not list those waters which are preserved.

Fly-only trout waters Because of the increasing popularity of still water fly fishing, the waters offering this kind of sport are given a special identification mark (●) to make them stand out in the list and provide a quick reference.

The Broads, The Lake District Since these are popular holiday areas for anglers, they are given separate headings in the list that follows.

Avon

Badminton Park Lake, Great Badminton.
C (DT Adv. from keeper or from Estate Office, Badminton. Rods limited to 15 anglers. Rod licence not needed).

Barrow Reservoirs, Barrow Gurney.
● T (DT Adv. ticket machine or from Bristol Waterworks Co., Woodford Lodge, Chew Stoke, near Bristol. Fly-only trout water. Stone banking makes them less popular than near-neighbours Chew and Blagdon, but they produce good fish averaging 2 lb and are additionally stocked with yearling fish. Three reservoirs, 1, 2 and 3, totalling about 120 acres. Rod licence incl.).

Bitterwell Lake, Westerleigh, near Bristol.
C (DT on bank. Very well stocked with carp, and holds tench, bream and rudd. Inclined to be crowded in school holidays. Wessex WA rod licence).

Blagdon Lake, Blagdon, near Bristol.
● T (DT Adv. ticket machines at Blagdon and Chew Valley Lake, or from Bristol Waterworks Co., Woodford Lodge, Chew Stoke, near Bristol. Fishes better from bank than Chew. The fly-only water held the 8 lb 8½ oz record rainbow, caught by Lt-Col. Creagh Scott, for many years. Rod licence incl. Rowing boats).

Cameley Lakes, Temple Cloud, near Bristol.
● T (DT Adv. Hillcrest Farm, Temple Cloud. Two fly-only lakes with 2 lb average weight fish. Open 1 Apr.–15 Oct. Wessex WA licence).

Chew Valley Lake, Chew Stoke, near Bristol.
● T (DT Adv. ticket machine or from Bristol Waterworks Co., Woodford Lodge, Chew Stoke, near Bristol. Fly-only water of considerable fame; fish average 2 lb but many are considerably bigger. Motor boats, must be booked. Rod licence incl. Open early Apr. to 15 Oct.).

Eastville Lake, Bristol.
C (Apply Bristol City Council, Recreations Office, Parks Dept, Cabot House, Deanery Road, Bristol. Wessex WA licence).

Henleaze Lake, Bristol.
C (DT Adv. at lake. A flooded quarry with good roach, also some carp. Wessex WA licence. Open first Saturday in May to last Sunday in Sept.).

Hutton Pond, Weston-super-Mare.
C (DT Adv. tackle shops, Weston. Wessex WA licence).

Locking Pit, Locking, Weston-super-Mare.
C (DT Adv. tackle shops, Weston. Wessex WA licence).
St George's Lake, Bristol.
C (Apply Bristol City Council, Recreations Office, Parks Dept, Cabot House, Deanery Road, Bristol. Wessex WA licence).

Bedfordshire

Leighton Buzzard Pits, Leighton Buzzard.
C (Season ticket through Leighton Buzzard AC. Main coarse species, plus carp to 30 lb and catfish. Anglian WA licence).
Little Heath Farm Lake, Gamlingay, Sandy.
● T (DT Adv. Little Heath Farm, Little Heath Road, Gamlingay, Sandy. Fly only, fish to 6 lb plus. Six acres. Evening tickets available).
Tingrith Trout Farm Lake, Tingrith, near Luton.
● T (DT Adv. Tingrith Trout Farm, Tingrith. Evening ticket available. Some big fish. Anglian WA licence).
Woburn Lakes, Woburn.
C (DT Adv. from keeper. Main coarse species, plus zander and catfish. Anglian WA licence).

Berkshire

Burghfield Pits, Burghfield.
C (WT Adv. tackle shop named on sign at entry or from Leisure Sport, RMC House, High Street, Feltham, Middx. Tench, roach, pike. Thames WA licence).
Dinton Pastures Lake (*Black Swan Lake*), Hurst.
● T (DT Adv. Dinton Pastures Trout Fishery, Davis Street, Hurst. Best rainbow tops 9 lb. Fly only, L–70. Open 1 Apr.–30 Nov. Thames WA licence).
Folley's Pit, Sonning.
C (DT on bank. Thames WA licence).

Horton Trout Fishery, Horton, Slough.
T (DT Adv. Kingsmead Trout Farms Ltd, Stanwell Road, Horton, Slough. Fourteen acres, stocked rainbows, fly, worm or spinning allowed. Thames WA licence).
Langham Pond, Runnymede.
C (DT on bank. Thames WA licence).
Queen Mother's Reservoir, Datchet.
● T (DT, fishing from boats only, Adv. from ticket office. Fly only, rowing boats. Stocked brown trout. Thames WA licence).
Stratfield Saye Lake, Stratfield Saye.
● T (DT Adv. from keeper. Fly only, trout to 7 lb. Thames WA licence).
Summerleaze Lake, Maidenhead.
C (DT Adv. J. Smith, tackle, 5 High Street, Maidenhead. Thames WA licence).
Theale Pits, Theale.
C (WT Adv. tackle shop named at entry to pits or from Leisure Sport, RMC House, High Street, Feltham, Middx. Pits hold roach, bream, tench and pike. Ticket covers Kennet backwater. Thames WA licence).
Windsor Great Park Lakes, Windsor.
C (Season permits for Johnson's Pond, Obelisk Pond and Virginia Water through Crown Estate Office, The Great Park, Windsor).

Broads (Norfolk)

NB. These and the Suffolk waters (see Broads (Suffolk) below) are covered by the Anglian WA rod licence, East Suffolk and Norfolk Rivers Division. For the rivers in the broads, see above, Anglian Water Authority rivers: Ant, Bure, Candle Dyke, Chet, New Cut, Thurne, Waveney, Wensum, Womack Water and Yare.
Alderfen Broad, Neatishead.
C (DT Adv. L–8 rods from 4 rowing boats, Haylett's Tackle, Wroxham. Main coarse species).
Barton Broad, Barton Turf.
C (Free fishing from boats only. Boat traffic can be heavy during day. Fishes well until late autumn. Boats from Barton Turf).

Heigham Sound, Hickling.

C (Free fishing from boats only, available at Hickling and Martham. Some limited bank fishing approachable by boat. Bream catches can be big, especially near Meadow Dyke).

Hickling Broad, Hickling.

C (Free fishing from boats only. Has suffered greatly from pollution, but bream show signs of recovery).

Horsey Mere, Horsey.

C (D T Adv. from keeper, Hall Cottage, Horsey, from Staithe Store, Horsey, or on bank. Boats from Martham or Hickling. Once a noted water for big pike, struck by pollution in the '60s. Smaller pike now recovering. Roach and bream good. Open 16 June–31 Oct. and 1 Feb.–14 Mar.).

Martham Broad, Martham Ferry.

C (D T on bank).

Ranworth Broad (*Malthouse Broad*), Ranworth.

C (D T Adv. Granary Stores, Ranworth, or The Maltsters, Ranworth. B available).

Ranworth Inner Broad, Ranworth.

C (D T Adv. Granary Stores, Ranworth, or The Maltsters, Ranworth. A nature reserve. B available).

Rockland Broad, Rockland St Mary.

C (Free fishing only from boats. A shallow broad with channel confining main boat traffic. B available at broad).

Salhouse Broad, Salhouse.

C (D T on bank or from keeper for boat fishing. Boats at Wroxham for Great Salhouse Broad; Little Salhouse Broad is private).

South Walsham Broad, South Walsham.

C (Free fishing from boats in outer broad; inner broad is private. Connected to Bure through Fleet Dyke. Boats from South Walsham).

Surlingham Broad, Surlingham.

C (Free fishing from boats, available at Brundall. Silting a problem. Shoals of smaller bream).

Wroxham Broad, Wroxham.

C (Free fishing from boats only, available at Wroxham. With inlets from the Bure it is one of the more popular broads, and maintains a good head of fish).

Broads (Suffolk)

See the introduction to the Norfolk Broads above for licence details.

Broome Pits, Broome.

C (Free fishing on 3 gravel pits).

Fritton Lake, Fritton.

C (D T Adv. lakeside café. Very pretty water offering excellent coarse fishing, especially for big bream. B available).

Ormesby Broads, Ormesby.

C (Free fishing from boats, banks inaccessible. Somewhat better than the other broads from the point of view of heavy boating. B available locally).

Oulton Broad, Lowestoft.

C (Free fishing from bank and boats, which are available at broad. Used to have reputation for big perch, now largely absent. Otherwise fair fishing).

Redgrave Lake, Botesdale.

C (D T on bank).

Station Pit, Bungay Common.

C (Free fishing).

N B. See also Norfolk and Suffolk (other still waters) under separate headings below.

Buckinghamshire

Blue Lagoon, Bletchley.

C (D T Adv. tackle shop, Bletchley, or Milton Keynes A A. Anglian W A licence).

Church Hill Farm Lake, Mursley.

● T (D T Adv. Church Hill Farm, Church Lane, Mursley. L–8; advance booking advised. Open 1 Apr.–30 Sept. Thames W A licence).

Claydon Lakes, Steeple Claydon.

C (Season membership only Leighton Buzzard A C. Pits contain main species, also catfish and zander. Anglian W A licence).

Colnbrook Lakes, Colnbrook.

C (Season only, William Boyer (Fishing), Trout Road, West Drayton, Middx).

Cosgrove Lodge Park Lane, Stony Stratford.
C (D T Adv. ticket office at park entrance. Anglian W A licence).
Kingsmead Pits, Horton.
C (W T Adv. for three pits, apply Leisure Sport, R M C House, High Street, Feltham, Middx).
Larbourne Farm Pits, Iver.
C (W T Adv. tackle shop named at entry to fishery or from Leisure Sport, R M C House, High Street, Feltham, Middx).
Latimer Park Lakes, Latimer.
● T (D T Adv. must be booked, tel. Little Chalfont 2396. Open 2 Apr.–30 Sept. No Sunday fishing. L–10. B available. Thames W A licence. Fly only).
Linford Lakes, Newport Pagnell.
● T (No day tickets but guests may have permit. Fly only).
Vicarage Spinney Lake, Little Linford.
● T (D T Adv. Mike Sando, 6 Kipling Drive, Newport Pagnell, Bucks. Fly only).
Wraysbury Pits, Wraysbury.
C (W T Adv. tackle shop named on notice-board at fishery, or from Leisure Sport, R M C House, High Street, Feltham, Middx. Excellent coarse fishing on two gravel pits).

Cambridgeshire

Barnwell Pit, Cambridge.
C (D T Adv. Cambridge Albion A S. Anglian W A licence).
Block Fen, Chatteris.
● T (D T Adv. ticket office, Chatteris Aqua Sports, Langwood Farm, Block Fen Drove, Mepal. Fly only. Open 1 Apr.–13 Oct. Rowing boats. Anglian W A licence).
Grafham Water, Buckden.
● T (D T Adv. ticket office. Probably the water which started the still water trout boom, and still a fine fishery, with fish of good average weight and some big fish. B available. Fly only. Open 1 May–13 Oct. Anglian W A licence).
Manea Pit, Manea.
C (D T on bank or from Manea A C).

The Pingles, Mepal.
C (D T Adv. Great Ouse Fishery Consultative Association, and free to affiliated clubs. Anglian W A licence).
Sibson Fisheries, Stibbington.
● T, C (D T Adv. Sibson Fisheries, New Lane, Stibbington. L–2. Trout and coarse water on this fishery, trout fly only. Open 1 Apr.–31 Oct. Anglian W A licence).

Cheshire

Bosley Reservoir, Macclesfield.
C (D T Adv. keeper, 1 Lake Side, Bosley. North-West W A licence).
Capesthorne Pools, Alderley Edge.
C (D T Adv. keeper, East Lodge, Capesthorne Hall).
Great Budsworth Mere, Northwich.
C (D T from keeper. North-West W A licence).
Lamaload Reservoir, Macclesfield.
● T (D T Adv. R. Newton, tackle, 5 Park Lane, Macclesfield. Fly only. L–5. North-West W A licence).
Leadbeaters Reservoir, Macclesfield.
C, T (D T Adv. R. Newton, tackle, 5 Park Lane Macclesfield. North-West W A licence).
Lymm Dam, Lymm.
C (D T on bank or from keeper or tackle shops in area, also from Church Hotel, Lymm. North-West W A licence).
Long Barn Park Pool, Warrington.
C (D T from keeper. North-West W A licence).
Newbridge Pool, Winsford.
C (D T on bank. North-West W A licence).
New Pool, Winsford.
C (D T Adv. Ashley and Harrison, tackle, Delamere Street, Winsford. North-West W A licence).
Oulton Mill Pool, Oulton.
C (D T Adv. R. Bennett, Pool Bank House, Oulton).
Pettypool, Winsford.
C (D T on bank. North-West W A licence).

Pritchard's Pits, Davenham.
C (DT from keeper. L–15. North-West WA licence).

Quoisley Mere, Quoisley.
C (DT from farm near Meres, near Nantwich. North-West WA licence).

Redesmere Pool, Macclesfield.
C (DT Adv. from keeper, East Lodge, Capesthorne. B available. North-West WA licence).

South Park Pool, Macclesfield.
C (DT on bank. North-West WA licence).

Tabley Mere, Knutsford.
C (DT from boats only. L–6. From Estate Office, Tabley, Knutsford. North-West WA licence).

Taxmere, Sandbach.
C (DT Adv. J. Fear, tackle, Wells Street, Sandbach. No rod licence needed).

Wide Hole, Poynton.
C (DT on bank or from Northern AA. North-West WA licence).

Winsford Flash, Winsford.
C (DT on bank. North-West WA licence).

Woods Meadow Pool, Northwich.
C (DT from keeper. North-West WA licence).

Cleveland

Lockwood Beck, Guiseborough.
● T (DT Adv. from ticket office. Fly only. B available. Stocked browns and rainbows. Open 1 May–31 Oct. Northumbrian WA licence).

Scaling Dam, Guiseborough.
T (DT ticket office. Spinning, worm allowed. Open 25 Mar.–31 Oct. Yorkshire WA licence).

Cornwall

Alderquarry Pond, Launceston.
C (DT Adv. Alder Farm, Lewdown. No close season. South-West WA licence).

Argal and College reservoirs, Falmouth.
● T (DT Adv. ticket machine. Fly only.

Fishery open 1 Apr.–12 Oct., with winter fishing for rainbows permitted. Boat for Argal. Rod licence incl.).

Carbis Moor Pool, Penwithick.
C (DT Adv. Treweek's tackle, 6 Victoria Place, St Austell. South-West WA licence).

Crowdy Reservoir, Camelford.
● T (DT Adv. ticket machine. Fly only. Open 1 Apr.–12 Oct. Rod licence incl.).

Drift Reservoir, Penzance.
● T (DT Adv. Driftways, at reservoir, or from South-West Water Authority, Chyandour Estate Office, Penzance. Open 1 Apr.–30 Sept. South-West WA licence).

Dutson Water, Launceston.
C (DT from keeper. South-West WA licence).

Lower Tamar and Upper Tamar lakes, Kilkhampton.
● T in part, C in part (DT Adv. ticket machine. Fly only Upper Tamar; coarse and trout Lower. B available. Open 1 Apr.–12 Oct., all year for rainbows. Rod licence incl.).

Porth Reservoir, Newquay.
● T (DT Adv. ticket machine. Fly only. B available. Rod licence incl.).

Sand Burrow, Bugle.
C (DT Adv. tackle shops at Truro, Newquay, St Austell and Bodmin. South-West WA licence).

Siblyback Reservoir, Liskeard.
● T (DT, WT Adv. Resident Warden, Tregarrick Lodge, Common Moor, St Cleer, Liskeard. B, MB available. Fly only. Open 1 Apr.–12 Oct. South-West WA licence).

Stithians Reservoir, Stithians.
● T (DT Adv. F. Hollis, tackle, Goonlaze, or Golden Lion, Menherion. Fly only. Open 16 Mar.–12 Oct. Rod licence incl.).

Stowford Pond, Launceston.
C (DT Adv. Peter Gardner, South Gate Street, Launceston. Open all year. South-West WA licence).

Tencreek Farm, St Austell.
● T (DT Adv., not in July and Aug., from ticket office. L–10. Fly only. South-West WA licence).

Tin Dene Lakes, Goldsithney.

C (D T Adv. G. J. Laity & Sons, Bostraze, Goldsithney. Has reputation of producing large carp and roach. L–12. B available. South-West W A licence).

Tredidon Barton Lake, Launceston.

C (D T Adv. ticket office or from Peter Gardner, South Gate Street, Launceston. Open all year. South-West W A licence).

Trerice Pool, Indian Queens.

C (D T Adv. Treweek's tackle, 6 Victoria Place, St Austell. South-West W A licence).

Tretheake Lake, Veryan.

C (D T Adv. Tretheake Manor Tourist Site. L–20. Open all year. South-West W A licence).

Wheal Rashleigh, St Blazey.

C (D T Adv. tackle shops, Truro, Newquay, St Austell, Bodmin. South-West W A licence).

Cumbria

See also Lake District under separate heading below.

North-West Water Authority rod licence needed.

Brayton Pond, Aspatria.

C (D T Adv. keeper's cottage, close to water).

Cogra Moss Reservoir, Cockermouth.

● T (D T Adv. tackle shops, Cockermouth. Fly only. Open 1 Apr.– 30 Sept.).

Eel Tarn, Boot.

T (Free fishing).

Ennerdale Lake, Cleator Moor.

T (D T Adv. Post Office, Wath Brow, Cleator Moor, or from Wath Brow and Ennerdale A A. Open 20 Mar.– 31 Oct.).

Inglewood Forest Pool, Armathwaite.

C (D T Adv. Wigan and Dist. A A. L–6).

Killington Reservoir, Kendal.

T, C (D T Adv. Kendal tackle shops or on bank. Open for trout Mar. to Sept., coarse fish June to Mar.).

Meadly Reservoir, Cleator Moor.

T (D T Adv. Post Office, Wath Brow,

Cleator Moor, or from Wath Brow and Ennerdale A A. Open 20 Mar.–31 Oct.).

Oakbank Pit, Longtown.

C (D T Adv. Border Coarse A C).

Ormsgill Lower Reservoir, Barrow-in-Furness.

C (D T Adv. Tally Ho, near Reservoir, or Furness F A. L–10).

Roanhead Ponds, Barrow-in-Furness.

C, T (D T Adv. kiosk at Roanhead summer only, or from Furness F A).

Thurstonfield Lough, Thurstonfield.

● T (D T Adv. from keeper. B available. Fly only).

Derbyshire

Allestree Park Lake, Derby.

C (D T Adv. from keeper or Derby tackle shops. Severn-Trent W A licence).

Bottoms Reservoir, Tintwistle.

T (D T Adv. ticket office or permit point at water. Normally open Good Friday to 30 Sept. North-West W A licence).

Butterley Reservoir, Ripley.

C (D T on bank. B available. Severn-Trent W A licence).

Combs Reservoir, Chapel-en-le-Frith.

C, T (D T on bank. Open all year. North-West W A licence).

Condor Park Reservoir, Condor Park.

C (D T on bank. Severn-Trent W A licence).

Cote Lodge Reservoir, Glossop.

T (D T on bank. Open Good Friday or 31 Mar. (whichever earliest) to 30 Sept. North-West W A licence).

Foremark Reservoir, Milton.

● T (D T Adv. at fishing lodge. Rainbows, browns and brooks, fly only. B available. Severn-Trent W A licence).

Hardwick Hall Lakes, Hardwick.

C (D T on bank. Yorkshire W A licence).

Harlesthorpe Dam, Clowne.

C, T (D T Adv. ticket office at water. Severn-Trent W A licence).

Highham Trout Fishery, Old Higham.

● T (D T Adv. Higham Farm Hotel, Old Higham. Open 1 Apr.–15 Oct. Severn-Trent W A licence. Fly only. L–4).

Ladybower Reservoir, Bamford.
- T (DT Adv. ticket office. Fly only. Severn-Trent WA licence).

Linacre Reservoir, Chesterfield.
- T (DT Adv. Severn-Trent WA, West Street, Chesterfield. Fly only. Open 1 Apr.–30 Sept. Severn-Trent WA licence).

Locko Park Lake, Derby.
- C (DT Adv. ticket office, Park Lodge. Severn-Trent WA licence).

Loscoe Dam, Loscoe.
- C (DT Adv. from keeper. L–25. Severn-Trent WA licence).

Markeaton Park Lake, Derby.
- C (DT Adv. from keeper. Severn-Trent WA licence).

Ogston Reservoir, Clay Cross.
- T (DT Adv. from New Napoleon public house, near reservoir, or from Severn-Trent WA, West Street, Chesterfield. Fly only. Open 1 Apr.–15 Oct. Severn-Trent WA licence).

Ringwood Park Lake, Hollingwood.
- C, T (DT Adv. ticket office. Yorkshire WA licence).

Shipley Country Park lakes, Shipley (incl. Mapperley Reservoir).
- C (DT at lakes from keeper. L–20. Severn-Trent WA licence).

Staunton Harold Reservoir, Melbourne.
- C (DT Adv. ticket office. Opens 16 June and closes 30 Sept. to maintain nature reserve. Good roach, big pike. L–40. Severn-Trent WA licence).

Swarkestone Gravel Pits, Swarkestone.
- C (DT Adv. tackle shops in area or from Crewe and Harpur public house, Swarkestone. Severn-Trent WA licence).

Todd Brook Reservoir, Whaley Bridge.
- C, T (DT on bank. North-West WA licence).

Troway Pond, Troway.
- C, T (DT on bank. Severn-Trent WA licence).

Vale House Reservoir, Tintwistle.
- T (DT Adv. Bottoms Reservoir office, or Vale House permit point. Open Good Friday or 31 Mar. (whichever earliest) to 30 Sept. North-West WA licence).

Devon

Abbrook Pond, Kingsteignton.
- C (WT Adv. tackle shops, Kingsteignton and Exeter. South-West WA licence).

Avon Dam, South Brent.
- (DT Adv. Anchor Inn, South Brent. Fly only. Open 1 Apr.–12 Oct. South-West WA licence).

Besley Lake, Holcombe Rogus.
- T (DT Adv. Lower Besley Farm, Holcombe Rogus. Fly only. South-West WA licence).

Bestridge Pond, Swimbridge.
- C (DT Adv. tackle shops, Barnstaple. South-West WA licence).

Burrator Reservoir, near Yelverton.
- T (DT Adv. ticket machine. Native browns, rainbows. Private water at head of lake. Fly only. Open 16 Mar.–30 Sept. Rod licence incl.).

Darracott Reservoir, Torrington.
- T, C (DT Adv. ticket machine. Brown trout 15 Mar.–12 Oct.; rainbows all year. Rod licence incl.).

East Batsworthy Lakes, Rackenford.
- T (DT Adv. ticket office. Fly only. Open 1 Mar.–30 Sept. L–6. South-West WA licence).

Fernworthy Reservoir, Chagford.
- T (DT Adv. ticket machine. Open 1 Apr.–12 Oct. Fly only. Rod licence incl.).

Gammaton and Jennets Reservoirs, Bideford.
- T (DT Adv. Petherick's tackle, High Street, Bideford. Open 15 Mar.–31 Oct. Fly only. South-West WA licence).

Haldon Ponds, Exeter.
- T (DT, telephone booking essential: Exeter 32967. Fly only. L–4. South-West WA licence).

Harcombe House Fishery, Chudleigh.
- T (DT Adv. Estate Office, Harcombe House. Fly only. Open 1 Apr.–30 Sept. South-West WA licence).

Home Farm Fishery, Kenton.
- T (DT, ½-day Adv. Home Farm. Open all year. Fly only. South-West WA licence).

Lake Pond, Barnstaple.
  C (DT Adv. tackle shop, Barnstaple. South-West WA licence).
Lee Quarry Lake, Lewdown.
  C, T (DT Adv. Blue Lion, Lewdown, or from The Manor, Coryton, Okehampton. South-West WA licence).
Little Dart Fishery, Witheridge.
  ● T (DT Adv. Dart Raafe Farm at water. Fly only. South-West WA licence).
Meldon Reservoir, Okehampton.
  ● T (DT Adv. ticket machine. Open 16 Mar.–30 Sept. Fly only. Rod licence incl.).
Payhembury Trout Ponds, Payhembury.
  ● T (DT Adv. farm at ponds. Fly only. B available. Open 1 May–30 Sept. South-West WA licence).
Preston Ponds, Kingsteignton.
  C (DT on bank, from keeper or local tacklists. South-West WA licence).
Rackerhays Pond, Newton Abbot.
  C (DT on bank, from keeper or tackle shop, Newton Abbot. Ponds complex offering roach, bream and carp. South-West WA licence).
Slade Reservoir, Ilfracombe.
  ● T (DT Adv. ticket machine. Fly only. Open 1 Apr.–12 Oct. Rod licence incl.).
Slapton Ley, Slapton.
  C (DT Adv. fishing from boats only, from Slapton Field Centre. Roach, rudd, perch and pike. Open all year. South-West WA licence).
Squabmoor Reservoir, Budleigh Salterton.
  T, C (DT Adv. Post Office, Knowle. Rod licence incl.).
Stafford Moor Lake, Dolton.
  ● T (DT Adv. ticket office at lake. Excellent fishery, offering some very big trout, regularly stocked. Normally open 1 Apr.–9 Oct. Rod licence incl. Fly only).
Stevenstone Lakes, Torrington.
  C (DT Adv. R. W. Parnell, Deer Park, Stevenstone. Open all year; roach, carp, rudd, perch. South-West WA licence).
Stover Lake, Bovey Tracey.
  C (DT Adv. tackle shop, Bovey Tracey. South-West WA licence).

Tinhay Lake, Lifton.
  ● T (DT Adv. Arundell Arms Hotel, Lifton. Guests have precedence for fishing permits. Fly only. B available. South-West WA licence).
Trenchford, Kennick and Tottiford reservoirs, Bovey Tracey.
  ● T (DT Adv. ticket machine. Fly only. Trenchford also holds brook trout. Rainbow fishing permitted through winter at Kennick. Rod licence incl.).
Venn Quarry, Shebbear.
  C (DT Adv. tackle shop, Barnstaple. South-West WA licence).
Wilminstone Lake, Tavistock.
  ● T (DT Adv. tackle shop, Tavistock, or from The Keep, Tavistock. Fly only. L–6. South-West WA licence).
Wistlandpound Reservoir, N. Devon.
  ● T (DT Adv. ticket machine. Open 1 Apr.–12 Oct. Fly only. Rod licence incl.).

Dorset

Wessex Water Authority rod licence needed.

Askers Farm pool, Askerswell.
  C (DT Adv. keeper, 25 Hutchins Close, Dorchester).
Flowers Farm Lakes, Hillfield, Dorchester.
  ● T (DT Adv. Flowers Farm. Booking essential. Fly only).
Kingsbridge Lakes, Organford, near Poole.
  ● T (DT Adv. 57 Dorchester Road, Lytchett Minster, Poole. Fly only).
Martin's Trout Lake, Wimborne.
  ● T (DT Adv. Martin's Farm, Woodlands, Wimborne. Fly only).
Nallers Farm Fishery, Bridport.
  C (DT Adv. The Tackle Shop, West Bay Road, West Bay, Bridport).
Pallington Lakes, Poole.
  ● T (DT Adv. through Wessex Water Authority, tel. Poole 7114. Fly only. Open 1 Apr.–15 Oct.).
Radipole Lake, Weymouth.
  C, T (DT Adv. tackle shop, 56 Park Street, Weymouth).

Tolpuddle Trout Fishery, Tolpuddle.
● T (DT Adv. Wessex Fly Fishing School, Tolpuddle. Fly only, open 1 May–7 Nov.).
Whitesheet Farm Fishery, Whitesheet.
● T (DT Adv. Whitesheet Farm, Wimborne. Fly only).

Durham

Northumbrian Water Authority rod licence needed.
Balderhead Reservoir, Middleton-in-Teesdale.
T (DT Adv. ticket office).
Blacktor Reservoir, Middleton-in-Teesdale.
T (DT Adv. ticket office).
Cow Green Reservoir, Middleton-in-Teesdale.
T (DT Adv. ticket office).
Derwent Reservoir, Edmundbyers.
● T (DT Adv. ticket office. Fly only. B, M B available. A very popular water offering 7 m of fishing from banks. Competitions to be arranged in advance. Open 1 May–14 Oct.).
Grassholme Reservoir, Middleton-in-Teesdale.
T (DT Adv. ticket office. B available).
Hury Reservoir, Middleton-in-Teesdale.
T (DT Adv. ticket office).
Selset Reservoir, Middleton-in-Teesdale.
T (DT Adv. ticket office).
Smiddy Shaw Reservoir, Consett.
T (DT Adv. ticket office. L–10).
Tunstall Reservoir, Wolsingham.
● T (DT Adv. ticket office. Open 1 May–31 Oct. Fly only).
Waskerley Reservoir, Consett.
T (DT Adv. ticket office. L–10).

Essex

Abberton Reservoir, Layer de la Haye.
C (DT Adv. ticket office. Holds large shoals of very big bream, although difficult to contact. Big pike. Anglian WA licence).
Abbey Trout Fishery, Fisher's Green, Waltham Abbey.
● T (DT Adv. Abbey Trout Fishery, Fisher's Green, Crooked Mile, Hayfields. Fly only. Large trout. Thames WA licence).
Aquatels Lake, Basildon.
C, T (DT Adv. from Site Shop or Aquatels Recreation Centre, Crane Farm Road, Basildon. Big carp, bream, also big trout. Open for trout 1 Apr.–31 Oct.; coarse, normal season. Anglian WA licence).
Ardleigh Reservoir, Colchester.
● T (DT Adv. ticket office, ticket machine, tackle shops in area or Wooden Fender or Fox and Hounds public houses, near reservoir. Fly only. Open last Saturday in March to last Sunday in Oct. Rowing boats. Anglian WA licence).
Central Park Lake, Chelmsford.
C (Free fishing. Anglian WA licence).
The Chase, Dagenham.
C (DT on bank or from keeper. Thames WA licence).
Chesterford Trout Fisheries, Great Chesterford.
● T (DT, ½-day Adv. Boro Farm, Great Chesterford, Saffron Walden. Fly only. Open 1 Apr.–29 Oct. Booking essential).
Corringham Pond, Corringham.
C (DT Adv. C. Wood, Culham House, Church Road, Corringham. Anglian WA licence).
Danbury Park Lake, Danbury.
C (DT on bank or from keeper. Anglian WA licence).
East Hanningfield Hall Lake, Chelmsford.
● T (DT Adv.; please book, tel. Chelmsford 400269. Fly only. B available. Open 19 Mar.–31 Oct. Anglian WA licence).
Epping Forest Ponds, Loughton.
C (DT for 2 ponds, rest free fishing. There are upwards of 100 ponds, some offering excellent coarse fishing, especially for big pike. Thames WA licence).
Gosfield Hall Lake, Gosfield.
C (DT Adv. shop on site. B available. Anglian WA licence).
Great Myles Lake, Ongar.
C (DT on bank. Thames WA licence).

Hatfield Forest Lake, Takeley.
C, T (DT Adv. from keeper or café at lake. B available. Thames WA licence).
Lake Meadows Lake, Billericay.
C (DT on bank or from keeper. B available. Anglian WA licence).
Lake Walk Lake, Clacton.
C (DT Adv. newsagents, 81 Coopers Lane, Clacton. Anglian WA licence).
Layer Pits, Colchester.
C (Season membership Colchester APS only. Big carp, bream. Anglian WA licence).
Little Easton Manor Lake, Dunmow.
C (DT Adv. ticket office, Little Easton Manor. L–20. Anglian WA licence).
Old Hall Lake, Herongate.
C (DT from keeper. Anglian WA licence).
Priory Park, Southend.
C (DT Adv. park keepers. Anglian WA licence).
Shoebury Park Lake, Shoeburyness.
C (DT Adv. from keeper. Anglian WA licence).
South Essex Carp Fisheries, South Ockendon.
C (DT on bank. Good carp fishing; most other still water species present. Anglian WA licence).
South Weald Lake, Brentwood.
C (DT on bank or from keeper. Thames WA licence).
Thorpe Pits, Thorpe-le-Soken.
C (DT from keeper. Anglian WA licence).
Wake Valley Pond, Loughton.
C (Free fishing. Thames WA licence).
The Warren Pits, Stanford-le-Hope.
C (WT at tackle shop named at entrance or from Leisure Sport, RMC House, High Street, Feltham, Middx. Anglian WA licence).

Gloucestershire

Hartpury Lake, Hartpury.
C, T (DT Adv. Watersmeet Hotel, Hartpury. Open all year. Rod licence incl.).
Horseshoe Lake, South Cerney.
● T (DT Adv. from office. Fly only.

Open from 16 Mar.–31 Oct. for browns and 3 Jan. for rainbows. Thames WA licence).
Lechlade Trout Farm Fishery, Lechlade.
● T (DT Adv. at farm. Fly only. Open 4 Apr.–31 Oct. Thames WA licence).
Lower Farm Lake, Somerford Keynes.
C (WT Adv. ticket machine. Thames WA licence).
South Cerney Pits, South Cerney.
C (WT Adv. ticket machine. Good all-round coarse fishing, especially for tench, bream. Thames WA licence).
Spinnaker Lake, *Snipe Lake*, Cerney Wick.
● T (DT Adv. ticket machine. Fly only. Thames WA licence).

Greater London

Alexandra Park Lake, Wood Green.
C (Free fishing. Thames WA licence).
Barn Elms Reservoirs, Barnes.
● T in part, C (DT Adv. from gatekeeper or from Thames Water Authority, Metropolitan Division, New River Head, Rosebery Avenue, London WC1. No. 5 Reservoir fly only, L–25. Rest C. Thames WA licence).
Battersea Park Lake, Battersea.
C (Free fishing. Thames WA licence).
Bedfont Pits, Feltham.
C (WT Adv. tacklist names on notice-board at water or from Leisure Sport, RMC House, High Street, Feltham, Middx. Thames WA licence).
Bedford Park Lake, Romford.
C (DT on bank. Thames WA licence).
Berwick Ponds, Rainham.
C (DT on bank. Thames WA licence).
Boyers Lakes, Enfield.
C (DT on bank or from keeper. Thames WA licence).
Chase Fishery, Romford.
C (DT on bank. Thames WA licence).
Clapham Common Ponds, Clapham.
C (Free fishing. Thames WA licence).
Connaught Water, Chingford.
C (Free fishing. Thames WA licence).
Crystal Palace Park Lake, Penge.
C (DT from keeper. Thames WA licence).

Dagnam Park Ponds, Romford.
C (Free fishing. Thames W A licence).
Eagle Pond, Snaresbrook.
C (Free fishing. Thames W A licence).
Finsbury Park Lake, Harringay.
C (Free fishing. Thames W A licence).
Grovelands Park Lake, Southgate.
C (D T on bank or from keeper. B available. Thames W A licence).
Hainault Forest Lake, Hainault.
C (D T on bank. Thames W A licence).
Hampstead and Highgate Ponds, Hampstead.
C (Free fishing. Thames W A licence).
Hampton Court, Bushey Park pools, Hampton.
C (Application to The Superintendent of Parks, Hampton Court Gardens, East Molesey, Surrey. Thames W A licence).
Hollow Pond, Whipps Cross.
C (Free fishing. Thames W A licence).
King George's Reservoir, Chingford.
C (Fishing through season membership, London A A. Thames W A licence).
Knighton Wood Pond, Woodford.
C (Free fishing. Thames W A licence).
Mayesbrook Park Lane, Barking.
C (Free fishing. Thames W A licence).
Osterley Park Lake, Osterley.
C (Fishing by application to The Superintendent of Parks, Hyde Park, London W2. Thames W A licence).
Parklands Lake, Upminster.
C (D T Adv. from keeper. Thames W A licence).
Raphael Park Lake, Romford.
C (D T on bank. Thames W A licence).
Royal Parks.
Applications, by letter, to superintendent of park concerned.
Serpentine, Hyde Park.
C (Application to the Superintendent of Parks, Hyde Park, London W2).
Tooting Common Lake, Tooting.
C (D T from keeper. Thames W A licence).
Trent Park Lake, Cockfosters.
C (D T Adv. ticket office or from Park Manager, The Rookery, Trent Park. L–20. Thames W A licence).

Victoria Park Lake, Bethnal Green.
C (Free fishing. Thames W A licence).
Walthamstow Reservoirs, Walthamstow.
● T in part, C (D T Adv. from gatekeeper or from Thames Water Authority, Metropolitan Division, New River Head, Rosebery Avenue, London WC1. Fly only for trout No. 1 Reservoir open 1 Apr.–30 Sept. Thames W A licence).
Wandsworth Common pools, Wandsworth.
C (Free fishing. Thames W A licence).
Wantz Boating Lake, Barking.
C (Free fishing. Thames W A licence).
Warren Pond, Chingford.
C (D T from keeper. Thames W A licence).

Greater Manchester

Blackley Lake, Higher Blackley.
C, T (D T Adv. McMahon's newsagents, Riverdale Road, Blackley. North-West W A licence).
Blackwater Flash, Wigan.
C (D T on bank. North-West W A licence).
Boggart Hole, Blackley.
C (D T from keeper. Open 1 Oct.–14 Mar. North-West W A licence).
Broadley Wood Pit, Rochdale.
C (D T Adv. Whitworth Valley A S. North-West W A licence).
Calderbrook Lake, Littleborough.
C, T (D T Adv. Steve's Tackle, Rochdale. North-West W A licence).
Crompton Lodge, Bury.
C (D T Adv. Fisherman's Way tackle, Boundary Street, Bury, or Angling Centre, Rochdale Road, Bury. North-West W A licence).
Debdale Reservoir, Gorton.
C (D T from keeper. Rod licence incl.).
Drinkwater Park Lake, Crumpsall.
C (D T on bank. North-West W A licence).
Elton Reservoir, Bury.
C (D T on bank. Very popular, especially for matches. L–180. North-West W A licence).

Firs Park Lake, Leigh.
C (DT from keeper. L–10. North-West WA licence).

Hindley Deep Pit, Wigan.
C (DT from keeper. North-West WA licence).

Hollingworth Lake, Rochdale.
C, T (DT on bank or from Hollingworth Lake AS. North-West WA licence).

Horseshoe Lodge Pit, Ramsbottom.
C (DT Adv. tackle shops, Bury. North-West WA licence).

King George V Pool, Altrincham.
C (DT Adv. ticket office. North-West WA licence).

Myrtle Road Reservoir, Middleton.
C (DT on bank. Not Sundays if matches booked. North-West WA licence).

Oldham Reservoirs, Oldham.
● T in part, C (DT Adv. Oldham tackle shops. Coarse fishing Ogden Reservoir, with Kitcliffe, Cattleshaw, Strinesdale trout, fly only. North-West WA licence).

Parkers Lodge Lakes, Bury.
C (DT tackle shops, Bury. North-West WA licence).

Pearson's Flash, Wigan.
C (DT on bank. North-West WA licence).

Pennington Flash, Leigh.
C (DT from keeper. L–10. North-West WA licence).

Pilsworthy Reservoir, Bury.
C (DT on bank. Open all year. North-West WA licence).

Platt Fields Park Lake, Rusholme.
C (DT on bank. L–50. Open 1 Oct.– 14 Mar. North-West WA licence).

Rhodes Reservoir, Middleton.
C (DT on bank. North-West WA licence).

Roman Lakes, Marple.
C, T (DT Adv. from keeper or café at water. No season. Rod licence incl.).

Scotsman's Flash, Wigan.
C (DT on bank. North-West WA licence).

Stamford Park Lake, Ashton-under-Lyne.
C (DT on bank. North-West WA licence).

Swineshaw Mill Dam, Stalybridge.
C (DT on bank or from Oldham and Dist. Amalgamated AA. North-West WA licence).

Hampshire

Avington Fishery, Avington.
● T (DT Adv., please book: tel. Itchen Abbas 312. Famed for the introduction of a fast-growing strain of rainbows, with the best fish now topping 20 lb. Open 2 Apr.–30 Sept. Fly only. Rod licence incl.).

Allens Farm Lake, Sandleheath.
● T (DT Adv. ticket office. Browns, rainbows; fly only. Open 26 Mar.– 16 Oct. Rod licence incl.).

Badshot Lea Ponds, Aldershot.
C (DT Adv. from keeper or tackle shop, Aldershot. Thames WA licence).

Bagwell Green Lakes, Winchfield.
● (DT Adv. Greenways Farm, Winchfield. Fly only. Open 1 Apr.–20 Oct. Thames WA licence).

Blashford Pits, Ringwood.
C (DT Adv. D. Swallow, tackle, The Bridges, West Street, Ringwood. Wessex WA licence).

Botleigh Grange Lakes, Botley.
● T (DT Adv. Botleigh Grange Hotel, Hedge End, Southampton. Fly only. Rod licence incl.).

Charlton Pits, Charlton.
C (Free fishing. Southern WA licence).

Damerham Fisheries, Damerham.
● T (DT Adv. from keeper. Fly only. Open 2 Apr.–31 Oct. Fish average 2 lb. Wessex WA licence).

Farnborough Pits, Farnborough.
C (DT Adv. J. Raison, tackle, Park Road, Farnborough. Thames WA licence).

Fishers Pond, Twyford.
C (DT from keeper. Southern WA licence).

Foxcote Lake, Charlton.
C (Fishing through Andover AC. Southern WA licence).

Frimley Lakes, Farnborough.
C (WT Adv. Leisure Sport, RMC

House, High Street, Feltham, Middx, or tacklist on notice-board at water. Thames WA licence).

Hatchet Pond, Beaulieu.
C (DT Adv. information caravan, camp site, Lyndhurst, or tackle shops in area. Forest pool with big bream, plus tench. Rod licence incl.).

Heath Lake, Petersfield.
C (Free fishing to Southern WA licence holders. B available through summer).

Hightown Pit, Ringwood.
C (DT Adv. D. Swallow, tackle, The Bridges, West Street, Ringwood. Wessex WA licence).

Horns Farm Lake, Eversley.
● T (DT Adv. Horns Farm, Lower Common, Eversley, near Basingstoke. Fly only. Open 1 Apr.–30 Sept. Thames WA licence).

John o'Gaunt Lake, King's Somborne.
● T (DT Adv., please book: A. Simms, How Park Farm, King's Somborne. Fly only. Open 2 Apr.–16 Oct. Wessex WA licence).

Kingfisher Lake, Ringwood.
C (DT Adv. Kingfisher House, North Poulner Road, Ringwood. L–8. Rod licence incl.).

Kingham Lakes, Winchester.
C (DT Adv. tackle shop, Upper Brook Street, Winchester, or from Winchester AC. Southern WA licence).

Ladywell Lakes, Alresford.
● T (DT Adv. except Mondays, Arle House, Ladywell Lane, Alresford; tel. Alresford 2317. Fly only. Open 1 Apr.–30 Sept. Southern WA licence).

Leominstead Fisheries, Emery Down.
● T (DT Adv. ticket office. Fly only. Open 1 Apr.–30 Oct. L–12. Southern WA licence).

Middle Lake, Bickton.
● T (DT Adv. bailiff at Bickton Mill. Fly only. Wessex WA licence).

Minstead Mill Lake, Lyndhurst.
C (DT Adv. Leominstead Trout Fishery, Emery Down. Southern WA licence).

Ringwood Fishery, Ringwood.
C (DT Adv. D. Swallow, tackle, The Bridges, West Street, Ringwood. Wessex WA licence).

Two Lakes, Crampmoor.
T (Season fishing only, fly only, by application to the fishery. Mentioned for the reason that it is an excellent still water trout fishery offering big fish, and served as the model for many later fisheries).

Waggoners Wells Lakes, Grayshott.
● T in part, C (DT on bank or Adv. The Warden, National Trust, Waggoners Wells, Grayshott, Hindhead, Surrey. One lake trout, fly only, and two lakes offering good coarse fishing. Rod licence incl.).

Hereford and Worcestershire

Castlemorton Lake, Ledbury.
C (Free fishing to Severn-Trent WA licence holders).

Kyre Pool, Tenbury.
C (DT Adv. Geltrend, Severnside South, Bewdley. Severn-Trent WA licence).

Trimpley Reservoir, Kidderminster.
T (Fishing managed by Trimpley AA, c/o Mr R. F. Pratt, 24 Lea Wood Grove, Kidderminster. Season membership, guests day tickets. Fly only. Severn-Trent WA licence).

Hertfordshire

Aldenham Reservoir, Elstree.
C (DT on bank or from Fisheries Inn. Thames WA licence).

Broxbourne Pits, Broxbourne.
C (WT Adv. from Leisure Sport, RMC House, High Street, Feltham, Middx, or tacklist named on notice-board at water. Most coarse species, tench, pike, roach and carp particularly big. Thames WA licence).

Cheshunt North Reservoir, Cheshunt.
C (DT Adv. from King's Arms, Cheshunt, or Cheshunt AS. L–12. Thames WA licence).

Crown Netherall Fishery, Hoddesdon.
T (DT Adv. ticket office. Stocked rainbows. Open 1 Mar.–30 Sept. Thames WA licence).

Croxley Hall Waters, Rickmansworth.
● T (DT Adv. Croxley Hall Farm, Rickmansworth. Fly only. Open 1 Apr.–30 Oct. Thames WA licence).
Fairlands Valley Lake, Stevenage.
C (DT on bank. Thames WA licence).
Hatfield Forest Lake, Bishops Stortford.
C (DT Adv. Shell House Café, Bishops Stortford. Thames WA licence).
Oughton Fisheries, Hitchin.
● T (DT Adv. ticket office. Fly only. L–8. Anglian WA licence).
Rickmansworth Aquadrome, Rickmansworth.
C (DT on banks or from keeper. Two lakes, Bury and Batchworth, holding bream, pike, carp and tench. Rod licence incl.).
Rickmansworth Fishery, Rickmansworth.
C (WT Adv. from Leisure Sport, RMC House, High Street, Feltham, Middx, or from tacklist named on notice-board at water. Thames WA licence).
Stanborough Lake, Welwyn Garden City.
C (DT on bank. Thames WA licence).
Stanstead Abbotts Pits, Stanstead Abbotts.
C (WT Adv. Leisure Sport, RMC House, High Street, Feltham, Middx, or from tackle dealer named on notice-board at water. Thames WA licence).
Tring Reservoirs (*Marsworth, Startops, Wilstone*), Tring.
C (DT from keepers. B available at Wilstone. Bream in quantity and of specimen size, also big pike and cat-fish. The British record catfish, 43 lb 8 oz, was taken in Wilstone in 1970. Thames WA licence).

Humberside

Barton Broads, Barton-on-Humber.
C (DT Adv. tackle shops or at site. Open all year. Anglian WA licence).
Brandesburton Ponds, Brandesburton.
C (Through season membership, Hull and Dist. AA. Some of the pools hold trout. Specimen tench have been

taken of late; also very big eels. Anglian WA licence).
Chapman's Pond, Cleethorpes.
C (DT Adv. Pet's Pantry, tackle, Cleethorpes. Anglian WA licence).
Hornsea Mere, Hornsea.
C (DT Adv. ticket office. B available. L–45. Has a reputation for big roach and pike, but has declined in recent years. Yorkshire WA licence).
Southfield Reservoirs, Cowick.
C (DT on bank. Yorkshire WA licence).

Kent

Bayham Lake, Lamberhurst.
● T (DT Adv. tel. 0892 890276. Stocked weekly. Fly only. B available. Open 3 Apr.–31 Oct. Southern WA).
Brooklands Lake, Dartford.
C (DT on bank. Big carp, tench. Thames WA licence).
Chiddingstone Castle Lake, Chiddingstone.
C (DT on bank. Noted for big bream. Southern WA licence).
Darenth Pits, Darenth.
C (Season only. Leisure Sport, RMC House, High Street, Feltham, Middx, or tacklist named on notice-board at water. Big carp, also roach, bream, tench and pike).
Hayes Farm Fishery, Bromley.
● T (DT Adv. Fishery, Hayes Lane, Bromley. Open 27 Feb. to end of Dec. Fly only. Thames WA licence).
Horton Kirby Lakes, Horton Kirby.
C (DT on bank. Big carp and roach. Southern WA licence).
Johnson's Lake, Larkfield.
C (DT on bank. Big tench and pike, also specimen crucians. Southern WA licence).
Keston Ponds, Keston.
C (DT on bank. Southern WA licence).
Mote Park Lake, Maidstone.
C (DT Adv. tackle shop, Maidstone, or Borough Engineer's Office, King Street, Maidstone. Southern WA licence).

Oare Pits, Faversham.
C (D T on bank. Noted for specimen carp. Southern W A licence).

Pett Pools, Maidstone.
C (D T Adv. Windmill Stores, Sea Road, Winchelsea, or from Southern W A. Southern W A licence).

Pooh Corner Pool, Rolvenden.
● T (D T Adv. booking essential; tel. Rolvenden 219. Fly only. Open 2 Apr.–31 Oct. Rod licence incl.).

Ruxley Pits, St Paul's Cray.
C (D T Adv. tackle shop, Orpington, or from Orpington and Dist. A A. Southern W A licence).

Tenterden Trout Waters, Tenterden.
● T (D T Adv. booking essential; tel. Tenterden 3201. Open 1 Apr.–31 Oct. Fly only. Southern W A licence).

Lake District

See also above, English Rivers, North-West Water Authority: Aira Beck, Brathay, Calder, Cocker, Crake, Derwent, Ehen, Esk, Gilpin, Goldrill, Greta, Grizedale Beck, Irt, Kent, Leven, Mint, Rothay, Sprint, Trout Beck, Ulverston Canal.

North-West Water Authority rod licence needed.

Angle Tarn, Beda Fell, Hartsop.
Private fishing.

Bassenthwaite, under Skiddaw.
T, C, some S (D T Adv. Post Office, Bassenthwaite. B available. Open all year).

Blea Tarn, Penrith.
T, C (D T Adv. Blea Tarn Farm).

Brotherswater, Hartsop.
T, C (Free fishing parts of bank; permission must be asked for private land).

Burnmoor Tarn, Boot.
T, C (Free fishing).

Buttermere, Buttermere Fell.
T, C and char (D T Adv. The Gun Shop, Cockermouth; Kirkstile Inn, Loleswater; Croft House Farm, Buttermere).

Codale Tarn, near Grasmere.
T, C (Free fishing).

Coniston Water, Coniston.
T, C and char (Free fishing. B available in area).

Crummock Water, Brackenthwaite Fell.
T, ST, S, C and char (D T Adv. The Gun Shop, Cockermouth, or Kirkstile Inn, Loleswater. B available. Trout best May–June, salmon and sea-trout from July. Char best late summer. Deep trolling usual method).

Derwentwater, Borrowdale.
T, C, some S (D T Adv. Temples tackle, Station Street, Keswick. M B available. Salmon from May on).

Drunken Duck Tarn, Ambleside.
● T (D T Drunken Duck Hotel, Ambleside. Fly only. Season varies).

Easdale Tarn, Grasmere.
Private fishing.

Elterwater, Chapel Stile.
T, C and char (Free fishing).

Ennerdale Water, Ennerdale Bridge.
T, S, ST and char (Fishing through local hotels).

Esthwaite Water, Windermere.
T, C (D T Adv. keeper, Hazel Seat Lodge, Graythwaite, near Newby Bridge. B available. Trout fishing 15 Mar.–30 Sept.; coarse, 16 June–14 Mar.).

Fisher Tarn, Kendal.
Private fishing.

Goats Water, Dow Crag.
T and char (Free fishing).

Grasmere, Grasmere.
T, C and char (Free fishing).

Grisedale Tarn, Patterdale Pass.
T (Free fishing).

Haweswater, Shap.
T, C, char, gwyniad (Fishing through local hotels).

High Arnside Tarn, Ambleside.
● T (D T Adv. tackle shops, Ambleside, Bowness and Windermere. Fly only).

Killington Reservoir, Killington.
T, C (D T Adv. at water).

Knotallow Tarn, near Ulverston.
Private fishing.

Little Langdale Tarn, Little Langdale.
Private fishing.

Loughrigg Tarn, near Windermere.
C (D T Adv. Tarn Foot Farm. Pike, perch).

Loweswater, Loweswater.
T, C (D T Adv. The Gun Shop, Cockermouth, or Kirkstile Inn, Loweswater. B available).

Marton Openworks Pool, near Marton.
T (D T Adv. Furness F A. Fly and worm only. Open 1 April. L–10).

Mockerin Lake, Mockerin.
C (Private, but permission sometimes granted by owner).

Rydal Water, Rydal.
T, C (D T Adv. tackle shops, Ambleside, Bowness and Windermere).

School Knot Tarn, Windermere.
● T (D T Adv. tackle shops Ambleside, Bowness and Windermere. Fly only).

Skelsmergh, near Kendal.
C (Free fishing. Also holds roach and rudd, rare in district).

Smallwater Tarn, Brampton.
T (Free fishing).

Talkin Tarn, Brampton.
C (Free fishing. B available. No Sunday fishing).

Tarn Hows, near Hawkshead.
Private fishing.

Thirlmere.
Preserved for North-West W A employees.

Ullswater, Glenridding.
T, ST, S, char, gwyniad and schelly (Free fishing, but permission must be sought for private land. Trout fishing 10 Mar.–15 Sept.; salmon, 15 Jan.–16 Oct.; sea-trout, 1 May–15 Oct.).

Wastwater, Copeland Forest.
T, ST, S, char (D T Adv. Estate Office, Cockermouth Castle, Cockermouth. Salmon fishing 1 Apr.–31 Oct.; sea-trout, 1 May–31 Oct.; trout, 20 Mar.–14 Sept. Salmon and sea-trout from late summer).

Watendlath Tarn, near Keswick.
T, C (Free fishing).

Whinfell Tarn, near Kendal.
C (D T Adv. farm at lakeside).

Windermere, Windermere.
T, C, char (Free fishing. B, M B available at Bowness. Trout can be big. Windermere and Ambleside best bets).

Yewtree Tarn, near Coniston.
T (D T Adv. tackle shop, Coniston).

Lancashire

North-West Water Authority rod licence needed.

Bank House Fly Fishery, Caton.
● T (D T Adv. please book; tel. Caton 770412. Big fish. Fly only, no lures. Open 1 Mar.–31 Oct.).

Barnsfold Waters, Longridge.
● T (D T Adv. 34 Blackburn Road, Ribchester, or tel. Chipping 583. Fly only. Open 1 Apr.–30 Sept. Must be booked).

Brenda Lodges, Tottington.
C (D T Adv. tackle shops, Bury).

Carr Mill Dam, St Helens.
C (Season membership only, St Helen's A A).

Deane Reservoir (*Earnsdale Reservoir*), Darwen.
T (D T Adv. County Sports, Duckworth Street, Darwen. L–2. Advance booking advised for weekends. Any method).

Fishmoor Reservoir, Blackburn.
T (D T Adv. tackle shop, 51 Whalley New Road, Blackburn. Open 1 Apr.–30 Oct.).

Foulridge Lower (*Burwains Reservoir*), Colne.
C, T (D T on bank or from keeper).

Grizedale Lea Reservoir, Garstang.
● T (D T Adv. Boulton's Tackle, 8 Preston Street, Kirkham. Fly only. L–4. B available).

Heapey Lodges, Chorley.
C, T (D T keeper at gate. Open all year).

Kirklees Lodges, Tottington.
C (D T Adv. tackle shops, Bury).

Parsonage Reservoir, Blackburn.
● T (D T Adv. J. Hoyle, tackle, 51 Whalley New Road, Blackburn. Fly only. Open 1 Apr.–30 Oct.).

Pennine Trout Fishery, Littleborough.
● T (D T Adv. Calderbrook Lakes, Calderbrook Road, Littleborough, or tel. 0706 78325. Fly only).

Rake Brook Reservoir, Brinscall.
C, T (D T Adv. A. Leach, tackle, Lee Lane, Horwich, or Salmons Café, Rivington Hall).

Rivington Reservoirs, Rivington.
● T in part, C, T in part (D T Adv. A.

Leach, tackle, Lee Lane, Horwich; R. P. Barton, tackle, Wigan Road, Hindley; or from North-West WA, Merton House, Stanley Road, Bootle. Four reservoirs, Anglezarke, Lower Rivington, Upper Rivington and Yarrow. Upper Rivington trout, fly only, and tickets additionally available from Resident Engineer).

Roddlesworth Reservoirs, Darwen.

● T in part, C, T in part (DT Adv. as Rivington Reservoirs above. Two reservoirs, Upper and Lower. Upper is trout, fly only).

Spring Lodge, Sabden.

C, T (DT Adv. from keeper, 2 Pendle Street West, Sabden, after 8 a.m. or T. Littler, tackle, Sabden, or from Accrington and Dist. FC. Open 1 Apr.–30 Sept. Roach, carp reputed to be good, also trout).

Stanley Park Lake, Blackpool.

C (DT Adv. ticket office. L–60).

Sunnyhurst Hey Reservoir, Darwen.

T (DT Adv. County Sports, Duckworth Street, Darwen. L–2. Booking advised for weekends).

Swantley Lake, Nether Kellet.

C (DT Adv. tackle shop, Lancaster, or from Lonsdale AC).

Urswick Tarn, Great Urswick.

C (DT on bank).

Leicestershire

Beedles Lake, Rearsby.

C (DT on bank at weekends, ticket office weekdays. Severn-Trent WA licence).

Belvoir Castle Lakes, Belvoir Castle.

C (DT from keeper or Estate Office, Belvoir Castle. No Sunday fishing. Severn-Trent WA licence).

Brooms Lane Pit, East Goscote.

C (DT on bank. Severn-Trent WA licence).

Eyebrook Reservoir, Uppingham.

● T (DT Adv. ticket machine or ticket office. Fly only. Open 1 Apr.–30 Sept. B available on advance booking from Corby District Water Co., Geddington Road, Corby. Anglian WA licence).

Frisby Gravel Pits, Asfordby.

C (Day block bookings for parties only through Asfordby Society of Anglers. Severn-Trent WA licence).

Kirby Bellars Lake, Kirby Bellars.

● T (DT Adv. ticket office weekdays and Saturday morning, on bank Saturday afternoon and Sunday. Fly only. Open 1 Apr.–30 Sept. Severn-Trent WA licence).

Knipton Reservoir, Knipton.

C (DT Adv. from keeper or Estate Office, Belvoir Castle. The water where in 1967 Clive Loveland caught a 39 lb pike. I was lucky enough to interview him just after the capture, and he said divers had seen even bigger fish. Bream, tench fishing also good. No Sunday fishing. Severn-Trent WA licence).

Mallory Park Lakes, Earl Shilton.

C (DT Adv. at racecourse ticket office. Big lake open all year; has produced big perch. Severn-Trent WA licence).

Mill Farm Fishery, Gilmorton.

● T (DT Adv. Mill Farm, Gilmorton, Lutterworth, or tel. Lutterworth 2392. Fly only. Severn-Trent WA licence).

Old Manor Pond, Long Clawson.

C (DT on bank. Severn-Trent WA licence).

Proctor's Park Lake, Barrow-on-Soar.

C (DT on bank or from ticket machine. Severn-Trent WA licence).

Rutland Water, Empingham.

● T (DT Adv. ticket machine, ticket office Whitwell. Fly only. This huge water, opened in 1977, covers over 3000 acres and has 24 m of bank space. Vast stocks of browns and rainbows have been introduced, and to date many big fish have been taken. The water is so big that the uninformed visitor should ask locally of the best prospects. Boats and motor boats are available and the rod licence is included in the permit price).

Saddington Reservoir, Wigston.

C (DT on bank. Severn-Trent WA licence).

Thornton Reservoir, Thornton.

● T (DT Adv. Bull's Head, Main Street,

128 · **English Still Waters**

Thornton. Fly only. B available.
Severn-Trent WA licence).

Willesley Lake, Ashby de la Zouch.
C (DT Adv. keeper's cottage, at lake,
or tackle shop, Measham. Severn-
Trent WA licence).

Lincolnshire

Anglian Water Authority rod licence
needed.

Boultham Park Lake, Lincoln.
C (DT on bank).

Brookside Fisheries, North Scarle.
C (DT Adv. booked through C. Booth,
tel. Spalford 234).

Buckminster Park Lake, Buckminster.
● T (Through Buckminster Trust Estate
Office, tel. Grantham 860472. Single
fly only).

Cartwright's Pond, South Somercotes.
C (DT on bank).

Chapel St Leonards Lakes, Chapel St
Leonards.
C, T (DT Adv. boating lake office.
Trout in one of three lakes, the other
two coarse fish).

Denton Reservoir, Denton.
C (DT Adv. tackle shop, Grantham, or
Watson's tackle, Nottingham).

Gouldsbra's Pit, Authorpe.
C (DT on bank).

Hartsholme Lake, Lincoln.
C (DT on bank).

Hill View Lakes, Hogsthorpe.
● T (DT Adv. from keeper or 19 St
Leonard's Drive, Chapel St Leonards,
near Skegness. Fly only. Open 2 Apr.–
31 Oct. Also coarse fishing one lake).

Lakeside Lido, North Somercotes.
C (DT Adv. caravan park office).

North Scarle Ponds, North Scarle.
C (DT on bank).

Revesby Reservoir, Revesby.
C (DT Adv. Revesby Estate Office,
Revesby).

Susworth Ponds, Susworth.
C (DT Adv. Harrison's newsagents,
Keadby Bridge; Bennet's tackle,
Scunthorpe, or White Swan, Slotter).

Swanholme Lakes, Lincoln.

● T in part, C in part (DT Adv. from
keeper, or tel. Lincoln 63175. Trout fly
only one water, open 1 Mar.–30 Sept.
Coarse fishing all year).

Toft Newton Reservoir, Market Rasen.
● T (DT Adv. ticket machine or ticket
office. Open 9 Apr.–30 Sept. Fly only.
L–40. Good fishing, although the
water is none too attractive).

Vicker's Pond, Saltfleetby.
C (DT Adv. Vicker's Shop by water.
Not open Sunday).

Merseyside

North-West Water Authority rod licence
needed.

Calderstones Lake, Liverpool.
C (DT on bank, from Liverpool tacklists or Liverpool and Dist. AA).

Greenbank Lake, Liverpool.
C (DT on bank, from Liverpool tacklists or Liverpool and Dist. AA).

Newsham Lake, Liverpool.
C (DT on bank, from Liverpool tacklists or Liverpool and Dist. AA).

Orrell Reservoir, Orrell.
C (DT on bank).

Sefton Park Lake, Liverpool.
C (DT on bank, from Liverpool tacklists or Liverpool and Dist. AA).

Stanley Lake, Liverpool.
C (DT on bank, from Liverpool tacklists or Liverpool and Dist. AA).

Walton Hall Lake, Liverpool.
C (DT on bank, from Liverpool tacklists or Liverpool and Dist. AA).

Norfolk

See also Broads (Norfolk) above.

Billingford Pit, Billingford.
C, T (DT on bank or from Fanthorpe's
tackle, Dereham. Anglian WA
licence).

Blickling Hall Lake, Aylsham.
C (DT Adv. C. Clarke, ironmonger,
Aylsham, or Anglian WA Fisheries
Department, Norwich. Anglian WA
licence).

Booton Claypits, Cawston.
C (D T on bank or from Clarke's tackle, Aylsham, or Fairfields Stores, Cawston. Anglian WA licence).
Bridge Lakes, Lenwade.
C (D T on bank. Anglian WA licence).
Burebank Trout Fishery, Itteringham.
● T (DT Adv. tel. Mr A. Green, Saxthorpe 666. Fly only. At time of going to press, this water was expected to be reopened shortly, after extensive work. Anglian WA licence).
Diss Mere, Diss.
C (DT Adv. tackle shop, Diss. A good carp water. Anglian WA licence).
Edgefield Hall Farm Lake, Edgefield.
● T (DT Adv. from farm or tel. Holt 2437. Fly only. Open 1 Apr.–29 Oct. Also evening and beginners' tickets. Anglian WA licence).
Elham Lake, Elham.
C (D T Adv. at gatehouse. Anglian WA licence).
Gunton Park Lake, Gunton.
C (D T on bank. Anglian WA licence).
Hardley Marshes (*Loddon Floods*), Loddon.
C (D T Adv. tackle shop, Market Place, Loddon. Anglian WA licence).
Haveringland Lake, Haveringland.
C (D T Adv. warden's caravan. Anglian WA licence).
Hevingham Lake, Hevingham.
C (DT at entrance. Big crucians and rudd. Anglian WA licence).
Holkham Lake, Wells-next-Sea.
C (DT Adv. Holkham Estate Office. Open 16 June–1 Sept.). No Sunday fishing. Anglian WA licence).
Letheringsett Lake, Letheringsett.
C (Free fishing. Anglian WA licence).
Norton Water, Hevingham.
C (DT at entrance. Anglian WA licence).
Poringland Pits, Poringland.
C (Free fishing. Anglian WA licence).
Reepham Trout Fishery, Reepham.
● T (D T Adv. at fishery or tel. Reepham 8178. Fly only. Open 1 Apr. 30–Oct. Anglian WA licence).
Ringland Lakes, Taverham.
C (DT Adv. from keeper or Wensum

Motors, West End, Old Costessey, Norwich. Big bream and tench. Anglian WA licence).
Station Lakes, Lenwade.
C (D T on bank. Anglian WA licence).
Swanton Morley Fishery, East Dereham.
C (DT Adv. tackle shop, Norwich Street, Fakenham, or the keeper, 12 North Park, Fakenham. Anglian WA licence. Permit covers stretch of Wensum).
Taverham Pits (*Costessey Pits*), Taverham.
C (Free fishing to Anglian WA licence holders. Big bream and carp).
Warren Lake, Lenwade.
C (DT Adv. postal application only to The Secretary, Warren Estates, Great Witchingham, Norfolk. B available. Good coarse fishing; many small pike. Anglian WA licence).
Waveney Valley Lakes, Wortwell.
C (D T Adv. caravan site shop. Big carp. Anglian WA licence).
Weybread Pits, Harleston.
C (D T Adv. tackle shop, Market Place, Harleston. Sizeable coarse fish. Anglian WA licence).
Wolterton Park Lake, Aylsham.
C (D T Adv. head gardener, Wolterton Hall. L–4. Good tench fishing. Anglian WA licence).
Womack Water, Ludham.
C (Free fishing from shore or boats. Anglian WA licence).

Northamptonshire

Abington Park Lake, Northampton.
C (Free fishing. Anglian WA licence).
Billing Aquadrome, Little Billing.
C (DT Adv. at gate. Big carp are a feature of the water. The fishery is open 16 June–9 Oct. only. Anglian WA licence).
Castle Ashby Lakes, Northampton.
C (D T on bank. Anglian WA licence).
Cosgrove Gravel Pits, Stony Stratford.
C (D T on bank. Anglian WA licence).
Cransley Reservoir, Kettering.
C (DT from keeper or Anglian WA,

Cliftonville, Northampton. Good tench fishing. Anglian W A licence).

Elinor Trout Fishery, Aldwincle.
● T (D T Adv. 40 North Street, Oundle, or tel. Oundle 3701. Fly only. Open 2 Apr.–23 Oct. Anglian W A licence).

Fawsley Park Lakes, Daventry.
C (D T on bank or from Northampton Nene A C. Anglian W A licence).

Ferrasands Pits, Rushden.
C (D T Adv. ticket office. L–20. Anglian W A licence).

Hollowell Reservoir, Hollowell.
C (D T from keeper. B available. Anglian W A licence).

Overstone Solarium Lakes, Northampton.
C (D T on bank. Anglian W A licence).

Pitsford Reservoir, Brixworth.
● T (D T Adv. ticket office, or from Anglian W A, Cliftonville, Northampton. Fly only. Open 1 Apr.–30 Sept. B, M B available. Anglian W A licence).

Ransome Road Gravel Pit, Northampton.
C (D T on bank or from Northampton Nene A C. Anglian W A licence).

Ravensthorpe Reservoir, Ravensthorpe.
● T (D T Adv. from keeper or from Anglian W A, Cliftonville, Northampton. Good fishing; surroundings quite lovely. Fly only. B available. Anglian W A licence).

Ringstead Grange Trout Fishery, Ringstead.
● T (D T Adv. at fishery or tel. Wellingborough 622960. Browns, rainbows and brook trout, fly only. Open 5 Apr.–29 Oct. Anglian W A licence).

Sulby Reservoir, Welford.
C (D T Adv. farm by water. Severn-Trent W A licence).

Thrapston Pits, Thrapston.
C (D T Adv. from keeper or on bank. 100 at weekends. Good coarse fishing, especially for bream. Anglian W A licence).

Northumberland

Bakethin Water, Kielder.
● T (D T Adv. from keeper. Fly only, stocked browns. B available. Open 1 May–30 Sept.).

Bolam Lake, Belsay.
C (Free fishing. Northumberland W A licence).

Fontburn Reservoir, off Scots Gap Road.
T (D T Adv. from keeper or Northumberland W A. Fly, worm or spinning. Northumberland W A licence).

Kielder Water, Kielder.
T (D T Adv. ticket office or from Northumberland W A. Fly, worm, spinning. B, M B available. Northumberland W A licence).

Sweethope Loughs, Kirkwhelpington.
● T in part, C (D T Adv. keeper at Lake House or Percy Arms Hotel, Otterburn. Fly only one lake, with B available and ghillie by prior arrangement. Northumberland W A licence).

Whittle Dean Reservoirs, Corbridge.
● T in part, rest T fly or spinning (D T Adv. keeper at reservoirs or tel. Wylam 3210. Fly only in one water; spinning allowed in others at certain parts of season. Open 1 Apr.–30 Sept. Northumberland W A licence).

Nottinghamshire

Severn-Trent Water Authority licence needed.

Attenborough Pits, Beeston.
C (D T Adv. from keeper or tackle shops, Derby. Has yielded big fish including a 3 lb roach).

Besthorpe Fleet, Besthorpe.
C (Free fishing).

Bulwell Hall Pond, Nottingham.
C (D T on bank).

Clumber Park Lake, Clumber Park.
C (D T on bank or from National Trust area office, Clumber Park, near Worksop. Good roach and pike water).

Colwick Fishery, Colwick.
● T in part, C in part (D T Adv. tacklists

in Carlton Road and Netherfield, Nottingham. Trout fly only in two pits; coarse fishing in three. One pit, now trout water, is thought to have produced a record roach of 4 lb 1 oz).

Colwick Ponds, Colwick.
C (D T on bank).

Coneygre Lake, Hoveringham.
C (D T Adv. Coneygre Farm).

Cromwell Lake, Cromwell.
● T (D T Adv. F. G. Gale, tackle, 26 Copley Road, Doncaster, or Carlton Service Station, Cromwell. Fly only. Open 18 Mar.–15 Nov.).

Dunham Lakes, Dunham Bridge.
C (D T Adv. Bridge Garage, Dunham).

Farndon Ponds, Farndon.
C (D T on bank).

King's Mill Reservoir, Sutton-in-Ashfield.
C (D T on bank).

Langold Lake, Langold.
C (D T on bank).

Lawn Dam, Sutton-in-Ashfield.
C (D T on bank).

Mapperley Reservoir, Mapperley.
C (D T on bank).

Martin's Pond, Nottingham.
C (D T on bank).

National Watersports Centre, Holme Pierrepont.
C (D T Adv. ticket office or Ranger's Post, Country Park, Holme Pierrepont. Fishing in two waters, the Winfield Lagoon and the Rowing Course, the latter producing numerous pike).

Sandhills Lake, Worksop.
C (D T on bank).

Spion Kop, Warsop.
C (D T on bank).

Vicar's Pond, Clipstone.
C (D T on bank).

Welbeck Abbey Lakes, Worksop.
C (D T only on special open days advertised in national angling press. Three lakes are fished regularly by local clubs on a rota, and no other anglers should attempt to fish outside the open days. Good fishing, when available, for roach, tench and pike).

Wollaton Park Lake, Nottingham.
C (D T on bank. Has produced big tench).

Oxfordshire

Thames Water Authority rod licence needed.

Blenheim Palace Lake, Woodstock.
C (D T Adv. fishing from punts only, no bank fishing, Estate Office, Blenheim Palace. Tench fishing especially good).

Buscot Lakes, Buscot.
C (D T on bank).

Bushyleaze Fishery, Lechlade.
● T (D T Adv. Rainbow's End, Lynch Hill Fishery, Stanton Harcourt, or tel. Standlake 774. Fly only. Open 15 Apr.–15 Oct.).

Clattercote Reservoir, Banbury.
C (D T Adv. tackle shop, Banbury, or from Banbury and Dist. A A).

Farmoor No. 2 Reservoir, Eynsham.
● T (D T Adv. at reservoir. No fishing No. 1 reservoir. Fly only; stocked browns and rainbows. Open 1 Apr.–30 Nov.).

Lynch Hill Fishery, Stanton Harcourt.
● T (D T Adv. as Bushyleaze Fishery above).

Shropshire

Blakemere, Ellesmere.
C (D T Adv. tackle shop, Ellesmere, or Red Lion public house, Ellesmere. Rod licence incl.).

Brown Moss Pools, Whitchurch.
C (D T Adv. from site warden. Severn-Trent W A licence).

Ellesmere, Ellesmere.
C (D T Adv. boat fishing only, Warden's bungalow, Cremorn Gardens. With Blakemere and Whitemere, the meres have produced big bream in quantity. Roach, tench, perch and pike are also caught. Rod licence incl.).

Hawkstone Park Lake, Hodnet.
C (D T on bank. Excellent catches of tench and carp on this National Trust water, also big pike. Severn-Trent W A licence).

Lake Vyrnwy, near Oswestry.
● T (D T Adv. Lake Vyrnwy Hotel, tel. 069 173 244. Fly only. Fishing free for hotel guests).

Marton Pool, Chirbury.
 C (DT Adv. public house at water. Severn-Trent WA licence).
Sunderton Lake (*Dell Lake*), Uffington.
 C (DT Adv. Ebrall Bros, tackle, Smithfield Road, Shrewsbury. Severn-Trent WA licence).
Trench Pool Reservoir, Trench.
 C (DT Adv. on bank or from Shropshire Arms, Trench. Not Sundays if water booked for match. Severn-Trent WA licence).
Walcot Lakes, Lydbury North.
 C (Fishing through membership of Birmingham AA. Severn-Trent WA licence).
Whitemere, Ellesmere.
 C (DT keeper's cottage near water or Red Lion, Ellesmere. Rod licence incl.).

Somerset

Ashford Reservoir, Bridgwater.
 C (DT Adv. tackle shops, Bridgwater, Langport and Highbridge. Wessex WA licence).
Chargot Water, Luxborough.
 ● T (WT Adv. keeper, Ponds Cottage, Chargot. Fly only. No Sunday fishing. Open 1 Apr.–30 Sept. Rod licence incl.).
Cheddar Reservoir, Axbridge.
 C (DT Adv. ticket machine, or tackle shop, Axbridge. Water is now administered by Cheddar anglers. Has reputation for big pike but also holds good roach and trout. Rod licence incl.).
Clatworthy Reservoir, Clatworthy.
 ● T (DT Adv. ticket office. Fly only. B available. Rod licence incl.).
Combwitch Ponds, Bridgwater.
 C (DT Adv. tackle shops, Bridgwater, Langport and Highbridge. Wessex WA licence).
Dunwear Ponds, Bridgwater.
 C (DT Adv. tackle shops in area. Wessex WA licence).
Durleigh Reservoir, Bridgwater.
 ● T (DT Adv. ticket office. Fly only. B available. Stocked browns and rainbows, some good fish. Rod licence incl.).

Exe Valley Fisheries, Dulverton.
 ● T (DT Adv. Exe Valley Fisheries, Exebridge, Dulverton; tel. Dulverton 23328. Open 4 Apr.–30 Sept. Fly only. South-West WA licence).
Hawkridge Reservoir, Spaxton.
 ● T (DT Adv. ticket machine. Fly only. Browns, rainbows. A 7 lb brown was taken in 1981. Rod licence incl.)
Newtown Pond, Highbridge.
 C (DT Adv. tackle shop, Church Street, Highbridge. Wessex WA licence).
Otterhead Lakes, Churchingford.
 ● T (DT Adv. ticket office. Fly only; browns and rainbows. Rod licence incl.).
Perry Street Pool, Chard.
 C (DT Adv. tackle shop, Chard. Wessex WA licence).
Screech Owl Pools, Bridgwater.
 C (DT Adv. local tackle shops. Wessex WA licence).
Sutton Bingham Reservoir, near Yeovil.
 ● T (DT Adv. ticket office at lodge. Fly only. B available. Good fishing for browns, rainbows, regularly stocked. Rod licence incl.).
Wimbleball Lake, Dulverton.
 ● T (DT Adv. ticket office or tel. Brompton Regis 372. Fly only; browns, rainbows and tigers. Open 1 May–31 Oct. B available to 12 Oct. only. Rod licence incl.).

Staffordshire

Severn-Trent Water Authority rod licence needed.
Bretby Pools, Burton-on-Trent.
 T, C (Fishery open to members of Birmingham AA. Trout pools fly only, rest general coarse species).
Hamps Valley Fishery, Winkhill.
 ● T (DT Adv. postal or telephone application, Hamps Valley Fishery, Winkhill, near Leek, Staffs; tel. Waterhouses 255. Fly only. Open 1 Apr.–31 Oct.).
Norton Pools, Brownhills.
 C (DT Adv. Whitmore Reans CAA).
Patshull Park Fishery, Pattingham.

● T (DT Adv. Patshull Fishery, Temple Hotel, Burnhill Green, Wolverhampton; tel. Pattingham 700100. Fly only. Open all year. Some big fish).

Rudyard Lake, Rudyard.

C (DT Adv. ticket office or Lake House, Rudyard. Matches to be booked through Warden, Lake House. B, MB available. Well stocked with coarse fish).

Shelmore Trout Fishery, near Gnosall.

● T (DT Adv. Brook Cottage, Norbury Junction; tel. Woodseaves 205. Fly only, barbless hooks. Open mid-Mar. to Christmas).

Swynnerton Lagoons, Millmeece.

C (DT Adv. Whitmore Reans CAA. Water shut during military training).

Tittesworth Reservoir, Leek.

● T (DT Adv. ticket office, lodge. Fly only. Open 10 Apr.–15 Oct. B available, also instructor. Well stocked).

Trentham Gardens Lake, Trentham.

C (DT Adv. ticket office. B available).

Weston Park Lake, Weston under Lizard.

C (DT Adv. from gatekeeper).

Suffolk

See also Broads (Suffolk) above.

Flixton Decoy, Lowestoft.

C (DT Adv. from keeper or tel. Lowestoft 730568. L–20. B available. Anglian WA licence).

Heveningham Lake, Heveningham.

C (DT afternoons only Adv. lake kiosk. Anglian WA licence).

Mill Lake, Holbrook.

C (DT Adv. Mill House, Holbrook. Anglian WA licence).

Wickham Skeith Mere, Wickham Skeith.

C (Free fishing to Anglian WA licence holders).

Surrey

Frensham Trout Lake, Frensham.

● T (DT Adv. Wishanger Stud, Frensham Lane, Churt; tel. Frensham 4175. Fly only, no lures. Open 1 Mar.–31 Oct. Thames WA licence).

Furnace Brook Trout Fishery, Cowbeach.

● T (DT Adv. from Fishery, Trolliloes, Cowbeach, Hailsham; tel. Rushlake Green 830298. Fly only).

Lambeth Reservoir, West Molesey.

C (No DT; fishing through membership of London AA. Water produced a record roach).

Littleton Lake, Shepperton.

C, T (DT on bank. Thames WA licence).

Lodge Pond, Farnham.

C (DT Adv. King & Sons, tackle, 3 South Street, Farnham. Thames WA licence).

Lodge Pond, Wrecclesham.

C (DT on bank or from tackle shops in area. Rods may be limited at bailiff's discretion. Thames WA licence).

Longfield Fishery, Staines.

C (WT Adv. Leisure Sport, RMC House, High Street, Feltham, Middx, or tacklist named on notice-board at water. Has good bream, roach. Thames WA licence).

Mytchett Lake, Camberley.

C (DT on bank or from keeper. Thames WA licence).

Old Bury Hill Lake, Dorking.

C (DT on bank. B available. Regular matches arranged by owner. Southern WA licence).

Papercourt Pits, Ripley.

C (WT Adv. from Leisure Sport, RMC House, High Street, Feltham, Middx, or tacklist named on notice-board at water. Good tench and bream catches. Thames WA licence).

Rushmore Trout Lakes, Rushmore.

● T (DT Adv. from fishery, Rushmore, near Hindhead; tel. Haslemere 2818. Single fly only, barbless hooks).

Shepperton Pits, Shepperton.

C (WT Adv. Leisure Sport, RMC House, High Street, Feltham, Middx, or tacklist named on notice-board at water. Roach, tench, bream and pike, also big eels. Thames WA licence).

Staines North Reservoir, Staines.

C (No DT; fishing through membership of London AA. Thames WA licence).

Tri-Lakes, Sandhurst.
C, T (DT Adv. from ticket office. Thames WA licence).

Waggoners Wells Lakes, Grayshott.
See under Hampshire.

Wattlehurst Farm Lake, Kingsfold.
● T (DT Adv. tel. Oakwood Hill 341. Fly only. Open 1 Apr.–31 Oct. Southern WA licence).

Willinghurst Lake, Shamley Green.
● T (DT Adv. tel. Cranleigh 2828. Fly only. Open 1 Apr.–31 Oct. Rod licence incl.).

Winkworth Lakes, Hascombe.
● T (DT Adv. by postal application only, marking envelope 'Fishing', to Cdr J. A. H. McKean, RN, Thicketts, Hascombe Road, Godalming. Two boats, 2 anglers each. Open 15 Apr.–30 Sept. Thames WA licence).

Wire Mill Lake, Lingfield.
C (DT on bank. Southern WA licence).

Yeoveney Fishery, Staines.
C (WT Adv. Leisure Sport, RMC House, High Street, Feltham, Middx, or tacklist named on notice-board at water. Holds big carp. Thames WA licence).

Yew Tree Trout Fishery, Rotherfield.
● T (DT Adv. tel. Rotherfield 2529. Fly only, barbless hooks. Open 1 Apr.–31 Oct.).

Sussex, East

Buckshole Reservoir, Hastings.
C (DT on bank from keeper. Southern WA licence).

Clive Vale Reservoirs, Hastings.
C (DT on bank or from 43 Rye Road, Hastings. Southern WA licence).

Crowhurst Lido, Hastings.
C (DT on bank or from keeper. Southern WA licence).

Darwell Reservoir, Robertsbridge.
● T (DT Adv. at fishing hut. Fly only. Open 1 Apr.–29 Oct. Southern WA licence).

Ecclesbourne Reservoir, Hastings.
C (DT on bank or from 43 Rye Road, Hastings. Southern WA licence).

Great Sanders Reservoir, Sedlescombe.
● T (DT Adv. at fishing hut. Fly only. Open 1 Apr.–29 Oct. B available. Southern WA licence).

Harmer's Pond, Hastings.
C (DT on bank or from keeper. Southern WA licence).

Peppingford Lakes, Nutley.
C (DT on bank. Southern WA licence).

Piltdown Pond, Uckfield.
C (Free fishing to Southern WA licence holders).

Weir Wood Reservoir, Forest Row.
● T (DT Adv. ticket machine or ticket office at reservoir. Fly only. Open 1 Apr.–30 Sept. B available. Southern WA licence).

Sussex, West

Buckan Park Lake, Crawley.
C (DT Adv. tackle shops, Crawley. Thames WA licence).

Burton Mill Lake, Petworth.
C (DT Adv. from keeper, 390a High Hoes, Petworth. L–16. Southern WA licence).

Chichester Pits, Chichester.
C (DT Adv. from tacklists in area or from Chichester AS. Southern WA licence).

Laybrook Lakes, Ashington.
C (DT Adv. tackle shops Worthing and Hove. Southern WA licence).

Peckham's Copse Fishery, North Mundham.
● T (DT Adv. ticket office or Southern Leisure Centre, Vinnetrow Road, Chichester. Fly only. Open 1 Apr.–29 Oct. Regularly stocked browns, rainbows. Southern WA licence).

Southern Leisure Centre Pits, Chichester.
C (DT Adv. ticket office. Southern WA licence. Coarse fish, some to specimen size).

Tyne and Wear

Killingworth Lakes, Newcastle upon Tyne.
C (Free fishing. Northumberland W A licence).
Throckley Flash (Throckley Reef), Throckley.
C (Free fishing. Northumberland W A licence).

Warwickshire

See also West Midlands still waters below.
Severn-Trent Water Authority rod licence needed.
Compton Verney Lakes, Kineton.
C (DT Adv. for North Lake, Kineton Garage. L–15. South Lake: Park Farm, Kineton).
Cuttle Mill Lake, Wishaw.
C (DT Adv. J. A. Brewer, Cuttle Mill, Wishaw, Sutton Coldfield. Open 16 June–30 Sept. Famed for large carp, many over 30 lb).
Draycote Water, Dunchurch.
● T (DT Adv. ticket office. Fly only. Open 8 Apr.–9 Oct. B, M B available. Well stocked; fish average 1½ lb).
Earlswood Lakes, Earlswood.
C (DT on bank).
Frankton Pool, Frankton.
C (DT on bank).
Kingsbury Pits, Kingsbury.
C (DT Adv. ticket machine).
Napton Reservoirs, Napton.
C (DT on bank, from tackle shops in area and at Coventry).
Newbold Quarry, Rugby.
C (DT on bank, from Banks and Burr tackle, Claremont Road, Rugby, or Empire A C).
Newbold Reservoir, Rugby.
C (DT on bank, tackle shop, Rugby, or Empire A C).

West Midlands

Severn-Trent Water Authority rod licence needed.

Arboretum Lake, Walsall.
C (DT Adv. from keeper. B available).
Brookvale Park Lake, Birmingham.
C (DT from keeper).
Cannon Hill Park Lake, Birmingham.
C (DT from keeper).
Coombe Abbey Lake, Coventry.
C (DT Adv. from keeper. Good fishing for bream, roach and tench with some big pike).
Edgbaston Reservoir, Birmingham.
C (DT from keeper).
Fox Hollies Park Lake, Birmingham.
C (DT from keeper).
Himley Hall Lakes, Dudley.
C (DT Adv. ticket office, Himley Hall. One lake trout only, restricted to residents of Dudley and Wolverhampton, who should apply through Dudley Metropolitan Borough Council).
Lifford Reservoir, Birmingham.
C (DT from keeper).
Lodge Farm Reservoir, Dudley.
C (Free fishing).
Norman Chamberlain Playing Fields Lake, Birmingham.
C (DT from keeper).
Packington Fisheries, Meriden.
● T in part, C in part (DT Adv. ticket office or ticket machine, or Packington Fisheries, Maxstoke Lane, Meriden, near Coventry. Advance booking recommended, as this is a popular venue. Some pits trout, fly only; rest coarse. Trout water open 18 Mar.–15 Nov. B available on some of water, and rod limits are applied. Excellent trout and coarse fishing).
Perry Park Lake, Birmingham.
C (DT from keeper).
Pool Hall Lake, Wolverhampton.
C (DT on bank).
Pype Hayes Park Lake, Birmingham.
C (DT from keeper).
Salford Park Lake, Birmingham.
C (DT from keeper).
Shustoke Reservoirs, Coleshill.
● T (DT Adv. Severn-Trent W A, Tame Division, 156–170 Newhall Street, Birmingham 3. Fly only. Open 16 Apr.–15 Oct. L–6. Advance booking recommended. B available).

Small Heath Park Lake, Birmingham.
C (DT from keeper).
Sutton Park Pools, Sutton Coldfield.
C (DT on bank).
Swanshurst Park Pool, Birmingham.
C (DT from keeper).
Trittiford Mill Lake, Birmingham.
C (DT from keeper).
Ward End Park Lake, Birmingham.
C (DT from keeper).

Wiltshire

Coate Water, Swindon.
C (DT Adv. at gate. Has produced large catches of big bream, but most of the fish at the margins small. Punts available. Thames WA licence).
Erlestoke Lake, Erlestoke.
C (DT Adv. from keeper, Badgerland, Lower Road, Erlestoke. L–12 rods, 6 for juniors only. Wessex WA licence).
Lower Moor Fishery, Oaksey.
● T (DT Adv. advance booking recommended from fishery, Oaksey, Malmesbury; tel. Minety 232. Fly only, lures on large lake only. Well stocked, some big fish. Open 24 Mar.–30 Nov. Thames WA licence).
New Lakes, Stourton.
● T in part, C in part (DT Adv. The House on the Lake, Stourton. Fly only on trout lakes. Wessex WA licence).
Steeple Langford Lakes, Steeple Langford.
C (DT on bank. Big carp and other coarse species. Wessex WA licence).
Wolverton Lake, Zeals.
● T (DT Adv. from keeper. Fly only. L–4. Open 1 Apr.–30 Sept. B available. Rod licence incl.).
Wroughton Reservoir, Swindon.
● T (DT Adv. Thames WA, Cotswold Division, 17 Bath Road, Swindon; tel. Swindon 24331. L–4. Booking essential. Fly only. Average fish 1 lb, with some big fish. Thames WA licence).

Yorkshire, North

Yorkshire Water Authority rod licence needed.
Castle Howard Great Lake, Malton.
C (DT on bank or from keeper. A good tench fishery, plus other species).
Cod Beck Reservoir, Osmotherby.
● T (DT Adv. Hambleton District Council, 72 High Street, Northallerton. Fly only; fish small on average, about ½ lb).
Elvington Lake, Elvington.
T, C (DT Adv. from keeper. Open 1 Apr.–28 Feb.).
Fairburn Ings, Fairburn.
C (DT Adv. tackle shop, Castleford).
Fewston and Swinsty Reservoirs, Harrogate.
● T in part, C (DT Adv. Keeper's Lodge, Fewston. Open 1 Apr.–29 Sept. Fly only at Fewston, minnow and fly at Swinsty).
Greenfield Lake, Buckden.
● T (DT Adv. Buck Inn, Buckden, near Skipton. Fly only. Open 1 Apr.–30 Sept. L–8).
Malham Tarn, Malham.
● T (DT Adv. ticket office, Malham Tarn Field Centre. B available. Open 1 May–30 Sept.).
Rogers' Quarry Pit, Ripon.
C (WT Adv. B. Wain, 82 Bondgate, Ripon, or Brewers Arms, 2 Bondgate Green, Ripon).
Scaling Dam Reservoir, Whitby.
T (DT Adv. ticket office. Open for brown trout 1 Apr.–30 Sept.; rainbows, 1 Apr.–14 Oct.).
Scarborough Mere, Scarborough.
C (DT on bank).
Semerwater, Bainbridge.
T, C (DT Adv. Countersett House, by lake, or Rose and Crown, Bainbridge. Has produced big catches of good bream and also holds perch and trout).
Thruscross Reservoir, Harrogate.
● T (DT Adv. ticket machine, keeper's lodge. Open 1 Apr.–29 Sept.).

Yorkshire, South

Arbourthorne Pond, Sheffield.
C (Free fishing. L–30. Yorkshire WA licence).

Askern Lake, Doncaster.
C (DT on bank or from ticket office. B available. Yorkshire WA licence).

Bramley Flash, Rotherham.
C (DT Adv. Dormer Sports AC. Yorkshire WA licence).

Crabtree Pond, Sheffield.
C (DT from keeper or warden at Earl Marshall Rec., Earl Marshall Road, Sheffield. Yorkshire WA licence).

Crookes Valley Dam, Sheffield.
C (DT from keeper. Rods limited to 40 from first Saturday in Apr. to last Sunday in Oct., then 80 until end of season. Yorkshire WA licence).

Cusworth Hall Lakes, Cusworth.
C (DT on bank. Yorkshire WA licence).

Cusworth Park Pits, Doncaster.
C (DT on bank. Yorkshire WA licence).

Dam Flask Reservoir, Sheffield.
T, C (DT Adv. ticket office. Heavily fished but holds good bream, roach and pike; also trout, some large. Open 1 Apr.–31 Jan. Yorkshire WA licence).

Elsecar Dam, Elsecar.
C (DT on bank. Yorkshire WA licence).

Fordholes Farm Pool, Braithwell.
C (DT Adv. T. E. Grice, tackle, Rotherham. Severn-Trent WA licence).

Forge Dam, Sheffield.
C (DT Adv. café at water. Trout also in this water. Open 1 Apr.–28 Feb. Yorkshire WA licence).

Frecheville Pond, Sheffield.
C (DT from keeper. L–30. Yorkshire WA licence).

Graves Park Pond, Sheffield.
C (DT Adv. from keeper. L–12. Yorkshire WA licence).

Lindholme Lake, Hatfield.
● T (DT Adv. F. G. Gale, tackle, Copley Road, Doncaster; Sportfishers, High Street, Hatfield; Sandtoft Filling Station or B. Lindley, Haverthward House, Burnham Road, Epworth. Fly only. Open 18 Mar.–16 Oct. Severn-Trent WA licence).

Milton Ponds, Hoyland.
C (DT Adv. Milton Arms. Yorkshire WA licence).

More Hall Reservoir, Ewden.
● T (DT Adv. Yorkshire WA, Castle Market Building, Exchange Street, Sheffield. Fly only. Yorkshire WA licence).

Rivelin Dams, Sheffield.
C, T (DT Adv. for 7 pools from keeper, or if not in attendance the assistant at the paddling pool. Rods limited according to pools. Yorkshire WA licence).

Scout Dike Reservoir, Penistone.
T (DT Adv. from ticket office, weekdays, or for weekends in advance from Yorkshire WA, Castle Market Building, Exchange Street, Sheffield. Yorkshire WA licence).

Ulley Reservoir, Rotherham.
C (DT Adv. T. E. Grice, tackle, Rotherham, or Mellor's tackle, Swallownest. Yorkshire WA licence).

Underbank Reservoir, Stocksbridge.
T, C (DT Adv. ticket office. Open 1 Apr.–31 Jan. Yorkshire WA licence).

Woodsetts Quarry, Woodsetts.
C (DT Adv. from keeper, 64 Kilton Glade, Worksop. Severn-Trent WA licence).

Yorkshire, West

Yorkshire Water Authority rod licence needed.

Chellow Dene and Leeming Reservoirs, Bradford.
C, T (Fishing through membership of Bradford City AA. Leeming stocked with brown trout).

Cromwell Lake, Brighouse.
● T (DT Adv. Grove Motel, Elland Road, Brighouse. Fly only. Open 1 Apr.–30 Oct. B available. Average fish 1 lb; some bigger).

Harold Park Lake, Bradford.
   C, T (DT Adv. tackle shops, Bradford).
Hill Top Reservoir, Slaithwaite.
   C (DT Adv. Wagstaff's tackle, Britannia Road, Slaithwaite).
Knotford Lagoon, Otley.
   C (DT Adv. The Gun Shop, Cross Green, Otley).
Middleton Park Pool, Leeds.
   C (DT from keeper. Fishing only during park hours).
Nostell Priory Lakes, Wakefield.
   C (DT Adv. Foulby Lodge, Nostell Priory, or F. Alexander, tackle, The Strings, Wakefield. Day permits one lake only; rest for season tickets, apply head bailiff at the Priory – one coarse lake, one trout).
Roundhay Park Lakes, Leeds.

C, T (DT Adv. tackle shops, Leeds, or Leeds Amalgamated SA. Upper Lake, coarse, open 1 June–27 Feb.; Waterloo Lake, trout and coarse, 25 Mar.–27 Feb.).
Sunnydale Reservoir, near Bingley.
   T (DT Adv. tackle shops, Bingley and Bradford, or from Bingley AC).
Wintersett Reservoir, Ryhill.
   C (DT on bank).
Worsborough Dam, Barnsley.
   C (DT Adv. from keeper. Open 1 June–28 Feb. No Sunday fishing. Has produced big bream catches and specimen roach).
Yeadon Tarn, Yeadon.
   T, C (DT Adv. Websters, grocers, High Street, and Denison's ironmongers, Town Street, Yeadon. B available. Open 1 Apr.–27 Feb.).

Three

Welsh Rivers
(Welsh Water Authority area)

As a contrast to England, most of the rivers of Wales hold game fish, and where coarse fish are present, in rivers such as the Wye, the Usk and the Dee, fishing for them comes second to game fishing, and restrictions may be enforced.

There is a contrast in scenery, too, with many of the rivers swelling from mountain sources and running brief, fast courses to the sea.

As explained in the section 'Water Authorities and Regulations', there are seven divisions within the Authority's region, these being the Taff Division, the Dee and Clwyd Division, the Wye Division, the Usk Division, the Gower Division, the West Wales Division and the Gwynedd Division (which includes Anglesey). Close seasons can differ between these divisions, and in some cases from water to water within a division, and anglers are advised to check the details in the rod licence entry carefully.

Aeron
Rises on Blaenpennal and runs 20 m through Llangeitho and Talsarn to the sea at Aberaeron.

Run of sea-trout and salmon begins June. Trout numerous but mostly small.

Abergorlech, Dyfed. 400 yds left bank on Teglan Waters (signposted).
S (WT Adv. D. H. Davies, Minyrafon, Abergorlech, Dyfed).

Lampeter, Dyfed. 1 m left bank near Ciliau Aeron on Lampeter–Aberaeron road.
S, ST, T (DT Adv. E. M. Davies, Tanyrallt Farm, Ciliau Aeron).

Talsarn. Dyfed. ¾ m above village.
S (DT Adv. M. Rogers Lewis, Abermeurig Mansion, Abermeurig, Lampeter).
West Wales Rivers Division.

Afan
Rises above Cymmer and runs south-east to the Bristol Channel at Port Talbot.

Mainly trout, with some sea-trout in lower reaches. Salmon rare.

Abarafan, W Glam. Most of water.
ST, T, S (DT Adv. S. Jenkins, 45 Station Road, Port Talbot, or Bakers, Cymmer. Fly only in Mar. and Oct.).
Gower Rivers Division.

Afon Llwyd
Rises north of Pontypool and runs south to join the Usk near Caerleon.

Trout fishing, regularly stocked in parts.

Cwmbran, Gwent. 2 m from Chapel Lane road bridge to biscuit factory.
T (DT Adv. tackle shops, Pontnewydd and Cwmbran).

Pontypool, Gwent. From Edlogan Way bridge upstream to Abersychan.
T (DT Adv. Pontypool AA, tackle shop, Pontypool, or Post Office, Pontmoile).
Usk Rivers Division.

Alaw
Rises near Rhosgoch on Anglesey and runs into Llyn Alaw Reservoir before running on to Holyhead Bay.

Trout and some sea-trout.

Llanfachraeth, Anglesey. Most of water.
T, ST (Free fishing, provided permission obtained from landowners).
Gwynedd Rivers Division.

Aled
Runs 10 m through Llansannon to join
the Elwey below Llanfair Talhaiarn.
Fair trout fishing.
Llansannen, Clwyd. 3 m upstream from
main road bridge.
T (DT Adv. Llansannen, Glasfryn
Stores. No Sunday fishing).
Tributary of Clywd system.
Dee and Clwyd Rivers Division.

Alwen
Runs from Alwen Reservoir through
Llanfihangel to the Dee above Corwen.
Holds trout, with some salmon.
Corwen, Clwyd. 1 m in area.
T, S (DT Adv. Cambrian Fly Fishery,
Old Vicarage, Trevor, Llangollen).
Llanfihangel, Clwyd. 1 m upstream from
Crown Hotel.
T (DT Adv. Crown Hotel, Llan-
fihangel).
Tributary of Dee system.
Dee and Clwyd Rivers Division.

Alyn
Rises near Llandegla and runs north to
Mold and then on through Caergwrle to
the Dee near Farndon.
Trout fishing fair, but nearly all water
is association-controlled, with no known
openings for day ticket anglers.
Caergwrle AC (R. Mathers, 29
Hawarden Road, Hope, Wrexham,
Clwyd) offers season membership.
Tributary of Dee system.
Dee and Clwyd Rivers Division.

Amman
Flows through Ammanford from source
in the Black Mountains to join the
Loughor.
Trout, with some salmon and sea-trout
late on.
Pontamman, Dyfed. Most of water.
S, ST, T (WT or 5-day, Adv. Club
Godier-Mynydd Du, 203 Cwmamman
Road, Glanamman).
Tributary of Loughor.
Gower Rivers Division.

Arddu
Small tributary of the Seiont.

Trout fishing.
Llanberis, Gwynedd. 1 m stretch from
mouth of Hwch.
T (DT Adv. tackle shops in area).
Tributary of Seiont.
Gwynedd Rivers Division.

Arrow
Rises to the east of Kington and runs to
join the Lugg below Leominster.
Like the Lugg and the Wye, the
Arrow offers some coarse fish, notably
dace and grayling, besides trout.
Salmon are rare. Although most of the
river is private, Birmingham AA holds
water.
Tributary of Wye system.
Wye Rivers Division.

Arth
A small water running to the Irish Sea to
the north of Aberaeron.
Trout, some sea-trout late on. No
known ticket opportunities, but inquiries to landowners can be worthwhile.
West Wales Rivers Division.

Artro
Rises on Moel Ysgyfarnogod and flows
into Cardigan Bay near Llanbedr.
Trout, with improving runs of sea-
trout and some salmon.
Lanbedr, Gwynedd. 4 m stretch.
T, ST, S (DT Adv. tackle shops in area,
or Post Office, Llanbedr. Fishery open
for salmon 2 Apr.–16 Oct.; trout,
4 Mar.–30 Sept.).
Gwynedd Rivers Division.

Bach Howey
Small tributary of Wye.
Trout fishing.
Hay-on-Wye, Powys. 1 m stretch.
T (DT Adv. tackle shop, Castle Street,
Hay-on-Wye).
Wye Rivers Division.

Braint
Runs inland along the line of the Menai
Strait, which it eventually joins below
Dwyram.
Trout, some sea-trout. No known

ticket opportunities, but farms are worth inquiry.

Gwynedd Rivers Division.

Bran

Rises on Crichan Forest slopes and runs to join the Towy at Llandovery.

Fair trout fishing.

Llandovery, Dyfed. Ystrad Walter Waters, 1 m.

T (DT Adv. Towy Vale Relays, D. C. Bancroft, Stone Street, Llandovery, or from Llandovery AA).

Tributary of Towy system.

West Wales Rivers Division.

Cadoxton Stream

Small water running to the Bristol Channel near Cadoxton.

Fair trout fishing. No known ticket opportunities, but worth inquiry to landowners.

Taff Rivers Division.

Cain (Gain)

Rises to the south of Trawsfynydd Lake and runs to join the River Mawddach near the Dolgellau Road.

Fair trout fishing.

Trawsfynydd, Merioneth. 5 m at Pistyllcain.

T (DT Adv. tackle shop, Trawsfynydd).

Tributary of Mawddach system.

Gwynedd Rivers Division.

Cefni

Rises in mid-Anglesey and feeds Llyn Frogwy and Cefni Reservoir before running over Malltraeth Marsh to the sea at the south end of the island.

Trout, with some sea-trout and salmon.

Llangefni, Anglesey. Whole water.

T (Free fishing, provided permission obtained from landowners).

Gwynedd Rivers Division.

Ceint

Another Anglesey trout water, the Ceint runs into the River Nodwydd.

Pentraeth, Anglesey. Whole water.

T (Free fishing, provided permission obtained from landowners).

Gwynedd Rivers Division.

Ceiriog

Rises in the Berwyn Mountains and runs to join the Dee near Chirk.

Trout, coarse fish and some sea-trout.

Chirk, Clwyd. 1 m from Ladies Bridge to fence above Pontyblew Farm, and fence below forge to Mouse Bridge.

T (DT Adv. Chirk AA. Fly only. L-2).

Llanarmon, Clwyd. Both banks upstream above village and ½ m downstream to Tregeriog.

T (2-day, fly only, Adv. from Mr Lowe, West Arms Hotel, Llanarmon).

Llwynmawr, Clwyd. Both banks downstream from Gatehouse to Pontfaen Bridge.

T, S (Residents only, Golden Pheasant Hotel, Llwynmawr, Dolywern, Wrexham. Fly only).

Tributary of Dee system.

Dee and Clwyd Rivers Division.

Cennen

Rises near the source of the Loughor and runs west then north to the Towy at Ffairfach.

Fair trout fishing.

Ffairfach, Dyfed. 3 m from Ffairfach to Derwydd.

T (DT Adv. tackle shops in area. Open 10 Mar.–30 Sept.).

Tributary of Towy system.

West Wales Rivers Division.

Chwefri

Trout river tributary of the Wye, joining near Builth Wells.

Cylmery, Powys. 1 m stretch.

T (Residents only, Lake Hotel, Llangammarch Wells).

Wye Rivers Division.

Cleddau (East)

The eastern branch of the system feeding the estuary complex leading to Milford Haven, rising above Clarbeston and running to Canaston Bridge.

Good sea-trout fishing from June to end of season, with some salmon. Trout fair.

Narberth, Dyfed. 1 m stretch of left bank from point 400 yds above Canaston Bridge.

T, ST, S (DT Adv. Bush Inn, Robeston Wathen, or Hunter's Lodge, Robeston Wathen. Fishery open 10 Mar.–7 Oct.).

West Wales Rivers Division.

Cleddau (West)

Rises above Treffgarn and runs to join the western arm of the Cleddau estuary complex.

Fishing as East Cleddau (above).

Haverfordwest, Pembrokeshire. 6 m of fishing in area.

T, ST, S (DT Adv. tackle shop, Haverfordwest).

West Wales Rivers Division.

Cleifon

Runs to the south of the A458 road to join the Dovey (or Dyfi) on its east bank.

Like the main river, the water is capable of producing big sea-trout, with some salmon. Trout fair. Most of the river preserved.

Mallwyd, Powys. ½ m from Dolgellau road bridge to Dovey.

ST, S (Residents only, Brigands Inn, Mallwyd).

Tributary of Dovey.

Gwynedd Rivers Division.

Clwyd

Rises to the north of Corwen and runs through the vale of Clwyd, passing Ruthin and St Asaph, to the sea at Rhyl.

Excellent sea-trout and salmon fishing. Salmon begin to move from Mar. to May, with the main run in July and Aug. The bigger sea-trout are taken in early summer, smaller fish moving later to September. Trout fishing fair to good.

Bontuchel, Clwyd. Stretch of right bank at hotel.

T, S (DT Adv. Bridge Hotel, Bontuchel).

Llanynys, Clwyd. 1¾ m stretch.

S, T (DT Adv. Liverpool and Dist. AA, J. Johnson, 97 Liverpool Road, North Maghull, near Liverpool).

Rhuddlan, Clwyd. 3 m from Rhuddlan to sea.

ST, S, C (Free fishing – mostly flounders, eels, with migratory fish moving straight through).

St Asaph, Clwyd. Stretch between old and new bridges.

T, ST (DT Adv. Bevins Newsagents, High Street, St Asaph, or Foxons Post Office, Penrhewl, St Asaph).

Tributaries: Aled, Clywedog, Elwy, Wheeler, Ystrad.

Dee and Clwyd Rivers Division.

Clywedog

Rises to the west of Ruthin to join the Clwyd below the town.

Good sea-trout and salmon fishing, but strictly preserved, with no known openings for visiting anglers.

Dee and Clwyd Rivers Division.

Conwy

Rises at Llyn Conwy, running through Pentrefoelas to the Conwy Falls above Betws-y-Coed, below which migratory species are taken. After Betws-y-Coed the river runs north through the Conwy Valley to the sea at Tal-y-Cafn.

The Conwy is rated among the best sea-trout rivers in England and Wales and has produced the second biggest fish of this species recorded – 21 lb 8 oz. In general the fish are big, to 15 lb, and there are also salmon, which run best at high water during May and June. The main runs of sea-trout are from June through to Sept. The trout fishing is fair.

Betws-y-Coed, Gwynedd. 7 m of fishing from Tyn-y-Cae pool to Trefriw Quay.

ST, S (DT Adv. Gwydyr Hotel, Betws-y-Coed).

Betws-y-Coed, Gwynedd. 1 m from Conwy Falls bridge to Rhydlanfair Bridge, excepting last field on right bank.

T (DT Adv. keeper, Bron Ruffydd, Pentrefoelas Road, Betws-y-Coed, or National Trust, North Wales Area, Dinas, Betws-y-Coed. Fly only except in flood. No Sunday fishing).

Dolgarrog, Gwynedd. Water within village boundaries.

T, ST, S (DT Adv. on weekends and public holidays only, from Dolgarrog FC. Salmon fishing to 31 Aug. L–6).

Llanrwst, Gwynedd. Over 1 m from old bridge upstream on right bank.

T, ST, S (WT Adv. tackle shop, Llanrwst. Fishery open 3 Mar.–19 Sept.).

Ysbyty Ifan, Gwynedd. 6 m from Llyn Conwy to A5.

T (DT Adv. Post Office, Ysbyty Ifan, or Voelas Arms, Pentrefoelas. Fly only except in flood; no Sunday fishing in parts of water).

Tributaries of Conwy: Crafnant, Cwm Penamnen, Ddu, Glasgwm, Gwyrd, Lledr, Llugwy, Machno, Nug, Roe, Serw, Ystumiau.

Gwynedd Rivers Division.

Cothi

The Towy's biggest tributary, the Cothi runs through Pumpsaint and Brechfa to the main river above Carmarthen.

Good sea-trout fishing; some salmon, best from June on. Trouting fair.

Brechfa, Dyfed. 1 m right bank from Brechfa to Parson's Pool.

T, S (DT Adv. Forest Arms Hotel, Brechfa. No Sunday fishing).

Nantgaredig, Dyfed. 1 m below road bridge at Pontargothi.

T, ST, S (WT Adv. tackle shops, Carmarthen, Llandeilo and Llanelli, also Post Office, Nantgaredig. Fishery open for salmon and sea-trout 10 Mar.–7 Oct.; trout, 10 Mar.–30 Sept.).

Pontargothi, Dyfed. Stretch of left bank near Pontargothi.

T, S (DT Adv. Cresselly Arms, Pontargothi).

Pumpsaint, Dyfed. 4½ m in area, plus stretch of Twrch.

T, ST, S (DT Adv. Dolaucothi Arms Hotel, Pumpsaint).

Tributary of Towy system.

West Wales Rivers Division.

Crafnant

Tributary of Conwy, running from Llyn Crafnant to main river below Trefriw.

Trout, including some rainbows.

Llyn Crafnant, Gwynedd. Most of water.

T (DT Adv. ticket office, lakeside café).

Gwynedd Rivers Division.

Cwm Penamnen

Small stream running into Lledr above Dolwyddelan.

Trout fishing.

Dolwyddelan, Gwynedd. 2 m to Tyn-y-cwm.

T (DT Adv. Forestry Commission, Forest Office, Dolwyddelan).

Tributary of Conwy system.

Gwynedd Rivers Division.

Cynfal

Small tributary of Dwyryd.

Trout fishing.

Ffestiniog, Gwynedd. 1½ m from source to Tal-y-Bont.

T (DT Adv. tackle shops in area).

Gwynedd Rivers Division.

Ddu

Small tributary of Conwy linking main river at Dolgarrog with Llyn Cowlyd Reservoir.

Some trout (reservoir free fishing with permit from Welsh Water Authority, Colwyn Bay).

Gwynedd Rivers Division.

Dee

From its source at Bala Lake down to Chester and its estuary, the Dee is one of Wales's most important fishing rivers. It is a noted salmon fishery, with fish to 30 lb, between Shocklach and Lake Bala, and in addition there are sea-trout (small in the main), brown trout (again on the small side) and coarse fish throughout. Grayling fishing can be excellent, and these fish are present to Bala. So are pike, which run to 20 lb and more. Below Llangollen, chub, roach and dace are found in numbers, and there are occasional reports of barbel, which are said to have been illegally placed in the river. Below Bangor the bream fishing is good. There is a spring run of salmon with the best catches from Mar. to June. The summer salmon run starts in July, when fish move progressively up from the lower river. The main sea-trout run is in July and Aug. Associations controlling water include St Helen's AA, Warrington AA, Llay AS, Liverpool and Dist. AA, and the Dee AA.

Bala, Gwynedd. 700 yds stretch down from Bala New Bridge.

T, C, some S (DT Adv. tackle shops, Bala).

Bangor-on-Dee, Clwyd. 4 m Bangor Bridge to Overton Bridge.

T, C, S (DT Adv. from keeper or tackle shop, Ruabon Road, Wrexham).

Cefn, Clwyd. 1½ m from Pontcysyllte Bridge to Viaduct Pool at Newbridge.

T, C (DT Adv. keeper, Mr Parry, Queen's Villa, Queen Street, Cefn, or from Maelor AC).

Chester, Cheshire. Left bank from Kissing Gates to Suspension Bridge; from Queensferry Old Bridge to sea; Chester Weir to Old Dee Bridge; left bank between Greenway Street and River Lane and from 1 meadow below Grosvenor Bridge to rail bridge.

C (Free fishing).

Chester, Cheshire. 1¾ m from meadow above Dirty Lane to Chester Weir, left bank.

C (DT Adv. tackle shops, Chester).

Chester, Cheshire. 2 m right bank from Holt to Lower Hall, plus ½ m at Berwyn.

C, T, S (DT Adv. Liverpool and Dist. AA).

Chester, Cheshire. 5 m Chester Weir to Queensferry Old Road Bridge.

C (DT Adv. Martin's Tackle, Bridge Street, Chester).

Chester, Cheshire. 3½ m from Crook o'Dee to Chester Weir.

C (Free fishing).

Coed Llwyd, Clwyd. 1 m right bank from Brickworks Pool, Little Gleisiad, to Sun Pool.

T (DT Adv. Chirk AA. Fly only. L–2).

Erbistock, Clwyd. Boat Inn water, left bank.

C, T, S (DT Adv. Boat Inn, Erbistock).

Erbistock, Clwyd. Stretch of right bank.

S, T (DT Adv. Golden Pheasant Hotel, Llwynmawr).

Farndon, Cheshire. Stretch of right bank upstream of Farndon Bridge beside car park.

C (Free fishing).

Farndon, Cheshire. 1 m left bank above Farndon Bridge.

C (DT Adv. Martin's Tackle, Bridge Street, Chester).

Llangollen, Clwyd. Left bank at Major Pool.

T, S (DT Adv. ticket office by bank or tackle shop, Llangollen. Fly only. L–2. Fishery open 1 Mar.–15 Oct.).

Llangollen, Clwyd. 400 yds left bank.

T, S, C (DT Adv. Ponsonby Arms, Llangollen).

Llangollen, Clwyd. ½ m left bank below vicarage.

C, T, S (DT Adv. Cambrian Fly Fishery, Old Vicarage, Trevor, Llangollen).

Newbridge, Clwyd. Wynnstay water between Tallyho Bridge and Ram Brook.

T, C, some S (DT Adv. Royal Oak, Newbridge. L–20).

Sun Trevor, Clwyd. 1½ m from golf links bridge.

C, T, S (DT Adv. Maelor AA. L–3 rods for salmon).

Tributaries of Dee: Alwen, Alyn, Ceiriog, Tryweryn, Worthenbury Brook.

Dee and Clwyd Rivers Division.

Dewi Fawr

A tributary joining the Taf (not Taff) at St Clears.

Fair trout fishing.

Mydrim, Dyfed. Pentowin Estate Water, Mydrim.

T (DT Adv. tackle shops, Carmarthen, Llandeilo, Llanelli, or Post Office, Nantgaredig. Fishery open 10 Mar.–30 Sept.).

West Wales Rivers Division.

Dovey (Dyfi)

Runs 30 m from source on Aran Mawddwy through Dines Mawddwy, Cemmaes and Machynlleth to estuary.

One of the prime sea-trout rivers of Wales, it boasts two fish in its records of more than 20 lb. The fish begin running in May and continue to Sept. The river also offers salmon fishing and brown trout of fair size.

Dinas Mawddwy, Gwynedd. ½ m from bridge downstream.

T, ST, S (DT Adv. Dolbrawd Maeth Hall Country House Hotel, Dinas Mawddwy. B available).

Machynlleth, Powys. 15 m left bank between Llyfnant stream and Nant Ty-Mawr.

ST, S (DT Adv. parts of water only, tackle shop, Dinas Mawddwy, garage, G. D. Evans, Cemmaes Road, or Post Office, Cemmaes. Fly only unless flags indicate otherwise. Fishery open 1 Apr.–17 Oct. No Sunday fishing).

Tributaries: Cleifion, South Dulas, Twymyn.

Gwynedd Rivers Division.

Dulais

Tributary of Towy, which it joins near Manordeilo.

Fair trout fishing.

Manordeilo, Dyfed. 2 m right bank from Manordeilo downstream.

T (DT Adv. tackle shops in area. Fishery open 10 Mar.–30 Sept.).

West Wales Rivers Division.

Dulais (Glamorgan)

Runs from the Seven Sisters to join the River Neath near Aberdulais.

Fair trout fishing.

Aberdulais, W Glam. 2 m stretch from Aberdulais towards Crynant.

T (DT Adv. Neath and Dulais A C. Fishery open 1 Mar.–30 Sept.).

Neath, W Glam. Stretches in area.

T (DT Adv. Neath and Dulais A C). Tributary of Neath system.

Gower Rivers Division.

Dulas

Joins the Wye tributary, the River Irfon, near Llangamarch Wells.

Fair trout fishing.

Llanwrtyd Wells, Powys. 1 m stretch.

T (DT Adv. Neuadd Arms, Llanwrtyd Wells).

Tributary of Wye system.

Wye Rivers Division.

Dwyfach

Runs across the Lleyn Peninsula to Cardigan Bay near Criccieth. Joins River Dwyfawr.

Offers sea-trout fishing from July to Oct., improving salmon fishing and fair trout fishing.

Garndolbenmaen, Gwynedd. Stretches in area, also on Dwyfawr.

ST, S, T (DT Adv. tackle shops in area).

Gwynedd Rivers Division.

Dwyfawr

Offers similar fishing to Dwyfach (see above).

Gwynedd Rivers Division.

Dwyryd

Rises west of Blaenau Ffestiniog and runs into Tan-y-Grisiau, afterwards heading south through Maentwrog to estuary north of Harlech.

Salmon and sea-trout from June. Trouting fair.

Maentwrog, Gwynedd. 2 m Llechrwd Farm to old laundry.

T, S (DT Adv. Grapes Hotel, Maentwrog).

Tributaries: Cynfal, Teigl.

Gwynedd Rivers Division.

Dyfi

See Dovey, above.

Dysynni

Runs from Cader Idris into Talyllyn, then to Peniarth and to estuary north of Towyn.

Sea-trout and salmon to lake, fair trout fishing.

Abergynolwyn, Gwynedd. 9 m of fishing in area.

T, ST, S (DT Adv. tackle shops in area or Railway Inn, Abergynolwyn. Fishery open 2 Mar.–17 Oct. No Sunday fishing).

Tywyn, Gwynedd. 3 m Llanegryn to Afon Fathew.

ST, S (DT Adv. tackle shop, College Green, Tywyn).

Gwynedd Rivers Division.

Ebbw Fach
Usk tributary. Polluted.

Ebbw Fawr
Usk tributary. Polluted.

Eden (Gwynedd)
Rises near Trawsfynydd Lake and runs to the Mawddach near Ganllwyd.
Sea-trout, salmon and trout.
Ganllwyd, Gwynedd. 4 m down to Mawddach.
T, S (D T Adv. tackle shops in area).
Ganllwyd, Gwynedd. From 200 yds below Dolgyfeilia Bridge to River Mawddach.
T, ST, S (D T Adv. Post Office, Ganllwyd. No Sunday fishing).
Gwynedd Rivers Division.

Elan
Forms the Elan Valley Reservoirs before joining the River Wye near Rhayader.
Mainly trout.
Rhayader, Powys. 1 m stretch.
T (Residents only, Lion Royal Hotel, Rhayader).
Wye Rivers Division.

Elwy
Rises near Llangernyw and runs east to the Clwyd at St Asaph.
A good sea-trout fishery (best fish 11 lb 8 oz), with fair trout and some salmon.
Rhyl, Clwyd. Gipsy Lane Water as permit.
T, ST, S (D T Adv. tackle shops in area or Rhyl and Dist. A A).
St Asaph, Clwyd. Several stretches in area.
T, ST, S (D T Adv. tackle shop, St Asaph).
Dee and Clwyd Rivers Division.

Erch
Runs off the Lleyn Peninsula into Cardigan Bay at Pwllheli.
Sea-trout, trout, some salmon.
Pwllheli, Gwynedd. 4 m from Four Crosses to Pwllheli.
T, S (D T Adv. tackle shop, Pwllheli).
Gwynedd Rivers Division.

Ffraw (Gwna)
A 6-mile stream running into Aberffraw Bay in south-west Anglesey. Above Llyn Coron known as River Gwna.
Trout, sea-trout.
Aberffraw, Anglesey. Entire water.
T, ST (Free fishing, provided permission given by landowners).
Gwynedd Rivers Division.

Frome (Hereford)
Rises above Bromyard and runs into the Lugg above Mordiford. No known openings for visiting anglers.
Tributary of Wye system.
Wye Rivers Division.

Gammarch
A tributary of the Irfon, which it joins near Llangammarch Wells.
Fair trout fishing.
Llangammarch Wells, Powys. Total of 3 m of fishing in area.
T (D T Adv. Cammarch Hotel, Llangammarch Wells).
Tributary of Wye system.
Wye Rivers Division.

Garw
Runs from Pontycymer to the Ogmore Valley above Aberkenfig.
Salmon, some sea-trout, trout.
Bridgend, Mid-Glam. 6 m Blaegarvy to Sarn.
S, T (D T Adv. F. Smiles, 3 Sweet Wells, Pontyrhyl, near Pontycymer. Fishery open for salmon 1 Mar.–31 Oct.; trout, 1 Mar.–30 Sept.).
Gower Rivers Division.

Glasgwm
Rises on Ro-wen to run into the Machno.
Trout.
Penmachno, Gwynedd. 3½ m source to Bron Graig.
T (D T Adv. Post Office, Penmachno, or National Trust, North Wales Area, Dinas, Betws-y-Coed. Fly only except in flood. No Sunday fishing).
Tributary of Conwy system.
Gwynedd Rivers Division.

Glaslyn

Rises on the southern slopes of Snowdon and runs through lake chain to Beddgelert and pass of Aberglaslyn, then on to Cardigan Bay near Porthmadog.

Good sea-trout, some salmon and fair trout fishing.

Porthmadog, Gwynedd. 7 m Beddgelert to Porthmadog, except private sections marked.

T, ST, S (DT Adv. tackle shop, High Street, Porthmadog).

Tributary: Nant Colwyn.

Gwynedd Rivers Division.

Gwaun

Runs off the Prescelly Mountains to Cardigan Bay at Fishguard.

Trout, sea-trout. No known openings for visiting anglers, but landowners worth inquiry.

West Wales Rivers Division.

Gwendraeth Fach

Rises near Porthrhyd and runs south-west to the Gwendraeth estuary.

Trout, some sea-trout and salmon.

Kidwelly, Dyfed. Stretches in area, and on Gwendraeth Fawr.

T, ST, S (DT Adv. tackle shops, Carmarthen, Llandeilo, Llanelli, or Post Office, Nantgaredig. Open 10 Mar.–30 Sept.).

West Wales Rivers Division.

Gwendraeth Fawr

Rises north of Gorslas and runs to the Gwendraeth estuary. Similar sport to Gwendraeth Fach (see above) and same access.

West Wales Rivers Division.

Gwili

One of the major tributaries of the Towy, rising to the north of Carmarthen and joining main river near Abergwili.

Sea-trout, with some salmon and trout.

Conwyl-Elfed, Dyfed. 3 m in area.

T, ST, S (DT Adv. ticket office, Avondale, Conwyl-Elfed).

Llanpumpsaint, Dyfed. 5 fields in area.

T (WT Adv. tackle shops, Carmarthen, Llandeilo, Llanelli, or Post Office, Nantgaredig. Open 10 Mar.–30 Sept.).

Tributary of Towy system.

West Wales Rivers Division.

Gwna

See Ffraw, above.

Gwyrd

Rises on Snowdon and runs to join the Llugwy at Capel Curig.

Mainly trout, with some access for visitors through hotels.

Tributary of Conwy system.

Gwynedd Rivers Division.

Gwyrfai

From Llyn Cwellyn the river runs across the west slopes of Snowdon to Betws Garmon and on to Llanwnda and the Menai Strait.

Trout, with runs of sea-trout and salmon.

Llyn Gadair, Gwynedd. Several stretches in area.

T, ST, S (DT Adv. tackle shops, post offices and newsagents in area).

Rhydd-Du, Gwynedd. Stretch from Llyn Cwellyn.

T (DT Adv. Welsh Water Authority, Gwynedd Division, Highfield, Caernarvon).

Gwynedd Rivers Division.

Hepste

Rises in the Brecon Beacons and runs to join the Mellte.

Fair trout fishing.

Glyn Neath, W Glam. ¾ m from Mellte.

T (DT Adv. Glyn Neath AA).

Tributary of Neath system.

Gower Rivers Division.

Hindwell Brook

Tributary of the Lugg offering some trout fishing through associations.

Wye Rivers Division.

Honddu

Tributary of the Monnow. Offers some trout fishing on hotel water.

Wye Rivers Division.

Honddu (Usk)

Runs through Upper and Lower Chapel to meet the Usk near Brecon.

Trout fishing, with some access through hotel and association water.

Tributary of Usk system.

Usk Rivers Division.

Hwch

Small tributary of the River Seiont.

Trout fishing.

Llanberis, Gwynedd. ½ m in area.

T (D T Adv. Welsh Water Authority, Gwynedd Rivers Division, Highfield, Caernarvon).

Gwynedd Rivers Division.

Irfon

Rises in the Cambrians and runs to join the River Wye at Builth Wells.

Trout, grayling and some salmon. Trout fishing good. Many hotels offer fishing for residents.

Builth Wells, Powys. ½ m stretch right bank.

C, T, S (WT Adv. tackle shop, High Street, Builth Wells. Also 3-day ticket).

Llangammarch Wells, Powys. 3 sections in area.

T, S (DT Adv. Cammarch Hotel, Llangammarch Wells).

Tributary of Wye system.

Wye Rivers Division.

Ithon

Runs south to Penybont, Llandrindod Wells and the Wye.

Good trout fishing, with coarse fish (especially chub) and occasional salmon. Many hotels offer fishing for residents.

Llandrindod Wells, Powys. 5 m stretch.

T (D T Adv. tackle shop, Park Crescent, Llandrindod Wells. Fly only to 1 Aug., when spinning permitted. Fishery open 1 Mar.–30 Sept.).

Penybont, Powys. 3 m from Brynthomas Bridge to Old Castle Farm, right bank.

C, T, S (DT Adv. tackle shop, Penybont, or Severn Arms Hotel, Penybont).

Tributary of Wye system.

Wye Rivers Division.

Kenfig

Rises south of Maesteg and runs to Swansea Bay near Kenfig.

A small water, it offers trout to 8 oz. Mostly preserved (Kenfig Hill and Dist. A A, 16 Marlas Road, Pyle).

Gower Rivers Division.

Lledr

From Snowdonia the Lledr runs through Dolwyddelan to the River Conwy, which it joins below the Conwy Falls and so attracts the salmon and sea-trout unable to progress through the main river. Summer and autumn are the best times for migratory fish.

Betws-y-Coed, Gwynedd. 7 m stretch of left bank from Plantation Pool.

S, S T (D T Adv. Gwydyr Hotel, Betws-y-Coed).

Dolwyddelan, Gwynedd. 3 m to Pont-y-Pant.

T, S (WT Adv. tackle shop, Dolwyddelan. Fishery open 3 Mar.–17 Oct.).

Tributary of Conwy system.

Gwynedd Rivers Division.

Llugwy

Another of the Conwy's tributaries, joining the main river near Betws-y-Coed.

Mostly preserved, with some trout fishing available, also salmon. Trout run to 2 lb.

Betws-y-Coed, Gwynedd. Left bank upstream of rail bridge to Swallow Falls and right bank upstream of Conwy junction to Swallow Falls.

T, S (DT Tan Lan Café, Betws-y-Coed. Spinning flood only).

Betws-y-Coed, Gwynedd. Mymbyr Lakes outfall to Swallow Falls.

T (D T Adv. Gwydyr Hotel, Betws-y-Coed. Fly only).

Tributary of Conwy.

Gwynedd Rivers Division.

Llyfni

From Llyn Nantle Uchaf the Llyfni runs to Llanllyfni and Caernarvon Bay at Pontllyfni.

Good sea-trout fishing with trout and salmon.

Penygroes, Gwynedd. Several stretches in area.

T, ST, S (DT Adv. from tackle shops, shops, post offices, garages etc. in area).

Gwynedd Rivers Division.

Llynfi

Feeds Llangorse Lake and then runs north to the Wye near Glasbury.

Trout and coarse fish, mostly preserved. Some hotels offer fishing for guests.

Glasbury-on-Wye, Powys. Stretches in area.

T, C (DT Adv. Treble Hill Cottage, Glasbury-on-Wye. Trout fly only. L–4. Fishery open for trout 1 Mar.–30 Sept.; coarse, 1 Oct.–28 Feb.).

Wye Rivers Division.

Loughor (Llychwr)

Rises in the Black Mountains and runs through Ammanford to the Bristol Channel near Pontardulais.

Trout, sea-trout and salmon. Migratory fish runs said to be improving steadily. Mostly preserved, with some hotels offering fishing for guests only.

Pontardulais, Dyfed. 4 m to Hendre Weir.

T, ST, S (DT Adv. tackle shop, St Teills Street, Pontardulais. L–25).

Tributary: Amman.

Gower Rivers Division.

Lugg

One of the Wye's main tributaries, the Lugg rises to the west of Presteigne and runs to Leominster and Marden and the Wye below Mordiford.

Excellent trout and coarse fishing, with some salmon. Birmingham AA and Hereford and District AA are among associations holding water on the Lugg.

Leominster, Hereford and Worcs. 750 yds stretch right bank at farm.

C, T (DT Adv. Marlbrook Farm, Fordbridge, Leominster).

Mordiford, Hereford and Worcs. Left bank for 200 yds upstream from Mordiford Bridge.

C (DT Adv. The Old Rectory, Mordiford).

Mordiford, Hereford and Worcs. ¼ m from bridge to Wye, left bank.

C (DT Adv. Mrs Bowcott, Yew Tree Cottage, Mordiford).

Moreton, Hereford and Worcs. ¾ m right bank downstream of Moreton.

T, C (DT Adv. Miss A. R. Dutson, Green Bank, Munderfield, Bromyard, Hereford).

Tributary of Wye system.

Wye Rivers Division.

Machno

Runs through Penmachno to join the Conwy above Conwy Falls.

Fair trout fishing.

Penmachno, Gwynedd. Several stretches in area.

T (DT Adv. National Trust, North Wales Area, Dinas, Betws-y-Coed. Fly only except in flood conditions. No Sunday fishing).

Penmachno, Gwynedd. Bennar Farm to River Conwy.

T (DT Adv. Mrs Jones, Pandymill Farm, Penmachno).

Gwynedd Rivers Division.

Marshfield Reens

Waters draining land between Rumney and Newport.

Some sections hold stocks of coarse fish, mainly roach and bream.

Newport, Gwent. Entire water.

C (DT Adv. tackle shop, Penarth Road, Cardiff).

Taff Rivers Division.

Mawddach

Rises to the south-east of Trawsfyndd Lake and runs south to Llanelltyd and west to Penmaenpool and the Irish Sea.

Fair runs of sea-trout and salmon, with reasonable trout fishing. Most of the water is privately owned, with some hotels offering fishing to guests.

Dolgellau, Gwynedd. Hengwrt Estate Water, 2 m from Whitestones to Penmaenpool Bridge.

T, ST, S (DT Adv. tackle shop, Eldon Square, Dolgellau).

Ganllwyd, Gwynedd. 1 m right bank near Ganllwyd.

T, ST, S (DT Adv. Dolmelynllyn Hall
Hotel, Ganllwyd).

Ganllwyd, Gwynedd. Over 1 m from
River Eden to Boyds, right bank.

T, ST, S (DT Adv. Post Office,
Ganllwyd. No Sunday fishing).

Tributaries: Cain, Eden (Gwynedd),
Wnion.

Gwynedd Rivers Division.

Mellte

Rises in the Brecon Beacons to feed the
River Neath.

Small trout, some salmon.

Glyn Neath, W Glam. 4 m from Nedd
Fach to Caves Ystradfellte.

T, S (DT Adv. Glyn Neath AA).

Gower Rivers Division.

Monmouth and Brecon Canal

Cut to provide link between Brecon and
Newport through the Usk valley, with a
branch from Newport to Crumlin. Well
stocked with coarse fish in most parts,
but some reaches suffer from breaches.

Abergavenny, Gwent. 33 m Brecon to
Pontypool, except sections below.

C (DT Adv. Section Inspector, British
Waterways Board, Canal Office,
Govilon, Abergavenny).

Cwmbran, Gwent. 4 m stretch.

C (DT Adv. tackle shop, Ponnewydd,
Cwmbran).

Mamhilad, Gwent. Bridge 62 to Bridge
58.

C (DT Adv. Pontllanfraith AC).

Newport, Gwent. 2 m Barrack Hill Tunnel
to Newport boundary.

C (DT Adv. tackle shop, Newport).

Pontypool, Gwent. $1\frac{1}{2}$ m Jockey
Bridge to Bridge Street, towpath.

C (DT Adv. Typoeth Stores, Pontypool).

Pontywain, Gwent. 5 m Pontywain to
Risca, Crumlin Arm.

C (DT on bank or from tackle shop,
Tredegar Street, Risca).

Usk Rivers Division.

Monnow

Rises north-west of Pandy to run
through Pontrilas and to Monmouth and
the Wye.

Good trout fishing, plus coarse fish.
Hotels offer fishing for guests, and
Birmingham AA is one of the associa-
tions holding water.

Grosmont, Gwent. Right bank stretch.

C, T (DT Adv. Lower Tresenny Farm,
Grosmont. L–5).

Hay-on-Wye, Powys. $1\frac{1}{2}$ m stretch at
Hay.

T (Residents only, Crown Hotel, Broad
Street, Hay. Fly only. Fishery open
1 Mar.–30 Sept.).

Monmouth, Gwent. $\frac{1}{2}$ m near town.

C, T (DT Adv. Monmouth and Dist.
AS. Fishery open for trout 1 Apr.–
30 Sept.; coarse fish, 1 Oct.–27 Jan.).

Skenfrith, Gwent. Over $\frac{1}{2}$ m right bank
upstream from Skenfrith Weir.

T, C (DT Adv. Malthouse Farm,
Skenfrith. L–20).

Wye Rivers Division.

Nant Bran

Runs through Llanfihangel Nant Bran to
Penpont and the Usk.

Fair trout fishing; inquiries to landowners worthwhile.

Llanfihangel Nant Bran, Powys. 800 yds
left bank.

T (DT Adv. Llwyncoed Farm. L–3).

Usk Rivers Division.

Nant Colwyn

Feeds the River Glasslyn above
Porthmadog.

Fair trout fishing, although fish generally small.

Beddgelert, Gwynedd. Right bank from
Beddgelert camping ground to Pont
Cae'r Gors.

T (DT Adv. Warden's Office, Snowdonia Forest Park Camp, Beddgelert).

Gwynedd Rivers Division.

Neath

Rises in the Brecon Beacons, running
south to Glyn Neath and then through
the Vale of Neath to the Bristol Channel
between Neath and Swansea.

In the past the Neath has suffered from
pollution, which resulted in most of its
migratory fish runs being lost; now,
with most of the pollution clear, sea-

trout runs are improving, but the salmon have yet to recover. Fair trout fishing.

Aberdulais, W Glam. 6 m Aberdulais road bridge to Rheola Estate.

T, ST, S (D T Adv. Neath and Dulais A C. Fishery open for trout 1 Mar.–30 Sept.; sea-trout, 1 Apr.–16 Oct.; salmon, 2 Mar.–31 Oct.).

Glyn Neath, W Glam. 8 m Resolven to Pont Nedd Fechan.

T, S (D T Adv. Glyn Neath A A).

Neath, W Glam. Sections in area.

T (D T Adv. Neath and Dulais A C).

Tributaries: Dulais, Hepste, Mellte, Nedd Fach, Pyrddin.

Gower Rivers Division.

Neath Canal

Cuts through the Vale of Neath.

Fair stocks of coarse fish; some trout.

Neath, W. Glam. 6 m Briton Ferry to Resolven.

C, T (D T Adv. Neath and Dulais A C. Fishery open for trout 1 Mar.–30 Sept.; coarse fish, 16 June–14 Mar.).

Gower Rivers Division.

Nedd Fach

Tributary of the Neath system.

Some trout fishing.

Glyn Neath, W. Glam. 4 m from junction with Mellte to Blaen Nedd.

T (DT Adv. Glyn Neath A A).

Gower Rivers Division.

Nevern

Source is above Whitechurch, from which the river runs to Cardigan Bay.

Fairly good sea-trout fishing, with some salmon.

Nevern, Dyfed. 1½ m from Penwaun.

T, S (D T Adv. keeper, 56 High Street, Fishguard. Fishery open 10 Mar.–7 Oct.).

Newport, Dyfed. 5 m near Crymmych and 5 m Newport to Nevern.

T, ST, S (DT Adv. Salutation Inn, Velindre. B, M B available part of water. Open 10 Mar.–7 Oct.).

West Wales Rivers Division.

Nug

Stream joining the Conwy near Pentrefoelas.

Trout. Worth inquiry to local landowners.

Gwynedd Rivers Division.

Ogwen

Runs from Ogwen Lake, Snowdonia, to Bethesda and the Menai Strait near Bangor.

Well stocked with brown trout, and fair sea-trout fishing. Salmon during autumn.

Bethesda, Gwynedd. 1½ m Ogwen Lake to Twy-y-naes and 3 m from Ponttwr to Halfway Bridge.

T, ST, S (D T Adv. Caxton House, High Street, Bethesda, or T. Jones, High Street, Bethesda).

Gwynedd Rivers Division.

Olway Brook

Rises near Trelleck and runs to the Usk near Llanllowell.

Trout mainly.

Usk, Gwent. 1½ m above and 1 m below Olway Inn.

T, C (D T Adv. Greyhound Inn, Usk).

Usk Rivers Division.

Prysor

Feeds the southern end of Trawsfynydd Lake.

Mainly trout, some coarse fish.

Trawsfynydd, Gwynedd. 4 m from lake to Dargaet.

T (D T Adv. tackle shop, Trawsfynydd. No Sunday fishing).

Gwynedd Rivers Division.

Pyrddin

Trout stream joining the River Neath at Pont Nedd Fechan.

Glyn Neath, W Glam. 2 m left bank Forestry water and right bank, Pont Lewsin.

T (D T Adv. Glyn Neath A A).

Gower Rivers Division.

Rheidol

Feeds Cwm Rheidol Reservoir before running to Capel Bangor and the sea at Aberystwyth.

Good run of sea-trout, sometimes large fish, with brown trout and salmon. Most of the river is preserved.

Aberystwyth, Dyfed. 20 m Llyn Llygad, Rheidol, to mouth, except for private stretches marked on permit.

T, ST, S (DT Adv. to 1 July, then WT Adv., L–3, to end of season, from tackle shops, Queen Street and North Parade, Aberystwyth, or Erwyd Garage, Ponterwyd).

West Wales Rivers Division.

Rhondda Fach

Runs parallel to the Rhondda Fawr, which it joins at Porth.

Fair trout fishing.

Maerdy, Mid-Glam. 6 m Maerdy to Porth.

T (DT Adv. 7 Richard Street, Maerdy, or 37 North Terrace, Maerdy. Fly only, fishery open 21 Mar.–30 Sept.).

Taff Rivers Division.

Rhondda Fawr

Runs through the Rhondda Valley to the Taff at Pontypridd.

Trout fishing fair.

Tonypandy, Mid-Glam. 6½ m Treorchy to Porth.

T (DT Adv. tackle shops, Tonypandy, Porth, Penygraig, Treorchy and Ystrad. Fishery open 1 Mar.–30 Sept.).

Treherbert, Mid-Glam. 4 m Treorchy to Blaencwm.

T (DT Adv. J. Colliver, Tydraw Farm, Blaencwm).

Taff Rivers Division.

Rhydhir

Runs beside River Erch to sea at Pwllheli.

Salmon, and stocked with brown trout to 11 in.

Pwllheli, Gwynedd. 4 m as marked on permit.

T, S (WT Adv. tackle shop, Pwllheli).

Gwynedd Rivers Division.

Rhymney

Runs through Rhymney, Caerphilly, to the Bristol Channel near Cardiff.

Polluted in lower reaches. Offers trout and some coarse fishing.

Llanbradach, Mid-Glam. 1 m Wingfield public house to Pwllypant, right bank.

C (DT Adv. tackle shop, Cardiff Road, Caerphilly).

New Tredegar, Mid-Glam. Rhymney Bridge to New Tredegar.

T, C (Free fishing).

Taff Rivers Division.

Roe

Runs through Roewen to join the Conwy. Worth local inquiry for fishing chances.

Gwynedd Rivers Division.

Sawdde

Joins the River Towy at Llangadog.

Trout.

Llangadog, Dyfed. Most of water.

T (Free fishing, provided permission obtained from landowners).

West Wales Rivers Division.

Seiont

Rises on Snowdon and runs through a series of lakes at Llanberis and then on to the Menai Strait at Caernarvon.

Sea-trout run from June, with salmon slightly earlier. Fair trout fishing.

Llyn Padarn, Gwynedd. Pengilfach to field below rail tunnel, and several other stretches throughout course.

T, ST, S (DT Adv. tackle shops, shops, public houses and garages in area).

Tributaries: Arddu, Hwch.

Gwynedd Rivers Division.

Senni

Trout stream rising on the Brecon Beacons and running to the River Usk at Sennybridge.

Sennybridge, Powys. 200 yds stretch of right bank from River Usk.

T (DT Adv. W. J. Davies & Sons, drugstores, Sennybridge. L–3).

Usk Rivers Division.

Serw

One of the feeder streams of the Conwy, which it joins at Blaen-y-Coed.

Trout fishing.

Ysbyty Ifan, Gwynedd. 4½ m Blaen-y-Coed to Llyn Serw.

T (D T Adv. Voelas Arms, Pentrefoelas; Bryn Conwy Café, Ysbyty Ifan; Post Office, Ysbyty Ifan; or from National Trust, North Wales Area, Dinas, Betws-y-Coed. Fishery open 1 June– 31 July only; fly only, except in flood conditions).
Gwynedd Rivers Division.

Shropshire Union Canal
Parts of this giant canal system fall within the Welsh Water Authority area (see also entries under Severn-Trent and North-West Water Authority areas).

A reasonable standard of coarse fishing is maintained throughout, and the main line, together with the Llangollen and Montgomery branches, have many stretches controlled by the Shropshire Union Canal A A, offering ticket facilities. The same organization has water on the short Prees branch. For the most part the tickets are available at locks and from tackle shops in the area.
Llanymynech, Powys. Bridges 92–4, Montgomery branch.
C (D T on bank or from Dolphin public house, Llanymynech).

Sirhowy
Runs south through Tredegar from the Brecon Beacons to join the Ebbw near Risca.
Fair trout fishing, with regular restocking.
Newport, Gwent. 10 m with some gaps from Cwmfelinfach to Ebbw Bridge, Newport.
T (D T Adv. tackle shop, Tredegar Street, Risca, or from Ebbw and Sirhowy A A. Fly only in parts).
Pontllanfraith, Gwent. 1 m in area.
T (D T Adv. keeper, L. Wilcox, 17 Pengram Street, Glay-y-Nant, Pengam).
Tributary of Usk system.
Usk Rivers Division.

South Dulas
North-flowing tributary of the Dovey, joining in the middle reaches.
Trout, some salmon. Mostly private or

season-ticket. Some hotel water for guests.
Tributary of Dovey system.
Gwynedd Rivers Division.

Taf
Not to be confused with the River Taff in Glamorgan, the Taf rises on Mynydd Prescelly and runs through Whitland and St Clears to Carmarthen Bay.
Salmon, best in late season, and sea-trout from June on, with fair trout fishing.
St Clears, Dyfed. 1 m left bank from Venture Life Bridge.
T, S T, S (D T Adv. tackle shops in area and Post Office, Nantgaredig. Fishery open for salmon and sea-trout 10 Mar.– 7 Oct.; trout, 10 Mar.–30 Sept.).
Whitland, Dyfed. 4 m in area.
T, S (D T Adv. tackle shops in area).
Tributary: Dewi Fawr.
West Wales Rivers Division.

Taff
Running through Merthyr, Pontypridd and Cardiff to the Bristol Channel, the Taff has suffered greatly from pollution, which even after repeated efforts at cleaning the river and restocking still has an effect.
Some of the upper river has recovered, and from time to time sea-trout manage to swim through. Much of the river is not worth serious consideration.
Treharris, Mid-Glam. 4 m Pontygwaith to Abercynon.
T (D T Adv. Treharris A A. L–10. Fishery open 1 Mar.–30 Sept.).
Tributaries: Taff Bargoed, Thondda Fach, Rhondda Fawr.
Taff Rivers Division.

Taff Bargoed
Small tributary of Taff.
Trout fishing.
Bedlinog, Mid-Glam. 7 m from Taf-Merthyr Colliery to Cwmbargoed.
T (D T Adv. E. Jones, 52 Hilton Terrace, Bedlinog).
Taff Rivers Division.

Tarrell

Flows off the Brecon Beacons to join the Usk at Brecon.

Trout. Only known access season membership (Merthyr Tydfil A A, 2 Wesley Close, Dowlais, Merthyr Tydfil).

Usk Rivers Division.

Tawe

Rises to the south of Fforest Ffawr and runs through the Swansea Valley to Swansea.

Trout fishing, with salmon and sea-trout returning following pollution clearance work in the lower river.

Swansea, W Glam. Most of water.

T, ST, S (D T Adv. tackle shops in area. Fishery open 10 Mar.–30 Sept.).

Gower Rivers Division.

Teifi

Runs through Tregaron, Lampeter, Llandyssul and Newcastle Emlyn to Cardigan.

Excellent trout fishing, especially in the Tregaron stretches, where salmon can also be good, with plenty of water in the river. Sea-trout runs rarely reach this high. There is a spring run of salmon, with summer fish running from July.

Lampeter, Dyfed. 740 yds left bank above Lampeter Bridge on Cwmann–Cellan road.

T, S (D T Adv. Mr J. H. Jones, Ffos-y-Ffin Farm, Cellan, Lampeter).

Llandyssul, Dyfed. Total of 14 beats in area – Pentre Farm, Llety Twppa, Cellan Fishery, Lampeter Waters, Cefnbryn Waters, Dolgwm Mill Waters, Maesisaf Waters, Brynhawk Waters, Church Farm Fishery, Mackwith Castle Waters, Porth Hotel Waters, Tyrdref Waters, Cilgwyn Estate Waters and Penbeili Fishing.

T, S (WT only Adv. Mr A. Jones, Shop-y-Jones, Llandyssul).

Llanybyther, Dyfed. 3 beats in area.

T, S (D T Adv. friends of members only, Llanybyther A A, Mr D. Jones, Lloyds Bank Ltd, Llanybyther).

Llanybyther, Dyfed. 1¼ m right bank above Llanybyther Bridge.

S (D T Adv. Highmead Hotel, Llanybyther).

West Wales Rivers Division.

Teigl

Short tributary of the Dwyryd.

Trout fishing.

Ffestiniog, Gwynedd. Whole water.

T (D T Adv. tackle shops in area).

Gwynedd Rivers Division.

Tennant Canal

Links Aberdulais with Swansea.

Fair stocks of coarse fish.

Aberdulais, W Glam. Whole water.

C (D T Adv. from Astley Samuel Leeder & Son, 49 Mansell Street, Swansea).

Gower Rivers Division.

Towy (Tywi)

One of the best game rivers of South-West Wales, the Towy rises in the Towy Forest and runs through a long valley, starting at Llandovery, to Carmarthen and the sea.

Salmon and sea-trout reach the middle stretches around Llandovery towards the end of the season but are present from mid-summer. Lower, the fish are earlier and tend to be bigger, with sea-trout of 10 lb and more (record: 16 lb 2 oz). The trout fishing is fair throughout the course.

Carmarthen, Dyfed. 2 long stretches in area.

T, ST, S (WT Adv. tackle shops in Carmarthen, Llandeilo, Llanelli, or Post Office, Nantgaredig. Season open for salmon and sea-trout 10 Mar.–7 Oct.; trout, 10 Mar.–30 Sept.).

Goldengrove, Dyfed. 8 m from Llandeilo Bridge to Glantowy footbridge.

T, ST, S (D T Adv. Cooke and Arkwright, Estate Office, Llangathen. L–10).

Llandeilo, Dyfed. 8 m from Llandeilo to Manordeilo.

T, ST (D T Adv. tackle shop, Llandeilo or Tregeyb Arms, Ffairfach, Llandeilo L–4. Fishery open 10 Mar.–7 Oct.).

Llandovery, Dyfed. ½ m from Chair Bridge upstream.

T, ST, S (D T Adv. E. Thomas, Tonn
Farm, Llandovery).
Llangadog, Dyfed. 1 m stretch.
T, ST, S (D T Adv. Black Lion Hotel,
Llangadog).
Pontargothi, Dyfed. 15 m Glantowy to
Bermalais.
T, ST, S (D T Adv. Cresselly Arms,
Pontargothi).
Tributaries: Bran, Cennen, Cothi,
Dulais, Gwili, Sawdde, Twrch.
West Wales Rivers Division.

Trothy
Rises near Grosmont and runs through
Skenfrith to join the Wye system below
Monmouth.
Most of the water is preserved.
Monmouth, Gwent. 5 m stretch of left
bank.
T, C (D T Adv. Monmouth and Dist.
A S. Fishery open for trout 1 Apr.–30
Sept.; coarse fish, 1 Oct.–27 Jan.).
Wye Rivers Division.

Tryweryn
Runs from Cwm Prysor Lake to feed Llyn
Celwyn, then running on to join Dee near
Bala Lake. No known openings for visit-
ing anglers.
Dee and Clwyd Rivers Division.

Twrch
A short feeder of the Cothi, which it joins
at Pumpsaint to form the Towy system.
No known openings for visiting anglers.
West Wales Rivers Division.

Twymyn
Rises near Dylife and runs to join the
River Dovey at Tafolwern.
Holds salmon, sea-trout and trout,
with some coarse fish.
Llanbrynmair, Powys. 8 m from
Talerddig to Cemmaes Road Village.
T, ST, S, C (D T Adv. D. Evans Service
Station, Cemmaes Road).
Gwynedd Rivers Division.

Tywi
See Towey, above.

Usk
One of the most prolific Welsh salmon

rivers, the Usk starts at Usk Reservoir
and runs through Sennybridge and
Brecon, then through Crickhowell and
Abergavenny to the Bristol Channel near
Newport.
With good rains salmon move to
Abergavenny and above early in the season, their size averaging around 10 lb,
but with the occasional 20-pounder
and a few fish of 30 lb or more. There
is a sea-trout run, but these are not so
prolific as the salmon. Fair brown trout
fishing throughout, with some big fish
where restocking takes place. The Usk
also carries a fair head of coarse fish,
notably roach and dace, the latter running to 1 lb (rumour has it that trout
anglers have caught several in excess of
the current British dace record, only to
discard them). Coarse fishing on the river
is often restricted to the winter.
Abergavenny, Gwent. Town Council
water from Llanfoist Bridge.
T, S (D T Adv. P M Tackle, Monk
Street, Abergavenny, or Bridge Inn,
Llanfoist. Trout fly only. Fishery open
for salmon 15 Feb.–30 Sept.; trout, 15
Mar.–30 Sept.).
Brecon, Powys. ½ m Llanfraes Bridge
to boathouse.
T, S (D T Adv. tackle shops, Brecon.
Fishery open for salmon 1 Feb.–15
Oct.; trout, 1 Mar.–30 Sept.).
Crickhowell, Powys. 1¾ m Danypark
to Glanusk.
T, S (D T Adv. Vine Tree public
house, Legar, Llangattock).
Crickhowell, Powys. 2 m plus on left
bank near Crickhowell.
T, S (D T Adv. Gliffaes Country House
Hotel, Crickhowell. Priority for hotel
guests. Fishery open for salmon 15
Feb.–30 Sept.; trout, 15 Mar.–30
Sept.).
Crickhowell, Powys. ½ m right bank.
T, S (D T Adv. Bell Hotel, Glan-
grwyney. L–4).
Sennybridge, Powys. 1 m from
Sennybridge to Gibraltar Wood end,
on right bank, and 1 m left bank from
Llwynce Bridge to Cilieni River.
T, S (D T Adv. W. J. Davies & Sons,
drugstores, Sennybridge. L–9).

Usk, Gwent. 2 m Usk Town Water.

T (DT Adv. Sweets Tackle, Porthy-carne Street, Usk. Fly only. Fishery open 15 Mar.–30 Sept.).

Usk, Gwent. Nearly 1 m near town.

T, S, C (DT Adv. L. H. Marshall, surveyor and land agent, 2 Bridge Street, Usk. L–2).

Usk, Gwent. 350 yds left bank downstream of Chainbridge.

T, C (DT Adv. Bridge Inn, Chainbridge, Usk. L–2).

Tributaries of Usk: Afon Llwyd, Ebbw Fach, Ebbw Fawr, Honddu, Nant Bran, Olway Brook, Senni, Sirhowy, Tarrell, Yscir.

Usk Rivers Division.

Wen

Runs off the Lleyn Peninsula to Cardigan Bay near Pwllheli.

Fair trout fishing, with some sea-trout. Farms in area worth inquiry.

Gwynned Rivers Division.

Wheeler

Tributary of the Clwyd joining the main river near Bodfari. No known openings for visiting anglers.

Dee and Clwyd Rivers Division.

Wnion

Runs through Bont Newydd and joins the River Mawddach below Dolgellau.

Fair trout fishing with runs of sea-trout and some salmon.

Dolgellau, Gwynedd. 5 m in area as outlined on permit.

T, S (DT Adv. tackle shop, Dolgellau). Gwynedd Rivers Division.

Worthenbury Brook

Runs by Worthenbury to join the River Dee above Farndon.

Coarse fish with some trout.

Worthenbury, Clwyd. 1 m from Brook Farm footbridge to River Dee.

C, T (DT Adv. Northern AA or on bank).

Dee and Clwyd Rivers Division.

Wye

Rises on Plynlimon to run through Rhayader, Builth Wells, Hay, Hereford, Ross and Monmouth to Chepstow and the Severn estuary.

Without a doubt the most famous salmon river of England and Wales, both for size and numbers of fish. The record for the water is just $\frac{1}{2}$ lb short of 60 lb, while every year the figures of fish taken range between 4000 and 8000. By and large the spring fish are biggest, although those of the summer run are around 10 lb. Late season fish are smaller. While sea-trout are caught in the Wye, they are not present in great numbers. Besides salmon the trout fishing is good, and the Wye is also a noted coarse water, producing large chub, dace and pike from time to time. Match records top 80 lb. Coarse fishing takes second place to the game fishing, and there are restrictions on the times allowed to fish for coarse fish and baits permitted. It would be fair to say that good salmon fishing on this river is likely to be expensive and may well be booked for some time ahead. Birmingham AA holds many stretches on the river.

Bredwardine, Hereford and Worcs. 8 m Turner's Boat to below Moccas Toll Bridge.

C, T, S (DT Adv. Red Lion Hotel, Bredwardine).

Brockweir, Gwent. 2¼ m to Llandogo.

C (DT Adv. keeper, Rock Cottage, Tintern).

Builth Wells, Powys. 3 m stretch.

C, T, S (DT Adv. Pencerrig Country Hotel, Builth Wells. Fly only in parts).

Builth Wells, Powys. Stretch in area.

T, S (DT Adv. Cammarch Hotel, Llangammarch Wells. L–2).

Builth Wells, Powys. 1½ m in area.

C, T, S (WT or 3-day Adv., tackle shop, High Street, Builth Wells).

Clifford, Hereford and Worcs. 2 m toll bridge to Winforton.

S (DT Adv. The Agent, Clifford Fishery, Whitney Court Estate Office, Whitney-on-Wye. L–3).

Fownhope, Hereford and Worcs. 1¼ m left bank from Lugg junction to below Holme Lacey.

C, T, S (DT, WT Adv. Perkins Tackle, Commercial Road, Hereford, or Hattons, St Owen Street, Hereford. No Sunday tickets 26 Oct.–14 Mar.).

Glasbury-on-Wye, Powys. 2 m stretch of right bank, plus 2 m at Hay.
C (DT Adv. Treble Hill Cottage, Glasbury-on-Wye. Fishery open 1 Oct.–24 Jan.).

Hay, Powys. 1¾ m right bank Hay Castle Water, and 1¼ m left bank Clypo Court Water.
C, T, S (DT Adv. keeper, Poolpardon Cottage, Clifford, near Hereford.

Hay, Powys. 300 yds right bank Hay Bridge to brook.
C, T, S (DT Adv. Grant's Tackle, Castle Street, Hay).

Hay, Powys. ¾ m right bank below Town free water.
C, T, S (DT Adv. Glanwye, Clifford Road, Hay).

Hay, Powys. 200 yds right bank below Hay Bridge. Town Water.
C, T, S (Free fishing).

Hereford, Hereford and Worcs. 1 m left bank from Eign to point above Carrotts Water (Field Farm Fishery).
C, T, S (DT, WT Adv. tackle shops, Commercial Road and St Owen Street, Hereford. No Sunday tickets 26 Oct.–14 Mar.).

Hereford, Hereford and Worcs. 4 m from Hereford to Eign.
C, T, S (DT, WT Adv. tackle shops, Commercial Road and St Owen Street, Hereford. No Sunday tickets 26 Oct.–14 Mar.).

Kerne Bridge, Hereford and Worcs. 3 m stretch.
C, S (DT Adv. Castle View Hotel, Kerne Bridge).

Llandogo, Gwent. 3 m Bigsweir Fishery Llandogo Church to Whitebrook.
C (DT Adv. 1 Oct.–31 Dec. only, Adv. J. Jones, The Rock, Tintern).

Llangurig, Powys. 8½ m Clochfaen Estate Water.
T, S (DT L–6, WT L–3, weekend ticket L–4; all Adv. from Llansevern Arms, Llangurig. Fly only).

Llangurig, Powys. 4 m Llangurig to Dernal.
T, S (DT Adv. Blue Bell Hotel, Llangurig. Fly only).

Llanwrthwl, Powys. 1200 yds left bank from 150 yds below Llanwrthwl Bridge to Doldowlod.
T, S (DT Adv. not Saturday or Sunday from Vulcan Inn, Llanwrthwl. Fly only).

Monmouth, Gwent. ½ m from Wye Bridge, Monmouth, to Trothy junction.
C (DT Adv. Monmouth and Dist. A S. L–2 rods. Fishery open 1 Oct.–27 Jan.).

Rhayader, Powys. 4 m at Rhayader.
T (DT, WT, tackle shop, West Street, Rhayader. Fly only at certain periods).

Ross-on-Wye, Hereford and Worcs. ½ m left bank Town Water, from Wilton Bridge to boathouse.
C, T, S (DT on bank or from tackle shop, Ross).

Ross-on-Wye, Hereford and Worcs. ½ m left bank from Awkward Stile to boathouse.
C, T (WT Adv. tackle shop, Ross. Open Apr. to Sept. only).

Tintern, Gwent. 1¼ m Brockweir Bridge to Tintern Abbey.
C (DT Adv. J. Jones, The Rock, Tintern).

Whitney-on-Wye, Hereford and Worcs. Stretch at inn.
C (DT Adv. Boat Inn, Whitney-on-Wye).

Wye tributaries: Arrow, Bach Howey, Chwefri, Dulas, Elan, Frome (Hereford), Gammarch, Hindwell Book, Honddu, Irfon, Ithon, Llynfi, Lugg, Monnow, Trothy.
Wye Rivers Division.

Wygyr
Rises in the northern part of Anglesey and runs to Cemaes Bay.
Fair trout fishing.

Llanfechell, Anglesey. 1½ m Tai Hen to Cemaes Bay.
T (DT Adv. Cefni Glas Inn, Llanfechell. Fly only. No Sunday fishing. Open 1 Mar.–30 Sept.).

Wyre

Small water running to the sea north of Aberaeron.

Trout, some sea-trout. No known ticket water. Farms in area worth an inquiry.

West Wales Rivers Division.

Yscir

Runs from Pont-faen to the River Usk at Aberyscir.

Trout fishing, but no known openings for visiting anglers.

Usk Rivers Division.

Ysgethin

Rises on Diffwys to feed Llyn Bodlyn, after which it runs to Tal-y-Bont and Cardigan Bay.

Trout and char.

Tal-y-Bont, Gwynedd. Entire water.

T (Free fishing).

Gwynedd Rivers Division.

Ystrad

Tributary of the Clwyd flowing from Denbeigh. Mostly private, with no known ticket opportunities.

Dee and Clwyd Rivers Division.

Ystumiau

Rises on Moel Siabod and runs to join the Lledr at Dolwyddelan.

Trout fishing.

Dolwyddelan, Gwynedd. 2 m on Forestry Commission estate.

T (DT Adv. Forestry Commission Office, Dolwyddelan).

Tributary of Conwy system.

Gwynedd Rivers Division

Ystwyth

Rises on Mynydd Bach and flows to Aberystwyth, to which it gives its name, and the sea.

Fair trout fishing, with runs of sea-trout and salmon.

Aberystwyth, Dyfed. 1 m Gosen Bridge to harbour.

T, ST, S (DT Adv. tackle shops, Queen Street and North Parade, Aberystwyth).

Llanilar, Dyfed. 10 m Llanfarian to Grogwynion Bridge, except where marked.

T, ST, S (DT Adv. J. Rosser, Aberystwyth, Royal Oak public house at Llanfarian, post offices at Crosswood and Llanilar, or Morfa Bychan caravan site).

West Wales Rivers Division.

Four

Welsh Still Waters

Clwyd

Acton Park Lake, Wrexham.
  C (Free fishing).
Aled Isaf, Llansannan.
  C (DT from keeper or Welsh WA, Plastirion, 91 Russell Road, Rhyl, Clwyd).
Alwen Reservoir, Cerrig-y-Drudion.
  ● T in part, C in part (DT Adv. ticket office. Open for trout 1 Mar.–30 Sept.; coarse, 16 June–14 Mar. Top section fly only for trout; rest spinner and bait fishing allowed for T and C).
Cambrian Fishery, Afonwen.
  ● T (DT Adv. Cambrian Fishery; tel. Caerwys 589. Fly only. Open 14 Mar.–28 Nov. Fish average over 1½ lb, some big fish).
Cilcain Fisheries, Cilcain.
  ● T (DT Adv. A. E. Williams, 9 Maes Cilan, Cilcain. Fly only. L–3).
Dolwen and Plas Uchaf reservoirs, Llannefydd.
  T (DT Adv. Welsh WA, Plastirion, 91 Russell Road, Rhyl. B available Dolwen. Both open 1 Mar.–30 Sept. L–6 Dolwen, 3 Plas Uchaf).
Llyn Aled, Llansannan.
  C (DT from keeper or Welsh WA, Plastirion, 91 Russell Road, Rhyl).
Llyn-y-Cawg, Llanrhaeadr-ym-Mochnant.
  T (Free fishing).
Penycae Reservoir, Penycae.
  ● T (DT Adv. keeper or Wrexham and Denbeighshire Water Co., 21 Egerton Street, Wrexham. Fly only; give 24 hours' notice).
Seven Springs Trout Fishery, Caerwys.
  ● T (DT Adv. A. D. Main, grocers, Water Street, Caerwys. Fly only.
L–4. B available. Open 1 Apr.–31 Oct.).
Trap Pool, Buckley.
  C (DT from keeper. Good mixed coarse fishing).

Dyfed

Berwen Lake, Tregaron.
  ● T (DT Adv. Barclays Bank, The Square, Tregaron. Fly only. No Sunday fishing).
Bosherton Ponds, Stackpole.
  C (DT Adv. tackle shops, Pembroke, Pembroke Dock and Tenby. Excellent tench fishing, plus big pike).
Bray's Pool, Aberystwyth.
  T (DT Adv. tackle shops, Aberystwyth).
Cwmrheidol Reservoir, Capel Bangor.
  T, ST, S (DT Adv. Rosser, tackle, Queen Street, Aberystwyth. One B available from 1 June. One of the few waters here taking salmon and sea-trout).
Eisteddla Curig Pool, Ponterwyd.
  T (DT Adv. tackle shops, Aberystwyth. B available).
Llanllawddog Lake, Carmarthen.
  ● T (DT Adv. Home Farm, Llanllawddog. Fly only. Open 10 Mar.–30 Sept. L–7. Browns, rainbows, average 1½ lb).
Lleidi Reservoirs, Llanelli.
  ● T in part, rest T other methods (DT Adv. ticket machine at entrance or from tackle shop, Llanelli. Upper reservoir fly only, browns and rainbows. Other methods permitted on lower reservoir. Open 1 Apr.–30 Sept.).

Llyn Blaenmelindwr, Aberystwyth.
T (DT Adv. tackle shops, Aberystwyth. B available).

Llyn Craig-y-Pistyll, Aberystwyth.
T (DT Adv. tackle shops, Aberystwyth).

Llyn Frongoch, Aberystwyth.
● T (DT Adv. tackle shops, Aberystwyth. B available).

Llyn Llgad Rheidol, Aberystwyth.
T (DT Adv. tackle shops, Aberystwyth).

Llyn Pendam, Aberystwyth.
T (DT Adv. tackle shops, Aberystwyth).

Llyn Rhosgoch, Aberystwyth.
● T (DT Adv. tackle shops, Aberystwyth).

Llyn Syfydrin, Aberystwyth.
● T (DT Adv. tackle shops, Aberystwyth. B available).

Llyn yr Oefa, Aberystwyth.
T (DT Adv. Rosser, tackle, Queen Street, Aberystwyth, or Sports Centre, North Parade, Aberystwyth).

Llys-y-Fran Reservoir, Llys-y-Fran.
T (DT Adv. ticket booth or Pembrokeshire Water Unit, Meyler House, Thomas Green, Haverfordwest. B available. Open 1 Apr.–30 Sept. Stocked browns, rainbows).

Newcastle Emlyn Trout Lake, Newcastle Emlyn.
● T (DT Adv. Emlyn Arms Hotel, Newcastle Emlyn. Fly only).

Prescelly Reservoir (*Rosebush Reservoir*), Maenclochog.
● T (DT Adv. from keeper. Fly only. Open 1 Apr.–30 Sept. B available).

Rheidol Fishery, Ponterwyd.
● T (DT Adv. tackle shops, Aberystwyth and Borth, Evans Garage, Ponterwyd, or CEGB, Bron Heulog, Conwy Road, Llandudno Junction, Gwynedd. Dinas and Nant-y-Moch reservoirs, Dinas providing bigger fish, with B available. Fly only).

Teify Pools, Strata Florida.
● T (DT Adv. tackle shops, Tregaron or Pontrhydfendigaid, or from Welsh WA, 19 Penyfai Lane, Llanelli. Fly

only. Open 1 Apr.–30 Sept. Now stocked with rainbows in addition to browns).

West Orielton Pool, Pembroke.
C (DT Adv. from keeper or David Mason, West Orielton, near Pembroke. Good tench catches).

Glamorgan, Mid

Caerphilly Castle Lakes, Caerphilly.
C (DT Adv. Mon.–Fri. only, Howell's, tackle, Cardiff Road, Caerphilly. No Sunday fishing. Good tench and bream water).

Castell Nos Reservoir, Maerdy.
● T (DT Adv. 7 Richard Street or 37 North Terrace, Maerdy. Fly only. Open 21 Mar.–30 Sept.).

Cwm Taf Fawr Reservoirs, Merthyr Tydfil.
● T in part, T other methods (DT Adv. ticket office, Llwyn-on-Water treatment works, Merthyr Tydfil. Open 1 Apr.–30 Sept. Two reservoirs fly only, one spinning allowed).

Cyfartha Park Lakes, Merthyr Tydfil.
C (DT Adv. from keeper or tackle shop, Merthyr).

Darren Lake, Ferndale.
C (DT from park keeper or tackle shop, Ferndale).

Fochriw Feeder Pool, Fochriw.
C (DT Adv. Post Office, Fochriw, or Rising Sun, Fochriw).

Kenfig Pool, Kenfig.
C, T (DT Adv. from keeper, tackle shop, Kenfig, Prince of Wales Hotel, Kenfig, or Kenfig Hill and Dist. AA. Reputed to hold huge tench, the water is, however, difficult to fish. No trout fishing 30 Sept.–1 Mar.).

Llwest Wen Reservoir, Maerdy.
● T (DT Adv. 7 Richard Street or 37 North Terrace, Maerdy. Open 1 Mar.–30 Sept. Fly only).

Llyn Fawr Reservoir, Treherbert.
● T (DT Adv. Tydraw Farm, Blaencwm. Fly only).

Newtown Pond, Bute Town.
C (DT Adv. Post Office, Middle Row, Bute Town).

Penywern Pond, Merthyr Tydfil.
C, T (D T from keeper or tackle shop, Merthyr).
Rhos-Las-Pond, Bute Town.
C (D T Adv. Post Office, Bute Town).
Taf Fechan Reservoirs, Merthyr Tydfil.
● T in part, T (D T Adv. ticket office or Welsh W A, Pentwyn Road, Nelson, Mid-Glam. Open 21 Mar.–30 Sept. Big cannibal browns have come from some of these waters. Pentwyn and Upper and Lower Neuadd offer trout fishing; Ponsticill offers trout and coarse. The former are fly only).
Tynywawn Pond, Bedlinog.
T, C (D T Adv. from keeper).

Glamorgan, South

Llanishen Reservoir, Cardiff.
● T (D T Adv. keeper at lodge or Water Engineer, Crwys House, 33 Crywys Road, Cardiff. Fly only. Open 1 Apr.–30 Sept.).
Lisvane Reservoir, Cardiff.
● T (D T Adv. Llanishen Reservoir Lodge or as Llanishen, above. Open 1 Apr.–30 Sept. Fly only).

Glamorgan, West

Eglwys Nunydd Reservoir, Port Talbot.
● T (D T Adv. B S C Steelworks entrance, Port Talbot. Fly only. Open 1 Mar.–30 Sept. Well-stocked water, fish averaging 1½ lb).
Glyn Clydach Pond, Neath.
C (D T Adv. Neath and Dulais A C).

Gwent

Cefn Golau Pond, Tredegar.
C (D T Adv. from keeper, 119 Gwent Way, Tredegar).
Cwmbran Boating Lake, Cwmbran.
C (D T Adv. ticket office. B available. L–20).
Glyn Pond, Pontypool.
T (D T Adv. tackle shop, Pontypool).
Liswerry Pond, Newport.
C (D T Adv. tackle shop, Newport).

Llandegfedd Reservoir, Pontypool.
● T (D T Adv. ticket machine or ticket office. Fly only. Open 15 Apr.–14 Oct. B, M B available. Said to have recovered well from fish disease, fish now averaging 1½ lb).
Machine Pond, Brynmawr.
C (D T Adv. tackle shops, Brynmawr and Ebbw Vale).
Tredegar House Lake, Newport.
C (D T Adv. from keeper, Tredegar House. B available).
Wentwood Reservoir, Newport.
● T (D T Adv. Reservoir Superintendent. Fly only. Open 4 Apr.–14 Oct. B available. Fish average under 1 lb, some bigger).
Ynysfro Reservoirs, Newport.
● T (D T Adv. Reservoir Superintendent. Fly only. Open 4 Apr.–14 Oct. Upper reservoir stocked rainbows; lower browns).

Gwynedd

Arran Lake, Dolgellau.
T (Free fishing).
Bala Lake (*Llyn Tegid*), Bala.
T, S, C and gwyniad (D T Adv. ticket office, Snowdonia National Park, Bala, or W. E. Pugh, tackle, High Street, Bala. Trout can run very big, and salmon are very occasionally taken. Of the coarse fish, roach, perch and pike predominate, with some big fish. The water also holds the rare gwyniad whitefish. The biggest natural still water in Wales).
Barlwyd Lake, Blaenau Ffestiniog.
T (D T Adv. tackle shop, Blaenau Ffestiniog. Well stocked and worth long walk).
Coedty Reservoir, Dolgarrog.
● T in part (D T Adv. for weekends and public holidays only, from Dolgarrog F C. Fly only, with small section where worm and spinning allowed at certain times).
Colwlyd, Dulyn and Melynllyn lakes, Bethesda.
● T (Free fishing only with prior permit

from Welsh WA, Conwy Valley Water Division, Colwyn Bay. Fly only).

Craigddrwg, Dywarshen Lake, Du Lake, Eiddewfach Lake, Eiddew-Mawr Lake, Harlech.
C (Free fishing).

Cwm Corsiog, Blaenau Ffestiniog.
T (DT Adv. tackle shop, Blaenau Ffestiniog. Hard to reach but some good fish).

Cwm Foel, Blaenau Ffestionig.
T (DT Adv. tackle shop, Blaenau Ffestiniog. Fish to 2 lb).

Cwmorthin, Blaenau Ffestiniog.
T (DT Adv. tackle shop, Blaenau Ffestiniog. Fish rather small on whole. B available).

Cwm Prysor Lake, Trawsfynydd.
● T (DT Adv. tackle shops, Bala. Fly only Mar.–Oct.).

Cwmystradllyn Reservoir, Porthmadog.
T (DT Adv. at water treatment works. Open 1 Apr.–30 Sept.).

Cyri Lake, Dolgellau.
T (Free fishing).

Dinas Lake, Beddgelert.
T, ST, S (DT Adv. Post Office, Beddgelert).

Dulbach Lake, Blaenau Ffestiniog.
T (DT Adv. tackle shop, Blaenau Ffestiniog. Trout smallish, water hard to reach).

Elsi Lake, Betws-y-Coed.
T (DT Adv. Gwydyr Hotel, Betws-y-Coed).

Gamallt Lakes, Llan Ffestiniog.
T (DT Adv. tackle shops in area. Very high and involve a goodish walk, fish up to 1 lb).

Glowwlyn Lake, Llanbedr.
T (DT Adv. Cwm-Yr Afon Farm, Llanbedr. Goodish walk).

Goddionduon Lake, Betws-y-Coed.
● T (DT Adv. Tan-Lan Restaurant, Betws-y-Coed. Fly only. B available. Trout smallish).

Idwal Lake, Bethesda.
T (DT Adv. Caxton House or T. Jones, High Street, Bethesda.).

Llanberis Lake, Llanberis.
T, S and char (DT Adv. tackle shop, Llanberis, or Railway Inn, Cwm-y-Glo. B available).

Llynaw Diwaunedd, Pen-y-Gwyrd.
T (Free fishing).

Llyn Bodlyn, Tal-y-Bont.
T, char (Free fishing).

Llyn Bychan, Betws-y-Coed.
● T (DT Adv. Tan-Lan Restaurant, Betws-y-Coed. Smallish fish).

Llyn Celyn, Bala.
T (DT Adv. tackle shops, Bala, or Post Office, Frongoch, Bala. Open 1 Apr.–30 Sept. Well stocked).

Llyn Crafnant, Trefriw.
T (DT Adv. from lakeside café. Trout to 1 lb. B available).

Llyn Cwellyn, Caernarvon.
T, ST, S (DT Adv. tackle shops, post offices and garages in area).

Llyn Cynwch, Dolgellau.
T (DT Adv. tackle shop, Dolgellau).

Llyn Gadair, Caernarvon.
T (DT Adv. tackle shops, post offices etc. in area).

Llyn Padern, Llanberis.
T, ST, S (DT Adv. tackle shops, post offices etc. in area).

Llyn Perfeddau, Llanbedr.
T (Free fishing).

Llyn-y-Gadair, Dolgellau.
T (Free fishing).

Llyn-yr-Gafr, Dolgellau.
T (Free fishing).

Manod Lake, Blaenau Ffestiniog.
T (DT Adv. tackle shop, Blaenau Ffestiniog).

Morwynion Lake, Llan Ffestiniog.
T (DT Adv. tackle shops in area. B available. Trout small).

Siabod Lake, Betws-y-Coed.
T (DT Adv. Gwydyr Hotel, Betws-y-Coed).

Tan-y-Grisiau Reservoir, Blaenau Ffestiniog.
T (DT Adv. Reception Centre, Ffestiniog Power Station, or tackle shops, stores and some hotels in area. Holds rainbows only and has produced a 10 lb 7 oz fish).

Trawsfynydd Lake, Trawsfynydd.
T (DT Adv. tackle shop, Trawsfynydd. Well stocked, fish averaging 1 lb. B,

M B available. Open 1 Feb.–30 Sept.).

Gwynedd, Anglesey

Cefni Reservoir, Llangefni.
● T (D T Adv. G. Daven, Rostrehwfa, Llangefni. Fly only. Average fish about 1 lb).

Dinas Lake, Valley.
C (Free fishing with permission from owner).

Geirian Lakes, Llanfechell.
● T (D T Adv. tel. Cemaes Bay 242. Fly only. Open 1 Mar.–30 Sept. B available. Some big fish).

Llyn Alaw, Llanerchymedd.
● T in part (D T Adv. from ticket office. Fly only north shore; worm and spinner allowed other banks. Open 1 Apr.–30 Sept. Fish average about 1 lb, but there are much bigger fish. B, M B available).

Llyn Coron, Aberffraw.
● T, S T (D T Adv. from keeper. Fly only. Trout run over 1 lb, and there are some sea-trout).

Llyn Hafodol, Rhosgoch.
● T, S T (D T Adv. tel. Cemaes Bay 245. Fly only. Open 1 Apr.–30 Sept. Trout averaging 1 lb, some sea-trout. B available).

Maelog Lake, Rhosneigr.
T, C (D T Adv. Maelog Lake Hotel).

Mynydd Badafon Lake, Mynydd.
C (Free fishing).

Penryn Lake, Dinas.
C (Free fishing with permission from bordering farms).

Traffwll Reservoir, Dinas.
C (Free fishing with permission from bordering farms).

Powys

Crai Reservoir, Sennybridge.
● T (D T Adv. from keeper. Fly only. L–6).

Cwm Taf Fawr Reservoirs, Brecon.
T (D T Adv. from reservoir keepers. Stocked browns and rainbows; fish on the whole small).

Dol-y-Gaer Reservoir, Ponsticill.
T (D T Adv. at filter house. Open 21 Mar.–30 Sept. Holds rainbows and browns).

Elan Valley Lakes, Rhayader.
● T except one water (D T Adv. ticket office, or Welsh W A, Area Estate Office, Elan Vallay, near Rhayader, Powys. Most of the lakes complex holds native browns averaging ½ lb, and some are stocked with rainbows. All fly only, except Craig Goch. Open 1 Mar.–30 Sept., except Caban Goch, Garreg Ddu and Pen-y-Garreg, usually opening Good Friday).

Fachwen Pool, Newtown.
● T (D T Adv. H. L. Bebb, tackle, 15 Short Bridge Street, Newtown, or from Grades Inn, Newtown. Open 1 Apr. Fly only. Severn-Trent W A licence needed).

Lake Vyrnwy, near Oswestry.
● T (See under English Still Waters, Shropshire).

Llangorse Lake, Llangorse.
C (D T Adv. tackle shop, Llangorse. B available. A good coarse fishery, with specimen perch, bream and roach. Some big pike).

Llyn Clywedog, Llanidloes.
● T (D T Adv. ticket office or tackle shops, Llanidloes and Welshpool. Fly only. Open 18 Mar.–15 Oct. Well-stocked water holding browns and rainbows. Severn-Trent W A licence needed).

Llyn Gwyn, Rhayader.
● T (D T Adv. tackle shop, Rhayader, or Nantymynach Farm, near Rake. Fly only. Open 1 Mar.–30 Sept.).

Llyn Tarw, Caersws.
● T (D T Adv. H. L. Bebb, tackle, 15 Short Bridge Street, Newtown. Fly only. L–12. Water also stocked with brook trout. Severn-Trent W A licence needed).

Maesmawr Pool, Welshpool.
C (D T Adv. keeper, Maesmawr Hall. L–12. Severn-Trent W A licence needed).

Talybont Reservoir, Talybont-on-Usk.
● T (D T Adv. ticket office. Fly only. Open 1 Apr.–14 Oct. B available).

Usk Reservoir, Trecastle.
   ● T in part (D T Adv. ticket machine. A fly-only zone, open 4 Apr.–14 Oct. M B available).

Ystradfellte Reservoir, Ystradfellte.
   ● T (D T Adv. ticket machine at Llwy-non Reservoir filter house, Merthyr Tydfil, or from keeper. Fly only. Open 21 Mar.–30 Sept.).

Five

The Isle of Man (rivers and lakes)

Freshwater fishing within the Isle of Man is controlled by the Isle of Man Board of Agriculture and Fisheries (see page 21). The island offers much in the way of fishing, with some salmon and sea-trout waters, although coarse fishing is rare. There is some preserved water, but many of the minor trout rivers are free, with permission from farmers and landowners.

Rivers

Ballaugh
Rises in hills west of Snaefel and runs to Ballaugh and then the Irish Sea. A small water, it contains a fair head of trout. Inquiries to farmers and landowners.

Colby
Short water running off Colby Glen to the sea near Port St Mary. Trout. Inquiries to farms.

Cornaa
Rises on Snaefel and runs east to the sea at Port Cornaa. Trout, with fair runs of salmon and sea-trout in the lower reaches. Mostly free fishing.

Dalby
Runs through Glen Maye and Dalby to the sea south of Peel. Trout. Inquiries to farmers.

Dhoo
Runs to Quarterbridge to meet the Glass and form the River Douglas. Mainly trout.

Union Mills. 1 m from Braddan Bridge to Snugborough.
T (Visitors' season ticket, Adv. from Angling Centre, Victoria Street, Douglas).
Tributary of Douglas.

Douglas
Formed at the meeting of the rivers Dhoo and Glass at Quarterbridge and runs through Crosby and the Baldwin Valley.
Trout, salmon. Salmon best late season.
Douglas. Parts of river.
T, S (Visitors' season ticket, Angling Centre, Victoria Street, Douglas).

Glass
Meets with the Dhoo at Quarterbridge to form the Douglas.
Trout, some salmon. Parts of river preserved.
Douglas. 2 m Quarterbridge to Tromode.
T, S (Visitors' season ticket, Angling Centre, Victoria Street, Douglas).

Glen Moor Burn
Small water running through Kirk Michael to the west coast. Trout, free fishing.

Glen Rushen
Drains Glen Maye in the south-west. Trout. Inquiries to farmers; mostly free fishing.

Groudle
Drains Glen Groudle on the east coast to the sea at Onchan Head. Trout, inquiries to farmers.

Laxey

Runs a 5 m course to the sea near Laxey Head on the east coast. Trout, some salmon.
Laxey. Most of water.
T, S (D T Adv. Commissioner's Offices, New Road, Laxey).

Neb (Peel River)

Rises above Little London and collects the Foxdale River and the Glen Maye. Trout and some salmon. Salmon best late in season. Mostly free fishing.

Port Soderick

Drains Port Soderick Glen. Trout; mostly free with permission from farms.

Santon Burn

Small stream running through Santon. Trout, mostly free.

Silverburn

Rises above Ballasalla and runs to the sea at Castletown. Mostly trout, with stretch above Castletown best. Mostly free fishing.

Sulby

Rises on Snaefel and runs through the Sulby Glen to Ramsey. Trout, with fair autumn runs of salmon and sea-trout. Mostly free fishing.

Wyllin Burn

Drains Glen Wyllin, near Kirk Michael. Trout, free fishing.

Still Waters

Ballure Reservoir, Ramsey.
T (D T Adv. Filter Station, Ballure Glen, or Isle of Man Water and Gas Authority, 16 Circular Road, Douglas. Board of Agriculture and Fisheries permit water, well stocked).
Block Eary Reservoir, Sulby Village.
T (D T Adv. Filter Station, Sulby Glen, or as Ballure Reservoir, above. Stocked trout fishery).
Brickworks Quarry, Peel.
T (D T Adv. tackle shop, West View, Peel. Stocked trout fishery).
Clypse Reservoir, Onchan Village.
● T (D T Adv. Reservoir Attendant's House, Clypse, or as Ballure Reservoir, above. Stocked trout fishery. Fly only).
Cringle Reservoir, Foxdale.
T (D T Adv. Filter House, Ballaganne, or as Ballure Reservoir, above. Stocked trout fishery).
Lake Fisheries, St Johns.
T (D T Adv. ticket office at lake. Well-stocked trout lake complex).
Kerrow Dhoo Reservoir, Onchan Village.
● T (D T Adv. Reservoir Attendant's House, Clypse Reservoir, or as Ballure Reservoir, above. Well-stocked trout fishery. Fly only).
West Baldwin Reservoir, West Baldwin.
T (D T Adv. Reservoir Attendant's House or as Ballure Reservoir, above. Well-stocked trout fishery).

Six

Scottish Rivers and Canals

Fishing in Scotland conjures up a picture of, first and foremost, mighty and prolific salmon rivers. It should be well noted, though, that the famous among these, waters such as the Tay, the Tweed, Aberdeen's Dee and the Spey, have little to offer the angler with a spur-of-the-moment urge to fish, for much of the water is private, or booked a lengthy time ahead. It can also be extremely expensive. Having mentioned that, there are a huge number of rivers which do offer high-quality fishing on a ticket basis, with the added advantage that a day's fishing does not cost the earth.

Besides the superb salmon fishing Scotland offers sea-trout waters in abundance, and the trout is ubiquitous. Its least rewarding stocks are those of coarse fish, but they do occur in numbers in some waters, notably the Tay, the Tweed, the Forth and the Clyde, and rivers of the Dumfries and Galloway area. Roach and chub are the main species, with perch extending beyond the range of these two species, but generally of poorer size than in English waters. There are pike too, those in some of the lochs growing to great size. Coarse fishing in Scotland is always of secondary importance to game fishing, and often where coarse fish are present they are required to be removed from the water as vermin.

Scotland's fishing regulations differ from those of the rest of Britain. There are no rod licence requirements, for a start, and throughout the whole of Scotland it is forbidden to fish for salmon and sea-trout on a Sunday. While trout and coarse fishing on Sundays is not prevented by statute, many waters do not allow it.

On the question of close seasons, these differ from river to river. Statutes cover the close times, and these are given in the entries for rivers where known; this does not, though, automatically mean that a river is open for fishing in the entirety of the open season, for individual fishery owners can impose altered close seasons inside the time allowed by statute.

Lastly, while a lot of trout fishing, and coarse fishing, is free in Scotland, it should never be assumed that there is a right to take a rod to any water and fish without permission. Without any exception, permission to fish should first be obtained by approaching the riparian owner or his agent.

Add

Runs through the vale between the Knapdale and Kilmichael forests.

Provides sea-trout and salmon fishing from late June, provided the water can carry them, fishing well for both species to the end of the season. Fair trout fishing. The ticket water available must be checked in advance.

Lochgilphead, Argylls, Strathclyde. Kilmichael to Billanoch.

T, ST, S(D T and WT Adv. Poltalloch Estate Office, Duntrune Castle, Lochgilphead. Fly only. L–6. Fishery open June–Oct. No Sunday fishing). Statutory season 16 Feb.–31 Oct.

Afton Water

A small tributary of the Solway's River Nith, which it joins at New Cumnock, offering ticket trout fishing.

New Cumnock, Ayrs., Strathclyde. Entire water (7 m).

T (WT Adv. J. Weir, blacksmith, New Cumnock; Tourist Information Centre, Glenafton Caravan Park; or Crown Hotel, New Cumnock).

Ailort

Links L. Eilt with L. Ailort sea loch, offering salmon and sea-trout. A noted spring run of sea-trout. Trout fair.

Glenfinnan, Inverness, Highland. 1½ m loch to river mouth.

T, ST, S (DT Adv. West Highland Estates Office, 33 High Street, Fort William. Fishery open 15 May–30 Sept. L–2).

Statutory season 11 Feb.–31 Oct.

Allan Water

Rises above Blackford and runs through Dunblane to the Forth near Bridge of Allan.

Fair trout fishing, with some sea-trout and salmon from late summer.

Dunblane, Perths., Central. Most of water, except private section marked.

T, S (DT Adv. Crockart & Son, tackle, Stirling, or Allanbank Hotel, Greenloaning. No Sunday fishing for salmon).

Almond

Rises near Whitburn, Midlothian, and runs to the Firth of Forth near Edinburgh. Stretch from Harthill to Calder, free trout fishing.

Almond (Tay)

Stream joining the Tay near Perth. Preserved salmon fishing; no known openings for visiting anglers.

Statutory season 15 Jan.–15 Oct.

Alness

Runs 15 m from L. Morie to the Cromarty Firth. Spate river with best salmon and sea-trout fishing from July on. One or two spring fish.

Alness, Ross and Crom., Highland. 2 m stretch from L. Morie.

T, S (DT Adv. tackle shop, Alness, or from The Factor, Novar Estates Office, Evanton. Fly only. No Sunday fishing. Ghillie available).

Alness, Ross and Crom., Highland. Six beats, covering 5 m in area.

T, ST, S (DT Adv. H. McKenzie, grocer, High Street, Alness. Fishery open for salmon 11 Feb.–15 Oct.; trout, 1 Apr.–10 Oct. Not Sunday).

Statutory season 11 Feb.–31 Oct.

Alyth

A short tributary of the River Isla which feeds the Tay. Trout fishing worth inquiry to landowners.

Annan

Rises close to the source of the Tweed and runs 35 m south-west through Beattock and Lockerbie to the Solway Firth.

Holds a few spring fish but most rated for summer and autumn spate runs, offering excellent sea-trout fishing, especially in middle reaches. The lower reaches are slow, with some coarse fish, especially chub (a 10½ lb fish held the British record, but has since been discredited). Chub are reported not so evident lately. Coloured in spates.

Annan, Dumfries, Dumfries and Gall. 2½ m from Annanbridge on Newbie Estates Water.

T, S (DT Adv. keeper, T. Nelson, Newbie Mill, Annan, or tackle shop, Annan. Fly only. Fishery open 20 Feb.–15 Nov. L–6).

Ecclefechan, Dumfries, Dumfries and Gall. 3 m Milk Foot to Mein Foot.

T, S (DT Adv. from keeper. L–16. Fishery open 25 Feb.–13 Nov. Fly only).

Lockerbie, Dumfries, Dumfries and Gall. Applegirth Estate Water plus parts of Kinnell and Dryfe Waters.

T, ST, S (WT Adv. A. Wright, Clock House, Millhouse Bridge, Lockerbie. No Sunday fishing).

Lockerbie, Dumfries, Dumfries and Gall. 4½ m Shillahill Bridge to Smallholm Burn, including Royal Four Towns Fishings.

T, ST, S (DT (L–20) and WT (L–30)

both Adv. from Commissioners of Royal Four Towns Fishings, Glenelg, High Tae, Lockerbie, or Castle Milk Estate Office, Norwood, Lockerbie. Fishery open for salmon 25 Feb.–15 Nov.; trout, 15 Mar.–6 Oct. No Sunday fishing).

Moffat, Dumfries, Dumfries and Gall. 4 m from Meeting of the Waters to Cogrie rail bridge.

T, S (DT Adv. Sports Shop, High Street, Moffat; Red House public house, Wamphray, or Beattock House Hotel, Beattock. No Sunday fishing. No day tickets after 15 Sept.).

St Mungo, Dumfries, Dumfries and Gall. 2 m Castle Milk water from Williamworth Bridge to Beckford.

T, S (DT Adv. Castle Milk Estate Office, Norwood, Lockerbie – closed Saturday. Fly only. No Sunday fishing). Tributaries of Annan: Milk, Moffat Water, Palmoodie Burn.

Statutory season 10 Feb.–15 Nov.

Annick Water

Rises to the north-east of Stewarton and runs to join the River Irvine.

Salmon and sea-trout, best in the latter half of the season.

Dreghorn, Ayrs., Strathclyde. 3½ m Cunningham Head to River Irvine.

T, S (DT Adv. tackle shop, Main Street, Dreghorn, or from Dreghorn AC. No Sunday fishing).

Kilmaurs, Ayrs., Strathclyde. 2½ m stretch in area.

T, ST, S (DT Adv. Kilmaurs AC. No Sunday fishing).

Stewarton, Ayrs., Strathclyde. Stretch as marked on ticket.

T, ST, S (DT Adv. Sports Centre, Stewarton, or A. Lawrie, painter, Stewarton; or from Stewarton AC).
Tributary of Irvine.

Statutory season 25 Feb.–31 Oct.

Ardle

Runs from L. Lnan Eun south-east through Strathardle to meet the Blackwater at Bridge of Cally, forming River Ericht.

Trout, salmon.

Bridge of Cally, Perths., Tayside. Stretch of left bank.

T, S (DT Adv. Carriefodly Hotel, Bridge of Cally).

Bridge of Cally, Perths., Tayside. 1 m stretch right bank.

T, S (DT Adv. Bridge of Cally Hotel. Fly only except 15 Jan.–15 Apr. No Sunday fishing).

Kirkmichael, Perths., Tayside. Stretch from bridge to weir.

T, S (DT Adv., free to hotel guests, Log Cabin Hotel, Kirkmichael. B available. Fishery open for salmon 11 Feb.–16 Oct.; trout, 15 Mar.–6 Oct. No Sunday fishing).

Statutory season 15 Jan.–15 Oct.

Arklet Water

Joins the west end of L. Arklet to the northern end of L. Lomond at Inversnaid. Trout, some salmon.

Inversnaid, Stirling, Central. 2 m Inversnaid to L. Arklet.

T (DT Adv. Inversnaid Hotel. No Sunday fishing).

Statutory season 1 Feb.–31 Oct.

Avon

Rises to the south of Falkirk and runs to the Firth near Grangemouth. Polluted in lower reaches. Trout fishing in upper reaches, free with permission from landowners.

Tributary of Forth system.

Avon (Banffs.)

Runs north from Tomintoul to the River Spey below the Bridge of Avon.

Trout, sea-trout and salmon.

Ballindalloch, Banffs., Grampian. 6 m in area.

T, ST, S (DT Adv. Delnasaugh Hotel, Ballindalloch. Fly only except at high water. No Sunday fishing. Fishery open 11 Feb.–30 Sept.).

Tributary of Spey system.

Avon Water

Small trout stream, tributary of the Clyde.

Stonehouse, Lanark, Strathclyde. 7 m Stonehouse to Strathaven.

T (DT Adv. Valley Sports, 134 Newmilns, Ayrshire. No Sunday fishing).

Awe

Runs a rapid course from L. Awe through the Pass of Brander to the sea.

Hydro-electric schemes have affected the flow in recent years, apparently without a great deal of effect on the fishing. However, the larger salmon for which the Awe is renowned have become scarcer. The biggest fish taken from the river, in 1921, weighed 57 lb. The river is mainly fished for its salmon, with the bigger fish in July and August. Ticket opportunities are limited.

Taynuilt, Argylls., Strathclyde. 1½ m barrage to viaduct.
S (Weekly bookings only, to Bell-Ingram, 7 Walker Street, Edinburgh. No Sunday fishing).
Tributaries: Lochy, Orchy.
Statutory season 11 Feb.–15 Oct.

Ayr

Rises in Glenbuck and runs 40 m to the sea, at Ayr Harbour.

Salmon, best in summer spates, sea-trout and trout to 2 lb. The river also offers grayling. This river was once hit by pollution but has recovered spectacularly to its present form.

Auchinleck, Ayrs., Strathclyde. 1 m left bank from Howford to Barskimince.
T, S (DT Adv. tackle shop, Main Street, Auchinleck, or from 21 Milne Avenue, Auchinleck).
Ayr, Ayrs., Strathclyde. Nearly 1 m Cemetery Burn to Craigie Pool.
T, S (DT Adv. ticket office, Kyle and District Council, Town Buildings, Ayr).
Catrine, Ayrs., Strathclyde. 2½ m bowling green dam to old Howford Bridge.
T, S (DT on bank or from TV shop, The Square, Catrine. Fishery open for salmon 15 Mar.–31 Oct.; trout, 15 Mar.–6 Oct. No Sunday fishing).
Muirkirk, Ayrs., Strathclyde. 8 m source to Sorn AC water boundary, Glenbuck.
T and grayling (DT Adv. Empire Bar, Muirkirk, or Muirkirk AC. Fishery open for trout 15 Mar.–6 Oct.; grayling all year).
Sorn, Ayrs., Strathclyde. 5 m stretch from Sorn.
T, S and grayling (DT Adv. Greyhound Inn, Sorn; Post Office, Sorn; Sorn Hotel or ICM Petrol Station, Sorn. Grayling fishing free 1 Nov.–14 Mar. No Sunday fishing).
Tributaries: Bellow, Coyle, Greenock, Lochar Water, Lugar.
Statutory season 11 Feb.–31 Oct.

Badachro

Small water running into Gairloch.
No real fishing until summer spates.
Gairloch, Ross and Crom., Highland. 1½ m stretch.
T, S (DT Adv. Shieldaig Lodge Hotel, Gairloch. B available, also ghillie. No Sunday fishing).
Statutory season 11 Feb.–31 Oct.

Balvag

A tributary of the River Teith joining L. Voil to L. Lubnaig.
Trout, some salmon.
Balquhidder, Perths., Central. 3 m L. Voil to L. Lubnaig.
T, S (DT on bank or from hotel, village shop or Sinclair Caravan Site. No Sunday fishing).
Tributary of Forth system.
Statutory season 1 Feb.–31 Oct.

Beauly

The system (River Glass) rises near the Atlantic coast and becomes the River Beauly at Struy.

The best fishing is lower at Lord Lovat's Estate below the hydro-dam at Kilmorock Falls, from where the river runs to the Moray Firth. Spring fishing poor, with spates from June onwards being best for sea-trout and salmon.

Beauly, Inverness, Highland. 5 m from Lovat Bridge to Beauly Firth.
T, ST, S (DT Adv. Lovat Estate Office, Beauly. Fishery open 13 Feb.–15 Oct. No Sunday fishing. Fly only).
Tributary: Glass.
Statutory season 11 Feb.–13 Oct.

Bellow
Small tributary of the Ayr at Lugar.
Trout fishing.
Cumnock, Ayrs., Strathclyde. 2 m stretch
at Lugar.
T (D T Adv. tackle shop at Cumnock).

Berriedale Water
Rises on Knockfin Heights and runs
across Maiden Pap slopes to the sea at
Berriedale.
Trout, with fair runs of sea-trout and
salmon in lower water.
Lybster, Caithness, Highland. 4 m in
area.
T, ST, S (Residents only, Portland
Arms, Lybster. Fishery open 28 Feb.–
15 Oct. Fly only. No Sunday fishing).
Statutory season 11 Feb.–31 Oct.

Bervie
Runs to the sea at Stonehaven between
the rivers Dee and Esk.
Trout and sea-trout, with some
salmon. Best in summer spates.
Inverbervie, Kincardines., Grampian.
Stretch from Ronalds Hole to sea.
T, ST, S (D T Adv. Joseph Johnston
& Sons, 3 America Street, Montrose.
L–6. Fishery open 25 Feb.–31 Oct. No
Sunday fishing).
Inverbervie, Kincardines., Grampian.
Water as on permit.
T, ST, S (Free fishing, but prior per-
mission essential from Kincardine and
Deeside District Council, Area Offices,
Burgh Chambers, Inverbervie. No
Sunday fishing).
Laurencekirk, Kincardines., Grampian.
Seven beats totalling 6½ m in area.
T, ST, S (D T Adv. Ticket Office,
Laurencekirk. Fishery open for salmon
and sea-trout 25 Feb.–31 Oct.; trout,
15 March–6 Oct. No Sunday fishing).
Statutory season 25 Feb.–31 Oct.

Blackadder
Rises near Greenlaw and runs to join the
Whiteadder at Chirnside.
Good trout fishing.
Greenlaw, Berwicks., Borders. 12 m.
T (D T Adv. Greenlaw A A).
Tributary of Tweed system.

Black Cart
Clyde tributary running through
Johnstone.
Fair trout fishing.
Howwood, Renfrews., Strathclyde.
2½ m in area.
T, some coarse (D T Adv. tackle shops
in area. Fishery open 15 Mar.–
30 Sept.).

Blackwater
Rises on the Perthshire and
Aberdeenshire border and runs through
Glenshee to the River Ericht at
Blairgowrie.
Trout and salmon.
Blairgowrie, Perths., Tayside. Stretch
from bridge to farm.
T, S (D T Adv. Dalruzion Hotel,
Blairgowrie. No Sunday fishing).
Tributary of Tay system.
Statutory season 15 Jan.–15 Oct.

Blackwater (Ross and Crom.)
Flows from L. Glascarnoch through
Garbat to join the River Conon.
Good summer salmon fishing, with
trout and sea-trout.
Contin, Ross and Crom., Highland. 1½ m
from Loch Na Croil to point up from
Rogie Falls.
T, S (D T Adv. Loch Achonachie A C.
Fishery open for salmon 1 June–
30 Sept.; trout, 1 Apr.–30 Sept. No
Sunday fishing).
Contin, Ross and Crom., Highland.
1½ m Middle Beat from Rogie Falls
to Contin Bridge on left bank.
T, ST, S (Guests only in Sept.,
Craigdarroch Lodge Hotel, Contin.
Usually heavily booked).
Garve, Ross and Crom., Highland. Left
bank stretch at Garve.
T mainly (D T Adv. Garve Hotel,
Garve. B available. No Sunday fish-
ing).
Garve, Ross and Crom., Highland. 6 m
L. Garve to Garbet.
T mainly (D T Adv. Strathgarve Lodge
Hotel, Garve. B, M B available. Fishery
open 1 May–30 Sept.).
Tributary of Conon system.

Bladnoch

Rises in Penninghame Forest and runs south-west through Kirkcowan to Wigtown Bay near Bladnoch.

Fair trout fishing, with late summer best for sea-trout and salmon. The river also holds perch and pike.

Kirkcowan, Wigtowns., Dumfries and Gall. 2 m stretch of right bank.

T, S (D T Adv. Tarff Hotel, Kirkcowan).

Newton Stewart, Wigtowns., Dumfries and Gall. 3 m at Waterside Farm.

T, S (D T Adv. hotels and caravan sites in area, or from Newton Stewart A A. Fishery open for salmon 1 Mar.–30 Sept.; trout, 15 Mar.–30 Sept. No Sunday fishing).

Tributary: Tarf.

Statutory season 11 Feb.–31 Oct.

Borgie

Rises to the north of Altnaharra and runs through L. Loyal and smaller lochs to the sea to the west of Naver estuary.

Trout, sea-trout and salmon, with some spring fish. Best summer and autumn. No known openings for visiting anglers, but local inquiries may prove worthwhile.

Statutory season 11 Feb.–31 Oct.

Bothwell Burn

Rises on Dunbar Common in East Lothian and runs to join the Whiteadder at Cranshaws.

Fair trout fishing.

Cranshaws, Berwicks., Borders. Most of water.

T (D T on bank or from keeper. Open 15 Mar.–30 Sept. No Sunday fishing).

Tributary of Tweed system.

Braan

Links L. Freuchie with the River Tay at Dunkeld after running through the Strathbraan Valley.

Trout, with some free fishing on inquiry from landowners.

Amulree, Perths., Tayside. 1 m in area, including stretch of Girron Burn.

T (D T Adv. Amulree Hotel, Amulree).

Breamish

Small water feeding the River Till, the tributary of the Tweed.

Trout, sea-trout. No known openings for visitors.

Broom

Rises in the Braemore Forest and runs to Loch Broom at Inverbroom.

Trout, sea-trout and salmon, with the best fishing July to Aug.

Ullapool, Ross and Crom., Highland. ½ m from river mouth upstream on left bank.

T, ST, S (D T Adv. tackle shop, Ullapool. L–2. No Sunday fishing. Fly only).

Statutory season 11 Feb.–31 Oct.

Brora

Rises to the north of Lairg and runs 20 m to L. Brora and on to the sea at Inverbrora.

Trout, sea-trout and salmon, with a spring run of the latter. Sea-trout best summer and autumn.

Brora, Sutherland, Highland. 3½ m right bank Brora to L. Brora.

T, ST, S (D T Adv. The Factor, Sutherland Estates, Golspie. Fly only. L–4. Fishery open for salmon 1 Feb.–15 Oct.; sea-trout, 1 June–15 Oct. Ghillie available. No Sunday fishing).

Brora, Sutherland, Highland. Fishing from 4 boats, including whole of L. Brora; no bank fishing.

T, ST, S (D T Adv. Gordonbush Estate Office, Brora. Fly only. No Sunday fishing).

Statutory season 1 Feb.–15 Oct.

Burn of Boyne

Rises on Knock Hill, running to the sea at Portsoy.

Trout, some salmon.

Portsoy, Banffs., Grampian. 4 m Cornhill to Boyne Mill.

T (D T Adv. Seafield Estate Office, Cullen, Buckie. No Sunday fishing).

Whitehills, Banffs., Grampian. Stretch in area.

T, S (D T Adv. Seafield Estate Office, Cullen, Buckie. No Sunday fishing).

Statutory season 11 Feb.–31 Oct.

Caddon Water
Tributary of the Tweed system draining
Great Law to Clovenfords.
Trout, mostly free fishing.

Cairnwater
Rises on Bogrie Hill and runs to
Moniaive and Dunscore, joining the
River Nith near Dumfries.
Trout, sea-trout, salmon.
Dumfries, Dumfries and Gall. Stretch
described on permit from Nith junction.
T, ST, S (D T Adv. Director of Finance,
Nithsdale District Council, Buccleuch
Street, Dumfries. No Sunday fishing
for salmon).
Dumfries, Dumfries and Gall. 30 m of
fishing in the area.
T, ST, S (D T Adv. McMillans tackle, 6
Friar's Vennel, Dumfries. L–5. Fishery
open 1 Apr.–30 Oct. No Sunday fish-
ing).
Moniaive, Dumfries, Dumfries and Gall.
2 m right bank from Craups Mill to Old
Crawfordton.
T (D T on bank or from Dellcairn
House, Moniaive).
Tributary of River Nith.
Statutory season 25 Feb.–30 Nov.

Calder (Renfrews.)
Runs south-east to Castle Semple L.
before joining Black Cart, a tributary of
the Clyde system.
Mainly trout.
Lochwinnoch, Renfrews., Strathclyde.
3 m from Castle Semple L. to
Tandlemuir.
T (D T Adv. Ticket Office, Castle
Semple L., or from St Winnoch A C.
Fishery open 15 Mar.–6 Oct.).

Carradale Water
Runs across the Kintyre Peninsula to
Kilbrannan Sound at Carradale.
Trout, salmon and sea-trout.
Carradale, Argylls., Strathclyde. 8 m Pool
Dhu to river mouth.
T, ST, S (D T Adv. from keeper or from
The Kennels, Carradale, by
Campbeltown. Fly only. No Sunday
fishing).
Statutory season 25 Feb.–31 Oct.

Carron
Rises on Ben Dearg and flows east to
Dornoch Firth near Bonor Bridge.
Salmon and sea-trout fishing, mostly
preserved but worth local inquiries.
Tributary of Oykel system.
Statutory season 11 Jan.–30 Sept.

Carron (Kincardines.)
Short Kincardines river which runs to the
sea at Stonehaven.
Trout, salmon and sea-trout, with the
best fishing from July to September.
Stonehaven, Kincardines., Grampian.
2½ m.
T, S (D T Adv. Gun Shop, Barclay
Street, Stonehaven. No Sunday fish-
ing).

Cassley
Rises on Ben More Assynt and joins
River Oykel near Rosehall.
Some spring fishing, with good runs
of sea-trout and grilse in summer spates.
Rosehall, Sutherland, Highland. 7 m in
area.
S (Weekly bookings only: Bell Ingram,
7 Walker Street, Edinburgh. Fly only.
No Sunday fishing).
Statutory season 11 Jan.–30 Sept.

Clyde
One of Scotland's best-known rivers,
rising not far from the source of the
easterly-flowing River Tweed and
running to Glasgow and the West
Coast.
Work continues on the massive pollution which has stopped all the game
runs up the Clyde, and there is hope that
some day migratory fish will be able to
return. Beyond the lower reaches, the
Clyde is a superb trout river (record 15 lb
4 oz) and in addition holds grayling and
stocks of large roach (best between
Hamilton and Rosebank). Trout fly patterns for the Clyde are usually lightly
dressed versions of standard patterns,
and bait is also used.
Permits for a good deal of water on
the Clyde and on its tributaries can be
obtained from Valley Sports, 134 Main
Street, Newmilns, Ayrshire.

Biggar, Lanarks., Strathclyde. 8 m
Roberton to Thankerton.
T (DT on bank. No Sunday fishing).
Lanark, Lanarks., Strathclyde. 4 m
Kirkfield to Easter Sills Farm.
T and grayling (DT on bank or from
Lanark and Dist. AC. Fishery open 15
Mar.–6 Oct.).
Motherwell, Lanarks., Strathclyde. 20 m
Motherwell to Elvanfoot, except
Lanark AC and Lamington AC waters.
T, C (DT Adv. tackle shops, Glasgow,
Motherwell, Edinburgh, Hamilton and
Wishaw; at Station Hotel, Carstairs, or
from United Clyde APA).
Tributaries: Avon Water, Black Cart,
Calder (Renfrews.), Gryfe, Leven (in
estuary).

Conglass

A small river running to join the Avon
(Banffs.) near Tomintoul.
Trout, with salmon and sea-trout
when conditions right.
Tomintoul, Banffs., Grampian. Most of
water.
T, ST, S (Guests only, Gordon Arms,
The Square, Tomintoul. Fishery
open 2 Feb.–30 Sept. No Sunday fish-
ing).
Tributary of Spey system.

Conon

Runs from Loch Luichart at Falls of
Conon, through Loch Achonachie to
long estuary at Dingwall.
Trout, sea-trout and salmon, with
summer sea-trout and grilse fishing
good.
Dingwall, Ross and Crom., Highland.
½ m.
T, S (DT Adv. tackle shop, Dingwall.
Fly only. Fishery open 26 Jan.–30
Sept. No Sunday fishing).
Strathpeffer, Ross and Crom., Highland.
Luichart Power Station to top of Loch
Achonachie.
T, S (DT Adv. Loch Achonachie AC.
Fly only. Fishery open 10 May–30
Sept. No Sunday fishing).
Tributary: Blackwater.
Statutory season 26 Jan.–30 Sept.

Cowie Water

Runs a 13-mile course to the sea at
Stonehaven.
Salmon, sea-trout, with the best fish-
ing from July to Sept. Fair trout fishing.
Stonehaven, Kincardines., Grampian.
1¼ m stretch.
T, S (DT Adv. Gun Shop, Barclay
Street, Stonehaven).

Coyle

A lower tributary of the River Ayr. Trout
and grayling fishing and some salmon.
Drongan, Ayrs., Strathclyde. 8 m of fish-
ing in area.
T, S, C (DT Adv. Drongon Youth Club
AC).
Statutory season 11 Feb.–31 Oct.

Crawick

Small tributary of the River Nith, joining
the north bank above the junction of the
River Euchan.
Trout, with sea-trout and salmon
when water levels up.
Sanquhar, Dumfries, Dumfries and Gall.
Stretch outlined on permit.
T, ST, S (DT Adv. Forsyth, solicitor,
100 High Street, Sanquhar. L–6. Fly
only, depending on water level.
Fishery open 15 Mar.–30 Sept. No
Sunday fishing).

Cree

Runs 25 m from L. Moan to Wigtown
Bay. A spate river, with spring runs said
to be improving.
Best salmon and sea-trout fishing in
summer spates.
Barrhill, Ayrs., Strathclyde. 7½ m from
Creebridge.
T, ST, S (DT Adv. Commercial Hotel,
Barrhill. Fishery open 15 Mar.–30
Sept. No Sunday fishing).
Drumlamford, Ayrs., Strathclyde. 3 m in
area.
T, ST, S, C (DT Adv. from W.
Stevenson, The Kennels, Drumlamford
Estate, Barrhill. L–40. Fishery open 1
Apr.–30 Sept. Fly only, except for C).
Newton Stewart, Wigtowns., Dumfries
and Gall. Town Beat of Cree.
T, ST, S (DT Adv. hotels and caravan

sites in area; also Newton Stewart A A.
Fishery open for salmon 1 Mar.–30
Sept.; trout, 15 Mar.–30 Sept. No
Sunday fishing).
Tributaries: Minnoch, Palnure Burn,
Penkiln Burn.
Statutory season 1 Mar.–30 Sept.

Crinian Canal
Runs through Knapdale Forest at north
end of Kintyre Peninsula between Sound
of Jura and L. Crinian.
Trout fishing, free.

Cruden Burn
Stream running into Cruden Bay,
Aberdeenshire.
Sea-trout and trout; few openings for
visitors.
Cruden Bay, Aberdeens., Grampian. 1 m.
T, ST (Guests only, Kilmarnock Arms,
Cruden Bay).
Statutory season 11 Feb.–31 Oct.

Cur
Source on Mulloch. Runs west to L.
Eyne at Strachur.
Trout, with salmon and sea-trout, best
late in season.
Strachur, Argylls., Strathclyde. Point
below junction with Colensluain to
head of L. Eck.
T, ST, S (D T Adv. J. McKinnell, mer-
chant, Strachur, or tackle shop,
Queen's Hall Buildings, Argyll Street,
Dunoon. Fishery open 1 Apr.–30 Sept.
No Sunday fishing).
Statutory season 16 Feb.–31 Oct.

Dee (Aberdeens.)
Rises in the Cairngorms and runs a 90-
mile course through Linn O'Dee to
Braemar. Because of its shallow, clear
nature the Dee has become one of the
best rivers for floating-line fly fishing for
salmon; indeed, in the 1920s Arthur
Wood, generally believed to have introduced floating-line fishing with small
salmon fly patterns to Britain, made excellent catches with this method on the
Cairnton beat.
The Dee's salmon begin to run from
February, and early catches can be excellent, especially following a mild wet
winter. Fish can be taken to Braemar
from opening day. Sea-trout fishing is
best in late June and July, with the trout
fishing only average. The record Dee
salmon weighed 56 lb.
Because salmon fishing on the river is
so popular, very early booking throughout is advised.
Aboyne, Aberdeens., Grampian. 2½ m
left bank from Aboyne.
S (WT Adv. Brodies, tackle, Aboyne.
July and Aug. bookings likeliest for
visitors, but reservations must be made
3 months ahead. Fly only. Fishery open
1 Feb.–30 Sept. No Sunday fishing).
Aboyne, Aberdeens., Grampian. 2¼ m
Aboyne Water, left bank.
T (D T Adv. July and Aug. only. Fly
only, except at high water. L–2.
Brodies, tackle, Aboyne. Ghillie avail-
able).
Aboyne, Aberdeens., Grampian.
Stretches in area.
T, ST, S (D T Adv. Huntley Arms Hotel,
Aboyne. Fishery open 1 Feb.–30 Sept.
No Sunday fishing).
Aboyne, Aberdeens., Grampian. 16 m
total Pannanich to Aboyne.
ST, S (D T Adv. (L– according to
number of bookings) Glen Tanar
Estate Office, Glen Tanar, Aboyne. Fly
only. Fishery open 1 Feb.–30 Sept. No
Sunday fishing. Ghillie available Feb.–
June.)
Ballater, Aberdeens., Grampian. 17 m left
bank Invercauld Bridge to Cambus
o'May.
S (D T Adv. Invercauld Estate Office,
by Ballater. Fly only. Ghillie available.
No Sunday fishing. Advance inquiry
essential).
Braemar, Aberdeens., Grampian. 4 m left
bank in area.
S, T (WT Adv. Mar Lodge Hotel,
Braemar. L–2. Ghillie available. No
Sunday fishing).
Dinnet, Aberdeens., Grampian. 5 m Dee
Castle and Dinnet beats.
T, ST, S (Inquiries to J. T. Sutherland,
chartered surveyor, Bank of Scotland
Buildings, Brechin, Angus. L–6. No
Sunday fishing).

Kincardine O'Neil, Aberdeens., Grampian. 6 m Ballogie and Carlogie beats.

T, ST, S (Inquiries as for Dinnet, above. Fishery open 15 Feb.–30 Sept. No Sunday fishing. L–7. Ghillie available).

Statutory season 1 Feb.–30 Sept.

Dee (Kirkcudbrights.)

System starts from lochs above L. Ken (famed for large pike), after which the river runs to the Solway Firth at Kirkcudbright.

Salmon and sea-trout, with the lower Dee giving the best salmon results, although most of the water is preserved. Trout fishing fair to good.

Kenbridge, Kircudbrights., Dumfries and Gall. ¾ m stretch of left bank from L. Stroan.

T, S (D T Adv. Cross Keys, Kenbridge; Kenmure Arms, Kenbridge; The Café, New Galloway. Fishery open 1 Apr.–30 Sept.).

Tributary: River Ken (Water of Ken).

Statutory season 11 Feb.–31 Oct.

Deveron

Rises not far from the Spey's headwaters and runs 60 m past Turriff to Banff and the sea.

The water is noted for occasional very big salmon (record 61 lb), usually late in the season. Sea-trout can run from June given enough water, and the same applies to the salmon fishing, which normally does not start until late summer. Spring trout fishing fair to good. A lot of the water is preserved, but there are some weekly opportunities.

Banff, Banffs., Grampian. ¾ m stretch upstream from Banff Bridge.

T, ST, S (WT tackle shop, Banff. No Sunday fishing. Fly only on right bank 1 June–31 Aug.).

Turriff, Aberdeens., Grampian. 2 m Laithers Beat, right bank.

T, ST, S (Inquiries Adv. to J. T. Sutherland, chartered surveyor, Bank of Scotland Buildings, Brechin, Angus. Fishery open 15 Mar.–31 Oct. No Sunday fishing. Ghillie available. L–4).

Turriff, Aberdeens., Grampian. Stretches shown by Turriff A A markers on Deveron Bridge map.

T, ST, S (WT Adv. J. Masson, tackle, 3 Sunnybrae, Turriff. Fly only June–Aug., except at some water levels. L–6. Fishery open for sea-trout, salmon 11 Feb.–31 Oct.; trout, 15 Mar.–6 Oct.).

Statutory season 11 Feb.–31 Oct.

Devon

From its source near Crook of Devon the river runs a course of 20 m through Dollar to the Forth below Stirling.

Trout fishing fair to good in spring, with summer and autumn sea-trout and salmon fishing.

Dollar, Clackmannans., Central. Most of river.

T (D T Adv. Hobby and Model Shop, New Row, Dunfermline. No Sunday fishing).

Tillicoultry, Clackmannans., Central. Most of river.

ST, S (D T Adv. autumn only (closing 31 Oct.) Mucishart Inn, Crook of Devon Inn, or Glendavon Hotel, Clackmannan, from tackle shops in area or from Devon AA. L–10. No Sunday fishing).

Tributary of Forth system.

Statutory season 1 Feb.–31 Oct.

Dochart

Runs through Glen Dochart and into the west of L. Tay.

Trout, with salmon running late summer and autumn. Mostly preserved, with no known openings for visiting anglers

Tributary of Tay system.

Statutory season 15 Jan.–15 Oct.

Don

Runs an eastward course, parallel to that of the Dee, to the north of Aberdeen.

Although a fine salmon river, boasting a record fish of 54 lb, the river has suffered from paper-mill pollution which is being cleared. Grilse run in summer, with the bigger fish late on. The sea-trout fishing is only average, but the trout fishing, especially dry fly fishing, can be very good indeed.

Alford, Aberdeens., Grampian. 7 m stretch right bank.

T, S (DT Adv. Haughton Arms Hotel, Alford. No Sunday fishing for salmon).

Alford, Aberdeens., Grampian. 2 m stretch left bank.

T, S (DT Adv. Ticket Office, Stone Circle, Glenkindie, or from Kildrummy Castle Hotel, Alford. Ghillie available. No Sunday fishing. Fly only trout, also salmon below high water).

Dyce, Aberdeens., Grampian. 5 m main road bridge to above Dyce church-yard.

T, S (DT Adv. tackle shop, Thistle Street, Aberdeen. Fly only. No Sunday fishing).

Glenkindie, Aberdeens., Grampian. 2 m stretch.

T., S (DT must be booked one day Adv. Glenkindie Arms Hotel, Glenkindie. No Sunday fishing).

Inverurie, Aberdeens., Grampian. 2 m left bank from Polinar Burn to River Ury.

T, S (DT Adv. tackle shop, West High Street, Inverurie; Bridge Bar, Port Elphinstone, Inverurie; or Inverurie AA. Trout fishing 1 Apr.–30 Sept. No Sunday fishing).

Kemnay, Aberdeens., Grampian. 1¾ m stretch right bank.

T, S (DT Adv. Mrs S. L. Milton, Kemnay House, Kemnay. L–6. No Sunday fishing).

Kintore, Aberdeens., Grampian. 1 m stretch left bank between Kintore AC markers.

T, S (DT Adv. Crown Hotel, Kintore. No Sunday fishing).

Monymusk, Aberdeens., Grampian. 10 m Monymusk Estate Waters.

T, S (Inquiries Adv. to Grant Arms Hotel, Monymusk. No Sunday fishing).

Strathdon, Aberdeens., Grampian. 9 m total on two stretches, Bahamm to Luib.

T (DT Adv. Colquhonnie Hotel, Strathdon. Fly only. No Sunday fishing).

Tributary: Ury.

Statutory season 11 Feb.–31 Oct.

Doon

Headwaters rise in the Kirkcudbright-shire borders, running to L. Doon, below which the river runs to the sea near Ayr, with excellent salmon water below Patna.

Hydro-electric installations at L. Doon provide compensation water for the lower river, giving good conditions for summer sea-trout and grilse runs. The upper river holds shoals of roach, some large.

Dalmellington, Ayrs., Strathclyde. 5 m B741 road bridge to Patna.

T, S (DT Adv. Palace Bar, Dunaskin Waterside. Fishery open for salmon 1 Mar.–31 Oct. No Sunday fishing).

Dalmellington, Ayrs., Strathclyde. 2 m right bank from Straiton road bridge.

C, T, S (DT Adv. public houses and hotels in area. L–10. No Sunday fishing).

Dalmellington, Ayrs., Strathclyde. 1½ m L. Doon to Lyn Bridge.

T, ST, S (DT Adv. Craigengillan Estates Co., Dalmellington. Fly only. L–4. No Sunday fishing).

Statutory season 11 Feb.–31 Oct.

Douglas Water

Rises on Beinn Dearg and runs to L. Fyne near Dalchenna.

An excellent summer and autumn sea-trout water.

Inveraray, Argylls., Strathclyde. Whole water.

ST (DT Adv. Argyll Estates Office, Cherry Park, Inveraray. Fishery open 16 May–15 Oct. Fly only. No Sunday fishing).

Statutory season 16 Feb.–31 Oct.

Dulnain

Flows 28 m from Monadhliath Hills to the Spey south-west of Grantown-on-Spey.

Trout and salmon.

Dulnain Bridge, Inverness, Highland. 12 m Invellaidnan Bridge to Spey.

T, S (DT Adv. tackle shop, 61 High Street, Grantown-on-Spey. Fishery open 11 Feb.–30 Sept. No Sunday fishing).

Dye Water

Rises in the Lammermuir Hills and runs through Longformacus to the River Whiteadder.

Mainly trout.

Longformacus, Berwicks., Borders. 3 m from Whiteadder up.

T (DT on bank or from keeper. Fishery open 15 Mar.–30 Sept. No Sunday fishing).

Tributary of Tweed system.

Earn

Runs from L. Earn through Comrie and Crieff and the Vale of Strathearn to the Firth of Tay below Bridge of Earn.

Trout, salmon, and fairly good sea-trout fishing.

Crieff, Perths., Tayside. 7 m Dalpatrick to Comrie.

T, ST, S (DT Adv. tackle shop, High Street, Crieff. Open 1 Feb.–15 Oct. No Sunday fishing. L–40).

Dunning, Perths., Tayside. 1 m Broomhill Fishing.

S (DT Adv. Hobby Model Shop, New Row, Dunfermline. L–4. No Sunday fishing).

Perth, Perths., Tayside. Left bank stretch outlined on permit.

T, ST, S (DT Adv. tackle shop, 46 South Methven Street, Perth. Fishery open 1 Feb.–31 Oct. No Sunday fishing. L–6).

St Fillans, Perths., Tayside. ¾ m St Fillans to Dundurn Mill.

T, ST, S (DT Adv. post offices, St Fillans and Lochearnhead. B, MB available. Fishery open 14 Feb.–15 Oct. No Sunday fishing).

Tributary of Tay system.

Statutory season 15 Jan.–15 Oct.

Ebrie

Runs south through Auchnagatt to River Ythen.

Trout, with sea-trout best during late season spates. Some free fishing, with permission from landowners at Auchnagatt.

Tributary of Ythan.

Statutory season 11 Feb.–31 Oct.

Eddleston Water

Tributary of the Tweed, joining at Peebles.

Trout fishing, mostly free.

Eden (Berwicks.)

A tributary of the Teviot, which it joins a few miles below Kelso.

Some trout fishing, with permission obtained locally.

Eden (Fifes.)

Rises in the Lomond Hills and runs east through Springfield and Cupar to the North Sea at Guardbridge.

Salmon and trout, some sea-trout.

Cupar, Fifes., Fife. 8 m Springfield to Guardbridge.

T, ST, S (DT Adv. tackle shop, Cupar, or from Eden AA. Fishery open for salmon and sea-trout 15 Feb.–15 Nov. No Sunday fishing).

Tributary: Moutray.

Statutory season 11 Feb.–31 Oct.

Endrick

Runs from Carron Valley Reservoir to L. Lomond near Drymen.

Trout, sea-trout and salmon, with large stocks of coarse fish, especially roach and pike, near its junction with L. Lomond. Fishing controlled by L. Lomond Angling Improvement Association, which, while allowing day and weekly tickets on the loch, offers only season fishing tickets for the Endrick and other waters running into the loch.

Statutory season 11 Feb.–31 Oct.

Ericht

Runs through Blairgowrie to join the River Isla.

Good trout fishing, with some salmon

Blairgowrie, Perths., Tayside. 3½ m stretch.

T, S (DT Adv. tackle shop, Blairgowrie Fishery open 15 Jan.–15 Oct.).

Bridge of Cally, Perths., Tayside. 2 m stretch right bank.

T, S (DT Adv. Bridge of Cally Hotel Fly only except 15 Jan.–15 Apr.).

Tributary of Tay system.

Statutory season 15 Jan.–15 Oct.

Esk (Border)

Rises as two headwaters, the White Esk and the Black Esk, in Eskdale, Dumfriesshire, and runs south-west to enter England and the Solway Firth.

A noted sea-trout river, with fish running from April to the end of September. The salmon fishing can also be good, with a spring run, but the best fishing is from April to October. The lower reaches of the Esk and the River Lyne hold big stocks of dace and chub. Most of the river is preserved, but some coarse fishing is allowed within restricted periods. Fair trout fishing, but fish mostly small.

Canonbie, Dumfries, Dumfries and Gall. 9 m Langholm to Scots Dyke, except stretch marked on permit.

T, ST, S (DT Adv. Riverside Inn, Canonbie. No Sunday fishing).

Langholm, Dumfries, Dumfries and Gall. 6 m Langholm to Canonbie.

T, ST, S (WT Adv. Eskdale Hotel, Langholm. No Sunday fishing).

A North-West Water Authority rod licence is needed to fish the English section of this river.

Tributaries: Kershope Burn, Liddel Water, Lyne.

Esk (North)

Rises near the Tayside–Grampian border, and runs east to mark the border in its lower reaches, before meeting the sea to the north of Montrose.

Rated an extremely prolific salmon river, with early runs in latter years, although it has been heavily netted. Sea-trout fishing best in summer, and the trout fishing can be good, although it is said it has not hit form in recent years.

Edzell, Angus, Tayside. 4 m in area.

T, S (DT Adv. Head Keeper, Millden, Glenesk. No DT after 8 Aug. No Sunday fishing).

Montrose, Tayside. 25 m of fishing Glenisla to Montrose.

T, ST, S (DT Adv. tackle shop, 180 High Street, Montrose. Fly only during March. Ghillie available. No Sunday fishing).

Tributaries: Luther Water, West Water.

Statutory season 16 Feb.–31 Oct.

Esk (South)

Rises to the south of the source of the North Esk and runs east to Montrose.

Like its northerly namesake, it is a good salmon river, with a good spring run. Summer sea-trout fishing good. Much of the water is preserved.

Bridge of Dun, Angus, Tayside. 1½ m stretch.

T, ST, S (DT Adv. only to people known to or accompanied by a Montrose A C member. Fly only).

Glen Clova, Angus, Tayside. 3 m in area.

T, ST, S (DT Adv. Ogilvy Arms Hotel, Glen Clova. Fishery open for trout 14 Mar.–7 Oct.; salmon, 16 Feb.–31 Oct. No Sunday fishing).

Kirriemuir, Angus, Tayside. 7 m of fishing in area.

T, ST, S (DT Adv. tackle shop, Kirriemuir, or from Kirriemuir AC. Fly only at low water. No Sunday fishing).

Tributary: Noran Water.

Statutory season 16 Feb.–31 Oct.

Ettrick Water

Flows through Selkirk to join the River Tweed at Galashiels.

Has a fair run of spring salmon in the lower stretches. Fair trout fishing, with regular stocking.

Selkirk, Selkirks., Borders. A total of 80 m on Ettrick and River Yarrow.

T (DT Adv. tackle shop, High Street, Selkirk; also hotels and post offices in area. Fishery open 1 Apr.–30 Sept. No Sunday fishing).

Tributary of Tweed system.

Statutory season 1 Feb.–30 Nov.

Euchan Water

A tributary of the upper Nith system.

Offers trout fishing, with salmon and sea-trout, best after spate.

Sanquhar, Dumfries, Dumfries and Gall. Stretch in area, as marked on permit.

T, ST, S (DT Adv. Forsyth, solicitor, 100 High Street, Sanquhar. Fly only at certain water levels. L–6. No Sunday fishing. Fishery open 15 Mar.–30 Sept.).

Statutory season 25 Feb.–30 Nov.

Euchar
A spate river running from L. Scamadale through Glen Euchar to L. Feochan.

Offers trout, sea-trout and salmon, the latter two needing spate to run. Can be good in right conditions.
Kilninver, Argylls., Strathclyde. 1 m at farm.

T, ST, S (DT Adv. Lagganmore Farm, Kilninver. Fly only. L–3. No Sunday fishing).
Kilninver, Argylls., Strathclyde. 1 m stretch.

T, ST, S (DT Adv., Monday, Tuesday and Thursday only, Major J. T. P. Mellor, Barndromin Farm, Knipoch, Argylls. L–2).
Statutory season 11 Feb.–31 Oct.

Ewe
Short water (2 m) draining L. Maree to the sea at Poolewe.

Salmon, sea-trout and trout. No known openings for visiting anglers.
Statutory season 11 Feb.–31 Oct.

Falloch
Runs into L. Lomond.

Offers game and coarse fishing, mostly association-controlled.
Ardlui, Dunbartons., Strathclyde. 1 m stretch left bank.

T, C (DT Adv. Ardlui Hotel, Ardlui. No Sunday fishing).
Statutory season 15 Jan.–15 Oct.

Faseny Water
Feeds Whiteadder Reservoir in the Tweed system.

Fair trout fishing.
Cranshaws, Berwicks., Borders. 2 m Snout Reservoir to Kilpallet.

T (DT on bank. Fishery open 15 Mar.–30 Sept. No Sunday fishing).

Feshie
Runs 23 m through Glen Feshie to the upper reaches of the Spey.

Trout, sea-trout and salmon.
Kincraig, Inverness, Highland. 2 m left bank from Black Mill to Saw Mill and stretch (both banks) from Mhor Burn to Black Mill.

T, ST, S (DT or WT Adv. the Paper Shop, Kingussie, or Black's, iron-mongers, Newtonmore. L–1 rod per pool. Fishery open for salmon, sea-trout, 11 Feb.–30 Sept.; trout, 15 Mar.–30 Sept.).
Statutory season 11 Feb.–30 Sept.

Fillan
Feeds the south-west end of L. Dochart.
Trout, with sea-trout and salmon.
Crianlarich, Perths., Central. Extensive stretches, including L. Dochart and parts of the River Cononish.

T, ST, S (DT Adv. Banmore Tea Room, Crianlarich. Fly only on parts of L. Dochart).
Tributary of Tay system.
Statutory season 15 Jan.–15 Oct.

Finart
Runs through Glen Finart to L. Long at Ardentinny.

Fair trout fishing, with some sea-trout and salmon.
Ardentinny, Argylls., Strathclyde. 4 m.

T (DT Adv. from keeper. No Sunday fishing).
Statutory season 11 Feb.–31 Oct.

Findhorn
This neighbour of the Spey shows all the characteristics of a salmon river, with rocky pools and fish moving through on spates. Offers some spring salmon fishing, but better from July onwards. Summer best for sea-trout. Fair trout fishing.
Forres, Morays., Grampian. 4 m from estuary up.

T, ST, S (WT Adv. only to visitors resident in Forres or Rafford, tackle shop, Tolbooth Street, Forres. Fishery open 11 Feb.–30 Sept. No Sunday fishing).
Forres, Morays., Grampian. Meads of St John Beat.

ST, S (WT Adv. Moray Estates Development Co.; tel. Forres 2213. No Sunday fishing).
Statutory season 11 Feb.–30 Sept.

Fleet
A small water rising south-east of Lairg and running through Pittentrail to

L. Fleet south-west of Golspie. Trout, sea-trout and salmon.

Aberscross, Sutherland, Highland. Left bank from pier to sea.

ST (DT Adv. Lindsay & Co., iron-mongers, Golspie).

Golspie, Sutherland, Highland. Little-ferry stretch.

ST, S (DT Adv. J. Baddon, tackle, Main Street, Golspie. Fishery open 1 Feb.–15 Mar. No Sunday fishing).
Statutory season 25 Feb.–31 Oct.

Fleet (Water of Fleet)

Runs to the Solway near Gatehouse, Galloway.

Trout, with good summer sea-trout fishing and an improving run of grilse. Mostly private.

Gatehouse, Kirkcudbrights., Dumfries and Gall. 2 m stretch.

T, ST, S (DT Adv. Fishing Office, Murray Arms Hotel, Gatehouse).

Forth

Running 80 m from Aberfoyle to the Firth of Forth, this is one of the few great Scottish waters which suffers from in-dustrial pollution.

Nevertheless it maintains runs of sea-trout and salmon, the latter having a reputation as big fish. It also offers fair trout fishing. Huge shoals of quality roach are found in some sections, especially near the junction of the River Teith. Coarse fishermen should approach riparian owners, who often offer the fishing free.

Aberfoyle, Perths., Central. 6 m Gartmoor Fishings on right bank from Aberfoyle.

T, ST, S (DT Adv. keeper at Gartmoor, tackle shops in Glasgow, Kirkintilloch and Stirling, or Rob Roy Hotel, Buchlyvie. Fishery open 1 Feb.–31 Oct. No Sunday fishing).

Aberfoyle, Perths., Central. 1½ m stretch in town.

T, ST, S (DT Adv. Ferguson, news-agent, Aberfoyle).

Stirling, Stirlings., Central. 3 m Lands of Hood to Teith.

T, S (DT Adv. Ticket Office, Municipal Buildings, Stirling, or tackle shop, Stirling. Fly only. No Sunday fishing). Tributaries of Forth: Allan Water, Almond, Avon, Balvag, Devon, Teith, Water of Leith.
Statutory season 1 Feb.–31 Oct.

Forth and Clyde Canal

Popular with North-of-England anglers as a close-season coarse fishery, and the venue for the Scottish coarse champion-ships. Built to link the North Sea and the Clyde; some stretches have since been filled in. Roach, often big, perch and pike predominate, with tench and carp in some stretches.

Dullatur, Stirlings., Central. 4 m stretch Wyndford Lock, Banknock, to Auchinstarry.

C (DT Adv. Glasgow and West of Scotland CFA).

Glasgow, Strathclyde. Whole water ex-cepting section above.

C (Season ticket only (but cost low) from British Waterways Board, Old Basin Works, Applecross Street, Glasgow C4).

Fruin

Runs through Glen Fruin to L. Lomond.

Trout, with sea-trout and salmon. Association-controlled (see L. Lomond under Scottish Still Waters below).

Fyne

Runs south-west through Glen Fyne to L. Fyne at Clachan.

Trout, sea-trout and salmon, with the best fishing June to Sept.

Cairndow, Argylls., Strathclyde. Whole water.

T, ST, S (DT Adv. Ardkingas Estate Office or Cairndow Estate Office, both Cairndow. L–4. Fishery open 1 June–15 Oct. No Sunday fishing. Ghillie available).
Statutory season 16 Feb.–31 Oct.

Gala Water

Rises south of Edinburgh and runs to the Tweed at Galashiels.

Good trout water, with free fishing for 9 m at Stow.

Garnock

Rises north of Kilbirnie and runs south through Dalry and Kilwinning to the Irvine estuary.

Trout, sea-trout and salmon.

Kilbirnie, Ayrs., Strathclyde. 8 m source to Kersland.

T, ST, S (DT Adv. Glendale Arms, Garnock. Fly only at low water. No Sunday fishing).

Kilwinning, Ayrs., Strathclyde. 5 m Dalgarven Dam to estuary.

T, ST, S (DT Adv. tackle shop, Kilwinning, or from Kilwinning Eglinton AC).

Statutory season 25 Feb.–31 Oct.

Garrel Burn

Small trout water running through Kilsyth, Stirlingshire.

Kilsyth, Stirlings., Strathclyde. Whole water.

T (DT Adv. Colzium Service Station, Stirling Road, Kilsyth, or from Kilsyth FPA. Fishing open 15 Mar.–7 Oct.).

Garron

Short water linking L. Dubh to L. Fyne.

Salmon and sea-trout, with the best fishing from June onwards.

Inveraray, Argylls., Strathclyde. Whole water plus L. Dubh.

T, ST, S (DT Adv. Argyll Estates Office, Cherry Park, Inveraray. Fly only. Fishery open 16 May–15 Oct. No Sunday fishing. L–6).

Garry

A tributary of the River Tummel in the Tay system.

Trout fishing good, but salmon badly affected by hydro-electric scheme, it is claimed. Inquiries to landowners could give trout fishing.

Garry (Ness system)

Links L. Quoich to L. Garry, then L. Oich at Invergarry.

Rated a fine early salmon river. Private water.

Statutory season 15 Jan.–15 Oct.

Gaur

Links L. Eigheach with L. Rannoch in the Tay system.

Fair trout fishing.

Rannoch Station, Perths., Tayside. 1 m L. Laidon to railway.

T (DT Adv. Moor of Rannoch Hotel, Rannoch Station. B available).

Girvan

Runs a course of 25 m to the sea at Girvan.

Salmon run to falls 5 m above Straiton. Reasonable trout fishing, with fair to good sea-trout fishing from July. Late salmon fishing best.

Barr, Ayrs., Strathclyde. 3½ m stretch.

T, ST, S (DT Adv. King's Arms Hotel, Barr. No Sunday fishing).

Girvan, Ayrs., Strathclyde. Stretch upstream from sea.

T, ST, S (WT Adv. tackle shop, Dalrymple Street, Girvan. Fishery open 25 Feb.–31 Oct. L–5. No Sunday fishing).

Straiton, Ayrs., Strathclyde. 2 m in area.

T, ST, S (DT Adv. Estate Keeper, Blairquhan Kennels, Straiton. L–12. Fishery open 1 June–31 Oct. No Sunday fishing).

Statutory season 25 Feb.–31 Oct.

Glass

Runs from its source near the West Coast to join the River Beuly above its estuary and Inverness.

Trout and salmon, with late salmon fishing good. Mostly private.

Cannich, Inverness, Highland. 1½ m stretch of left bank.

T, S (Residents only, Glen Affric Hotel, Cannich. B and ghillie available. No Sunday fishing).

Statutory season 11 Feb.–15 Oct.

Glass (Allt Grand)

Runs from L. Glass to the Cromarty Firth.

Sea-trout, trout and salmon.

Evanton, Ross and Crom., Highland. 1 m stretch in area.

T, S (DT Adv. tackle shops in area or from The Factor, Novar Estates Office,

Evanton. Fly only. No Sunday fishing).

Glazert
A tributary of the Irvine, which it joins near Kilmaurs.
Trout and salmon.
Kilmaurs, Ayrs., Strathclyde. 2 m stretch in area.
T, ST, S (DT Adv. Kilmaurs AC. No Sunday fishing).
Stewarton, Ayrs., Strathclyde. Stretch in area.
T, ST, S (DT Adv. tackle shop, Sports Centre, Stewarton; A. Lawrie, painter, Stewarton, or Stewarton AC).
Statutory season 25 Feb.–31 Oct.

Glentarken Burn
Short tributary of the Earn in the Tay system, joining the north shore of L. Earn.
Fair trout fishing.
St Fillans, Perths., Tayside. 2 m from loch.
T (DT Adv. post offices, St Fillans and Lochearnhead. Open 15 Mar.–7 Oct.).

Goil
Runs through Ardgoil Estate to L. Goil at Lochgoilhead.
Salmon, trout and sea-trout.
Arrochar, Argylls., Strathclyde. As marked on ticket.
ST, S (DT Adv. Chief Forester, Forest Office, Ardgartan Forest, Arrochar. No Sunday fishing).
Statutory season 11 Feb.–31 Oct.

Greenock
Runs from the north to join the Ayr system below Muirkirk.
Offers trout and grayling fishing.
Muirkirk, Ayrs., Strathclyde. Whole water.
T, grayling (DT Adv. Empire Bar, Muirkirk, or from Muirkirk AC. Fishery open for trout 15 Mar.–6 Oct.; grayling, all year).

Gryfe
Links Gryfe Reservoir through Strathgryfe to the Clyde.
Trout and grayling fishing.

Bridge of Weir, Renfrews., Strathclyde. 3½ m Bridge of Weir to Roman Bridge.
T, grayling (DT Adv. from keeper or tackle shop, Bridge of Weir. Grayling fishing Nov.–Feb. needs special permission).
Kilmacolm, Renfrews., Strathclyde. Kilmacolm to Low Gryfe Reservoir.
T (DT Adv. Cross Café, Kilmacolm. Lower reaches fly only).

Halladale
Runs a 20-mile course to the sea at Melvich.
Trout, sea-trout and salmon, with some early runs of salmon. Most of the water is private, and early booking is advisable for the accessible stretches.
Forsinard, Caithness, Highland. 7 m in area.
T, ST, S (DT Adv. Forsinard Hotel, Forsinard. Fishery open for salmon and sea-trout 2 Jan.–30 Sept.; trout, 15 Mar.–15 Oct. No Sunday fishing. Hotel also arranges fishing on lochs in area, with boats and ghillies available. Fly only).
Melvich, Sutherland, Highland. Considerable amount of water in area.
T, S (DT Adv. Mrs J. Atkinson, Liberton Estate Office, 8 Sinclair Street, Thurso. Early booking advised. Fishery open 12 Feb.–30 Sept. No Sunday fishing).
Statutory season 12 Jan.–30 Sept.

Helmsdale
Runs south off the north-east projection of Scotland to Helmsdale.
Salmon, with diminished spring runs in recent years but excellent summer results. Trout fishing poor; the water is largely private, with no known openings for visitors.
Statutory season 11 Jan.–30 Sept.

Inver
Runs from L. Assynt to the sea at Lochinver.
Good salmon fishing from summer on, but the river is mostly private.
Statutory season 11 Feb.–31 Oct.

Irvine

A noted trout water, the Irvine runs by Kilmarnock to Irvine and its common estuary with the Garnock.

Salmon and sea-trout fishing said to be improving.

Dreghorn, Ayrs., Strathclyde. 6½ m Laigh Milton Mill to River Annick.
T, S (DT Adv. W. M. Steen, Main Street, Annick, or Dreghorn AC. No Sunday fishing).

Hurlford, Ayrs., Strathclyde. 3½ m Kilmarnock to Galston.
T, ST, S (DT Adv. Post Office, The Cross, Hurlford. L–6 on Saturdays. No Sunday fishing).

Irvine, Ayrs., Strathclyde. 5 m from estuary, including stretch of Annick Water.
T, ST, S (DT Adv. not Saturdays, tackle shop, Irvine. Fishery open for salmon fishing 1 Mar.–31 Oct. No Sunday fishing).

Kilmarnock, Ayrs., Strathclyde. 15 m in area.
T, S (DT Adv. McCrirck & Sons, tackle, 38 John Finnie Street, Kilmarnock. L–5).

Newmilns, Ayrs., Strathclyde. 3 m Darvel Old Sewage Works to Haggs Burn, Newmilns.
T, ST, S (DT Adv. Valley Sports Tackle, 134 Main Street, Newmilns. No Sunday fishing).
Tributaries: Annick Water, Garnock, Glazert, Lugton Water.
Statutory season 25 Feb.–31 Oct.

Isla

Rises in Angus and runs south, then south-west to Alyth and the River Tay below Kinclaven.

Best-known for its trout and grayling fishing, although there are some salmon. Some big pike have been taken from the lower reaches.

Airlie, Perths., Tayside. Upstream from Airlie Castle.
T (Free fishing).

Meigle, Perths., Tayside. 3 m stretch.
T (DT Adv. tackle shop, Meigle. Fly only).
Tributary of Tay system.
Statutory season 15 Jan.–15 Oct.

Jed Water

Rises in the Cheviots and runs north through Jedburgh to the River Teviot.
Fair trout fishing.

Jedburgh, Roxburghs., Borders. Most of water, including part of River Oxnam.
T, C (DT Adv. The Gun Shop, Kenmore Toll, Jedburgh, or J. Lunn, Cannongate, Jedburgh. No Sunday fishing).
Tributary of Tweed system.

Kale Water

Another Teviot tributary, which joins near Eckford.
Trout fishing and some roach.

Eckford, Roxburghs., Borders. 1½ m upstream from Teviot.
T, C (DT Adv. Keeper's House, Eckford. L–6. Fishery open 1 Apr.–30 Sept. No Sunday fishing).
Tributary of Tweed system.

Kello

Tributary of the River Nith.
Offers game fishing. Spates provide best fishing.

Sanquhar, Dumfries, Dumfries and Gall. Stretch as permit.
T, ST, S (DT Adv. Forsyth, solicitor, 100 High Street, Sanquhar. L–6 rods. Fishery open 15 Mar.–30 Sept. No Sunday fishing. Fly only if water conditions warrant).
Statutory season 25 Feb.–30 Nov.

Ken (Water of Ken)

Runs off Windy Standard south-west to L. Kendoon, then Dalry and L. Ken at New Galloway.

Trout and some salmon, with some coarse fishing in the lower reaches.

Carsphairn, Kirkcudbrights., Dumfries and Gall. Stretches on Lorgue and Holme Estates.
T (WT Adv. J. Weir, blacksmith, New Cumnock; Tourist Information Centre, Glenafton Caravan Park; or Crown Hotel, New Cumnock).

New Galloway, Kirkcudbrights., Dumfries and Gall. 3 m from above Ken Bridge, New Galloway, to L. Ken, including part of Garple Burn.

T, S, C (DT Adv. tackle shops in area or from Cross Keys, Kenmure Arms, Ken Bridge. Fishery open 1 Apr.– 30 Sept. No Sunday fishing). Tributary of Dee (Kirkcudbrights.) system.

Kerbet Water
A tributary of Dean Water which runs to the River Isla in the Tay system.

Trout fishing and some grayling.

Forfar, Angus, Tayside. 2 m marked by Forfar Canmore AC notice-boards.

T (DT Adv. C. Kerr, tackle, 1 West High Street, Forfar. Fly only. Fishery open 15 Mar.–6 Oct.).

Kershope Burn
Rises on the English border to run to the River Liddel in the Border Esk system.

Trout, with some sea-trout, salmon. Access limited.

Penton, Cumbria. 2½ m stretch.

T, ST, S (Residents only, Kershope House Estate Guest House. Fly only in parts. Fishery open 1 May–30 Sept.). Visitors are reminded that for fishing waters on the English side of the border in parts of Cumbria, a North-West Water Authority rod licence is necessary.

Kinglas
Runs through Glen Kinglas to L. Fyne at Cairndow.

Trout, sea-trout and salmon, with the best fishing from June to September.

Cairndow, Argylls., Strathclyde. 2 m Bendarroch Bridge to Butterbridge.

T, S (DT Adv. Cairndow Estate Office, Cairndow. L–3. Fishery open 1 June– 15 Oct. No Sunday fishing). Statutory season 16 Feb.–31 Oct.

Kirtle Water
Rises on Grange Fell and runs through Kirtlebridge and Kirkpatrick Fleming to the Solway Firth.

Fair fishing for trout and sea-trout, and the water has produced some big chub. Sea-trout are best from midsummer.

Kirtlebridge, Dumfries, Dumfries and Gall. Stretch in town.

T, ST (Free fishing).

Rigg, Dumfries, Dumfries and Gall. 2½

m from river mouth to Rigg.

T, ST (DT Adv. Rigg Shop, Rigg; Hunters Lodge or Solway Lodge, Gretna Green, or from Gretna Green AA. Fishery open for trout 15 Mar.– 7 Oct.; sea-trout and herling, 15 Mar.– 31 Oct.).

Kyle of Sutherland
Extends from the meeting of the Oich and Cassley rivers 12 m to Bonar Bridge and below, forming the neck of the Dornoch Firth.

Trout, sea-trout and salmon.

Bonar Bridge, Sutherland, Highland. Whole water.

T, ST, S (DT Adv. W. A. Macdonald, tackle, Castle Street, Dornoch, or from Burghfield House Hotel, Dornoch. No Sunday fishing). Statutory season 11 Jan.–30 Sept.

Leader
Rises south of Edinburgh and runs through Lauderdale and Lauder to the Tweed below Earlston.

Fair to good trout fishing; fish mostly small.

Earlston, Berwicks., Borders. Stretches as marked on permit.

T (DT Adv. McQuillan & Wilson, High Street, Earlston. Fishery open 15 Mar.– 30 Sept. No Sunday fishing).

Lauder, Berwicks., Borders. 6 m from upper boundary, Wiselaw Mill Farm, to Whitslaid Bridge, except for Thirlestone Castle policies fishery, and including fishing on tributaries in area.

T (DT Adv. Post Office, Lauder; J. Bell, Barns Cottages, Lauder, or Dod Mill, Lauder; or from Lauderdale AA. Fishery open 15 Mar.–6 Oct.). Tributary of Tweed system.

Leet Water
Rises to the north of Coldstream and runs to join the Tweed, where remarkable catches of quality roach have been made, especially when the Tweed is high. Some trout.

Coldstream, Berwicks., Borders. Left bank from road bridge in town to River Tweed.

C, T (DT from keeper).

Leithen Water
Rises south-west of Moorfoot Hills and runs to join the River Tweed at Inner Leithen.

Trout; most of the water free fishing.

Leven (Dumbarton)
Short water linking the south end of L. Lomond to the Clyde estuary at Dumbarton.

Trout, sea-trout and salmon, with some coarse fish.

Balloch, Dumbartons., Strathclyde. 22 m of fishing in area.

T, S (Residents only, Tullichewan Hotel, Balloch. B, M B available).

Statutory season 11 Feb.–31 October.

Leven Cut
Runs from L. Leven.

Mostly trout.

Scotlandwell, Kinross, Tayside. 3 m Sluice House to Auchmuir Bridge, on right bank.

T (D T Adv. Sluice House. Fishery open 15 Mar.–6 Oct.).

Liddel Water
Follows the English border from north of Nook to junction with the Border Esk.

Fair game fishing, as River Esk.

Canonbie, Dumfries and Gall. 12 m Newcastleton to Scots Dyke.

T, ST, S (D T Adv. Riverside Inn, Canonbie. No Sunday fishing).

Liever
Runs through Glen Liever to L. Etive.

Mostly trout.

Ford, Argylls., Strathclyde. Stretches in area.

T (D T Adv. keeper, Inverliever Lodge, Ford).

Little Ferry
A small water running into the Dornoch Firth at Dornoch.

Fair sea-trout fishing and trout.

Dornoch, Sutherland, Highland. 400 yds left bank old pier to sea.

T, ST (D T Adv. tackle shop, Castle Street, Dornoch. No Sunday fishing).

Livet
Runs 8 m through Glenlivet to the River Avon (Banffs.) near Drumin Castle.

Trout, sea-trout and salmon.

Tomintoul, Banffs., Grampian. 2 m from mouth of Livet, right bank.

T, S T, S (Residents only, Gordon Arms Hotel, The Square, Tomintoul. Fishery open 12 Feb.–30 Sept. No Sunday fishing. Fly only Sept.).

Tomnavoulin, Bannfs., Grampian. Glenlivet A A water.

S T, S (D T Adv. Mr Duff, Excise House, Tomnavoulin Distillery. Fishery open 11 Feb.–19 Aug. No Sunday fishing). Tributary of Spey system.

Loanan Water
Runs from L. Awe, Sutherland, north to L. Assynt.

Trout, sea-trout and salmon, with the best fishing from June onwards. Some hotels offer fishing.

Lochar Water
Runs from Locharbridge south to the Solway Firth below Bankend.

Trout, sea-trout and salmon, with most of the water free fishing, provided permission is obtained from riparian owners.

Lochay
Runs through Glen Lochay to Dochart at the west end of L. Tay.

Trout and grayling, with some salmon lies near the loch.

Killin, Perths., Tayside. 1 m stretch of right bank.

T, S and grayling (D T Adv. W. Allan, tackle, Main Street, Killin. B, M B available).

Tributary of Tay system.

Lochy (Highland)
Runs from L. Lochy to be joined by the River Spean and reach the sea near Fort William.

Mostly salmon and sea-trout, with the best fishing from summer spates onwards. Trout fishing good in parts.

Fort William, Inverness, Highland. Stretch from rail bridge to river mouth.

S, ST (DT Adv. tackle shop, Fort William. L–20, 8 reserved for visitors. Fly only in parts of fishery. No Sunday fishing).
Tributaries: Roy, Spean.
Statutory season 11 Feb.–31 Oct.

Lochy (Strathclyde)
Runs through Glen Lochy to the Orchy at Inverlochy.
Fair trout fishing.
Tyndrum, Perths., Central. 2 m downstream from loch, including fishing in Lochan Nabi.
T (DT Adv. L. Musk, Caravan Site, Tyndrum, or Ben More Tea Room, Tyndrum. Fly only. Fishery open 15 Mar.–6 Oct.).
Tributary of Awe system.

Lossie
Runs 25 m from L. Trevie to Lossiemouth on the Moray Firth.
Fair trout fishing, with sea-trout and salmon from late summer onwards.
Elgin, Morays., Grampian. 10½ m Calcot's rail bridge to Leaoch Burn.
T, ST, S (DT Adv. tackle shop, Elgin. Fishery open for trout 15 Mar.–6 Oct.; salmon and sea-trout, 11 Feb.–15 Oct. No Sunday fishing).
Lossiemouth, Morays., Grampian. 6½ m Coopers Burn to Bin Mill rifle range.
T, ST, S (DT Adv. tackle shop, Lossiemouth, or from Lossiemouth AA. Open 1 Mar.–15 Oct. No Sunday fishing).
Statutory open season 11 Feb.–15 Oct.

Ludgate Water
Small tributary of the Tweed at Stow, Midlothian.
Trout fishing; mostly free, with permission from riparian owners.

Lugar
Rises near Cumnock and runs to join the Ayr south of Mauchline.
Sea-trout, salmon and trout, also grayling.
Auchinleck, Ayrs., Strathclyde. 4 m to Mauchline.

T, S (DT Adv. tackle shop, Main Street, Auchinleck, or from 21 Milne Avenue, Auchinleck. Fishery open 15 Mar.–31 Oct. No Sunday fishing).
Cumnock, Ayrs., Strathclyde. 5 m to Dalblair.
T, with S on season ticket only (DT Adv. tackle shop, Cumnock. No Sunday fishing).
Tributary of Ayr system.
Statutory season 11 Feb.–31 Oct.

Lugton Water
Rises near Lugton and runs south-east through Kilwinning to join the River Garnock north-west of Irvine.
Trout, sea-trout and salmon.
Kilwinning, Ayrs., Strathclyde. 5½ m from Montgrennan Estate to River Garnock.
T, ST, S (DT Adv. tackle shop, Kilwinning, or from Kilwinning Eglinton AC. No Sunday fishing).
Stewarton, Ayrs., Strathclyde. Stretch outlined on permit.
T, ST, S (DT Adv. Sports Centre, Stewarton, or from A. Lawrie, painter, Stewarton).
Statutory season 25 Feb.–31 Oct.

Lunan
Runs 13 m from near Forfar to the sea between Montrose and Arbroath.
Good trout fishing, and good sea-trout fishing late in the season if there is water for them. Some salmon.
Arbroath, Angus, Tayside. 8 m Friockheim to river mouth.
T, ST, S (DT Adv. tackle shop, High Street, Arbroath. No Sunday fishing).
Tributary: Vinney.
Statutory season 16 Feb.–31 Oct.

Luther Water
A small tributary of the North Esk.
Good sea-trout fishing.
Laurencekirk, Kincardines., Grampian. 6 m Thornton Estate to North Esk.
ST, S (DT Adv. Ticket Office, Thornton Estate).
Laurencekirk, Kincardines., Grampian. 7 m Thornton Estate Water.
ST, S (DT Adv. Ticket Office,

Thornton Estate. Fishery open 25 Feb.–31 Oct. No Sunday fishing). Statutory season 16 Feb.–31 Oct.

Lyne
Runs through border country to join the Border Esk.

Fair trout fishing, sea-trout. Some riparian owners offer fishing if permission is sought.

Lyne Water
Rises to the north of West Linton and runs south to the River Tweed near Drochil Castle.

Mainly trout.

Peebles, Peebles, Borders. Flemington Bridge to River Tweed.

T (DT Adv. tackle shops, Peebles and Innerleithen; George Hotel and Tweed Valley Hotel, Walkerburn; or Post Office, Stobo. Fishery open 1 Apr.–30 Sept. Fly only in parts. No Sunday fishing).

Lyon
Runs from L. Lyon and through Stronvich Reservoir and Fortingall to the River Tay.

Offers salmon, some of them early, and fair trout fishing.

Fortingall, Perths., Tayside. 6 m stretch of left bank.

T, S (DT Adv. Fortingall Hotel, Fortingall. Ghillie available. No Sunday fishing).

Tributary of Tay system.

Statutory season 15 Jan.–15 Oct.

Machrihanish Water
A small water of the Kintyre Peninsula, entering the sea near Machrihanish.

Trout fishing, mostly free.

Megget Water
Small stream flowing into the west end of St Mary's Loch in the Tweed system.

Salmon, trout and some coarse fish.

Cappercleuch, Selkirks., Borders. 7 m from Tala to loch.

T, S, C (DT Adv. Rodono Hotel, Cappercleuch. No Sunday fishing). Statutory season 1 Feb.–30 Nov.

Mennock
Small tributary of the River Nith, joining below Sanquhar.

Trout, salmon and sea-trout, with the best fishing when there is plenty of water.

Sanquhar, Dumfries, Dumfries and Gall. As outlined on permit.

T, ST, S (DT Adv. Forsyth, solicitor, 100 High Street, Sanquhar. L–6. Fishery open 15 Mar.–30 Sept. No Sunday fishing).

Statutory season 25 Feb.–30 Nov.

Milk
South-flowing tributary of the Annan, joining the main river above Annan.

Fair to good trout fishing, with some sea-trout and salmon; also coarse fish, with some big chub.

Lockerbie, Dumfries, Dumfries and Gall. 1 m below Kettleholme Bridge and 7 m above Scroggs Bridge.

T, ST (DT Adv. Castle Milk Estate Office, Norwood, Lockerbie. Fly only. No Sunday fishing).

Statutory season 10 Feb.–15 Nov.

Minnoch (Water of Minnoch)
Tributary of the Cree system.

Like the parent river, it offers its best fishing after spates wash through its gorges. When conditions are right the salmon and sea-trout fishing can be good, especially from August onwards.

Newton Stewart, Wigtowns., Dumfries and Gall. 2 m left bank stretch above Glentrool.

T, S (DT Adv. hotels and caravan sites in area or from Newton Stewart AA. Fishery open for trout 15 Mar.–30 Sept.; salmon, 1 Mar.–30 Sept. No Sunday fishing).

Moffat Water
Another tributary of the Annan system.

Fair trout fishing, with occasional salmon and some coarse fish.

Moffat, Dumfries, Dumfries and Gall. ½ m from Drumcrief Bridge to Meeting of the Waters, left bank.

T (DT Adv. Sports Shop, High Street, Moffat; Red House Hotel, Wamphray;

Beattock House Hotel, Beattock. No Sunday fishing).

Moffat, Dumfries, Dumfries and Gall. 5 m stretch.

T, S (Residents only, Craigieburn Hotel, Moffat).

Statutory season 10 Feb.–15 Nov.

Moidart

Runs off the Inverness Mountains, then south-east to L. Moidart near Ardmolich.

A spate river, it offers good sea-trout fishing from mid-June to August, with salmon and some trout.

Kinlochmoidart, Inverness, Highland. 2 m lochans to sea, including trout fishing on lochans.

T, ST, S (DT Adv. Mrs Bley, West Lodge, Kinlochmoidart. L–4 on river section).

Statutory season 11 Feb.–31 Oct.

Monynut

Rises to the south of Bransley Hill and runs to the River Whiteadder below Abbey St Bathans.

Fair trout fishing.

Abbey St Bathans, Berwicks., Borders. 1½ m Bankend to Whiteadder.

T (DT on bank or from keeper. Fishery open 15 Mar.–30 Sept. No Sunday fishing).

Tributary of Tweed system.

Moriston

Runs from L. Cluanie and L. Loyne through Glen Moriston to L. Ness at Invermoriston.

Fair salmon fishing, said to be influenced by hydro-electric scheme. Good trout fishing.

Invermoriston, Inverness, Highland. 12 m on Glenmoriston Estate from estuary to Torgoyle Bridge.

T, S (DT Adv. Glenmoriston Estate Office, Invermoriston, or from village shop or Glenmoriston Arms Hotel, Invermoriston. Advance booking essential. B, MB and ghillie available. Fishery open for trout 15 Mar.–30 Sept.; salmon, 15 Jan.–30 Sept. Fly only on Dundreggan Beat).

Moutray

A tributary of the Eden (Fife).

Fair trout fishing, mostly free.

Mudale

Rising to the east of Mudale to run to the River Naver near Altnaharra.

Trout, sea-trout and salmon.

Altnaharra, Sutherland, Highland. 3 m in area.

T, ST, S (DT Adv. Altnaharra Hotel. Fly only. B and ghillie available. Fishery open for salmon 12 Jan.–30 Sept. No Sunday fishing).

Nairn

Rises on the north slopes of Monadhliath Mountains and runs north-east through Strathnairn and Drummossie Muir to the sea at Nairn.

Trout, salmon, sea-trout.

Nairn, Nairns., Highland. 7½ m harbour to Kilravock Castle.

T, ST, S (DT Adv. P. Fraser, tackle, High Street, Nairn. Fly only except in spate. Fishery open 11 Feb.–30 Sept. Not Sundays).

Naver

Rises above Altnaharra and runs 24 m to the sea near Bettyhill.

Good salmon fishing, with a spring run, but the fishing is mostly preserved. Fishing in the estuary below Naver Bridge is free.

Tributary of the Mudale.

Open season 12 Jan.–30 Sept.

Ness

Flows from the north of L. Ness to the Moray Firth.

Fair to good fishing for salmon and sea-trout; some trout.

Inverness, Inverness, Highland. 3 m in town boundaries.

T, ST, S (DT Adv. tackle shop, Inverness. Fishery open 15 Jan.–15 Oct.).

Inverness, Inverness, Highland. 2½ m Clachnahaig Stone to estuary.

T, ST, S (DT Adv. J. Graham, tackle, 27 Union Street, Inverness (not open Saturday). No Sunday fishing).

Tributaries: Garry, Moriston, Oich.

Nith
Rises above Dalmellington, Argylls, and
runs 55 m to the sea.

Offers improving salmon fishing after
first being hit by pollution to the turn of
the century and salmon disease from the
1960s. The best salmon run late and can
be big, with a 67-pounder reported to
have been poached in the last century.
Also contains sea-trout, trout, and some
grayling.

Dumfries, Dumfries and Gall. 3 m.

T, ST, S (DT Adv. McMillans tackle, 6
Friar's Vennel, Dumfries. L–5. No
Sunday fishing).

Dumfries, Dumfries and Gall. Section as
marked on permit, including stretch of
Cargen Burn.

T, ST, S and grayling (DT Adv.
Director of Finance, Nithsdale District
Council, Buccleuch Street, Dumfries.
Fishery open for trout 15 Mar.–6 Oct.;
salmon, 25 Feb.–30 Nov. Not
Sundays).

New Cumnock, Ayrs., Strathclyde. 9 m
source to Ayrs.–Dumfries boundary.

T, S (WT Adv. J. Weir, blacksmith,
New Cumnock; Tourist Information
Centre, Glenafton Caravan Park; or
Crown Hotel, New Cumnock).

Sanquhar, Dumfries, Dumfries and Gall.
11 m from Ayrs.–Dumfries boundary.

T, ST, S (DT Adv. Forsyth, solicitor,
100 High Street, Sanquhar. L–6. Fly
only depending on water level.
Fishery open for salmon and sea-
trout 15 Mar.–30 Nov. No Sunday
fishing).

Thornhill, Dumfries, Dumfries and Gall.
5 m from Thornhill downstream.

T, S (DT Adv. Ticket Office or tackle
shop, Thornhill. Fly only at low water.
Fishery open for trout 1 Apr.–30 Sept.;
salmon, 25 Feb.–30 Nov. L–8).

Tributaries: Afton Water, Cairnwater,
Crawick, Euchan Water, Kello,
Mennock.

Statutory season 25 Feb.–30 Nov.

Noran Water
Tributary of the South Esk, joining near
Netherton.

Fair trout fishing.

Forfar, Angus, Tayside. Stretch marked
by Forfar Canmore AC notice-boards.
T (DT Adv. C. Kerr, tackle, 1 West
High Street, Forfar. Fly only. Fishery
open 15 Mar.–6 Oct.).

North Ugie
Tributary of the Ugie.

Trout fishing, mostly free on inquiry to
riparian owners.

Oich
Joins the east end of L. Lochy to L. Ness
at Fort Augustus.

Salmon, sea-trout and trout.

Fort Augustus, Inverness, Highland.
Beats in area.

S (DT Adv. Outdoor Shop, Fort
Augustus. L–4. No Sunday fishing).

Tributary of Ness system.

Statutory season 15 Jan.–15 Oct.

Orchy
Rises L. Tully and runs through Glen
Orchy to L. Awe below Dalmally.

Fair trouting, with salmon when water
allows. Can yield spring fish before the
Awe.

Bridge of Orchy, Argylls., Strathclyde.
2 m stretch left bank.

S (DT Adv. Inveroran Hotel, Bridge of
Orchy. Fishery open mid-June to 15
Oct.).

Dalmally, Argylls, Strathclyde. 6½ m
upstream from L. Awe.

S, T (DT Adv. Dalmally Hotel or
Croggan Crafts, Dalmally. No Sunday
fishing).

Tributary of Awe system.

Statutory season 11 Feb.–15 Oct.

Oykel
Rises on Ben More Assynt and runs to L.
Ailsh, then south to Oykel Bridge and on
to Dornoch Firth.

Good salmon fishing, with a spring run
especially on the lower beats. Also offers
sea-trout, trout.

Rosehall, Sutherland, Grampian. Whole
river.

S (DT Adv. Benmore Estate Office,
Bonar Bridge. Fishery open 11 Jan.–

30 Sept. No Sunday fishing. Fly only. Ghillie available).
Tributaries: Carron, Cassley, Shin.

Palmoodie Burn

Small tributary of the Annan, entering near Moffat.

Trout.

Moffat, Dumfries, Dumfries and Gall. Stretch near Moffat.

T (Residents only, Craigieburn Hotel, Moffat).

Palnure Burn

Rises at Brockloch Hill and runs south-west to join the River Cree below Palnure.

Fair to good fishing for salmon and sea-trout.

Newton Stewart, Wigtowns., Dumfries and Gall. Left bank from Cree upstream.

T, ST, S (DT Adv. hotels and caravan sites in area or from Newton Stewart AA. Fishery open for trout 15 Mar.–30 Sept.; salmon, 1 Mar.–30 Sept. No Sunday fishing).

Penkiln Burn

Another Cree tributary, rising in Kirroughtree Forest and running south-west to Newton Stewart.

Trout, sea-trout and salmon.

Newton Stewart, Wigtowns., Dumfries and Gall. From above Mattie White's Bridge to source.

T, ST, S (DT Adv. hotels and caravan sites in area or from Newton Stewart AA. Seasons as Palnure Burn, above. No Sunday fishing).

Polly

Rises some 20 m from Ullapool in north-west Scotland to run into Enard Bay.

Good salmon and sea-trout fishing. The Royal Hotel in Ullapool offers fishing for guests.

Roy

Runs through Glen of Roy to join Spean River near Inverroy.

Salmon, sea-trout and trout, with the best fishing from July onwards.

Roybridge, Inverness, Highland. Whole river.

S, ST (DT Adv., L–4 rods to Roybridge Hotel, Speanbridge Hotel and Stranrossit Hotel, and 4 more from The Manager, River Roy Fisheries, Braeroy, Roybridge (total 8 rods). No Sunday fishing).

Tributary of Lochy system.

Statutory season 11 Feb.–31 Oct.

Ruel

Runs into L. Riddon below Clachan.

Offers salmon, sea-trout and trout, with the best fishing from July onwards.

Clachan of Glendaruel., Argylls., Strath-clyde. Left bank from church to Otter Ferry road bridge.

T, ST, S (DT Adv. Glendaruel Hotel, Clachan of Glendaruel. Fly only).

Statutory season 16 Feb.–31 Oct.

Sark

Runs 10 m to join the Solway Firth near Gretna Green.

Fair to good fishing for trout and sea-trout, with some big chub.

Gretna Green, Dumfries, Dumfries and Gall. Right bank from mouth to A75 at Gretna.

T, ST, C (DT Adv. Rigg Shop, Rigg; hotels in area or from Gretna Green AA. Fishery open for trout 15 Mar.–7 Oct.; sea-trout and herling, 15 Mar.–31 Oct.).

Shee Water

Small tributary of the Tay system.

Some trout fishing.

Glenshee, Perths., Tayside. 1 m stretch.

T (DT Adv. Spittal Hotel, Glenshee. Fly only. No Sunday fishing).

Shiel

A small (3 m) West Coast river.

Good runs of salmon and sea-trout. Preserved, with no known openings for visiting anglers.

Statutory season 11 Feb.–31 Oct.

Shin

Runs from L. Shin, Lairg, to the River Oykel below Achinduich.

Hydro-electric schemes have had some effect on salmon runs, but they remain good, with spring fish from March to May and moderate summer runs. Trouting fair. Mostly preserved, but the Sutherland Arms Hotel, Lairg, offers fishing to guests.

Statutory season 11 Jan.–30 Sept.

Shinary

Drains L. Sandwood in north-west Scotland near Cape Wrath.

Salmon, sea-trout.

Kinlochbervie, Sutherland, Highland. 4 m source to Sandwood.

ST, S (D T Adv. Garbet Hotel, Kinlochbervie. No Sunday fishing).

Statutory season 11 Feb.–31 Oct.

Shira

Runs from Lochan Sron Mor, Argylls, through Glen Shira to L. Dubh.

Fair to good fishing for salmon and sea-trout.

Inveraray, Argylls., Strathclyde. Whole river

ST, S (D T Adv. Argyll Estates Office, Cherry Park, Inveraray. L–4. Fishery open 16 May–15 Oct. No Sunday fishing).

Small Echaig

Runs from Clachaig to Holy Loch and the Firth of Clyde near Dunoon.

Fair to good fishing for salmon, sea-trout and trout.

Dunoon, Argylls., Strathclyde. 1½ m stretch from Clachaig.

T, ST, S (D T Adv. Ballochyle House, Dunoon. Fishery open 1 Apr.–31 Oct. No Sunday fishing).

Southwick Water

Short tributary of the River Urr, between the Dee and the Nith.

Salmon and sea-trout from summer on, given water. No fishing is allowed in droughts.

Dalbeattie, Kirkcudbrights., Dumfries and Gall. Whole water.

T, ST, S (D T Adv. from keeper. No Sunday fishing).

Statutory season 25 Feb.–29 Nov.

Spean

Runs from Tulloch Station, L. Laggan,

through Braes o'Lochaber to Spean Bridge.

Trout and salmon, with some sea-trout. Best fishing from June onwards given spates.

Spean Bridge, Inverness, Highland. Left bank from old rail viaduct to High Bridge.

T, ST, S (D T Adv. Spean Bridge Hotel, Spean Bridge. No Sunday fishing).

Tributary of Lochy system.

Statutory season 11 Feb.–31 Oct.

Spey

This famous salmon river runs a 100-mile course, with the last 60 m below L. Insh holding quantities of good salmon. Below Grantown, where most of the water is preserved, lie the best salmon beats.

There is a good spring run of salmon, with sea-trout appearing from March to April. The trout of the Spey are often big, but fishing for them is secondary to salmon and sea-trout fishing. A powerful, fast-running water, it makes for exciting fishing.

Aberfour, Banffs., Grampian. 1 m right bank Delagyle Beat.

T, ST, S (Inquiries to J. T. Sutherland, chartered surveyors, Bank of Scotland Buildings, Brechin, Angus. L–4. No Sunday fishing).

Aberlour, Banffs., Grampian. Aberlour A A Fishing.

T, ST, S (D T Adv. for bona fide visitors staying in Aberlour, from J. A. J. Munro, tackle, 95 High Street, Aberlour. No Sunday fishing).

Aberlour, Banffs., Grampian. Stretch in area.

S, ST (Residents only, Downans Hotel, Aberlour. No Sunday fishing).

Aviemore, Inverness, Highland. Three sections.

T, ST, S (D T Adv. Osprey Fishing School, The Fishing Centre, Aviemore Centre. Facilities for disabled anglers. Ghillie available).

Boat of Garten, Inverness, Highland. 5½ m Abernethy A I A waters.

T, ST, S (D T Adv. for temporary residents in area only, from Kelman's

Stores, Boat of Garten; Boat Hotel or Craigard Hotel, Boat of Garten; Nethy Bridge Hotel, Nethy Bridge. Fishery open 11 Feb.–30 Sept. No Sunday fishing. Fly only when water conditions warrant).

Fochabers, Morays., Grampian. 1½ m Castle Water.

T, S (D T Adv. from mid-May to 31 Aug. only, from Miss J. Murray, 38 High Street, Fochabers – advance booking requested. L–4. Fly only when water conditions warrant. No Sunday fishing).

Fochabers, Morays., Grampian. 1½ m Braehead Pool to sea.

T (D T Adv. from keeper, 2 Bogmoor, Speybay by Fochabers. No inquiries on Sunday. Fly only. Fishery open 1 Apr.–14 May and 1 July–26 Aug. No Sunday fishing).

Fochabers, Morays., Grampian. Stretch in area.

ST, S (Residents only, Gordon Arms Hotel, Fochabers. No Sunday fishing).

Grantown-on-Spey, Morays., Highland. 8 m Tulchan Estate waters.

T, ST, S (D T Adv. Tulchan Lodge, Grantown-on-Spey. Rods limited depending on advance booking. B and ghillie available. Fishery open 11 Feb.–30 Sept. No Sunday fishing).

Grantown-on-Spey, Morays., Highland. 7 m Strathspey A I A waters from Old Spey Bridge to Broomhill Bridge.

T, S (D T Adv. G. Mortimer, tackle, High Street, Grantown-on-Spey. Ghillie by special arrangement. Fly only when water levels warrant. Fishery open 11 Feb.–30 Sept. No Sunday fishing).

Newtonmore, Inverness, Highland. 15 m Spey Dam to River Tromie.

T, S, some pike (D T Adv. or WT Adv. The Paper Shop, Kingussie, or Black's, ironmongers, Newtonmore. Fishery open for trout 15 Mar.–30 Sept.; salmon, 11 Feb.–30 Sept.).

Spey tributaries: Avon (Banffs), Conglass, Dulnain, Feshie, Livet, Truim.

Statutory season 11 Feb.–30 Sept.

Stinchar
Runs 30 m to the sea at Ballantrae.

Trout, sea-trout and salmon, with the best fishing late in the season. Salmon can be big.

Barr, Ayrs., Strathclyde. 1½ m right bank to Milton.

T, ST, S (D T Adv. King's Arms Hotel, Barr. Fly only. No Sunday fishing).

Colmonell, Ayrs., Strathclyde. 3 m stretch.

T, ST, S (D T Adv. keeper, Knockdolian Estate, Colmonell. Ghillie available. Fishery open 1 Mar.–31 Oct. No Sunday fishing).

Pinwherry, Ayrs., Strathclyde. Fishing in area.

T, S (D T Adv. Daljarrock Hotel, Pinwherry).

Statutory season 25 Feb.–31 Oct.

Tarf
Rises on Eldrig Fell and runs south-east to join the River Bladnoch near Kirkcowan.

Trout, with some sea-trout and salmon.

Kirkcowan, Wigtowns., Dumfries and Gall. Tarf Bridge to Airyligg.

T, S (D T Adv. Three Lochs Caravan Park, Kirkcowan).

Kirkcowan, Wigtowns., Dumfries and Gall. 6 m left bank.

T, S (D T Adv. Tarf Hotel, Kirkcowan).

Statutory season 11 Feb.–31 Oct.

Tay
Recognized as one of the world's great salmon rivers, the Tay has a 160-mile course from L. Tay to Perth and is the main channel of a huge watershed which gives it its wide, deep character.

The river produced the British record salmon of 64 lb (Miss G. W. Ballantine, 1922). Salmon run in spring, although this feature has recently declined, with the bigger fish generally taken in late season. Besides the salmon, the Tay offers excellent trout fishing, and has a head of roach and grayling. Roach of more than 2 lb have been taken, although they are seen as detrimental to the salmon fisheries and a by-law is in force that all roach caught must be killed.

Because of its fame, it is advisable to book very early to fish the Tay.

Aberfeldy, Perths., Tayside. 2½ m right bank as permit.

T (DT, WT, tackle shop, Aberfeldy. Fly only. Sunday fishing permitted on weekly ticket only).

Aberfeldy, Perths., Tayside. 2½ m Menzies Castle to Tirinie.

S (WT Adv. Major Neil Ramsay & Co., Farleyer, Aberfeldy. B and ghillie available. Fishery open 15 Jan.–15 Oct. No Sunday fishing).

Aberfeldy, Perths., Tayside. 1½ m left bank from Boltachan Burn to Cluny Cottages.

T, S (DT Adv. Killiechassie Estate Office, Aberfeldy. L–4. No Sunday fishing).

Birnam, Perths., Tayside, 2 m.

S (Inquiries well in advance to I. Redford, Holmlea, Station Road, Errol, or Birnam Hotel. B, MB available. Fishery open 15 Jan.–15 Oct.).

Dunkeld, Perths., Tayside. 1½ m Kinnaird Beat.

S, T (Advance inquiries to J. T. Sutherland, chartered surveyor, Bank of Scotland Buildings, Brechin, Angus. B, MB and ghillie available. Fishery open 15 Jan.–30 Sept. No Sunday fishing).

Dunkeld, Perths., Tayside. 2 m right bank.

T, S (DT Adv., if fishing not booked by guests, from Dunkeld House Hotel. Trout fly only. MB and ghillie available. No Sunday salmon fishing).

Dunkeld, Perths., Tayside. 4 m right bank Inchmagranachan Farm to Dunkeld bridge.

T (DT Adv. R. Scott Millar, tackle, Atholl Street, Dunkeld. Fly only).

Errol, Perths., Tayside. 2 m.

T, S (DT Adv. Holmlea, Station Road, Errol. B, MB and ghillie available. No Sunday fishing).

Grandtully, Perths., Tayside. To Ballechin.

T, grayling (DT Adv. Grandtully Hotel. Salmon fishing for residents).

Kinclaven, Perths., Tayside. Beats in area.

S (WT advance inquiries to J. G. Forsyth, Ballathie Estate Office,

Balamains, near Stanley, Perths. B and ghillie available.).

Logierait, Perths., Tayside. 6 m Logierait towards Aberfeldy.

T, S, C (DT Adv. Logierait Hotel, Logierait. B, MB and ghillie available. No Sunday salmon fishing).

Perth, Perths., Tayside. 3 m North Inch to harbour and beyond.

T, ST, S, C (DT Adv. Director of Finance, Perth and Kinross District Council, 1 High Street, Perth. L–20. Fly only in parts).

Perth, Perths., Tayside. 12 m Redgorton to Ballathie.

T, ST, S, C (DT Adv., but not required for coarse fish, from P. D. Malloch, tackle, 24 Scott Street, Perth. B, MB and ghillie available. No Sunday fishing).

Stanley, Perths., Tayside. 1½ m right bank Stanley Water.

S (DT Adv., in Jan. and Feb. only, from Ballathie Estate Office, Balamains, near Stanley, Perths. Fishery open 15 Jan.–28 Feb. No Sunday fishing).

Stanley, Perths., Tayside. 1½ m Taymont Estate Water.

S (WT advance inquiries only to Bell-Ingram, 7 Walker Street, Edinburgh 3. B and ghillie available. Fly only. No Sunday fishing).

Weem, Perths., Tayside. 1½ m Weem Water, Twin Trees to Aberfeldy.

T, S (DT Adv. Weem Hotel, Weem. No Sunday fishing).

Tay tributaries: Almond, Alyth, Ardle, Blackwater (Perths), Braan, Dochart, Earn, Ericht, Fillan, Garry, Gaur, Glentarken Burn, Isla, Kerbet Water, Lochay, Lyon, Shee Water, Tummel, Water of Dean.

Statutory season 15 Jan.–15 Oct.

Teith

Rated the main salmon water in the Forth system, the Teith runs from L. Venacher through Callander to the Forth near Stirling.

Often a good March salmon run, generally with a bigger run later in the season, and fair trout and sea-trout fishing.

Callander, Perths., Central. 3 m Bullshed Pool to Gart March, except stretches marked on ticket.

T, S (D T Adv. tackle shops in area or from Stirling District Council, Municipal Buildings, Stirling. Fly only. No Sunday fishing).

Statutory season 1 Feb.–31 Oct.

Teviot

A major Tweed tributary, rising in hills above Hawick to run to the Tweed at the famed Junction Pool, Kelso.

Spates can give a good spring run of salmon. Excellent trout fishing, plus grayling.

Eckford, Roxburghs., Borders. 1 m stretch right bank.

S, ST, T, grayling (D T Adv. Keeper's House, Eckford. L–6. Fishery open 1 Apr.–30 Sept. for trout).

Hawick, Roxburghs., Borders. Extensive fishing in area, including Teviot tributaries; map available.

T, S, C (D T Adv. Mon.–Fri. only Stothart's Tackle, Hawick, or from Horse and Hounds, Bonchester. Fishery open 6 Mar.–30 Sept. No Sunday fishing).

Jedburgh, Roxburghs., Borders. 2 m Oxnam Mouth to Nine Wells.

T, S, C (D T Adv. The Gun Shop, Kenmore Toll, Jedburgh, and J. Lunn, Cannongate, Jedburgh. L–2 rods for salmon. Salmon permits only from J. Lunn. No Sunday fishing).

Kelso, Roxburghs., Borders. Sunlaws Salmon Fishery.

S (D T Adv. Redpath & Co., tackle, Horse Market, Kelso. L–4).

Kelso, Roxburghs., Borders. Stretches in area.

T, C (D T Adv. Kelso tacklists or R. Gibson, Boathouse, Sprouston. Fly only in April).

Statutory season 1 Feb.–30 Nov.

Thurso

Rises near the Sutherland border and runs 20 m to L. More.

An excellent spring salmon water, opening on 11 Jan. Compensation water from Loch can assist summer sport, with the best fishing in July and August. Trout fishing of little note.

Thurso, Caithness, Highland. Whole river.

T, S (D T Adv., depending on bookings, from River Superintendent, Ulbster Arms, Halkirk, from 8.30 a.m. to 10 a.m. Mon.–Sat.; longer periods through hotel residence only, or from Thurso Fisheries Ltd, Estate Office, Thurso East. B and ghillie available. Fishery open 11 Jan.–5 Oct. No Sunday fishing).

Till

Rises north-west of Alnwick, Northumberland, and runs north through the Cheviots to the Tweed at Tillmouth, below Coldstream.

Good sea-trout fishing; some salmon, trout and coarse fish (lower reaches).

Cornhill-on-Tweed, Northumb. 3 m to Tweed.

T, ST, S, C (D T Adv., provided fishing not booked by hotel guests, otherwise with residence, from Tillmouth Park Hotel, Cornhill. Fly only 1–14 Feb. and 14 Sept.–30 Nov. Coarse fishing reserved for residents at hotel's self-catering cottages. Ghillie available. No Sunday fishing).

Statutory season 1 Feb.–30 Nov.

Truim

Runs through Glen Truim to join the River Spey above Newtonmore.

Good salmon and trout fishing.

Newtonmore, Inverness, Highland. As marked on ticket.

T, S (D T, WT Adv. J. Dallas, High Street, Kingussie. L–6. Fishery open 11 Feb.–30 Sept.).

Tummel

Links L. Rannoch with L. Tummel and the Tay at Ballinluig.

An interesting feature is the Pitlochry visual fish pass, open to visitors to inspect the running fish scaling the dam. Salmon fishing good, with fair trout fishing, and occasional sea-trout. Also holds pike and perch.

Kinloch Rannoch, Perths., Tayside. ½ m
West Tempar Estate.

T, S (D T Adv. Main House, West Tempar
Estate, Kinloch Rannoch. L–6).

Kinloch Rannoch, Perths., Tayside. 2 m
L. Rannoch to L. Dunalastair.

T, S (D T Adv. Dunalastair Hotel,
Kinloch Rannoch. Fly only).

Pitlochry, Perths., Tayside. 1½ m Port-
na-Craig Fishery below Pitlochry
Dam.

S (D T Adv. Pitlochry A C, c/o
Pitlochry Tourist Office for fishing on
Tuesday, Thursday and Saturday, and
Pine Trees Hotel, Pitlochry, for
Monday, Wednesday and Friday.
Advance booking usually essential).

Pitlochry, Perths., Tayside. 5 m to
Ballinluig.

T, grayling (D T Adv. Pitlochry Tourist
Office; C. Stuarts, ironmonger, Atholl
Road, Pitlochry; Milton of Fonals
Caravan Site, Pitlochry; McDonalds
Tackle, Kirkmichael; Post Office,
Ballinluig).

Statutory season 15 Jan.–15 Oct.

Tweed

Springs 1500 ft up in the Hills of
Tweedsmuir and runs a 100-mile course
to the North Sea at Berwick, draining
over 1000 square miles through its many
tributaries.

Although it has suffered a decline
(now checked) from the results that put
it among rivers like the Tay, it can still
offer excellent game fishing. There is a
spring run of salmon to 10 lb, with the
bigger fish going over 20 lb in late
summer and autumn. The sea-trout, too,
are large, with reports of fish to 30 lb
being netted. The largest Tweed salmon
is reckoned to be a 69 lb 12 oz fish
caught by the Earl of Home in 1730, not
allowed as a British record through lack
of details.

It is an excellent trout water, famous
among other things for the invention of
the Greenwell's Glory fly, still popular on
the water. Spring and summer are best
for trout. Shoals of roach to 2 lb inhabit
the lower reaches, although there are
signs that fishery policies of slaughtering

them are having a marked effect. The
river also offers fine grayling.

Coldstream, Berwicks., Borders. 600 yds
left bank Leet Water to road bridge.

T, S, C (D T Adv. from keeper).

Cornhill-on-Tweed, Northumb. 4 m
Coldstream Bridge to Drieper Island.

T, S T, S (Fishing available, if not taken
by guests, from Tillmouth Park Hotel,
Cornhill. Fly only. B and ghillie available. No Sunday fishing).

Galashiels, Selkirks., Borders. 9 m
Thornilee to Ellwyn Burn.

T (D T Adv. Mon.–Fri. J. and A.
Turnbull, tackle, 30 Bank Street,
Galashiels, or Gala A A. No Sunday
fishing).

Horncliffe, Berwicks., Borders. 8 m from
island above Horncliffe to sea.

T, C (Free fishing).

Kelso, Roxburghs., Borders. 2¼ m
Merton to Makerstoun.

S (W T Adv. inquiries only Bell-
Ingram, 7 Walker Street, Edinburgh 3.
B and ghillie available. Fly only. No
Sunday fishing).

Kelso, Roxburghs., Borders. Stretches in
area.

T, C (D T Adv. Mon.–Fri. from tackle
shop, Kelso, or R. Gibson, Boathouse,
Sprouston. Fly only 1–30 Apr. No
Sunday fishing).

Melrose, Roxburghs., Borders. 1½ m
from St Helens.

T (D T Adv. J. Stewart, ironmonger,
Melrose, or from keeper, W. Murray,
Drygrange, Melrose. Fishery open 1
Apr.–6 Oct. No Sunday fishing.

Norham, Northumb. 3 m stretch.

T, C (D T Adv. Masons Arms, Norham.
No Sunday fishing).

Peebles, Peebles, Borders. Peebles Town
Water from Manor Bridge to Priorsford
Bridge.

T, S (D T Adv. I. Fraser, tackle,
Northgate, Peebles. L–20. No Sunday
fishing).

Peebles, Peebles, Borders. Stretches in
area as marked on ticket.

T (D T Adv. tackle shops, Peebles and
Innerliethen; George Hotel and Tweed
Valley Hotel, Walkerburn; or Post
Office, Stobo. Fly only at times.

Fishery open 1 Apr.–30 Sept. No Sunday fishing).

Peebles, Peebles, Borders. 12 m Wire Bridge Cottage to Selkirk boundary, except for private stretches.

T, S (D T Adv. I. Fraser, tackle, Northgate, Peebles, or Blackwood & Smith, 39 High Street, Peebles. Fly only 14 Sept.–30 Nov. Rods limited after 14 Sept. to 20 weekdays, 30 weekends. Fishery open 21 Feb.–30 Nov. No Sunday fishing).

St Boswells, Roxburghs., Borders. 4½ m stretch as shown on permit.

T (D T Adv. tackle shop, St Boswells; Dryburgh Abbey Hotel, Dryburgh; Lilliards Caravan Park; or St Boswells AA. Fishery open 15 Mar.–6 Oct. No Sunday fishing).

Walkerburn, Peebles, Borders. 10 m Holylee to Peebles.

T, ST, S (D T Adv. Tweed Valley Hotel, Walkerburn. Fly only when conditions warrant. Fishery open for trout 1 Apr.–30 Sept.; salmon, 21 Feb.–30 Nov. Hotel also offers tuition and special game fishing weeks).

Tweed tributaries: Blackadder, Bothwell Burn, Breamish, Caddon Water, Dye Water, Eddleston Water, Eden (Berwicks), Ettrick Water, Faseny Water, Gala Water, Jed Water, Kale Water, Leader, Leet Water, Leithen Water, Ludgate Water, Lyne Water, Megget Water, Monynut, Teviot, Till, Watch Water, Whiteadder, Yarrow Water.

Statutory season 1 Feb.–30 Nov.

Tyne

Rises in the Lammermuir Hills and runs 25 m through East Lothian to the sea near Dunbar.

Good trout fishing. Pollution, said to be improving, has affected the sea-trout runs, but a considerable number get through towards the end of the season. Like the Tweed, this river has a head of roach to 2 lb, although netting in recent years has reduced the shoals markedly.

East Linton, East Lothian, Lothian. 200 yds left bank stretch.

T (D T Adv. Harvesters Hotel, East Linton. Fly only. No Sunday fishing).

Haddington, East Lothian, Lothian. 20 m High Reaches to East Linton.

T (D T Adv. tackle shops, East Linton, Haddington and Edinburgh. Fishery open 15 Mar.–6 Oct. No Sunday fishing. Fly only).

Statutory season 1 Feb.–31 Oct.

Ugie

A good sea-trout water of the North-East Coast, running 20 m to the sea at Peterhead.

Trout fishing is also of good quality; some salmon.

Peterhead, Aberdeens., Grampian. Whole river except sections outlined on ticket.

T, ST, S (DT, WT Adv. from A. Mitchell, The Cruives, Inverugie, or G. Morrison, c/o Bruce, ironmongers, Chapel Street, Peterhead. Fly only at certain times. Fishery open 12 Feb.–31 Oct. No Sunday fishing).

Tributary: North Ugie.

Ullapool

Runs a short course through Glen Achall to L. Broom at Ullapool.

Fair to good fishing for sea-trout and salmon. Fair trout fishing.

Ullapool, Ross and Crom., Highland. 1 m from Loch to Black Pools.

T, ST, S (DT Adv. Highland Coastal Estates, Coulmore, Kessock, by Inverness. L–2. Fishery open 28 May–8 Oct. No Sunday fishing).

Urr

Runs to the Solway Firth below Dalbeattie between the Dee and the Nith.

Fair to good trout fishing, especially early in the season. Sea-trout run in May, but the best fishing for them and for salmon is from summer onwards.

Castle Douglas, Kirkcudbrights., Dumfries and Gall. To point near East Logan.

T, S (DT Adv. Tommy's Sports, 20 King Street, Castle Douglas. L–10. No Sunday fishing).

Dalbeattie, Kirkcudbrights., Dumfries and Gall. 3½ m from port.

T, ST, S (WT Adv. N. Parker, 30 High Street, Dalbeattie. No Sunday fishing).
Tributary: Southwick Water.
Statutory season 25 Feb.–29 Nov.

Ury

A tributary of the River Don, joining at Inverurie.

Good trout and salmon fishing, with some sea-trout.

Inverurie, Aberdeens., Grampian. 4 m right bank Howeford Bridge to Don.
T, S (D T Adv. Duncan's tackle, 4 West High Street, Inverurie; Bridge Bar, Port Elphinstone, Inverurie; or from Inverurie AA. Fishery open for trout fishing 1 Apr.–30 Sept. No Sunday fishing).
Statutory season 11 Feb.–31 Oct.

Vinney

A small water joining the River Lunan near Friockheim.

Trout and sea-trout, with some late salmon.

Friockheim, Angus, Tayside. 1 m stretch.
T, ST, S (D T Adv. T. Clark & Sons, tackle, High Street, Arbroath. No Sunday fishing).
Statutory season 16 Feb.–31 Oct.

Watch Water

Tributary of the Tweed system, rising at Blythe Edge, feeding Watch Water Reservoir, then running to Dye Water at Longformacus.

Fair to good trout fishing.

Longformacus, Berwicks., Borders. 2 m Longformacus to reservoir.
T (D T on bank or from keeper. Fishery open 15 Mar.–30 Sept. No Sunday fishing).

Water of Dean (Dean Water)

Tributary of the River Isla, joining near Glamis Castle.

Fair trout fishing, also grayling.

Forfar, Angus, Tayside. Left bank stretch marked by Forfar Canmore A C boards.
T (D T Adv. C. Kerr, tackle, 1 West High Street, Forfar. Fly only. Fishery open 15 Mar.–6 Oct.).

Meigle, Perths., Tayside. 2 m Braidston Mill to Isla.
T (D T Adv. G. Dick, tackle, Meigle. Fly only).
Tributary of Tay system.

Water of Leith

Tributary of the Forth system running north-east to Edinburgh.

Recovering from pollution and now regularly restocked with trout. Free fishing, but season permit must be obtained in advance from Lothian Regional Council, Dept of Admin., George IV Bridge, Edinburgh.

Water of Luce

Small water flowing 6 m to Luce Bay at Glenluce.

Sea-trout and salmon, with some trout.

Glenluce, Wigtowns., Dumfries and Gall. 1 m road to Linfoot.
ST, S, T (D T Adv. Three Lochs Caravan Park, Newton Stewart. Ghillie available).

Stranraer, Wigtowns., Dumfries and Gall. Stretch from Quarter Bridge.
T, ST, S (D T Adv., except Saturday, from hotels, tackle shops and camping sites in area, or from Stranraer and Dist. A A. No Sunday fishing).
Statutory season 25 Feb.–31 Oct.

Water of Nevis

Runs from Ben Nevis through Glen Nevis to L. Linnhe at Fort William.

Can offer good sea-trout and salmon fishing, given water.

Fort William, Inverness, Highland. 6 m river mouth to lower falls.
ST, S (D T Adv. tackle shop, Fort William. L–6 adult rods, 4 juveniles under sixteen. Fishery open 11 Feb.–16 Oct. No Sunday fishing).

West Water

A tributary of the North Esk, rising at West Knock and running to the main river below Inchbane.

Trout, sea-trout and salmon.

Edzell, Angus, Tayside. 1 m right bank stretch.

T, S (DT Adv. Glenesk Hotel, Edzell).

Edzell, Angus, Tayside. 5 m March to river mouth.

ST, S (DT Adv. T. Clark & Sons, tackle, High Street, Arbroath. L–4. No Sunday fishing).

Statutory season 16 Feb.–31 Oct.

Wester Water

Feeds Loch of Wester, running on into Sinclairs' Bay.

Trout, with fair salmon fishing when conditions are right.

Wick, Caithness, Highland. Left bank of whole river, including fishing in loch.

T, S (DT Adv. C. Dunnet, Auckhorn Farm, Lyth, by Wick. B available from 1 Aug. on. Fishery open 1 Apr.–31 Oct. No Sunday fishing).

Whiteadder

Rises in East Lothian and runs through the Lammermuir Hills to join the River Tweed above Berwick.

Fair trout fishing.

Berwick-upon-Tweed, Northumb. 7 m Canty's Bridge to Allanton.

T (DT Adv. Corporation Arms, Canty's Bridge; Red Lion Hotel, Allanton; Country House Hotel, Chirnside; or Berwick and Dist. A A. Fly only to 1 May. No Sunday fishing).

Duns, Berwicks., Borders. 25 m Chirnside to source.

T (DT on bank or from keeper. No Sunday fishing).

Wick

A small water offering improving sea-trout and salmon fishing encouraged by the local angling association. Fair trout fishing, especially in middle reaches. Migratory fish from summer on.

Wick, Caithness, Highland. 12 m whole river.

ST, S (DT Adv. tackle shop, Wick. No Sunday fishing).

Statutory rod season 11 Feb.–31 Oct.

Yarrow Water

Links St Mary's Loch with the Ettrick at Selkirk.

Trout, sea-trout and salmon, with late fishing best. Trout restocked regularly by Selkirk A A.

Selkirk, Selkirks., Borders. Considerable stretches; also fishing in River Ettrick.

T (DT Adv. D. and H. MacDonald, tackle, High Street, Selkirk; Gordon Arms Hotel, Tushielaw; Post Offices at Ettrick, Yarrowford, Yarrow and Ettrick Bridge. Fishery open 1 Apr.–30 Sept. No Sunday fishing).

Tributary of Tweed system.

Statutory season 1 Feb.–30 Nov.

Ythan

Runs a 30-mile course and is rated among Scotland's best sea-trout fisheries, especially in the tidal pool, 4 m in extent, at Newburgh.

Sea-trout fishing is best June to Oct. There are a few salmon in Mar. and May, but the best runs are from summer on.

Ellon, Aberdeens., Grampian. Ellon Castle Estate Water.

T, ST, S (DT Adv. Buchan Hotel, Ellon. Fishery open 11 Feb.–31 Oct. No Sunday fishing).

Fyvie, Aberdeens., Grampian. 3 m left bank Ardlogie to Fetterletter.

T, ST, S (DT Adv. Vale Hotel, Fyvie. Fly only June–Aug. No Sunday fishing).

Methlick, Aberdeens., Grampian. Haddo Estate Water.

T, ST, S (DT Adv. tackle shop, Methlick, or Haddo Estate Trust, Estate Office, Haddo House, Aberdeen. Fishery open 11 Feb.–31 Oct. No Sunday fishing).

Methlick, Aberdeens., Grampian. 2½ m left bank stretch.

T, S (DT Adv. J. Somers & Son, tackle, Thistle Street, Aberdeen. No Sunday fishing).

Methlick, Aberdeens., Grampian. Right bank, Waterloo Bridge to Tangland Bridge.

T, ST, S (DT Adv. tackle shop, Methlick. No Sunday fishing).

Newburgh, Aberdeens., Grampian. 3½ m Snub to sea.

T, ST, S (DT Adv. ticket machine, Udny and Dudwich Estates Office, The Stables, Udny Green, or Udny Arms Hotel, Newburgh. Reduced fishing for residents, and B and ghillie by arrangement. No Sunday fishing).

Tributary: Ebrie.

Statutory season 11 Feb.–31 Oct.

Seven

Scottish Still Waters (by region)

The waters in this section are listed under county headings, with the counties grouped together inside their regional boundaries – Borders, Central, Dumfries and Galloway etc.

Berwickshire, Borders

Loch Coldingham, Coldingham.
● T (DT Adv. Westloch House, Coldingham; tel. Coldingham 270. Please book. Fly only. Open 15 Mar.– 6 Oct. L–25. Good loch fishing, with some big fish).
Watch Reservoir, Longformacus.
● T (DT Adv. from keeper or Rathbourne Hotel, Longformacus. Fly only. Open 15 Mar.–30 Sept. B available).

Peebleshire, Borders

Fruid Reservoir, Broughton.
● T (DT Adv. for fishing from 2 boats only, must be booked a month in advance, from Lothian Regional Council, Water Supply Services, 55 Buckstone Terrace, Edinburgh. Fly only. Open 15 Apr.–30 Sept. No Sunday fishing).
Talla Reservoir, Tweedsmuir.
● T (DT Adv. ticket office for bank fishing, and Lothian Regional Council, Water Supply Services, 55 Buckstone Terrace, Edinburgh, for boat fishing. Open 1 Apr.–30 Sept. No Sunday fishing).

Roxburghshire, Borders

Acreknowe Reservoir, Hawick.
T (DT Adv. tackle shop, Hawick. B available).
Alemore Loch, Hawick.
T, C (DT Adv. tackle shop, Hawick. B available. Trout and pike).
Cauldshiels Loch, Melrose.
C (Free fishing. Mainly perch).
Crooked Loch, Hawick.
T (DT Adv. tackle shop, Hawick).
Goose Loch, Hawick.
T (DT Adv. tackle shop, Hawick).
Hellmoor Loch, Hawick.
T (DT Adv. tackle shop, Hawick).
Williestruther Loch, Hawick.
T (DT Adv. tackle shop, Hawick).
Windylaw Loch, Hawick.
T (DT Adv. tackle shop, Hawick).

Selkirkshire, Borders

St Mary's Loch, Cappercleuch.
T, C, S (DT Adv. Gordon Arms or Rodono Hotel, Cappercleuch, or from St Mary's A C. Trout, pike and perch, with occasional salmon. Open 1 Apr.– 30 Sept. No Sunday fishing, except for guests of club members. B available).

Perthshire, Central

Doine Loch, Balquhidder.
● T (DT Adv. from keeper. B available).
Glen Finglas Reservoir, Callander.
● T (DT Adv. for boat fishing only, L–3, from Water Dept, Strathclyde Regional

Council, 419 Balmore Road, Glasgow, or sub-office at Stronachlachar. Open 1 Apr.–30 Sept.).

Lake of Menteith, Port of Menteith.
● T (D T Adv. Lake Hotel, Port of Menteith. B available. Open 9 Apr.– 6 Oct. No Sunday fishing).

Lochan-na-Laraig, Killin.
● T (D T Adv. tackle shop, Main Street, Killin. Fly only).

Lochan Reoidhte, Aberfoyle.
T (D T Adv. Ferguson, newsagent, Aberfoyle).

Loch Ard, Aberfoyle.
● T, pike (D T Adv. Ferguson, newsagent, or Forest Hills Hotel, Aberfoyle. Trout fly only. B available. Some very big pike have come from this water; inquire locally for permission).

Loch Chon, Aberfoyle.
T, C, S (Free fishing. Migratory fish rod season 1 Feb.–31 Oct. No Sunday fishing).

Loch Drunkie, Aberfoyle.
T (D T Adv. Chief Forester, Forest Office, Achray Forest, Aberfoyle).

Loch Katrine, Aberfoyle.
● T (D T Adv. from Water Dept, Strathclyde Regional Council, 419 Balmore Road, Glasgow, or sub-office at Stronachlachar. Fishing from boats only. L–15. Open 1 Apr.–30 Sept. Fly only).

Loch Lubnaig, Callander.
T, ST, S, char (D T Adv. from keeper or tackle shops locally. Migratory fish rod season 1 Feb.–31 Oct. B available).

Loch Tay, Killin.
T, S (D T Adv. tackle shop, Main Street, Killin; Killin Hotel or Clachaig Hotel, Killin. B, M B and ghillie available. Salmon can be big, and trolling is the usual method. Migratory fish rod season 15 Jan.–15 Oct. No Sunday fishing for salmon).

Loch Venacher, Callander.
T, ST, S (D T Adv. tackle shop, Main Street, Callander, from keeper, or from Stirling District Council, Municipal Buildings, Stirling. B through tackle shop. Game fishing fly only, but the water has produced big pike; inquire

locally for permission. Migratory fish rod season 1 Feb.–31 Oct.).

Loch Voil, Balquhidder.
● T (D T Adv. from keeper. B available).

Stirlingshire, Central

Carron Valley Reservoir, Denny.
● T (D T Adv. Finance Director, Central Regional Council, Viewforth, Stirling. Must be booked. L–12. B, M B available. Fly only).

Loch Arklet, Inversnaid.
● T (D T Adv. Water Dept, Strathclyde Regional Council, 419 Balmore Road, Glasgow, or sub-office at Stronachlachar. Fishing from boats only. L–5. Open 1 Apr.–30 Sept.).

Loch Coulter, St Ninians.
● T (D T Adv. Larbert and Stenhousemuir A C. Boat only; no bank fishing. Fly only. L–4. Open 1 Apr.–30 Sept. No Sunday fishing).

Dumfriesshire, Dumfries and Galloway

Barscobe Loch, Balmaclellan.
● T (D T Adv. Barscobe Cottage, Barscobe, or Milton Park Hotel, Dalry. Fly only. L–4. B available. Browns and rainbows).

Black Esk Reservoir, Boreland.
T (D T Adv. from keeper or Sandyford Filter Station, Boreland. L–8. Fishing from boats only. Open 15 Apr.–30 Sept.).

Castle Loch, Lochmaben.
C (D T on bank or from W. Marshall, Lochfield, near Lockerbie. B available. Big bream in quantity and tench and carp. Pike to 20 lb. The water also holds vendace. Open all year).

Glenkiln Reservoir, Dumfries.
● T (D T Adv. from keeper or Director of Water and Sewerage, 70 Terregles Street, Dumfries. B available. Fly only. Open 1 Apr.–30 Sept. No Sunday fishing).

Hightae Mill Loch, Lochmaben.
C (D T Adv. Moss Side, Hightae.

Fishing limited to fishing from 4 boats; no bank fishing. Water produces big bream and pike and also holds tench, carp and roach).

Kirkcudbrightshire, Dumfries and Galloway

Brack Lock, Dalry.
● T (D T Adv. Milton Park Hotel, Dalry. Fly only. L–4. B available. No Sunday fishing. Water stocked with rainbows and brook trout).
Bush Moss Loch, Gatehouse of Fleet.
● T (D T Adv., for 2 fishing from one boat only (no bank fishing), from McMurray Bros, tackle, 10 High Street, Gatehouse, or McKinnel, tackle, 15 St Cuthbert Street, Kirkcudbright. Fly only).
Carlingwark Loch, Castle Douglas.
C (Free fishing. B available).
Clatteringshaws Loch, New Galloway.
T, C (D T Adv. tackle shop, Ken Bridge; Cross Keys or Kenmure Arms, Ken Bridge; The Café, High Street, Ken Bridge; or Newton Stewart A A. Trout can run big, and the pike fishing is good. Open 15 Mar.–30 Sept.).
Dalbeattie Reservoir, Dalbeattie.
● T (D T Adv. from café, 30 High Street, Dalbeattie. Fly only. Open 15 Apr.–30 Sept. Regular stocking with browns and rainbows).
Earlston Loch, Dalry.
● T (D T Adv. Glenkens Café, Dalry. B available).
Howie Loch, Dalry.
T, S (D T Adv. Milton Park Hotel, Dalry. Migratory fish rod season 11 Feb.–31 Oct. No Sunday fishing).
Lairdmannoch Loch, Castle Douglas.
● T (D T Adv. from keeper or Lidderdale and Gillespie Ltd, Castle Douglas. Fly only. L–8 rods fishing from boats; no bank fishing. Open 1 Apr.–30 Sept. No Sunday fishing).
Loch Fleet, Gatehouse of Fleet.
T (D T Adv. tackle shops, High Street, Gatehouse, or St Cuthbert Street, Kirkcudbright).
Loch Grannoch, Gatehouse of Fleet.

T (D T Adv. as Loch Fleet, above. B available).
Loch Ken, New Galloway.
T, C, S (Free fishing on west bank, by road; rest private. Good trout fishing, with occasional salmon. The water has a reputation for big pike, producing a 40-pounder in recent years. A legendary monster which cannot be substantiated was said to weigh 70 lb. Salmon rod season 11 Feb.–31 Oct.).
Loch Lochenbreck, Gatehouse of Fleet.
● T (D T Adv. tackle shops as Loch Fleet, above. Fly only. B available).
Loch Stroan, New Galloway.
T, C (D T Adv. Cross Keys or Kenmure Arms, Ken Bridge, or The Café, High Street, Ken Bridge. Open 1 Apr.–30 Sept.).
Skerrow Loch, Gatehouse of Fleet.
T (D T Adv. as Loch Fleet, above. B available).
Whinyeon Loch, Gatehouse of Fleet.
● T (D T Adv. as Loch Fleet, above).
Woodhall Loch, Castle Douglas.
T, C (Fishing for residents, Kenmure Arms, New Galloway, and Culgruff House Hotel, Crossmichael, the latter offering a boat. No Sunday fishing).

Wigtownshire, Dumfries and Galloway

Black Loch, Kirkcowan.
● T (D T Adv. ticket office at Three Lochs Caravan Park. B available. L–12. Open Easter to 6 Oct.).
Bruntis Loch, Newton Stewart.
T (D T Adv. hotels and caravan parks in area or from Newton Stewart A A. Open 15 Mar.–30 Sept.).
Dindinnie Reservoir, Stranraer.
● T (D T Adv. hotels, tackle shops and camping sites in area or from Stranraer and Dist. A A. Fly only. No Sunday fishing).
Kirriereoch Loch, Newton Stewart.
T (D T Adv. hotels and camping sites in area or Newton Stewart A A. Open 15 Mar.–30 Sept.).
Knockquhassen Reservoir, Stranraer.
T (D T Adv. hotels, tackle shops and

camping sites in area or from Stranraer and Dist. AA. No Sunday fishing).

Loch Dunalgar, Kirkcowan.
● T (DT Adv. Tarff Hotel, Kirkcowan. Fly only).

Loch Heron, Kirkcowan.
C (DT Adv. Three Lochs Caravan Park. Open Easter to 31 October. B available).

Lochnaw, Stranraer.
● T (DT Adv. Lochnaw Castle Hotel. Fly only. L–6. No Sunday fishing).

Loch Ochiltree, Newton Stewart.
T, pike (DT Adv. hotels and camping sites in area or from Newton Stewart AA. Open 15 Mar.–30 Sept.).

Loch Ree, Stranraer.
T (DT Adv. hotels, tackle shops and camping sites in area or from Stranraer and Dist. AA. B available. No Sunday fishing).

Loch Ronald, Kirkcowan.
C (DT Adv. Three Lochs Caravan Park. B available. Open Easter to 31 October).

Penwhirn Reservoir, Stranraer.
T (DT Adv. hotels, tackle shops and camping sites in area or from Stranraer and Dist. AA. B available. No Sunday fishing).

Soulseat Loch, Stranraer.
T (DT Adv. hotels, tackle shops and camping sites in area or from Stranraer and Dist. AA. B available. No Sunday fishing).

Wee Glenamour Loch, Newton Stewart.
T (DT Adv. hotels and camping sites in area or from Newton Stewart AA. Open 15 Mar.–30 Sept.).

Fifeshire, Fife

Ballo Reservoir, Leslie.
● T (DT Adv. for fishing from 1 boat; please book: Water Division, Fife Regional Council, Craig Mitchell House, Flemington Road, Glenrothes. Open 1 Apr.–30 Sept. No Sunday fishing. No bank fishing).

Cameron Reservoir, St Andrews.
● T (DT Adv. from keeper. Fly only. Open 16 Apr.–1 Oct. B available.

L–25 bank rods, 18 boats. Well stocked, fish averaging over 1 lb. No Sunday fishing).

Carlhurlie Reservoir, Leven.
● T (DT Adv. Hutchison, tackle, College Street, Buckhaven. Fly only. Open 1 Apr.–30 Sept. L–4. No Sunday fishing).

Clatto Loch, Cupar.
● T (DT Adv. The Factor, Crawford Priory Estate, 2 Bonnygate, Cupar. Fly only. Open 1 Apr.–30 Sept. L–10).

Gally Loch, Cowdenbeath.
C (Free fishing. Water offers big perch and average pike, with occasional big fish).

Harper Lees Reservoir, Leslie.
● T (DT Adv. please book for 2 fishing from one boat, A. Constable, tackle, 39a High Street, Kirkcaldy. Fly only. Open 1 Apr.–30 Sept. No Sunday fishing).

Holl Reservoir, Leslie.
● T (DT Adv. please book for 2 fishing from one boat, Water Division, Fife Regional Council, Craig Mitchell House, Flemington Road, Glenrothes. Fly only. Open 1 Apr.–30 Sept. No Sunday fishing).

Lindores Loch, Newburgh.
● T (DT Adv. F. G. A. Hamilton, Drummond Street, Comrie, Perths. Please book. Fly only. Open 15 Mar.– 6 Oct. Stocked browns, rainbows, some big).

Loch Fitty, Dunfermline.
● T (DT Adv. Game Fisheries Ltd, Loch Fitty, Kingseat, Dunfermline; tel. Dunfermline 23162. Fly only. B available. Stocked browns and rainbows).

Loch Glow, Kelty.
T (DT Adv. Hobby and Model Shop, New Row, Dunfermline).

Raith Lake, Kirkcaldy.
● T (DT Adv. Game Fisheries Ltd, as Loch Fitty, above. Fly only. B available).

Aberdeenshire, Grampian

Aboyne Loch, Aboyne.

C, T (DT Adv. ticket office. Mainly pike and perch, some big. No Sunday fishing).

Loch Loirston, Aberdeen.

T (DT Adv. J Somers & Son, tackle, Thistle Street, Aberdeen).

Loch of Strathbeg, St Combs.

● T (DT Adv. The Tufted Duck, St Combs. No tickets from 1 September. Fly only. B available).

Red Loch, Fraserburgh.

● T (DT Adv. A. P. Brown & McRae, solicitors, 35 Frithside Street, Fraserburgh; tel. Fraserburgh 2922. B available. Fly only).

Kincardineshire, Grampian

Loch Saugh, Fettercairn.

T (DT Adv. tackle shops, Brechin and Drumtochty, or Ramsay Arms, Fettercairn, which also offers salmon stretch on South Esk).

Morayshire, Grampian

Bishopmill Trout Fishery, Elgin.

● T (DT Adv. Bishop Mill Fisheries, Spynie Churchyard Road, Elgin; tel. Elgin 3875. Fly only).

Blairs Loch, Forres.

● T (DT Adv. The Smokers' Shop, High Street, Forres. Fly only. B available. No Sunday fishing).

Easter Bauds Farm Fishery, Fochabers.

● T (DT Adv. Easter Bauds Farm; tel. Fochabers 456. Fly only).

Glen Letterach Reservoir, Elgin.

● T (DT Adv. Grampian Regional Council, Water Services, Grampian Road, Elgin; tel. Elgin 7102. Fly only).

Loch Dallas, Forres.

● T (DT Adv. The Smokers' Shop, High Street, Forres. Fly only. B available. No Sunday fishing).

Millbuies Lochs, Elgin.

● T (DT Adv. Dept of Recreation, Moray Dist. Council, High Street, Elgin; tel. Elgin 45121. L–4 rods fishing from boats only. Fly only).

Argyllshire, Highland

Loch Shiel, Acharacle.

T, ST, S (DT Adv. Creel Fishing Facilities, Creel Cottage, Acharacle, or Dalilea Farm House Hotel, Acharacle. Fishing from boats only. B, M B available. Open 28 Feb.–30 Oct. No Sunday fishing. Sea-trout best from summer onwards).

Loch Sunart, Strontian.

T, ST, S (DT Adv. Kilcamb Lodge Hotel, Strontian, free for guests at hotel. B, M B available. Migratory fish best from late summer. Rod season 11 Feb.–31 Oct.).

Caithness, Highland

Loch Scarmelate, Dummet.

● T (DT Adv. Northern Sands Hotel, Dummet. Fly only. Open 14 Mar.–14 Sept. No Sunday fishing. B, M B available).

Loch Watten, Wick.

● T (DT Adv. Melvich Hotel, by Thurso, Sutherland. Fly only. No Sunday fishing. A good trout water, with fish averaging 1 lb).

Inverness-shire, Highland

Avielochan, Boat of Garten.

T (DT Adv. Ticket Office, Avielochan, Aviemore; G. Mortimer, tackle, High Street, Grantown-on-Spey, or Craigard Hotel, Boat of Garten. Open 1 Apr.–30 Sept. B available through hotel; please book. L–10).

Clunas Reservoir, Inverness.

● T (DT Adv. J. Graham, tackle, Union Street, Inverness. Fly only. L–6).

Loch Arkaig, Spean Bridge.

T, ST, S (DT Adv. Lochyview, Bunarkaig, Spean Bridge; tel. Gairlochy 217. B, M B available. Open 1 Apr.–15 Oct.).

Loch Benevean, Fasnakyle.

T (DT Adv. J. MacPherson & Sons, tackle, Inglis Street, Inverness. Fishing from boats only. Open 1 Apr.–30 Sept. No Sunday fishing).

Loch Boath, Inverness.
- T (D T Adv. tackle shop, Union Street, Inverness. Fly only. B available).

Loch Bran, Whitebridge.
- T (D T Adv. Whitebridge Hotel, Whitebridge. Fly only. Open 1 May to first Sunday in October. B available).

Loch Cuaich, Dalwhinnie.
  T (D T Adv. The Paper Shop, Kingussie; Blacks, ironmongers, Newtonmore, or keeper's house at loch. B available. Open 15 Mar.–30 Sept. excepting 12 Aug.–15 Sept. No Sunday fishing).

Loch Dallas, Boat of Garten.
  T (D T Adv. G. Mortimer, tackle, High Street, Grantown-on-Spey, or Craigard Hotel, Boat of Garten. B available through hotel. Open 1 Apr.–30 Sept. No Sunday fishing).

Loch Eilt, Glenfinnan.
- T, ST, S (D T Adv. West Highland Estates Office, 33 High Street, Fort William. Fly only. Open 15 May–30 Sept. No Sunday fishing. B available. L–6).

Loch Farraline, Foyers.
  T (D T Adv. Foyers Hotel, Foyers. B, M B available).

Loch Garten, Boat of Garten.
  T (D T Adv. Craigard Hotel, Boat of Garten. B available through hotel. No Sunday fishing).

Loch Garth, Foyers.
  T (D T Adv. Foyers Hotel, Foyers. B, M B available).

Loch Gynack, Kingussie.
- T (D T Adv. for 2 rods fishing from boat only, The Paper Shop, Kingussie. Open 1 Apr.–30 Sept. No Sunday fishing).

Loch Inchlaggan, Invergarry.
- T (D T Adv. Tomdoun Hotel, Invergarry. Fly only. L–35. B available).

Loch Killin, Foyers.
  T (D T Adv. Foyers Hotel, Foyers. B, M B available).

Loch Killin, Whitebridge.
  T (D T Adv. Whitebridge Hotel, Whitebridge. Open 1 May to first Sunday in October. B, M B available).

Loch Knockie, Whitebridge.
- T (D T Adv. Whitebridge Hotel, Whitebridge. Fishing in west and east ends of water only. Fly only. Open 1 May to first Sunday in October. B available).

Loch Lochy, Spean Bridge.
  T (D T Adv. Lochyview, Bunarkaig, Spean Bridge; tel. Gairlochy 217. M B available).

Loch Morlich, Aviemore.
  T (D T Adv. from Warden, Glenmore Forest Park. B available).

Loch Ness, Fort Augustus.
  T, ST, S (D T Adv. fishing from boats only, Outdoor Shop, Fort Augustus; Foyers Hotel, Foyers; Whitebridge Hotel, Whitebridge. Salmon run early in this famous loch, which can be hard to fish without a local ghillie, which can be organized with a boat through the Fort Augustus shop. The salmon and sea-trout fishing can be good, and again, with such a huge water, local advice is useful. No Sunday fishing).

Loch Quoich, Glen Garry.
- T (D T Adv. Tomdoun Hotel, Invergarry. Fly only. No Sunday fishing. B, M B available).

Loch Ruthven, Inverness.
- T (D T Adv. tackle shop, Union Street, Inverness. B available. L–2. No Sunday fishing).

Loch Ruthven, Whitebridge.
- T (D T Adv. Whitebridge Hotel, Whitebridge. Open 1 May to first Sunday in October. Fly only. No Sunday fishing. B available).

Loch Tarff, Whitebridge.
- T (D T Adv. Whitebridge Hotel, Whitebridge. Fly only. Open 1 May to first Sunday in October. B available).

Loch Unagar, Fort Augustus.
  T (D T Adv. Outdoor Shop, Fort Augustus. B, M B available).

Loch Vaa, Boat of Garten.
- T (D T Adv. G. Mortimer, tackle, High Street, Grantown-on-Spey, or Craigard Hotel, Boat of Garten. Fly only. Open 1 Apr.–30 Sept. No Sunday fishing. B through hotel).

Morar Loch, Mallaig.
  T, ST, S (D T Adv. from keeper, Park Mhor, Glas Nacerdoch, Mallaig. B

M B available. Migratory fish rod season 11 Feb.–31 Oct.).

Sailbanoch Loch, Cannich.
C (Free fishing).

Spey Dam, Laggan.
● T (DT, WT Adv. The Paper Shop, Kingussie, or Blacks, ironmongers, Newtonmore. B available. Fly only. Open 15 Mar.–30 Sept. No Sunday fishing).

Morayshire, Highland

Lochindorb, Grantown-on-Spey.
T (DT Adv. Moray Estates Development Office, Forres; tel. Forres 2213. L–4, fishing from 2 boats only. Open 1 Apr.–30 Sept. No Sunday fishing).

Loch Pityoulish, Grantown-on-Spey.
T (DT Adv. G. Mortimer, tackle, High Street, Grantown. Open 1 Apr.–30 Sept. No Sunday fishing. B available).

Ross and Cromarty, Highland

Goose Loch (Loch A'bhaid Luachraich), Aultbea.
● T (DT Adv. National Trust Information Centre, Inverewe House, Poolewe; tel. Poolewe 229. Fly only. Open 1 Apr.–6 Oct. No Sunday fishing. B available).

Lean Cow Loch (Loch Na Ba Caoile), Poolewe.
● T (DT Adv. as Goose Loch, above).

Loch Dubh, Ullapool.
T, ST (DT Adv. Royal Hotel, Ullapool. B, M B available. Rod open season 11 Feb.–31 Oct. No Sunday fishing).

Loch Ghuiragarstidh, Poolewe.
● T (DT Adv. as Goose Loch, above. Fly only).

Loch Glascarnoch, Garve.
T (DT Adv. Aultguish Inn, by Garve).

Loch Glass, Evanton.
● T (DT Adv. Factor, Novar Estates Office, Evanton. Fly only. B, M B available. No Sunday fishing).

Loch Ketchnsary, Poolewe.
● T (DT Adv. as Goose Loch, above. Fly only).

Loch Luichart, Garve.
T, C (DT Adv. J. J. Shanks & Son, tackle, Dingwall. Open 15 Mar.–6 Oct. No Sunday fishing).

Loch Maree, Gairloch.
T, ST, S (WT Adv. Shieldaig Lodge Hotel, by Gairloch. Essential to book. L–2. B available. No Sunday fishing. Rod open season 11 Feb.–31 Oct. Salmon from April, and excellent summer sea-trout fishing, especially with dapped flies. A very popular water).

Loch Meig, Contin.
● T (DT Adv. Loch Achonachie A C. Fly only. Open 1 June–30 Sept. No Sunday fishing. B available).

Loch Morie, Evanton.
● T (DT Adv. Evanton tacklist, or Factor, Novar Estates Office, Evanton. Fly only. No Sunday fishing. B available).

Loch Nan Dailthean, Poolewe.
● T (DT Adv. as Goose Loch, above. B available. No Sunday fishing).

Shieldaig Forest Waters, Gairloch.
T and S in 1 loch (DT Adv. Shieldaig Lodge Hotel, by Gairloch. Series of waters, of which Loch Badachro takes salmon. B available on some waters, most fly only, and a ghillie can be arranged. No Sunday fishing).

Sutherlandshire, Highland

Gillaroo Loch, Inchnadamph.
● T (DT Adv. Inchnadamph Hotel; tel. Assynt 202. Fly only. No Sunday fishing).

Kinbrace Lochs, Kinbrace.
● T (DT Adv. Garvault Hotel, Kinbrace. Fly only fishing on 13 lochs in area. B available some waters. No Sunday fishing).

Lairg Lochs, Lairg.
● T (DT Adv. Altnacealgach Hotel, by Lairg. Lochs Cama, Urigill and Veyatie offer good trout fly fishing. B available. No Sunday fishing).

Loch-an-Ruathair, Helmsdale.
● T (DT Adv. Navidale House Hotel, Helmsdale. Fly only. B available. No Sunday fishing).

Loch Assynt, Inchnadamph.
- T, S (3 only day permits if not taken by guests, Inchnadamph Hotel; tel. Assynt 202. Trout and chance of salmon, fly fishing only. Rod season 11 Feb.–31 Oct. No Sunday fishing).

Loch Boarrian, Elphin.
- T (D T Adv. Altnacealgach Hotel. B available. No Sunday fishing).

Loch Brora, Brora.
- T, ST, S and char (D T Adv. fishing from boats only, Links Hotel and Royal Marine Hotel, Brora, or Sutherland Arms Hotel, Golspie. Fly only. Open 1 May–15 Oct. No Sunday fishing).

Loch Cama, Elphin.
- T (D T Adv. Altnacealgach Hotel. Fly only. B available. No Sunday fishing).

Loch Craggie, Tongue.
- T (D T Adv. Tongue Hotel and Ben Loyal Hotel, Tongue. Fly only. B available. No Sunday fishing).

Loch Farlary, Golspie.
  T (D T Adv. Lindsay & Co., ironmongers, Golspie, or tackle shop, Main Street, Golspie. B available. No Sunday fishing).

Loch Ghriam, Overscaig.
  T (D T Adv. Overscaig Hotel, Overscaig. B available).

Loch Ghubais, Dornoch.
- T (D T Adv. MacDonald, tackle, Castle Street, Dornoch. Fly only. No Sunday fishing. L–4).

Loch Hakel, Tongue.
- T (D T Adv. Ben Loyal Hotel, Tongue. Fly only. No Sunday fishing).

Loch Hope, Hope.
- T, ST, S (D T Adv. Altnaharra Hotel and Tongue Hotel, Tongue. Fly only. B and ghillie available. No Sunday fishing. This is one of Britain's best sea-trout lakes and it fishes best from summer onwards. Migratory fish rod season 12 Jan.–30 Sept.).

Loch Horn, Golspie.
  T (D T Adv. tackle shop, Main Street, Golspie, or Lindsay & Co., ironmongers, Golspie. B available. No Sunday fishing).

Lochinver Lochs, Lochinver.
  T, some ST, some S (D T Adv. Tourist Information Office, Lochinver, Culag

Hotel, Lochinver; Kylesku Hotel, Kylesku; Drumbeg Hotel, Drumbeg; or Post Office, Stoer. Most waters fly only – there are upwards of 30 in area – and some take sea-trout and salmon. There are also boats on some waters. No Sunday fishing. Open 15 Mar.–15 Oct.).

Loch Lannsaidh, Dornoch.
- T (D T Adv. MacDonald, tackle, Castle Street, Dornoch. Fly only. B available. No Sunday fishing).

Loch Laoigh, Dornoch.
- T (D T Adv. tackle shop, Dornoch. Fly only. B available. No Sunday fishing).

Loch Loyal, Tongue.
- T (D T Adv. Ben Loyal Hotel or Tongue Hotel, Tongue. Fly only. B, M B available. No Sunday fishing).

Loch Lundie, Golspie.
  T (D T Adv. tackle shop, Golspie. B available. No Sunday fishing).

Loch Merkland, Overscaig.
  T (D T Adv. Overscaig Hotel. B, M B available. No Sunday fishing).

Loch Naver, Altnaharra.
- T, S (D T Adv. Altnaharra Hotel. Fly only. B available. No Sunday fishing. Loch takes salmon. Rod season 12 Jan.–30 Sept.).

Loch Shin, Lairg.
  T (D T Adv. fishing hut at water or Overscaig Hotel, Overscaig, or Sutherland Arms Hotel, Lairg. Open 15 Apr.–30 Sept. No Sunday fishing. Good trout fishing).

Loch Slaim, Tongue.
- T (D T Adv. Tongue Hotel, Tongue. Fly only. B, M B available. No Sunday fishing).

Loch Vayatie, Elphin.
- T (D T Adv. Altnacealgach Hotel. Fly only. B available. No Sunday fishing).

Loch Urigill, Elphin.
- T (D T Adv. Altnacealgach Hotel. B available. No Sunday fishing. Fly only).

Melvich Lochs, Melvich.
  T (D T Adv. Melvich Hotel, Melvich. B available some waters).

Scourie Lochs, Scourie.
- T (D T Adv. for many lochs in area, A. Mackay, Choc Bhuan, or H. Macleod

Arch Cottage, Scourie. Fly only. B available some waters. No Sunday fishing).

East Lothian, Lothian

Danskine Loch, Gifford.
C (D T Adv. from keeper. Water holds carp and tench. Open all year).
Donolly Reservoir, Gifford.
● T (D T Adv. Water Supply Services, Alderston House, Haddington, East Lothian. Fly only. Open 15 Apr.–30 Sept. No Sunday fishing. B available).
Hopes Reservoir, Gifford.
● T (D T Adv. as Donolly Reservoir, above. Fly only. No Sunday fishing).
Whisky Bottle Reservoir, North Berwick.
● T (D T Adv. 6 rod only keeper or North Berwick A C. Fly only. No Sunday fishing).
Whiteadder Reservoir, Duns.
● T (D T Adv. 4 rods only as Donolly Reservoir, above. Fly only. B available. No Sunday fishing).

Midlothian, Lothian

Clubbiedean Reservoir, Edinburgh.
● T (D T Adv. 2 rods from one boat, ticket office or Lothian Regional Council, Water Supply Services, 55 Buckstone Terrace, Edinburgh. Fly only. No Sunday fishing).
Duddingston Loch, Edinburgh.
C (Free fishing only with permit from Property Services Agency, Dept of the Environment, Room J708, Argyle House, 3 Lady Lawson Street, Edinburgh. Open all year. Roach, carp, tench).
Gladhouse Reservoir, Penicuik.
● T (D T Adv. as Clubbiedean Reservoir, above. L–6 rods from boats only. Fly only. No Sunday fishing).
Glencorse Reservoir, Penicuik.
● T (D T Adv. as Gladhouse Reservoir, above. 6 rods, fly only from boats).
Rosebery Reservoir, Gorebridge.
● T (D T Adv. as Clubbiedean Reservoir, above. 2 rods, fly only).

West Lothian, Lothian

Harperrig Reservoir, West Calder.
● T (D T Adv. ticket office or Lothian Regional Council, Water Supply Services, 55 Buckstone Terrace, Edinburgh. Fly only. Open 1 Apr.–30 Sept. No Sunday fishing. Limited to 4 bookings. B available).
Humbie Quarry, Humbie.
C (Free fishing).
Linlithgow Loch, Linlithgow.
● T (D T Adv. tackle shop, Gowan Avenue, Falkirk. Fly only. L–14 on bank. B available).

Argyllshire, Strathclyde

Argyll Estates Hill Lochs, Inveraray.
● T (D T Adv. Argyll Estates Office, Cherry Park, Inveraray. Fly only. Open 15 May–6 Oct. No Sunday fishing. L–6).
Ascog Loch, Tighnabruaich.
● T (D T Adv. tackle shops, hotels and post offices in area. Fly only. Open 15 Mar.–5 Oct.).
Auchalochy Loch, Campbeltown.
● T (D T Adv. tackle shops, Campbeltown. Fly only).
Cam Loch, Ford.
T (D T Adv. keeper, Inverliever Lodge, Ford. B available).
Castle Fisheries, Inveraray.
T (D T Adv. ticket office. Open all year).
Crosshill Loch, Campbeltown.
T (D T Adv. tackle shops, Campbeltown).
Dubh Loch, Inveraray.
● T (D T Adv. Argyll Estates Office, Cherry Park, Inveraray. Fly only. Open 16 May–15 Oct. No Sunday fishing. Permit also covers for stretch of River Garron. L–6. One B available).
Dubh Loch, Kilninver.
T (D T Adv. Barndromin Farm, Knipoch. Limited to fishing from one boat).
Dunoon Reservoirs, Dunoon.
● T (D T Adv. tackle shop, Queens Hall Buildings, Argyll Street, Dunoon. Fly

only. Open 15 Mar.–30 Sept. No
Sunday fishing. L–12).
Glen Dubh Reservoir, Barcaldine.
T (DT Adv. Forest Office, Barcaldine,
Connel).
Hospital Lochan, Ballachulish.
T (DT Adv. Glencoe Campsite office
or Chief Forester, Glencoe Forest,
Ballachulish).
Inverliever Loch, Ford.
● T (DT Adv. keeper, Inverliever Lodge,
Ford. B available).
Knapdale Forest Lochs, Lochgilphead.
● T (DT Adv. Forestry Commission,
Knapdale Forest, Cairnbarn, Loch-
gilphead. Fly only. No Sunday fish-
ing. B available. L–5 rods on each
water).
Knapdale Hill Lochs, Lochgilphead.
● T (DT Adv. P. Davidson, tackle,
Colchester Square, Lochgilphead. Fly
only. No Sunday fishing).
Lettermay Loch (*Lochain Cnainh*),
Lochgoilhead.
● T (DT Adv. Forestry Office, Ardgar-
tan, Arrochar. Fly only. No Sunday
fishing).
Lochan Dubh, Barcaldine.
T (DT Adv. Forest Office, Barcaldine,
Connel).
Lochan Lariche, Achnamara.
● T (DT Adv. Post Office, Achnamara.
Fly only. One B).
Loch Avich, Dalavich.
T (DT Adv. Forestry Office, Dalavich.
B, MB available. No Sunday fish-
ing).
Loch Awe, Lochaweside.
T, S, ST, C (The fishing is free with
charges for boats, arranged through
Carraig Thura Hotel, Lochawe; Ford
Hotel, Ford; Portsonachan Hotel,
Lochaweside. The water produces fair
trout, although it has not been so pro-
ductive in recent years. Salmon run
early, and most are taken near Kilchurn
Castle. Some big pike have also been
taken in this area).
Loch Barnluasgan, Cairnbaan.
● T (DT Adv. limited to fishing from
2 boats from Chief Forester,
Knapdale Forest Office, Cairnbaan.
Fly only).

Loch Coille Bhar, Cairnbaan.
● T (DT Adv. as Loch Barnluasgan,
above. Limited to fishing from 2 boats.
Fly only).
Loch Eck, Kilmun.
T, ST, S (DT Adv. Loylet Hotel or
Whistlefield Inn, Loch Eck. B, MB
available. No Sunday fishing for
salmon and sea-trout. Migratory fish
rod season 16 Feb.–31 Oct.).
Loch Goil, Carrick Castle.
T, ST, S (DT Adv. Forestry Office,
Ardgartan, Arrochar, or Carrick Castle
Hotel. Migratory fish rod season 11
Feb.–31 Oct.).
Loch Lussa, Campbeltown.
● T (DT Adv. tackle shops
Campbeltown, or Kintyre AC. Fly only.
B available).
Loch Nant, Kilchrenan.
● T (DT Adv. Kilchrenan Trading Post.
Fly only).
Loch Nell, Oban.
T (DT Adv. from keeper. B avail-
able).
Loch Restil, Cairndow.
T (DT Adv. Cairndow Estate Office,
Cairndow. Open 20 May–20 Sept. No
Sunday fishing. L–6).
Loch Tarsan, Dunoon.
● T (DT Adv. Scott, ironmongers,
Argyll Street, Dunoon, or tackle shop,
Queens Hall Buildings, Argyll Street,
Dunoon. Fly only. Open 1 Apr.–30
Sept. No Sunday fishing. B avail-
able).
Loch Tromlee, Kilchrenan.
C (DT Adv. Kilchrenan Trading Post.
Mostly pike).
Loch Seil, Kilninver.
T (DT Adv. limited to fishing from
one boat, Barndromin Farm,
Knipoch).
Oude Reservoir, Oban.
T (DT Adv. Oban and Lord AC. Open
15 Mar.–5 Oct.).
Powder Dam Reservoir, Tighnabruaich.
● T (DT Adv. tackle shops and post
offices in area. Fly only. Open 15 Mar.–
5 Oct.).
Tangy Loch, Campbeltown.
● T (DT Adv. at loch. B available. Fly
only).

Ayrshire, Strathclyde

Bogton Loch, Dalmellington.
T, C and char (Free fishing. Trout small. The water is said to hold big pike).

Boreland Reservoir, Cumnock.
T (D T Adv. tackle shop, Cumnock).

Braehead Dam, Cumnock.
T (D T Adv. Blackwood, tackle, Glaisnock Street, Cumnock).

Brickwork Loch, Cumnock.
T (D T Adv. tackle shop, Cumnock).

Burnfoot Reservoir, Kilmarnock.
T (D T Adv. McCririck & Sons, tackle, John Finnie Street, Kilmarnock. B available).

Camphill Reservoir, Largs.
● T (D T Adv. Area Engineer, Water Dept, Strathclyde Regional Council, 19 Underwood Road, Paisley. Fly only, limited to 6 rods fishing from 3 boats only).

Corsehouse and Cocklebie Pits, Stewarton.
T (Sports Centre, Stewarton, or Stewarton A C).

Craigendunton Reservoir, Kilmarnock.
T (D T Adv. McCririck & Sons, tackle, John Finnie Street, Kilmarnock. L–5).

Kilbirnie Loch, Kilbirnie.
T, C (D T Adv. D. Lennie, jeweller, Main Street, Kilbirnie, or Glendale Arms, Glengarnoch. Water holds roach and perch in addition to trout).

Lady's Loch, Dalmellington.
T (D T Adv. from keeper. B available. L–2).

Loch Bradan, Straiton.
T (D T Adv. Head Ranger, Tallaminnoch, Straiton, or from ticket machine. B available. Fish average around 1 lb, with some bigger).

Loch Brecbowie, Straiton.
● T (D T Adv. Head Ranger, Tallaminnoch, Straiton. Fly only. B available).

Loch Dhu, Straiton.
● T (D T Adv. as Loch Brecbowie, above. Fly only. L–2).

Loch Doon, Dalmellington.
T, C, S (Free fishing. Salmon occasionally, and pike and char in addition to trout).

Loch Skelloch, Straiton.
T (D T Adv. as Loch Brecbowie, above. B available. L–20).

Martnaham Loch, Ayr.
C (Free fishing).

Mill Reservoir, Ardrossan.
● T (D T Adv. tackle shop, Ardrossan. Fly only).

Penwhapple Reservoir, Girvan.
● T (D T Adv. ticket office or King's Arms, Barr. Fly only. Open 1 Apr.–15 Sept. No Sunday fishing. B available. L–30).

Prestwick Reservoir, Prestwick.
T (D T Adv. tackle shop, Main Street, Prestwick, or Wheatsheaf Inn, Monkton. Open 15 Apr.–4 Oct. Good trout fishing).

Tarmac Loch, Auchinleck.
T (D T Adv. tackle shop, Auchinleck).

White Loch Reservoir, Stewarton.
● T (D T Adv. Sports Centre, Stewarton, or Stewarton A C. Fly only).

Dunbartonshire, Strathclyde

Loch Lomond, Balloch.
T, ST, S, C (D T, WT Adv. boat hirers and hotels near loch and tackle shops at Clydebank, Dumbarton and Glasgow. N B. Fishing on waters running into loch for members only, Loch Lomond Angling Improvement Association. Best coarse fish catches come from the lower loch, with big pike and roach, and the areas around its inlets. Trout fishing is fair, and there have been some big fish. The loch also holds the rare powan and takes a run of salmon and sea-trout. Migratory fish rod season 11 Feb.–31 Oct. Boat hire is abundant).

Loch Sloy, Tarbet.
T (D T Adv. Loch Sloy Power Station, Arrochar, or Loch Lomond Caravan Park, Inveruglas, Arrochar).

Lanarkshire, Strathclyde

Bothwellhaugh Pool, Hamilton.
C (Free fishing).

Clyde Park Pond, Motherwell.
C (Free fishing).
Daer Reservoir, Elvanfoot.
● T (D T Adv. Finance Dept, Strathclyde Regional Council, Hamilton. Fly only. No Sunday fishing. B available).
Glen Finglas Reservoir, Brig O'Turk.
● T (D T Adv. limited to 6 anglers in 3 boats (no bank fishing), from Water Dept, Strathclyde Regional Council, 419 Balmore Road, Glasgow. Fly only).
Hillend Reservoir, Airdrie.
T (D T Adv. from keeper or Turf Hotel and Forresfield Hotel, Airdrie).
Hogganfield Loch, Glasgow.
C (Free fishing. Park opening hours only).
Lily Loch, Airdrie.
T (D T Adv. as Hillend Reservoir, above).
Roughriggs Reservoir, Airdrie.
● T (D T Adv. Finance Dept, Strathclyde Regional Council, Hamilton. Fly only. No Sunday fishing. B available).
Roukenglen Park Pond, Glasgow.
C (Free fishing).
Springfield Reservoir, Carluke.
● T (D T Adv. tackle shop, Carluke, or United Clyde A P A. Fly only).

Renfrewshire, Strathclyde

Camphill Reservoir, Largs.
● T (D T Adv. 8 rods from boats only (no bank fishing) from Water Dept, 19 Underwood Road, Paisley. Fly only).
Castle Semple Loch, Lochwinnoch.
C (D T Adv. ticket office at loch or St Winnoch A C. Open 15 Mar.–6 Oct.).
Glenburn Reservoir, Paisley.
● T (D T Adv. as Camphill Reservoir, above. Fly only. L–10).
Greenock Reservoirs, Greenock.
● T (D T Adv. tackle shop, Greenock, farms at reservoir or from Greenock and Dist. A C. Four waters. Fly only. No Sunday fishing).
Harelaw Loch, Port Glasgow.
T (D T Adv. Port Glasgow A C).
Howwood Reservoirs, Howwood.
● T (D T Adv. as Camphill Reservoir,

above. Fly only. L–4, giving access to Rowbank and Barcraigs reservoirs. No Sunday fishing).
Knocknair Loch, Port Glasgow.
T (D T Adv. Port Glasgow A C).
Loch Thom, Greenock.
● T (D T Adv. tackle shop, Greenock, or Greenock and Dist. A C. Fly only. Open 15 Mar.–30 Sept. No Sunday fishing).
Lower Loch Gryffe, Kilmacolm.
T (D T Adv. Port Glasgow A C. Open 15 Mar.–6 Oct.).
Mill Dam, Port Glasgow.
T (D T Adv. Port Glasgow A C).
Picketlaw Reservoir, Eaglesham.
● T (D T Adv. limited to 2 rods from one boat (no bank fishing), from Water Dept, 55 Burnfield Road, Glasgow. Fly only. No Sunday fishing).
Whittlemuir Dam, Howwood.
● T (D T Adv. General Store, Station Road, Howwood. Fly only. Open 1 Apr.–30 Sept.).

Stirlingshire, Strathclyde

Banton Loch, Kilsyth.
T (D T Adv. Calzium Motor Sales, Stirling Road, Kilysyth. B available. L–4. No Sunday fishing).
Birkenhead Reservoir, Kilsyth.
T (D T Adv. as Banton Loch, above, or from Kilsyth F P A).

Angus, Tayside

Blackwater Dam, Kirriemuir.
● T (D T Adv. Tayside Regional Council, Water Services Dept, 10 Ward Road, Dundee. Fly only. Open 2 Apr. to last Sat. in Sept. L–12 rods bank, 15 boats. No bank rods Sunday until all boats taken).
Crombie Reservoir, Dundee.
● T (D T and season as Blackwater Dam, above. Fly only. L–6 rods fishing from 3 boats).
Forfar Loch, Forfar.
● T in part (D T Adv. tackle shop, West High Street, Forfar. Fly only on south bank).

Glenogil Reservoir, Forfar.
- T (D T Adv. tackle shop, Forfar. Fly only. No Sunday fishing).

Lintrathen Loch, Kirriemuir.
- T (D T Adv. as Blackwater Dam, above. Fly only. L–15 rods fishing from boats only).

Loch Lee, Edzell.
- T (D T Adv. for fishing from 3 boats only, Head Keeper, Tavermark, Glenesk; tel. Tarfside 208. Fly only. No Sunday fishing).

Monikie Reservoir, Dundee.
- T (D T Adv. as Blackwater Dam, above. L–14 rods from boats only. Fly only).

Rescobie Loch, Forfar.
- T (D T Adv. from keeper. Fly only. B available).

Saugh Loch, Brechin.
- T (D T Adv. Sports Shop, High Street, Brechin. Fly only).

Kinross-shire, Tayside

Loch Leven, Kinross.
- T (D T Adv. Loch Leven Fisheries, The Pier, Kinross. Boat fishing only, L–126. Fly only. This famous water holds the silvery strain of trout which runs to 5 lb and more, and the average weight is around 1½ lb. The water can be dour but is said to be recovering from a recent fall in catch totals. There is a booking wait of up to six months).

Perthshire, Tayside

Butterstone Loch, Dunkeld.
- T (D T Adv. Lochend Cottage at loch. Fly only. Open 1 Apr.–6 Oct. B available).

Carsebreck Loch, Braco.
- T (D T Adv. from keeper or Ardoch Farming Co. Ltd, Estate Office, Keir, Dunblane. Fly only. Open 1 Apr.–30 Sept. No Sunday fishing).

Dunalastair Loch, Kinloch Rannoch.
- T, S (D T Adv. Dunalastair Hotel, Kinloch Rannoch. Fly only. Migratory fish rod season 15 Jan.–15 October. B and ghillie arranged. No Sunday fishing).

Glenfarg Reservoir, Glenfarg.
- T (D T Adv. for 3 boats (no bank fishing) from Water Division, Fife Regional Council, Craig Mitchell House, Flemington Road, Glenrothes. Fly only. Open 1 Apr.–30 Sept. No Sunday fishing).

Loch Bainnie, Glenshee.
  T (D T Adv. Spittal Hotel, Glenshee. B available. No Sunday fishing).

Loch Bhac, Pitlochry.
- T (D T Adv. West Lodge, Faskally, Pitlochry, or Pitlochry A C, Pitlochry Tourist Office. Fly only. L–12 rods from bank. B available).

Loch Earn, Lochearnhead.
- T (D T Adv. post offices, Lochearnhead and St Fillans. Fly only. B, M B available).

Loch Eigheach, Kinloch Rannoch.
- T (D T Adv. Moor of Rannoch Hotel, Rannoch Station, or The Garage, Kinloch Rannoch. Fly only).

Loch Faskally, Pitlochry.
- T, S (D T Adv. Boating Station at loch or tackle shop, Pitlochry. Trout fly only. Open 15 Mar.–6 Oct., with chance of salmon, which run through the famous Tummel fish pass. The trout can be big. B, M B available).

Loch Finnart, Kinloch Rannoch.
- T (D T Adv. Forestry Commission Office, Kinloch Rannoch; tel. Kinloch Rannoch 335. L–4 rods fishing from boats only. Fly only. No Sunday fishing).

Loch Horn, Methven.
- T (D T Adv. Forest Office, Inverpark, Dunkeld; tel. Dunkeld 284. Fly only. L–2 rods fishing from one boat only).

Loch Kinnardochy, Tummel Bridge.
- T (D T Adv. Queen's View Visitors' Centre, Allean, near Pitlochry; tel. Killiecrankie 223. Fly only. L–2 rods fishing from one boat only).

Loch Laidon, Rannoch Station.
  T (D T Adv. Moor of Rannoch Hotel, Rannoch Station. M B available).

Loch Monzievaird, Ochertyre.
- T (D T Adv. keeper's cottage at entrance or tel. Comrie 273. B available.

Fly only. Water stocked with brook trout and rainbows besides browns.).

Loch Rannoch, Kinloch Rannoch.

T, S (DT Adv. Dunalastair Hotel or Bunrannoch Hotel, Kinloch Rannoch. Fly only. B, M B and ghillie available. Most fish under 1 lb, but some big. Water also takes salmon).

Loch Tay, Kenmore.

T, S (Fishing for guests only, Kenmore Hotel, Kenmore, and Tigh an Loan Hotel, Fearnan. B and ghillie available. Open 15 Jan.–15 Oct. No Sunday fishing).

Loch Tulloch Curran, Kirkmichael.

T (DT Adv. Log Cabin Hotel, Kirkmichael. No Sunday fishing).

Loch Tummel, Tummel Bridge.

T, C (DT Adv. Loch Tummel Hotel, Tummel Bridge. B available. No Sunday fishing. A good trout water, it also holds perch and pike).

Loch Vrotigan, Glenshee.

● T (DT Adv. Spittal Hotel, Glenshee. Fly only. No Sunday fishing).

Lower Glendevon Reservoir (Frandy Loch), Auchterarder.

● T (DT Adv. Waterman's House, Upper Glendevon Reservoir, or Water Division, Fife Regional Council, Craig Mitchell House, Flemington Road, Glenrothes. Fly only. Open 1 Apr.–30 Sept. B available).

Mharaich Loch, Kirkmichael.

● T (DT Adv. The Forester, Sillerburn, Kirkmichael; tel. Strathardle 343. Fly only. L–2 rods fishing from one boat only. Open 1 May–15 Sept. No Sunday fishing).

Old England Loch, Stanley.

● T (DT Adv. Ballathie Estate Office, near Stanley, Perth. Fly only. L–3. B available).

Turret Loch, Crieff.

● T (DT Adv. tackle shop, Crieff, or Central Scotland Water Development Board, 30 George Square, Glasgow. Fly only. No Sunday fishing).

Upper Glendevon Reservoir, Auchterarder.

● T (DT Adv. as Lower Glendevon Reservoir, above. Limited to fishing from 3 boats; no bank fishing. Fly only. Open 1 Apr.–30 Sept. No Sunday fishing).

Eight

The Scottish Islands (rivers and lochs)

The islands as a whole, many laced with lochs and streams, offer a wealth of fishing, some virtually untouched. For convenience of reference, rivers and still waters are given under each island heading.

Arran

The rivers running to the west coast of the island offer the best migratory fish runs, usually fishing well late in the season. Trout fishing in the lochs and smaller waters can be good, and local inquiries will find the best prospects.

Rivers

Kilmory

Runs west off the central hills.
 Good salmon and sea-trout fishing.
Kilmory. Whole river.
 T, ST, S (DT Adv. Lagg Hotel, Kilmory, or Post Office, Lagg. No Sunday fishing).

Machrie

Runs west, like the Kilmory, and offers similar prospects. Best from July onwards.
Blackwater Foot. 3 m from river mouth.
 ST, S (DT Adv. J. Boscawen, Killiechassie Estate Office, Aberfeldy, Perths., or from Lagg Hotel, Kilmory. Fishery open 1 June–15 Oct. No Sunday fishing. L–6).

Benbecula

Fishing for trout and occasional sea-trout in the island's many lochs can be arranged through the hotel at Creagorry.

Bute

Alone, in this part of the world, the island offers coarse fishing in L. Fad and L. Ascog, the former producing roach to 2 lb and pike of 20 lb and more. L. Quien is an excellent trout water.

Kilfinan River

Runs to L. Fyne and offers trout, salmon and sea-trout.
Kilfinan. 3 m High Fence to L. Fyne.
 T, ST, S (DT Adv. Kilfinan Hotel, Kilfinan. Ghillie by arrangement with hotel. No Sunday fishing).

Lochs

Loch Ascog
 ● T (DT Adv. Bute Estate Office, Rothesay. Fly only. No Sunday fishing).

Loch Fad
 ● T (DT Adv. Bute Estate Office, Rothesay. Fly only. No Sunday fishing).

Meldalloch
 ● T (DT Adv. Kilfinan Hotel, Kilfinan. B available. Fly only. No Sunday fishing).

Loch Quien
 ● T (DT Adv. Bute Estate Office, Rothesay. Fly only. B available. No Sunday fishing).

Coll

Plentiful trout, if small, in the lochs, which fish best in late spring. Inquiries for ticket fishing to The Gamekeeper, The Lodge, Arinagour, or from Isle of Coll Hotel, Arinagour.

Harris

The lochs offer trout fishing, and those linked to the sea have sea-trout and salmon runs from July onwards. Inquiries to hotels and estates in the island: Factor, Borve Lodge, Scarista (L. Borve, L. Carron, L. Fincastle, L. Laxdale, L. Sluice); D. Bertram, Estate Factor, Invercarse, Kendebig (L. Collam, L. Drinishader, L. Grose Bay); Tarbert Hotel, Tarbert (Lacasdale lochs); Laig Guest House, Drinishadder (Loch-na Haidh and Loch-na Croath).

Islay

Has two main rivers, the Laggan and the Machrie, offering salmon and sea-trout sport, with the best fishing from late summer onwards. Most of the lochs offer reasonable trout fishing, controlled by hotels and estates. Inquiries for loch fishing to: Port Askaig Hotel, Port Askaig (L. Allan, L. Ballygrant, L. Lossit); Head Keeper, Islay House (L. Finlaggan, L. Gorm).

Rivers

Laggan

Offers trout and salmon fishing, best late in season for salmon.
Port Askaig. 4 m of fishing in area.
T, S (DT Adv. The Keeper, Keills, by Port Askaig, or from Port Askaig Hotel, Port Askaig. Ghillie by arrangement. No Sunday fishing).

Machrie

Trout, with salmon and sea-trout. Migratory fish best late in season.
Port Ellen. Stretch near hotel.
T, ST, S (Residents only, Machrie Hotel, Port Ellen. Fly only. No Sunday fishing).

Lewis

With 600 or more lochs, Lewis offers a wealth of trout fishing, although good salmon fishing is preserved to a degree and may not be available without booking. On the preserved Grimersta Fishings in the 1880s, it is recorded, a Mr Naylor landed 54 salmon on fly in one day. Inquire locally for loch trout fishing, which may often be had for the asking, although hotels control some water.

Stornaway River

Offers good salmon and trout fishing.
Stornaway. Whole river, including fishing in lochs in area.
T, S (WT Adv., early booking preferred, from Estate Factor, 13 Kenneth Street, Stornaway. B available for loch fishing. Fly only. No Sunday fishing).

Mull

The main river, the Forsa, offers runs of salmon and sea-trout and fishes best late in the season. The lochs offer trout fishing, with L. Frisa taking salmon and sea-trout.

Forsa River

Good salmon and sea-trout fishing, best in late season.
Salen. Whole river.
T, ST, S (DT Adv. Glenforsa Hotel, Salen. Ghillie available. Fishery open mid-June to mid-Oct. No Sunday fishing).

Lochs

Loch Frisa

T (DT Adv. Ticket Office, The Forestry Commission, Isle of Mull; Browns, hardware, Tobermory; Bellacrom Hotel, Dervaig. B available).

Loch Mishnish

T (DT Adv. Browns, hardware, Tobermory, or Bellacrom Hotel, Dervaig. B available. Fishery open 15 Mar.–30 Sept. No Sunday fishing.)

North Uist

The lochs and loch chains on this island offer a wealth of trout fishing, while the Loch Skealtar chain has a run of salmon, with some spring fish. Contact the Keeper or the Dept of Agriculture and Fisheries for Scotland, Area Sub-Office, Balivanich, Isle of Benbecula, for: Loch-na Ceardaich, Loch An Duin, L. Fada, Deadmans L., Nam Geadh, Traigh Ear Pools (ST, fly only), L. Tergavat, L. Vergavat. Loch fishing permits also from Lochmaddy Hotel, which offers boats and a ghillie by arrangement.

Orkney Islands

Very few of the lochs in the islands attract migratory fish, and the main sport is with trout, often big, like the 17-pounder which is the record for L. Harray in the main island. Fishing on L. Boardhouse, L. Harray and L. Swanney is free, with the Smithfield Hotel arranging boats and motor boats for all three, and Merkister Hotel at the loch offering boats and a ghillie service on Harray.

Other lochs
Muckle Water
- T (DT Adv. Major Ritchie, Trumland House, Rousay. One boat; L–6 rods from shore. Fly only).

Wasbister
- T (DT Adv. ticket office or from Major Ritchie, Trumland House, Rousay. Fly only. Rods limited. B available).

Raasay

Lochs all offer trout fishing, generally free.

Shetland Islands

The inland lochs of the Shetlands offer excellent trout fishing, but the group is more famous for the sea-trout and grilse runs in the voes, or inlets, around the shores. Here, much of the fishing is of high quality and free, although permits are needed for some voes. Shetland AA controls a number of lochs, including L. Spiggie, with a reputation for big trout. Shetland AA day tickets can be had from the Bank of Scotland, Commercial Street, Lerwick. Other permits from tackle shop, Lerwick, Spiggie Hotel, Scousburgh, and Baltasound Hotel, Unst. No Sunday fishing throughout the islands.

Skye

Blessed with a number of game rivers, the island also offers loch fishing, with some of them taking sea-trout and salmon. Most of the hotels on the island control some fishing. For hill loch fishing in the Camus Croise area, contact Hotel Tigh-Osda Eilean Larmain, Camus Croise; for the Storr lochs at Portree contact the College of Agriculture, The Square, Portree. There is no Sunday fishing on the Camus Croise lochs or the Portree lochs.

Rivers

Broadford
Offers trout, salmon and sea-trout.
Broadford. Stretch in area.
- T, ST, S (DT Adv. Broadford Hotel, Broadford. No Sunday fishing).

Eishort
A short river of 1 m or so, offering good sport, with sea-trout and trout.
Sleat. Most of river to Lochanan Dubha.
- T, ST (DT Adv. Hotel Tigh-Osda Eilean Larmain, Camus Croise. Ghillie by arrangement. No Sunday fishing).

Hinnisdal
Has a course of roughly 5 m, and offers good trout and salmon fishing.
Uig. Most of river.
- T, S (DT Adv. Tourist Office, Portree, or Uig Hotel, Uig – fishing free to hotel guests, loch fishing also arranged. Fly only on river. No Sunday fishing).

Horavaig

Offers salmon and sea-trout fishing, with some trout.

Teangue. Stretch from hotel to boat-house.

T, ST, S (Residents only, Toravaig House Hotel, Knock. Hotel also arranges loch fishing for non-residents on L. Dalival, L. Dougall and L. Torscavaig. Boats available. No Sunday fishing).

Ord

Another short river offering fair sport, with sea-trout, plus trout.

Sleat. Whole river.

T, ST (DT Adv. Hotel Tigh-Osda Eilean Larmain, Camus Croise. Ghillie by arrangement. No Sunday fishing).

Snizort

One of the main rivers of the island, offering good sport, with salmon and sea-trout.

Skeabost Bridge, 8 m from river mouth.

T, ST, S (DT Adv. Skeabost House Hotel, Skeabost Bridge. Hotel also offers loch fishing in area. Ghillie by arrangement. Fishery open 1 June–31 Oct. No Sunday fishing).

South Uist

The sea-linked lochs of the island offer excellent sea-trout fishing, although the best water is preserved. Good trout fishing throughout the island, with west coast lochs considered best. The only salmon fishing of note is on L. Bharp. The Lochboisdale Hotel, Lochboisdale, offers fishing on many lochs, mainly L. Bharp, Castle Loch, L. Fada, L. Grogarry, Lower Bornish Loch, Lower L. Kildonan, L. Roag, L. Stilligarry, Upper Kildonan Loch and West Olay Loch. Most of the water is fly only, and the hotel offers boats on many waters. The season usually in force is 15 July–31 Oct., with no Sunday fishing).

Nine

Northern Ireland Rivers

The visiting angler in Northern Ireland will be amazed by the amount of free fishing offered, often of superb quality, on coarse and game waters. While the best of the salmon and sea-trout fishing is preserved, the rest can often be extremely productive. Good trout fishing can often be had for the asking, while the coarse fishing is by and large all free. Another attractive aspect is that there is no coarse fishing close season.

Visitors are reminded that an appropriate rod licence, either Foyle Fisheries Commission (Foyle and Finn systems) or Fisheries Conservancy Board, must be carried. There is no need for a coarse fishing rod licence in the Foyle Fisheries Commission area.

Besides the waters listed in this guide the Department of Agriculture has developed many free fisheries, mostly coarse fishing, through arrangements with landowners. Many are signposted.

Agivey
Formed from the Big Agivey and the Wee Agivey, the river runs to join the Bann system above Coleraine.

Trout, with some salmon. Some fishing with prior permission from landowner.

Tributary of Bann system.

Fisheries Conservancy Board licence.

Arney
Links Lower L. Macrean with Upper L. Erne near Rossdoney and Inishmore Island.

Excellent catches of roach and bream have been taken in the lower river. Some trout.

Sessiagh West, Co. Fermanagh. Stretch in area.

T, C (D T Adv. Dept of Agriculture, Fisheries Dept, 2–4 Queen Street, Belfast).

Tributary of Erne system.

Fisheries Conservancy Board licence.

Ballinamallard
Runs from L. Galballs to Lower L. Erne at St Angelo, where, on the aerodrome water, catches of roach and bream to 100 lb have been frequent. The river also holds trout, with some salmon.

Ballinamallard, Co. Fermanagh. 1 m above and below Kilgortnaleague Bridge.

C, T, S (D T Adv. J. A. Knaggs, Ballinamallard; J. Ruddy, Irvinestown; R. Dickie & Sons, Irvinestown; or Mahon's Hotel, Irvinestown).

Tributary of Erne system.

Fisheries Conservancy Board licence.

Ballinderry
Rises near Dungannon and runs north to Cookstown then east to L. Neagh.

Trout, including dollaghan, and salmon. Fishing mostly free, with permission from landowners.

Tributary of Bann system.

Fisheries Conservancy Board licence.

Bann
The Upper Bann rises in the Mourne Mountains, Co. Down, and runs northeast through Banbridge and Portadown to L. Neagh, the largest lake in the British Isles. The river then runs out of the lough at Toome Bridge through Portglenone to Kilrea and the sea.

Salmon run begins in June, some going through L. Neagh to upper river. Trout fishing is good, and includes the localized race, the dollaghan trout, peculiar to this system. The largest Bann trout is believed to be a 14 lb 5½ oz fish taken by Sir Arthur Algeo in 1967. The system holds good stocks of coarse fish, notably rudd, roach, bream, perch and pike. The upper river between Point of Whitecoat and L. Neagh is rated best for coarse fish.

Banbridge, Co. Down. 12 m Lenaderg to Katesbridge.

C, T, ST, S (DT Adv. Coburn's tackle, 32 Scarva Street, Banbridge, or Angler's Rest, Corbet. Salmon by fly only in parts. No Sunday fishing in parts. L–40).

Portadown, Co. Armagh. Point of Whitecoat to L. Neagh.

C, T, ST (DT Adv. Dept of Agriculture, Fisheries Dept, 2–4 Queen Street, Belfast. Trout fishing 1 Mar.–31 Oct.; coarse all year).

Rathfriland, Co. Down. 9 m Katesbridge Bridge to Hilltown Bridge.

T, S (DT Adv. W. Trimble, tackle, Downpatrick Street, Rathfriland. Fishery open 1 Mar.–31 Oct. No Sunday fishing in parts).

Tributaries: Agivey, Ballinderry, Blackwater (Armagh), Clady, Claudy, Kells Water (Glenwherry), Lower Bann Navigation, Main, Moyola, Six Mile Water.

Fisheries Conservancy Board Licence.

Blackwater (Co. Armagh)

Rises south of Caledon and runs north through Moy to L. Neagh.

The upper river is preserved salmon and trout water. Below Moy there are bream to 7 lb, good roach and pike to 20 lb and more. The fishing here is mostly free, with permission from landowners.

Fisheries Conservancy Board licence.

Burndennet

Flows close to the Tyrone–Londonderry border and offers trout and sea-trout fishing. Mostly free, with permission from riparian owners.

Tributary of Foyle system.

Foyle Fisheries Commission licence.

Burren

A tributary of the River Shimna.

Fair trout fishing, with some sea-trout and salmon.

Newcastle, Co. Down. Stretch in area including parts of River Shimna.

T, ST, S (DT Adv. J. Mackie, tackle, 125 Main Street, Newcastle (closed on Sunday). Fishery open 1 Mar.–31 Oct.).

Fisheries Conservancy Board licence.

Bush

Rises on the north slopes of the Antrim Mountains and runs west to Conagher Bridge, then north to the sea at Bushmills.

To a large extent dependent on spates, offering good salmon and sea-trout fishing when the conditions are right. Trout fishing fair.

Ballymoney, Co. Antrim. 25 m Ballymoney to Bushmills, except water at Benvarden Bridge.

S, ST, T (DT Adv. Dept of Agriculture, Fisheries Dept, 2–4 Queen Street, Belfast).

Bushmills, Co. Antrim. ½ m stretch.

S, ST, T (DT from ticket office or from Dept of Agriculture, Fisheries Dept, 2–4 Queen Street, Belfast).

Fisheries Conservancy Board licence.

Camowen

Joins the Drumragh River to form the River Strule at Omagh.

Trout and sea-trout, with some salmon, also coarse fish.

Omagh, Co. Tyrone. 7 m stretch.

T, C, ST, S (DT, WT Adv. G. Flanagan, Sedan Avenue, Omagh. Fishery open 1 Apr.–20 Oct. Coarse fishing free on application).

Tributary of Foyle system.

Foyle Fisheries Commission licence.

Carey

Runs west from Ballyvoy Bridge to Glenshesk above Ballycastle.

Offers sea-trout and salmon, with fair trout fishing.

Ballycastle, Co. Antrim. 2½ m stretch.

T, S T, S (D T Adv. R. Bell, 38–40 Ann Street, Ballycastle, or from Dept of Agriculture, Fisheries Dept, 2–4 Queen Street, Belfast).

Tributary of Margy system.

Fisheries Conservancy Board licence.

Clady Water

A short river feeding Six Mile Water.

Reasonable trout fishing, with coarse fish in lower reaches.

Portglenone, Co. Antrim. 5 m stretch, most of water.

T, S and C in lower mile (D T Adv. Wild Duck, Port Glenone; McErleans Bar, Clady; Wairs Service Station, Clady Road, Port Glenone. L–12. Open for game fishing 1 Mar.–31 Oct.).

Tributary of Bann system.

Fisheries Conservancy Board licence.

Claudy

Rises to the north of Maghera and runs east to the Lower Bann near Port Glenone.

Trout, some salmon. Some fishing available on request to local riparian owners.

Tributary of Bann system.

Fisheries Conservancy Board licence.

Colebrook

Rises to the north of Creagh and runs past Lisnaskea to Upper L. Erne.

Trout, some salmon, with coarse fishing especially good in the Creamery length, Lisnaskea. Salmon run from August.

Lisnaskea, Co. Fermanagh. Most of river.

C, T, S (Free fishing, provided prior permission sought).

Fisheries Conservancy Board licence.

Derg

Runs from L. Derg north-east through Castlederg to the Mourne near Millbrook.

Offers trout, sea-trout and salmon,

with an improving run of grilse, also coarse fish. Free stretches at Spamount and Greenville.

Castlederg, Co. Tyrone. 7 m stretch.

T, S T, S, C (D T, W T Adv. S. Faulkner, 24 Eden Park, Castlederg. Fishery open 1 Apr.–20 Oct. Coarse fishing free, with permission).

Tributary of Foyle system.

Foyle Fisheries Commission licence.

Drumragh

Joins the Camowen at Omagh to form the River Strule.

Trout, coarse fish and some salmon.

Omagh, Co. Tyrone. 4 m stretch.

T, S, C (D T, W T Adv. G. Flanagan, Sedan Avenue, Omagh. Trout and salmon fishing 1 Apr.–20 Oct. Coarse fishing free, with permission).

Tributary of Foyle system.

Foyle Fisheries Commission licence.

Erne

Forming the backbone of the Fermanagh lakes system, including the huge Upper and Lower L. Erne, the Erne drains a vast area and offers fishing unrivalled in Britain, probably in Europe. This is particularly true of the coarse fishing. Splendid work has been done by the Agriculture Department and the Fisheries Conservancy Board to provide fishing stands and access paths. Bream and roach are a feature of the upper lough, with vast weights taken at a sitting. The hot spot is undoubtedly the upper end of the lough near Inishmore Island. In the lower lough the lower sections and tributaries produce similar results. Huge pike inhabit the system, and trolling is the main approach.

The system's trout should not be overlooked, for they run big and produced the British record brown of 19 lb 4½ oz (lower lough). Again, trolling is used to locate fish in this huge amount of water. Although there is an appreciable salmon run, the Erne is not rated as highly as other Irish waters. Most fish are taken by spinning in the lower lough. Permits and rod licences for the Erne and Upper and Lower L. Erne are available at numerous points, listed below, and visiting anglers are asked to inquire closely about the kind of rod licence needed for their choice of fishing, since there are localized restrictions.

Permits, licences: Enniskillen.
Lakeland Tackle, Henry Street; Post Office, East Bridge Street; J. E. Richardson (Inniskillen) Ltd, East Bridge Street; A. C. Rutledge, 16 High Street; Robert Dickie & Sons Ltd, High Street; Fermanagh Tourist Information Centre, Townhall Street; Thornton Bros, Church Street; all Enniskillen.

Lower L. Erne.
Manor House Hotel, Killadeas; Roscor Post Office; Thomas Flynn, Kesh; Blaney Service Station; Mrs E. Graham, Manville House, Letter; Casey's Lake Hotel, Garrison; Lough Erne Hotel, Kesh; Leggs Post Office; Kesh Post Office; Brendan Faughan, Leggs; T. Daly, Belleek; Carlton Hotel, Belleek; Lough Naver Forest Office, Derrygonelly; Mahon's Hotel, Irvinestown; R. Dickie & Sons, High Street, Irvinestown.

Upper L. Erne
Post offices, Bellanaleck and Maguiresbridge; John Meldrum, Main Street, Lisnaskea; W. R. Nawn, Main Street, Lisbellaw; Lakeland Hotel, Bellanaleck.

Boats for hire: Carrybridge Angling Centre, Lisbellaw; Lough Erne Hotel, Kesh; Lakeland Tackle, Henry Street, Enniskillen; J. Graham, Manville House, Aughablaney.

Tributaries: Arney, Ballinamallard, Colebrooke, Kesh River, Sillees River.

Fairy Water
Joins the River Strule at Poe Bridge.

Made famous in the late 1950s for huge catches of roach. Mainly coarse fish, with some sea-trout and trout. Best stretch in lower river below creamery to Strule.

Omagh, Co. Tyrone. From old rail bridge, Strule.
C (Free with permission from Nestle's Condensary, Coneywarren, near Omagh).

No rod licence needed for coarse fishing.

Finn
Runs from L. Finn, Co. Donegal, and crosses border below Castlefinn.

Salmon, with a good spring run. Mostly preserved, but worth local inquiries.
Foyle Fisheries Commission licence.

Foyle
Formed at the confluence of the Mourne and Finn at Lifford; runs through L. Foyle to the sea below Londonderry.

An important salmon fishery, with some fish running from March. Also sea-trout, with the best fishing from June onwards. Trout fishing can be good.

The river has some huge shoals of roach, which appeared comparatively recently.

Fishing on the Foyle (no rod licence needed for coarse fish) is available on a season permit only from the Foyle Fisheries Commission, 8 Victoria Road, Londonderry, Co. Derry, where rod licences are also available. Permits and rod licences must be obtained through an application to the Commission's address.

Tributaries: Burndennet, Camowen, Derg, Drumragh, Fairy Water, Faughan, Finn, Glen, Mourne, Owenkillew, Roe, Strule.

Glen
Rises in the Sperrin Mountains and runs west to Plumbridge and then south to Owenkillew east of Newtonstewart.

Salmon, sea-trout and coarse fish.
Omagh, Co. Tyrone. Stretch in area.
S, ST, C (D T Adv. Mon.–Fri. only. Gaff A C).
Tributary of Foyle system.
Foyle Fisheries Commission licence.

Glenshesk
Rises in the northern Antrim Mountains and runs through Craigban to Carey.

Trout, sea-trout and salmon.
Ballycastle, Co. Antrim. 1½ m stretch.
T, ST, S (D T Adv. R. Bell, 38–40 Ann

Street, Ballycastle, or from Dept of Agriculture, Fisheries Dept, 2–4 Queen Street, Belfast).

Tributary of Margy.

Fisheries Conservancy Board Licence.

Kells Water (Glenwherry)

Rises at the southern end of the Antrim Mountains and runs west to join the Main below Kells.

Trout fishing (including Dollaghan) good. Some salmon.

Kells, Co. Antrim. 7 m Kells to Battery Bridge and 4 m Colin Bridge to Kells Bridge.

T, S (D T Adv. L. Gillen, tackle, Castlegore Road, Moorfields, or Texaco Filling Station, Kells).

Tributary of Bann system.

Fishery Conservancy Board licence.

Kesh River

Runs into Lower L. Erne at Kesh.

Trout and coarse fish. Fishing free, on application to landowners.

Fishery Conservancy Board licence.

Lagan

Rises in Co. Down and runs north-east through Dromore and Lisburn to Belfast Lough.

The upper reaches offer fair trout fishing, with good coarse fishing in the lower river.

Dromore, Co. Down. 12 m stretch.

T (D T Adv. T. McCann, tackle, 7 Gallows Street, Dromore. Fly only. Fishery open 1 Mar.–30 Sept.).

Lisburn, Co. Antrim. 4 m Spences Bridge to Halftown Bridge.

T, C (Free fishing. Trout season 1 Mar.–31 Oct.; coarse all year).

Lurgan, Co. Armagh. 14 m stretch.

T (D T Brownlow Arms Hotel, Lurgan. Fly only. Fishery open 1 Mar.–30 Oct.).

Tributary: Ravarnette.

Fisheries Conservancy Board licence.

Lower Bann Navigation

Canalised section of the River Bann from Toome, L. Neagh, to Kilrea.

Mainly coarse.

Toome Bridge, Co. Antrim. Fisheries at Toome, Portna and Movanagher developed by Dept of Agriculture.

C (D T Adv. Dept of Agriculture, Fisheries Dept, 2–4 Queen Street, Belfast).

Fisheries Conservancy Board licence.

Main

Rises in the north of Antrim and runs south to L. Neagh at Randalstown.

Trout, sea-trout and salmon.

Ballymena, Co. Down. Bridgend to Galgorm Bridge.

T, ST, S (D T Adv. McCord's Tackle, Bridgend, Ballymena).

Cullybackey, Co. Antrim. 4 m from Cullybackey Bridge; also 4½ m Cullybackey to Glavay Ford.

T, ST, S (D T Adv. R. Getty, Pottinger Street, Cullybackey. No Sunday fishing. Fishery open 1 Mar.–31 Oct.).

Randalstown, Co. Antrim. 4 m from Randalstown.

T, S, C (D T Adv. tackle shop, Randalstown).

Templepatrick, Co. Antrim. 6 m Antrim to Doagh.

T, S (D T Adv. Esso Filling Station, Templepatrick. L–25. Fly only to 31 Aug.).

Tributary of Bann system.

Fisheries Conservancy Board licence.

Margy

Formed by the confluence of the Carey and Glenshesk rivers near Ballycastle.

Good sea-trout fishing, with a small run of salmon. Trout fishing fair.

Ballycastle, Co. Antrim. Stretch on golf course lands.

T, ST, S (D T Adv. R. Bell, 38–40 Ann Street, Ballycastle, or from Dept of Agriculture, Fisheries Dept, 2–4 Queen Street, Belfast. L–8).

Tributaries: Carey, Glenshesk.

Fisheries Conservancy Board licence.

Mourne

Formed by the rivers Strule and Owenkillew at Newtonstewart; runs west to the Foyle below Strabane.

Small run of salmon from May, with a

later main run of grilse. Sea-trout best in June and July. Coarse fishing, mainly roach, is good from Strabane to the Foyle.

Omagh, Co. Tyrone. 1 m below junction of Owenkillew, including $1\frac{1}{2}$ m on Owenkillew.

T, ST, S, C (D T, WT Adv. D. Flanagan, Sedan Avenue, Omagh. Game fish 1 Apr.–20 Oct. Coarse fishing free on application).

Sion Mills, Co. Tyrone. 5 m below Sion Mills Weir to Victoria Bridge.

T, ST, S, C (D T, WT Adv. A. Annesley, 10 Albert Place, Sion Mills, or filling station, Victoria Bridge. Coarse fishing free on application).

Sion Mills, Co. Tyrone. $1\frac{1}{4}$ m at Victoria Bridge and $\frac{3}{4}$ m at Lisky.

T, ST, S, C (D T Adv. R. Cunningham, 10–12 Bridge Street, Strabane, or D. Flanagan, Sedan Avenue, Omagh. Fishery open 1 Apr.–20 Oct.).

Strabane, Co. Tyrone. Clayholes stretch below old rail bridge.

C (Free fishing, with permission from S. Rule, Khiva, Urney Road, Strabane, or T. H. Graham, Lifford Road Filling Station, Strabane).

Tributary of Foyle system.

Foyle Fisheries Commission licence.

Moyola

Rises in Co. Londonderry and runs east past Draperstown, Castledawson, to L. Neagh near Lower Bann.

Trout and some salmon, usually late. Some fishing on request from local landowners.

Tributary of Bann system.

Fisheries Conservancy Board licence.

Owenkillew

Joins the River Strule to form the River Mourne at Newtonstewart.

A good sea-trout run, with salmon on late spates. Trout fishing fair and some coarse fish.

Omagh, Co. Tyrone. Water in area.

T, ST, S, C (D T Adv. Mon.–Fri. only from Gaff A C).

Tributary of Foyle system.

Foyle Fisheries Commission licence.

Quoile

Rises near Ballynahinch and runs south through Downpatrick to Strangford Lough at Quoile.

Trout fishing is fair, but coarse fishing, especially for rudd, is good. Perch and pike also taken.

Downpatrick, Co. Down. Old barrier, Quoile Bridge, to new barrier, Strangford Lough Head.

T, C (D T Adv. H. Dickson & Son, Irish Street, Downpatrick; A. Patton, 56 Mill Street, Comber; T. West, tackle, Castle Street, Comber; Black and White Garage, Church Street, Downpatrick; F. Magee, Down Sports Centre, Market Street, Downpatrick).

Fisheries Conservancy Board licence.

Ravarnette

Tributary of the Lagan.

Fair trout fishing; mostly free, on application to local landowners.

Fisheries Conservancy Board licence.

Roe

Runs through Dungiven and Limavady to L. Foyle below Ballycarton.

Sea-trout, salmon. Can be good after spates.

Dungiven, Co. Derry. 4 m Ross's Mill to Burnfoot Bridge.

T, ST, S (D T, WT Adv. S. Doran, hairdresser, Main Street, Dungiven, or Strangemoor Farm, Dungiven. Fishery open 1 Apr.–20 Oct.).

Limavady, Co. Derry. 20 m Burnfoot to sea, excepting two sections.

T, ST, S (D T Adv. tackle shop, Limavady. L–20. Fishery open 1 Apr.–20 Oct.).

Limavady, Co. Derry. $1\frac{1}{4}$ m from Dog Leap Bridge.

T, ST, S (D T Adv. F. J. Mullen & Co., Main Street, Limavady. Fishery open 1 Apr.–20 Oct.).

Tributary of Foyle system.

Foyle Fisheries Commission licence.

Shima

Rises in the south of the Mourne Mountains and runs to the sea at Newcastle, Co. Down.

Salmon fishing can be good, given spates. Sea-trout from July on.

Newcastle, Co. Down. 1½ m Tollymore Park boundary to sea; also trout only above Tollymore Park and 1½ m River Burren above confluence.

T, ST, S (DT Adv. J. Mackie, tackle, 125 Main Street, Newcastle. L–6. Fishery open 1 Mar.–31 Oct.).

Newcastle, Co. Down. 2½ m stretch near Newcastle.

T, ST, S (DT Adv. Keeper, Forest Office, Tullymore Forest (closed at weekends). L–6).

Fisheries Conservancy Board Licence.

Sillees River

Runs south from Ross L. to Glencunny Wood, then east to Erne near Enniskillen.

Good coarse fishing in this often-coloured water, with some trout. Most of the fishing is free on application to landowners.

Tributary of Erne system.

Fisheries Conservancy Board licence.

Six Mile Water

Rises near Ballyclare and runs east to L. Neagh at Antrim.

Trout, including stocked rainbows, and some salmon. Some free fishing through local inquiries.

Tributary of Bann system.

Fisheries Conservancy Board licence.

Strule

Runs from Omagh to Newtonstewart.

Good trout fishing; also some sea-trout and salmon. Coarse fish.

Omagh, Co. Tyrone. 8 m stretch.

T, C, ST, S (DT, WT Adv. G. Flanagan, Sedan Avenue, Omagh. Game fishing 1 Apr.–20 Oct. Coarse fishing free on application).

Tributary of Foyle system.

Foyle Fisheries Commission licence.

Ten

Northern Ireland Still Waters

Lough Neagh, the biggest still water in Britain, sharing borders with many Northern Ireland provinces, holds trout and coarse fish. It is hardly ever fished, for the reason that the many waters which feed it are far more productive.

This section barely touches the huge amount of fishing, much of it free, in Northern Ireland, where a local inquiry for permission to fish is generally all that is needed. The entries below offer organized fishing where, in some instances, additional stocking takes place. See the section on Northern Ireland in 'Water Authorities and Regulations' above.

Co. Antrim

Dungonnell Reservoir, Ballymena.
    T (D T Adv. Fyfe's Stores, Glenravel Road, Cargan, or Dept of Agriculture, 2–4 Queen Street, Belfast. Open 1 Mar.–31 Oct.).
Killylane Reservoir, Larne.
    T (D T Adv. Glenwherry Service Station, Ballymena; Foster Sports, Main Street, Larne, or Mairs Gift Shop, Main Street, Ballyclare. Open 1 Mar.–31 Oct.).
Leatherstown and Stoneyford Reservoirs, Lisburn.
    ● T in part (D T Adv. Stoneyford Cash Stores, Stoneyford, Lisburn, or Dept of Agriculture, 2–4 Queen Street, Belfast. Letherstown Reservoir fly only. Open 1 Mar.–31 Oct.).
Woodburn Reservoirs, Carrickfergus.
    ● T in part (D T Adv. Cambridge Tackle, High Street, Carrickfergus, or

Dept of Agriculture, 2–4 Queen Street, Belfast. Fly only in Upper South, Lower South and Copeland reservoirs. Fish of good average size and some big).

Co. Armagh

Carnagh Forest Lakes, Keady.
    C (D T Adv. J. McKeever, hardware shop, Keady. Open all year).
Clay Lake, Keady.
    C (D T Adv. as Carnagh Forest Lakes, above. Open all year).
Craigavon Park Lakes, Craigavon.
    T (D T Adv. Golden Arrow Sports, Lurgan, S. Beckett, 54 High Street, Lurgan, or Silverwood Garage, Kiln Lane, Lurgan. Open 1 Apr.–31 Oct.).
Glasdrumman Lake, Crossmaglen.
    T (D T Adv. Dept of Agriculture, 2–4 Queen Street, Belfast. Open 1 Mar.–31 Oct.).
Keady Trout Lakes, Keady.
    ● T in part (D T Adv. H. McGinnity, 70 Victoria Street, Keady; J. McKeever, hardware shop, Keady, or Dept of Agriculture, 2–4 Queen Street, Belfast).
Shaw's Lake, Markethill.
    T (D T Adv. J. Hale Ltd, 5 Kildare Street, Newry, or Dept of Agriculture, 2–4 Queen Street, Belfast. Open 1 Mar.–31 Oct.).

Co. Derry

Altnaheglish Reservoir, Dungiven.
    T (D T Adv. Esso Service Station, Dungiven, or Shell station, Derry-

chrier, Dungiven. Open 1 April–20 Oct.
Rod licence incl).
Binevenagh Dam, Limavady.
 ● T (D T Adv. F. J. Mullen & Co., Main
Street, Limavady. Fly only. Open 1
Mar.–20 Oct. Rod licence incl.).
Enagh Lough, Campsie.
 C (D T Adv. Enagh House, Campsie).

Co. Down

Ballykeel Lougherne, Ballynahinch.
 ● T (D T Adv. Dept of Agriculture, 2–4
Queen Street, Belfast. Fly only. Open
1 Mar.–31 Oct. Stocked browns and
rainbows).
Castlewellan Lakes, Castlewellan.
 ● T in part (D T Adv. Castlewellan
Forest Park Office or Dept of
Agriculture, 2–4 Queen Street, Belfast.
Boat anglers fly only. Open 1 Apr.–31
Oct. One water, Slieve-na-Slat,
stocked rainbows; rest browns. B
available).
Corbet Lough, Banbridge.
 T (D T Adv. Angler's Rest, Corbet,
Banbridge. L–6).
Fofanny and Spelga Reservoirs,
Hilltown.
 T (D T Adv. W. R. Trimble Ltd, 25
Downpatrick Street, Rathfriland, or
Thieraforth Inn, Kilcoo, Castlewellan.
Open 1 Mar.–31 Oct.).
Grinan Lake, Newry.
 T (D T Adv. D. O'Hare, The Mall,
Newry; B. Breen, Church Street,
Newry).
Hillsborough Lake, Hillsborough.
 ● T (D T Adv. Sports Centre, Smithfield
Square, Lisburn. Fly only. Open 1
May–31 Oct. Manager advises book-
ing).
Lough Brickland, Banbridge.
 ● T (D T Adv. James Coburn & Sons,
Scarva Street, Banbridge, or Lake
View Service Station, Lough Brickland.
Fly only. Open 1 Mar.–31 Oct.).
Lough Cowey, Portaferry.
 T, C (D T Adv. J. M. Clegg, 48 Regent
Street, Newtonards, or Black and
White Garage, 10 Church Street,
Downpatrick. Open all year).

Lough Money, Downpatrick.
 T, C (D T Adv. Black and White
Garage, Church Street, Downpatrick.
Rainbows in this water. Open all
year).
Mill Dam, Warrenpoint.
 T (D T Adv. P. Grant, Church Street,
Warrenpoint, or Begg's Café, The
Square, Warrenpoint).
Portavoe Reservoir, Donaghadee.
 T (D T Adv. J. M. Clegg, 48 Regent
Street, Newtonards, or tel. Groomsport
221. Open 1 Mar.–31 Oct. L–20).
Waterworks Pool, Warrenpoint.
 T (D T Adv. as Mill Dam, above).

Co. Fermanagh

Coolyermer Lough, Enniskillen.
 ● T (D T Adv. Post Office, Letterbreen,
Coolyermer. Fly only. Open 1 Mar.–
30 Sept. B available).
Lough Erne, Upper and Lower,
Enniskillen.
 T, S, C (See under River Erne in
'Northern Ireland Rivers', above).
Lough Keenaghan, Belleek.
 ● T (D T Adv. Thomas Daly, Belleek, or
Carlton Hotel, Belleek. Fly only. Open
1 Mar.–30 Sept.).
Lough Melvin, Garrison.
 T, S, C and char (D T Adv. for Northern
Ireland area of lough only, Lake Hotel,
Garrison, or Carlton Hotel, Belleek.
Salmon run early, from Feb., and can
be big. Summer grilse run. The trout
fishing is good, and the water also has
perch and char).
Lough Scolban, Belleek.
 T, C (D T Adv. Thomas Daly, Belleek,
or Carlton Hotel, Belleek. Open all
year).
Mill Lough, Bellanaleck.
 ● T (D T Adv. for fishing from boats,
G. A. Cathcart, Bellanaleck. Fly only.
Open 1 Mar.–30 Sept.).
Navar Lakes, Derrygonnelly.
 T (D T Adv. Lough Navar Forest
Office; Thomas Daly, Belleek, or
Derrygonnelly Autos, Main Street,
Derrygonnelly. Open 1 Mar.–30
Sept.).

Rosle Loughs, Rosle.

T, C (D T Adv. Coranny Post Office. Rainbow trout only in Lough Coranny; browns Escleagh and Corry; mixed in Killyfoyle, which also holds pike. Open 1 Mar.–30 Sept.).

Co. Tyrone

Baronscourt Lakes, Newtonstewart.

C (D T Adv. Estate Office, Baronscourt, Newtonstewart. B available. Said to be the water responsible for the introduction of roach into Northern Ireland after being stocked with the species from the south in order to feed the lake pike. A flood in 1929 pushed water over the banks and into the Foyle system. Today the water offers bream in quantity, roach, and pike, some of them big).

Brantry Lough, Benburb.

● T (D T Adv. from Liam Donnelly, 127 Moor Street, Aughnacloy, or Deer Park Inn, Caledon. Fly only. Water is stocked with rainbows only and is open 1 July–31 Dec.).

Enagh Lough, Caledon.

C (D T Adv. Deer Park Inn, Caledon. Open all year. Good pike fishing).

Lough Ash, Donemana.

T (D T Adv. R. Cunningham, 10–12 Bridge Street, Strabane. Open 1 Mar.– 20 Oct. Rod licence incl.).

Lough Bradan, Drumquin.

T (D T Adv. D. Flanagan, Sedan Avenue, Omagh. Open 1 Mar.–20 Oct. Rod licence incl.).

Lough Creeve, Benburb.

C (D T Adv. Deer Park Inn, Caledon. Open all year. Holds big pike and perch).

Lough Lee, Drumquin.

T (D T Adv. D. Flanagan, Sedan Avenue, Omagh. Open 1 Mar.–20 Oct. Rod licence incl. Good trout fishing).

Lough Muck, Omagh.

C (D T Adv. Lakeview House, Lough Muck).

Lough Screeby, Five Mile Town.

C (D T Adv. J. Creighton, Main Street, Tempo, and L. Donnelly, 127 Moor Street, Aughnacloy. Open all year. Water holds pike, perch, bream and tench).

Moor Lough, Donemana.

T (D T Adv. as Lough Ash, above).

Mountfield Loughs, Omagh.

T (D T, WT Adv. D. Flanagan, Sedan Avenue, Omagh. Fair trout fishing in a series of lakes).

Roughan Lough, Coalisland.

T (D T Adv. K. Cahoon, 2 Irish Street, Dungannon, or James Beggs, 54b Scotch Street, Dungannon. The water is stocked with rainbows only, which run big. Open 1 July–31 Dec.).

White Lough, Aughnacloy.

C (D T Adv. Deer Park Inn, Caledon. Open all year).

Eleven

Irish Republic Rivers

If the waters of Northern Ireland offer fishing of astounding quantity and quality, those of the Republic surpass them, in quantity at least. Here, fishermen of all persuasions will find fishing to their liking, and often for a nominal charge or free (a rod licence is required for sea-trout and salmon fishing – see under 'Water Authorities and Regulations' above). It stands to reason, though, that the game rivers of fabulous repute, such as the Munster Blackwater or some of the Connemara sea-trout lough chains, will be expensive and heavily booked.

Trout fishing of quality is still free in many places, largely governed by their remoteness from big centres, but of late pressure has been growing to preserve the better trout waters. Nevertheless, the visiting angler will find that even a season ticket for trout fishing will often cost less than is paid in England for a day's fishing.

Coarse fishing is, by and large, free for the asking, although it must be stressed that unless a water is known to be free or is signposted so, an inquiry is both necessary and courteous before fishing starts. This is especially true of coarse fishing on game rivers.

A good deal of trout fishing in the Republic was formerly managed by the Inland Fisheries Trust, now reorganized into the Central Fisheries Board. An annual subscription (£5 in 1982) to the board opens a number of good trout and coarse fisheries to members, while visitors may take advantage of them for a small daily charge (£2 in 1982).

The Central Fisheries Board has also amalgamated several of the seventeen former Fishery Districts in the Republic into seven Regional Fishery Boards. The address of the Central Fisheries Board is Weir Lodge, Earl's Island, Galway, and the addresses of the Regional Boards (all supplying local information and permits) with the former fishery districts in brackets are:

Eastern Region (Dundalk, Drogheda, Dublin and Wexford), 58 Dame Street, Dublin 2.

Southern Region (Waterford and Lismore), Gladstone Street, Clonmel, Co. Tipperary.

South-Western Region (Cork and Kerry), Macroom, Co. Cork.

Shannon Region (Limerick, including all River Shannon lakes and tributaries), Thomond Weir, Limerick.

Western Region (Galway, Connemara and Ballinskill), Weir Lodge, Earl's Island, Galway.

North-Western Region (Ballina, Bangor and Sligo), Abbey Street, Ballina, Co. Mayo.

Northern Region (Ballyshannon and Letterkenny), College Street, Ballyshannon, Co. Donegal.

Another body of interest to anglers is the Electricity Supply Board (ESB), which is responsible for hydro-electric schemes on Irish rivers and holds some fisheries. These are run by the Fisheries Manager, Electricity Supply Board, 27 Lower Fitzwilliam Street, Dublin.

Visitors are reminded that it is forbidden to bring maggots, worms and some other baits and groundbaits into Ireland. There are limited supplies at main centres (it is wise to order in advance of your visit) but locally dug worms are your best bet.

Standard coarse fishing methods are useful throughout Ireland, but trolling either a bait or a spoon is a useful method for pike on some of the bigger loughs. It is also useful for the larger trout and, in some cases, salmon. Fishing with a dapped fly in the mayfly and daddy-longlegs seasons on some loughs can be exciting.

Aherlow
Enters the River Suir above Cahir.

Good trout fishing. Local inquiries essential, as pollution in recent years has led to some clubs withdrawing visitors' tickets.

Cahir, Tipperary. Water in area.

T (D T Adv. Cahir Estate Office, Cahir).

Trout season 1 Mar.–30 Sept.

Southern Region.

Allow
A fair-sized stream entering the River Blackwater at Banteer.

Fair trout fishing. Some free fishing; inquire locally.

Trout season 15 Feb.–30 Sept.

Southern Region.

Annagh
A tributary of the Erne system.

Fair trout fishing, with some fish to 4 lb. Offers dry and wet fly water. Some free fishing; inquire locally.

Trout season 1 Mar.–30 Sept.

Northern Region.

Annagheragh
A spate river entering the sea between Doonbeg and Quilty.

Some salmon when conditions right; trout mainly small. Some free fishing; inquire locally.

Trout season 15 Feb.–30 Sept.; salmon, 1 Mar.–31 Aug.

Shannon Region.

Annalee
Another Erne system tributary offering trout fishing, with occasional big fish.

Some free fishing; inquire locally.

Trout season as Annagh, above.

Northern Region.

Annascaul
A rapid, rocky stream of some 4 m, draining L. Annascaul to Dingle Bay.

Good sea-trout; salmon when conditions right, usually from summer onwards. Mostly preserved, but worth local inquiry.

Trout and sea-trout season 12 Mar.–12 Oct.; salmon, 17 Mar.–31 Aug.

South-Western Region.

Anner
Joins the River Suir between Clonmel and Kilsheelan.

Trout. Some free fishing, or for nominal charge. Inquire locally.

Trout season 1 Mar.–30 Sept.

Southern Region.

Argideen
Rises in Clonakilty and runs to Courtmacsherry Bay at Timoleague.

A good run of sea-trout and some summer grilse. Trout small but numerous.

Timoleague, Cork. Water in area, except Lisselan Estate water.

T, ST, S (By arrangement with Argideen A A, Bandon, Co. Cork).

Trout and sea-trout season 15 Feb.–12 Oct.; salmon, 15 Feb.–31 Aug.

South-Western Region.

Avoca
Formed from the Avonmore and Avonbeg rivers; runs from the Wicklow Mountains to Arklow and the coast.

Trouting fair, but fish on small side. Parts of lower river polluted.

Aughrim, Wicklow. Water in area.

T (D T Adv. Aughrim Post Office).

Trout season 1 Mar.–30 Sept.

Eastern Region.

Awbeg
Flows through Buttevant, Doneraile and Castletownroche to the River Blackwater.

Good dry fly trout water. Some water available through Castletownroche A C; inquire locally.

Doneraile, Cork. Doneraile Estate Water.
T (D T Adv. Estate Agent, Doneraile).
Trout season 15 Feb.–30 Sept.
Southern Region.

Ballisodare

A 5½-mile water formed by the junction of the Arrow and Owenmore.

Good for wet and dry fly fishing. Trout to 4 lb. Some salmon fishing, mostly preserved – the river has the earliest salmon ladder made in Ireland (1852). Sea-trout and brown trout fishing sometimes available; inquire locally.

Bandon

Rises in west Cork and runs through Dunmanway, Ballineen, Enniskean, Bandon and Innishannon to the sea at Kinsale, covering some 45 m.

Stretches can be low and weedy after May. Good run of spring salmon, although declining in recent years. Sea-trout from July to September. The trout are mainly small. Coarse fishing on the river is virtually unexplored, but it is known to hold tench in addition to the usual species and is worth local inquiries. Some of the best salmon water is preserved.

Bandon, Cork. Water in area.
T, ST, S (D T, WT tackle shop, Bandon).

Ballineen, Cork. Water in area.
T, ST, S (D T Adv. Ballineen and Enniskean A C, Mrs P. Fehilly, Ballineen. Fly only).
Trout and sea-trout season 15 Feb.–30 Sept.; salmon 15 Feb.–31 Aug.
South-Western Region.

Bansha

Runs through Tipperary to the River Suir.

Good trout fishing; worth local inquiry.
Trout season 1 Mar.–30 Sept.
Southern Region.

Barrow

Rises in the Bog of Allen and runs 120 m

via Athy, Carlow and New Ross to join the Nore.

The canalized upper section, inclined to run low in summer, holds good stocks of coarse fish, including tench. The best coarse water is said to be from St Mullins up, with the tidal water beginning just downstream. Early runs of salmon and sea-trout, with a grilse run in wet years. Trout good. Some free water in the Carlow area.

Athy, Kildare. 8 m in area.
T (D T Adv. Monasterevan and Dist. A A, Paul Cullen, Main Street, Athy).

Carlow, Co. Carlow. Fishing in area.
T, ST, S (D T Adv. Gavin's tackle, Carlow).
Tributaries: Triogue, Owenass, Greese, Lerr, Burren, Owenduff, Corock, Nore.
Trout season 1 Mar.–30 Sept.; sea-trout, 1 Feb.–30 Sept.; salmon, 1 Feb.–31 Aug.
Southern Region.

Behy

A swift stream draining a number of loughs before entering Rossbehy Creek.

Some good pools. Trout small; best fishing for summer sea-trout and some grilse given water.

Glenbeigh, Kerry. Fishing in area.
T, ST, S (Inquire locally).
Trout season 15 Feb.–12 Oct.; sea-trout, 17 Jan.–12 Oct.; salmon, 17 Jan.–31 Aug.
South-Western Region.

Black River

Runs through Strule to Corrib.

A fair limestone stream offering good trout fishing, but can be weedy in summer. Some free fishing, with permission from owners; some Central Fisheries Board water.
Trout season 1 Mar.–30 Sept.
Western Region.

Blackwater (Cork)

Joins the River Bandon north-west of Ballineen.

A fair trout water.

Manch, Cork. Fishing in area.
T (Inquire Railway Hotel, Manch).

Trout season 15 Feb.–30 Sept.
South-Western Region.

Blackwater (Kells)

Rises near Virginia and runs through L. Ramor to the River Boyne at Navan.

A good dry fly water, with trout to 7 lb. Pike fishing can be good. Some spring salmon. Local associations hold some water. Inquire locally.

Trout season 15 Feb.–15 Sept.; salmon, 1 Feb.–31 Aug.

Eastern Region.

Blackwater (Kenmare)

A 7-mile water draining L. Brin. The upper river is called the River Kealduff.

Trout, sea-trout and salmon, but worth inquiry to Kenmare Estate Office, Kenmare.

Trout and sea-trout season 15 Mar.–12 Oct.; salmon, 15 Mar.–31 Aug.

South-Western Region.

Blackwater (Munster)

Runs 85 m through Rathmore, Millstreet, Banteer, Mallow, Fermoy, Lismore and Cappoquin to sea at Youghal.

A streamy river with glides and good pools, it is one of Ireland's best salmon rivers. Of latter years it has also gained a reputation as a fine coarse water, especially for its shoals of roach and dace at Cappoquin, Fermoy and Mallow. Most of the trout fishing is preserved by associations, but the game fisheries listed will give permits to trout anglers. Also inquire at Barbers Tackle, Fermoy.

Ballyduff, Waterford. 25 m plus 2 m of South Bride.

S, ST, T (DT Adv. if fishing not booked by guests, otherwise through residence, Blackwater Lodge Hotel, Ballyduff. B and ghillies available. Advance booking usually essential).

Conna, Cork. 9 m of water with 20 pools.

S, ST, T (DT Adv. Peter Demster, Carrigeen, Conna. Ghillies, tackle, advice available).

Fermoy, Cork. Fermoy Salmon A A water.

S, ST (Inquiries to Jack O'Sullivan, 41 Patrick Street, Fermoy).

Lismore, Waterford. Lismore Estates water.

S, ST (Inquiries to Lismore Estates Office, Lismore).

Tributaries: Owentaraglin, Finnow, Allow, Awbeg, Funshion, North Bride, Lickey, Tourig.

Trout season 15 Feb.–30 Sept.; sea-trout, 1 Feb.–30 Sept.; salmon, 1 Feb.–31 Aug.

Southern Region.

Bonet

Feeds L. Gill.

A good salmon water, with fair fishing for trout to 1 lb or so.

Dromhaire, Leitrim. Water in area.

S, T (Inquiries to Abbey Hotel, Dromhaire).

Trout season 15 Feb.–30 Sept.; salmon, 1 Jan.–31 Aug.

North-Western Region.

Boyle

Flows from L. Gara through Boyle into L. Key.

Fair trout fishing, with some good fish. Excellent coarse fishing, especially for bream.

Boyle, Roscommon. Water in area.

T, C (DT Adv. tackle shop, Boyle. Coarse fishing in area free on application).

Trout season 1 Mar.–30 Sept.

Shannon Region.

Boyne

Rises near Idenderry Mountains and flows through Trim, Navan and Slane to tidal water at Drogheda.

A good trout water, taking salmon and sea-trout. Most of the salmon fishing is preserved, but inquire locally for hotel and association water.

Trout season 15 Feb.–15 Sept.; sea-trout, 1 Feb.–15 Sept.; salmon, 1 Feb.–31 Aug.

Eastern Region.

Brinny

Joins the River Bandon near Innishannon.

Fair trout fishing; worth local inquiries.

Trout season 15 Feb.–30 Sept.
South-Western Region.

Broadmeadow
Small water running into the Malahide
Inlet near Dublin.

Trout, with some sea-trout in the lower
reaches. Mostly preserved by Swords
A C, with little chance of opening.
Eastern Region.

Brosna
Runs from L. Ennell through Bally-
nagore, Kilbeggan, Clara, Ballycumber
and Ferbane to Shannon at Shannon
Harbour.

Good pools and glides for wet and dry
fly fishing, with trout to 3 lb. Good
coarse fishing in the slower stretches,
especially for pike. Much of the water is
controlled by the Central Fisheries Board
(see introduction to this section). Some
salmon.
Tributaries: Clodiagh, Frankford,
Silver, Little Silver.
Trout season 15 Feb.–30 Sept.
Shannon Region.

Brown Flesk
The main tributary of the River Maine.

Fair trout fishing, with sea-trout
and salmon, generally arriving late.
Some lengths free fishing; inquire
locally.
Trout season 15 Feb.–12 Oct.; sea-
trout, 17 Jan.–12 Oct.; salmon,
17 Jan.–31 Aug.
South-Western Region.

Bundrowes (Drowes)
Drains L. Melvin into Donegal Bay.
Salmon fishing, preserved. Season 1
Jan.–31 Aug.
Northern Region.

Bunowen (Mayo)
Flows to Clew Bay near Louisburg.
Salmon from June, sea-trout from
July. Inquiries to Sligo Estate Agent,
Estate Office, Westport.
Sea-trout season 1 Apr.–12 Oct.;
salmon, 1 Apr.–31 Aug.
Western Region.

Bunowen
Tributary of the Suck.
A fair trout water, if rather heavily
fished by local anglers. Controlled by the
Central Fisheries Board (see the intro-
duction to this section).
Trout season 1 Mar.–30 Sept.
Shannon Region.

Bunree
Rocky water flowing into Moy estuary.
Fair trout fishing and good for sea-
trout when conditions right. Worth local
inquiries.
Trout season 15 Feb.–10 Oct.; sea-
trout, 1 Feb.–10 Oct.
North-Western Region.

Burren
Joins the River Barrow in Carlow.
Fair trout fishing; worth local in-
quiries.
Trout season 1 Mar.–30 Sept.
Southern Region.

Camcor
Enters the River Brosna at Birr.
Holds good trout, with the best fish
from August onwards. Central Fisheries
Board water (see the introduction to this
section).
Trout season 15 Feb.–30 Sept.
Shannon Region.

Camog (Camogue)
Flows through Grange, Meanus and
Monaster to the River Maigue near
Cherrygrove Bridge.
A good trout water, but liable to dry
up in droughts. Mostly free fishing.
Trout season 15 Feb.–30 Sept.
Shannon Region.

Caragh
A swift stream running into Rossbehy
Creek.
Excellent salmon and sea-trout, but
with few spring fish. Trout mostly
small, with bigger fish in the loughs
on its course. Fishing through the
Tower Hotel, Glenbeigh Hotel,
Glenbeigh.
Trout season 15 Feb.–12 Oct.; sea-

trout, 17 Jan.–12 Oct.; salmon, 17 Jan.–31 Aug.

South-Western Region.

Cashla

Drains a series of lakes into Cashla Bay at Costello.

The sea-trout fishing is excellent, among the best in Ireland. They run from July to September. Salmon from June to August.

Costello, Galway. Water in area.

ST, S (D T Adv. rods sometimes available through Costello Lodge Hotel, Connemara).

Trout season 15 Feb.–12 Oct.; sea-trout, 1 Feb.–12 Oct.; salmon, 1 Feb.–31 Aug.

Tributaries: Fermoyle, Clohir.

Western Region.

Clady

Water draining L. Nacung and L. Dunlewy to Gweedore Bay at Bunbeg.

A fair run of sea-trout, but salmon to some extent discouraged by hydro scheme. Trout fishing can be good. Mostly preserved, but Electricity Supply Board has some water (see the introduction to this section).

Trout season 15 Feb.–12 Oct.; sea-trout, 2 Feb.–12 Oct.; salmon, 2 Feb.–31 Aug.

Northern Region.

Clare

Twenty-mile tributary of the Corrib system.

Salmon April to July, but affected by drainage work. Trout fishing can be good. Some free fishing; inquire locally.

Trout season 1 Mar.–30 Sept.; salmon, 1 Feb.–31 Aug.

Western Region.

Clodiagh

A tributary of the Brosna system.

Fair trout fishing. The Central Fisheries Board has water in area (see the introduction to this section).

Trout season 15 Feb.–30 Sept.

Shannon Region.

Clodiagh

Tributary of the Suir, joining below Holycross.

Fair trout fishing. Clubs in area have recently stopped visitors' tickets because of pollution on the Suir, so inquire about the latest position at tackle shops in Thurles, Cashel, Cahir, Clonmel and Carrick.

Trout season 1 Mar.–30 Sept.

Southern Region.

Clohir

Tributary of the Cashla system.

Trout, sea-trout and salmon, best June–July onwards. Inquire locally.

Trout season 15 Feb.–12 Oct.; sea-trout, 1 Feb.–12 Oct.; salmon, 1 Feb.–31 Aug.

Western Region.

Cloonaghmore
(Palmerstown River)

Enters Killala Bay on west shore.

Occasional salmon, with a fairly good sea-trout run. Trout small. Some free fishing in area.

Palmerstown, Mayo. Stretch near Palmerstown Bridge.

T, ST, S (D T Adv. from waterkeeper).

Trout season, tidal water, 1 June–12 Oct.; sea-trout, 1 Feb.–12 Oct.; salmon, 1 June–31 Aug.

North-Western Region.

Cloonee (Clonee)

Drains Cloonee lakes and L. Inchiquin.

Fair summer fishing for sea-trout and salmon. Inquiries to Lansdowne Estate Office, Kenmare.

Trout and sea-trout season 15 Mar.–12 Oct.; salmon, 15 Mar.–31 Aug.

South-Western Region.

Colligan

Enters sea at Dungarvan Harbour.

Has a run of sea-trout, with occasional summer salmon. Trout fishing fair. Inquiries to John Casey, tackle, Dungarvan.

Trout season 1 Mar.–30 Sept.; sea-trout, 1 Feb.–30 Sept.; salmon, 1 Feb.–31 Aug.

Southern Region.

Coomhola

A small stony stream running 11 m to the sea between Glengarriff and Bantry.

Small trout, with some salmon and sea-trout on summer floods. Worth local inquiry.

Trout and sea-trout season 17 Mar.–12 Oct.; salmon, 17 Mar.–31 Aug.
South-Western Region.

Corock

A fair trout stream running to the south-east of New Ross, a tributary of the Barrow system. Worth local inquiries.

Trout season 1 Mar.–30 Sept.
Southern Region.

Corrib

Runs a short (6-mile) course, draining loughs Carra, Mask and Corrib.

Good game water, with salmon from March to September (they do not enter L. Mask or L. Carra). Trout fishing good.

Galway, Co. Galway. State Fishery waters.

S, ST, T (DT and ½-day, Adv. The Salmon Fishery, Nun's Island, Galway. L–5).

Tributaries: Clare, Owenriff, Joyce.

Trout and sea-trout season 1 Mar.–30 Sept.; salmon, 1 Feb.–31 Aug.
Western Region.

Cottononers

A small tributary of the River Laune.

Fair trout fishing. Worth local inquiries.

Trout season 15 Feb.–12 Oct.
South-Western Region.

Cree

Flows to sea 1 m north of Doonbeg.

Mainly trout, but fish small. Inquire locally.

Trout season 15 Feb.–30 Sept.
Shannon Region.

Crumlin

A short river draining the hill loughs Fadda, Ugga Beg, etc.

Summer salmon; good sea-trout fishing.

Crumlin, Galway. Crumlin Fishery waters.

S, ST (DT Adv. The Caretaker, Crumlin Fishery, Crumlin, Inverin).

Trout and sea-trout season 1 Feb.–12 Oct.; salmon, 1 Feb.–31 Aug.
Western Region.

Culfin

Drains L. Fee and L. Muck into Killary Harbour.

Good summer salmon fishing and sea-trout. Trout mainly small. Preserved, but worth local inquiry.

Trout season 15 Feb.–12 Oct.; sea-trout, 1 Feb.–12 Oct.; salmon, 1 Feb.–31 Aug.
Western Region.

Cullenagh (Inagh)

Enters Liscannor Bay at Lahinch after running through Ennistymon, where there is a fish ladder.

Some summer salmon and sea-trout, but the best fishing is generally late. Trout small. West Clare AA holds water; inquire locally. Fishing for guests at Falls Hotel, Ennistymon.

Trout season 15 Feb.–30 Sept.; sea-trout, 1 Mar.–30 Sept.; salmon, 1 Mar.–31 Aug.
Shannon Region.

Cummeragh

Runs a 5-mile course draining a chain of lakes, including Derriana, Namona and Cloonakin, before running into the northern end of L. Currane.

Salmon February to May, with grilse May to August. Sea-trout June to September. Some hotel water; inquire locally.

Trout season 15 Feb.–12 Oct.; sea-trout, 17 Jan.–12 Oct.; salmon, 17 Jan.–31 Aug.
South-Western Region.

Dargle

Formed by the junction of the rivers Glencullen and Glencree, running to the sea at Bray Harbour.

Trout fishing fair, with a good late run of sea-trout.

Bray, Wicklow. Fishing in area.
> T, ST, S (WT Adv. Owens Tackle, Bray).
> Trout season 1 Mar.–30 Sept.; sea-trout, 1 Feb.–12 Oct.
> Eastern Region.

Dawros
Drains Kylemore lakes 6 m to Ballinakill Harbour.
> Salmon in August; good sea-trout from July to September. Trout small. Preserved, but worth inquiry to Kenmare Estate Office, Kenmare.
> Trout season 15 Feb.–12 Oct.; sea-trout, 1 Feb.–12 Oct.; salmon, 1 Feb.–31 Aug.
> Western Region.

Dealagh
Enters Liscannor Bay to the north of Lahinch.
> Small brown trout. Inquire locally.
> Trout season 15 Feb.–30 Sept.
> Shannon Region.

Dee (Dundalk)
Runs through Ardee to join the Glyde and enter the sea at Annagassan.
> Good trout fishing, with fish to 4 lb. Early salmon, best February to May depending on spates, then from June onwards, given water. Sea-trout only between Drumcar Weir and Willistown Head Weir. Some free fishing; inquire locally.
> Trout season 15 Feb.–30 Sept.; sea-trout, 1 Feb.–31 Aug. and in tidal water, 12 Feb.–19 Aug.; salmon, 1 Feb.–30 Sept. and in tidal water, 12 Feb.–19 Aug.
> Eastern Region.

Deel
Flows through Crossmolina to L. Conn.
> A rocky river offering fair trout fishing, with some summer salmon, given water. Inquire locally.
> Trout season 15 Feb.–10 Oct.; salmon, 1 Feb.–31 Aug.
> North-Western Region.

Deel
Enters the Shannon estuary below Limerick.
> Early salmon; sea-trout from summer. Fair to good trout fishing.

Rathkeale, Limerick. Water in area.
> T, ST, S (D T Adv. J. McEnnery, tackle, Rathkeale).
> Trout and sea-trout season 1 Mar.–30 Sept.; salmon, 1 Mar.–31 Aug.
> Shannon Region.

Deel
Enters the River Boyne near Longwood.
> Mainly trout; worth local inquiries.
> Trout season 15 Feb.–15 Sept.
> Eastern Region.

Derreen
Fairly big tributary of the River Slaney, which it joins near Clonegal.
> Fair trout fishing; worth local inquiry.
> Trout season 25 Feb.–31 Aug.
> Eastern Region.

Derry
A fair trout water, entering the River Slaney below Tullow. Best at high water. Worth local inquiry.
> Trout season 26 Feb.–31 Aug.
> Eastern Region.

Devlin
Enters the sea north of Balbriggan.
> Fair trout fishing, with sea-trout, best June to September. Worth local inquiries.
> Trout season 15 Feb.–15 Sept.; sea-trout, 12 Feb.–15 Sept.
> Eastern Region.

Dinin
Flows through Castlecomer to the River Nore.
> Fair trout fishing, with occasional big fish. Inquiries to tackle shop, Kilkenny.
> Trout season 1 Mar.–30 Sept.
> Southern Region.

Dodder
A moorland stream rising in the Dublin Mountains and running through Bohernabreena, Firhouse, Templelogue

and Rathfarnham to the Liffey estuary at Dublin.

Trout small in upper river, bigger in lower reaches. Intermittently polluted. Some free fishing on application to land-owners.

Trout season 1 Mar.–30 Sept.
Eastern Region.

Doonbeg

Flows through Cooraclare to the sea at Doonbeg.

Mainly small trout. Inquire locally.
Trout season 15 Feb.–30 Sept.
Shannon Region.

Drish

Flows from east of Thurles to join the River Suir below the town.

Fair trout fishing. Inquire locally.
Trout season 1 Mar.–30 Sept.
Southern Region.

Drumcliff

A 5-mile water draining L. Glencar to Drumcliff Bay north of Sligo.

A good salmon and sea-trout water. Trout mainly small. Inquire locally.

Trout season 15 Feb.–12 Oct.; sea-trout, 1 Feb.–12 Oct.; salmon, 1 Feb.–31 Aug.
North-Western Region.

Duff (Bunduff)

Runs a 13-mile course to Donegal Bay west of Bundoran.

Salmon from June to July, especially in lower reaches, and fair runs of sea-trout. Brown trout mainly small. Worth local inquiries.

Trout season 15 Feb.–30 Sept.; sea-trout, 1 Feb.–30 Sept.; salmon, 1 Feb.–31 Aug.
Northern Region.

Dungloe

Drains a chain of lakes, including Rosses Fishery.

Fair trout fishing; good sea-trout fishing. Some free fishing in area. Inquire from Mr H. O'Donnell, The Lodge, Doochary; tackle shop, Glenties; or Sweeney's Hotel, Dungloe.

Trout season 15 Feb.–12 Oct.; sea-trout, 2 Feb.–12 Oct.; salmon, 2 Feb.–31 Aug.
Northern Region.

Durrus

Flows into the head of Dunmanus Bay.

Brown trout, mainly small. Inquire locally.

Trout season 17 Mar.–12 Oct.
South-Western Region.

Easkey

Drains L. Easkey, running 12 m to Sligo Bay.

Some summer salmon and good sea-trout fishing. Inquire locally.

Trout season 15 Feb.–12 Oct.; sea-trout, 1 Feb.–12 Oct.; salmon, 1 Feb.–31 Aug.
North-Western Region.

Eriff

Flows into Killary Harbour north-east of Leenane (7 m).

Good salmon and sea-trout water, given spates. Trout small. Inquire locally.

Seasons as Easkey, above.
Western Region.

Erkina

Flows by Rathdowney and Durrow to the River Nore.

Has been the subject of drainage work. Trout mostly small, with occasional big fish in recent years. Information from Kilkenny tackle shops.

Trout season 1 Mar.–30 Sept.
Southern Region.

Erne

Part of a complex of lakes and tributaries. The Erne proper begins at L. Gowna.

Trout fishing can be good, with fish to 4 lb, especially in the mayfly season. Salmon fishing has been uncertain since the hydro scheme was started. Much free fishing; inquire from tackle shops in Ballyshannon.

Tributaries: Finn, Annagh, Annalee, Laragh.

Trout season 1 Mar.–30 Sept.
Northern Region.

Eske
Drains L. Eske.
 Salmon July–Aug.; sea-trout fishing good. Mostly preserved.
 Northern Region.

Fane
Rises near Castleblaney and runs through L. Muckno and L. Ross to Dundalk Bay.
 Trout fishing good. Some spring salmon, but best in summer and autumn, though not after August. Late spates are good for sea-trout. Some free water and ticket water; inquire from tackle shops in Dundalk.
 Trout and sea-trout season 1 Mar.–12 Oct.; salmon, 1 Mar.–31 Aug.
 Eastern Region.

Feale
Flows 46 m to the Shannon estuary south of Ballybunion.
 Good spring and summer salmon runs; sea-trout from July on. Trout small but numerous. Since drainage work it is subject to violent spates.
Listowel, Kerry. 2 m stretch near Listowel.
 T, ST, S (DT Adv. Tralee and Dist. AA, T. Hennebery, Castle Countess, Tralee, Co. Kerry).
Listowel, Kerry. 15 m in area.
 T, ST, S (DT Adv. North Kerry Salmon AA, North County Guest House, 67 Church Street, Listowel).
 Tributaries: Smerlagh, Galey.
 Trout season 15 Feb.–30 Sept.; sea-trout, 1 Mar.–15 Sept.; salmon, 1 Mar.–31 Aug.
 Shannon Region.

Feoghanagh
Six-mile water flowing into Smerwick Harbour.
 Sea-trout from June to October. Fair trout fishing, mostly small fish. Worth local inquiries.
 Trout and sea-trout season 1 May–30 Sept.
 South-Western Region.

Fergus
A limestone water draining the Clare plateau. Runs into Inchiquin L., to Ballyteige L. and Ennis, then to tidal barrage at Clarecastle.
 Salmon in lower reaches. Good trout fly water, but can dry up in parts in droughts. Mostly free fishing; some Central Fisheries Board water.
 Trout season 15 Feb.–30 Sept.; salmon, 1 Mar.–31 Aug.
 Shannon Region.

Fermoyle
Tributary of the Upper Cashla system.
 Good salmon and sea-trout fishing, especially late in season.
Costello, Galway. Fermoyle Fishery water.
 ST, S (DT Adv. rods sometimes available through The Agent, Fermoyle Lodge, Costello).
 Sea-trout season, 1 Feb.–12 Oct.; salmon, 1 Feb.–31 Aug.
 Western Region.

Ferta
An 8-mile water entering the River Valentia east of Cahirciveen.
 Small trout, with summer salmon and sea-trout. Inquire locally.
 Trout and sea-trout season 1 Apr.–12 Oct.; salmon, 1 Apr.–31 Aug.
 South-Western Region.

Finn
Somewhat sluggish tributary of the Erne, joining near Beltgurbet.
 Some trout, mainly coarse fish. Free fishing.
 Trout season 1 Mar.–30 Sept.
 Northern Region.

Finnglas
Tributary of the River Laune.
 Fair trout fishing. Inquire locally.
 Trout season 15 Feb.–12 Oct.
 South-Western Region.

Finnow
Enters the River Blackwater at Millstreat
 Fair trout fishing. Inquire locally.
 Trout season 15 Feb.–30 Sept.
 Southern Region.

Finny

Joins L. Nafooey to L. Mask and holds big trout from L. Mask from August onwards. Inquire locally.

Trout season 1 Mar.–30 Sept.
Western Region.

Flesk

A large tributary of the Laune, feeding L. Leane and running over a stony course.

Trout, sea-trout and salmon. Fishing through Lough Leane A A, Joan Fleming, 25 High Street, Killarney.

Trout season 15 Feb.–12 Oct.; sea-trout, 17 Jan.–12 Oct.; salmon, 17 Jan.–31 Aug.
South-Western Region.

Foherish

Joins the River Sullane, a tributary of the Lee system, west of Aracroom.

Fair trout fishing, with some free fishing.

Trout season 15 Feb.–12 Oct.
South-Western Region.

Francis

A tributary of the River Suck.

Fair trout fishing. Central Fisheries Board water (see the introduction to this section).

Trout season 1 Mar.–30 Sept.
Shannon Region.

Frankford

Tributary of the Brosna system.

Trout fishing. Central Fisheries Board water (see introduction to this section).

Trout season 15 Feb.–30 Sept.
Shannon Region.

Funshion

A fairly good stream, inclined to be weedy, rising north of Mitchelstown and running to the Blackwater near Fermoy.

Trout can be good. Dace and rudd fishing free on application; details from Barber's Tackle, Fermoy.

Trout season 15 Feb.–30 Sept.
Southern Region.

Gaddagh

Tributary of the Laune system.

Trout fishing. Inquire locally.

Trout season 15 Feb.–12 Oct.
South-Western Region.

Galey

A tributary of the River Feale.

Fair trout fishing, with summer runs of sea-trout and salmon. Inquire locally.

Trout season 15 Feb.–30 Sept.; sea-trout, 1 Mar.–15 Sept.; salmon, 1 Mar.–31 Aug.
Shannon Region.

Garvogue (Sligo River)

Drains L. Gill into Sligo Harbour.

Trout to $\frac{3}{4}$ lb; some salmon. Fishing through Abbey Hotel, Dromhaire, Leitrim.

Tributary: Bonet.

Trout season 15 Feb.–30 Sept.; salmon, 1 Jan.–31 Aug.
North-Western Region.

Glen

Runs 12 m, entering Tawny Bay at Carrick.

Salmon from April on; best June to October. Good sea-trout late in season. Fishing through Slieve League Hotel, Carrick.

Tributary: Yellow.

Trout and sea-trout season 1 Mar.–9 Oct.; salmon, 1 Mar.–31 Aug.
Northern Region.

Glenamoy

A 7-mile water entering Sruwadaccon Bay.

Salmon and sea-trout. Preserved.
North-Western Region.

Glencree

Forms the River Dargle at junction with the Glencullen near Enniskerry.

Mainly trout. Mostly preserved.
Eastern Region.

Glencullen

See the Glencree, above. Mostly preserved.

Eastern Region.

Glengarriff

A 7-mile spate water.

Salmon in the summer and sea-trout from May, provided there is water. Trout fishing poor. Glengarriff AA has water; inquire locally.

Sea-trout season 17 Mar.–12 Oct.; salmon, 17 Mar.–31 Aug.
South-Western Region.

Glyde
Runs through Tallanstown and Castlebellingham, joining the River Dee close to the sea at Dundalk Bay.

Good spring run of salmon, with a few grilse on summer floods. Trout good (4–5 lb). Can be weedy after June. Some coarse fish, especially pike and bream. Some free water, excepting Bellingham Castle Estate and water at Tallanstown. Dee and Glyde F D A hold water.

Trout season 15 Feb.–30 Sept.; sea-trout, 1 Feb.–31 Aug. and 12 Feb.–19 Aug. in tidal water; salmon, 1 Feb.–30 Sept. and 12 Feb.–19 Aug. in tidal water.
Eastern Region.

Grand Canal
Main line runs from Dublin west towards Shannon.

Still a navigable waterway ($\frac{1}{2}$-in-to-mile maps available through Irish Ordnance Survey: sheet 15, western section; sheet 16, eastern section). Mainly coarse fishing, although there are some big trout. The best coarse sections are reckoned to be Gollierstown; from Lock 13 at Celbridge; Sallins; Digby Bridge (Lock 16); Cock Bridge; Lowtown (Barrow line joins here); Allenwood (which has a match length, providing good weights); Ticknevin; Lock 24, near Tullamore; Locks 30–31, where catches of 100 lb have been taken regularly; Ferbane; Belmont; Shannon Harbour. Free fishing.

Greese
Enters the River Barrow between Athy and Carlow.

A good trout water.
Carlow, Co. Carlow. Water in area.
T (D T Adv. tackle shop, Carlow).
Trout season 1 Mar.–30 Sept.
Southern Region.

Gully
A tributary of the Nore, joining north of Durrow.

Fair trout fishing. Inquiry locally.
Trout season 1 Mar.–30 Sept.
Southern Region.

Gweebarra
Drains L. Barra into Gweebarra Bay.

Fair trout fishing. Salmon, sea-trout in lower river Apr. to May, upper river July to September. Fishing by application to riparian owners.

Trout season 15 Feb.–12 Oct.; sea-trout, 2 Feb.–12 Oct.; salmon, 2 Feb.–31 Aug.
Northern Region.

Gweedore (Crolly)
Drains L. Anure into Gweedore Bay.

Salmon, sea-trout Apr. through to Aug. Apply Mr Gallagher, Crolly Bridge.
Seasons as Gweebarra, above.
Northern Region.

Gweestin
A tributary of the Laune.

Fair trout fishing. Inquire locally.
Trout season 15 Feb.–12 Oct.
South-Western Region.

Ilen
Rises near the Cork–Bantry road and runs to Skibbereen, where it becomes tidal, then to Baltimore Harbour.

Some good pools. Fair run of salmon from April, with grilse from June. Sea-trout good summer and autumn. Trout mainly small.
Skibbereen, Cork. Water in area.
T, ST (D T Adv. tackle shop, Skibbereen).
Trout season 15 Feb.–12 Oct.; sea-trout, 1 Feb.–12 Oct.; salmon, 1 Feb.–31 Aug.
South-Western Region.

Inny (Kerry)
A spate river running 12 m to Ballinskelligs Bay north of Waterville.

Trout fair, salmon and sea-trout best in late heavy water. Fishing available through hotels in Waterville.

Trout season 15 Feb.–12 Oct.; sea-trout, 17 Jan.–12 Oct.; salmon, 17 Jan.–31 Aug.
South-Western Region.

Inny (Limerick)
Flows from L. Sheelin through Finea into L. Kinale.
Good pools near Ballymahon. Advisable to check on fishing results following drainage work. Central Fisheries Board water (see the introduction to this section). Trout, coarse fish.
Trout season 1 Mar.–30 Sept.
Shannon Region.

Island
A tributary of the Suck system.
Fair trout fishing. Central Fisheries Board water (see the introduction to this section).
Trout season 1 Mar.–30 Sept.
Shannon Region.

Joyce (Baelanabrack)
Flows into Maambay, Mask.
Trouting fair, and can hold big fish late in season. Inquire locally.
Trout season 17 Mar.–15 Sept.
Western Region.

Kilcolgan
Enters Galway Bay at Kilcolgan.
Fair fly water; some big trout. Best water preserved, but inquire locally for prospects.
Trout season 17 Mar.–15 Sept.
Western Region.

Killeglan
A tributary of the Suck system.
Fair trout fishing. Can run low in the summer. Central Fisheries Board water (see the introduction to this section).
Trout season 1 Mar.–30 Sept.
Shannon Region.

King's River
A moorland water offering small trout. Runs into Poulaphouca Reservoir at Valleymount. Inquiries to Dublin tackle shops.

Trout season 1 Mar.–30 Sept.
Eastern Region.

King's River (Kilkenny)
Flows through Callan to the River Nore.
Fair trout fishing, but patchy; some late salmon. Pike fishing good. Inquiries at Abbeyleix, Leix.
Trout season 1 Mar.–30 Sept.; salmon, 1 Feb.–31 Aug.
Southern Region.

Lacklagh
Drains Glenlough to head of Sheephaven Bay.
Fair trout fishing, with good runs of salmon and sea-trout May to September. Fishing through Rosapenna Hotel.
Trout season 15 Feb.–12 Oct.; sea-trout, 1 Jan.–30 Sept.; salmon, 1 Jan.–31 Aug.
Northern Region.

Laney
Joins the River Sullane at Macroom.
A good wet fly stream. Fishing through Macroom A A, B. Baker, South Square, Macroom.
Trout season 15 Feb.–12 Oct.
South-Western Region.

Laragh
Enters River Annalee in the Erne system between Cootehill and Ballyhaise.
Trout small but numerous. Inquire locally.
Trout season 1 Mar.–30 Sept.
Northern Region.

Laune
A 14-mile water draining Killarney lakes to the head of Dingle Bay.
Excellent salmon fishing, with sea-trout mainly in lower reaches. Some free fishing at Killorglin Bridge. Fishing through Tower Hotel, Glenbeigh Hotel, Glenbeigh, Co. Kerry.
Killorglin, Kerry. Water in area.
T, S T, S (D T Adv. permits obtainable in Killorglin and Milltown).
Tributaries: Flesk, Gaddagh, Gweestin, Finnglas, Cottoners.
Trout season 15 Feb.–12 Oct.; sea-

trout, 17 Jan.–12 Oct.; salmon, 17 Jan.–31 Aug.
South-Western Region.

Lee
A 10-mile water running into Tralee Bay at Tralee.

Salmon, sea-trout after summer spates. Trout fishing fair. Inquire locally.
Trout and sea-trout season 1 Apr.–30 Sept.; salmon, 1 Apr.–31 Aug.
South-Western Region.

Lee (Cork)
Flows 53 m by Ballingeary, Inchigeelagh, Macroom, Inniscarra and Cork to the sea.

Sandstone bed with natural lakes on its course, and some hydro work. Trout small above Ballingeary, otherwise fair. Some spring salmon below Inniscarra; best fishing preserved. Much free fishing above reservoirs and on tributaries. Fishing also through Macroom AA, B. Baker, South Square, Macroom.
Cork, Co. Cork. Fishing in area.
   ST (DT Adv. Cork Fishing Centre, MacCurtain Street, Cork).
   Tributaries: Toon, Sullance, Laney, Foherish, South Bride.
   Trout season 15 Feb.–12 Oct.; sea-trout, 1 Feb.–12 Oct.; salmon, 1 Feb.–31 Aug.
   South-Western Region.

Lennon
Originates in L. Gartan and runs 15 m through L. Fern to the sea at L. Swilly.

Good salmon lower reaches Feb. to May, middle reaches Apr. to June, upper reaches June to Aug. Trout mainly small. Permits from landowners, also tackle shops in area.
   Trout season 1 Mar.–12 Oct.; sea-trout, 2 Feb.–12 Oct.; salmon, 2 Feb.–31 Aug.
   Northern Region.

Lerr
Runs through Castlemount to the River Barrow above Carlow.

Good trout fishing.
Carlow, Co. Carlow. Stretch near Carlow.
   T (DT Adv. tackle shop, Carlow).
   Trout season 1 Mar.–30 Sept.
   Southern Region.

Lickey
A small stony stream with some pools entering the Blackwater estuary.

Some summer grilse when conditions right. Inquire locally.
   Trout season 15 Feb.–30 Sept.; salmon, 1 Feb.–31 Aug.
   Southern Region.

Liffey
Dublin's river. Rises to the south-west of the city and runs 80 m through Poulaphouca Reservoir, Kilcullen, Clane and Lucan to the Dublin boundary.

Despite some pollution of lower reaches, the river has some fair salmon runs with spring fish. Trout run to 1 lb on average. There is a good deal of pressure on Liffey trouting, most of it now being taken up by associations.
Clane, Kildare. Water in area.
   T (WT Adv. M. Casey, Firmount, Clane).
Newbridge, Kildare. 30 m in area.
   T, S (Inquire North Kildare Trout and Salmon AA, P. Byrne, 33 College Park, Newbridge).
Straffan, Kildare. Stretch in area and water at Ballymore Eustace, Clane and Celbridge.
   T (DT, WT Adv. Dublin Trout AA, M. Donahoe, Clonkeen Road, Deansgrange, Co. Dublin).
   Tributaries: King's River, Lisheen, Rye Water, Dodder.
   Trout season 1 Mar.–30 Sept.; sea-trout, 1 Jan.–30 Sept.; salmon, 1 Jan.–31 Aug.
   Eastern Region.

Lisheen
A stream running into the upper Liffey.

Trout occasionally bigger than in main river. Inquire from tackle shops in Dublin.
   Trout season 1 Mar.–30 Sept.
   Eastern Region.

Little Brosna

Fair to good dry fly water at Roscrea, Brosna and Sharavogue. Enters Shannon at Meelick. Salmon enter lower reaches. Trout to 2 lb. Central Fisheries Board water (see the introduction to this section).
Tributary: Camcor.
Trout season 15 Feb.–30 Sept.; salmon, 1 Mar.–31 Aug.
Shannon Region.

Little Silver

A tributary of the Brosna system.
Trout, mostly on small side. Some free fishing. Inquire locally.
Trout season 15 Feb.–30 Sept.
Shannon Region.

Mahon

Runs to sea at Bunmahon after passing through Kilmacthomas.
Fair wet fly trout fishing; some sea-trout. Inquiries to John Casey, tackle, Dungarvan, Co. Waterford.
Trout season 1 Mar.–30 Sept; sea-trout, 1 Feb.–30 Sept.
Southern Region.

Maigue

A fair limestone stream with big trout and some salmon. Dredging work makes fishing chances uncertain; inquire locally.
Tributaries: Morning Star, Camog.
Shannon Region.

Maine

A 20-mile water running to the head of Dingle Bay.
Sea-trout and salmon. Trout fishing fair. Late fishing best. Some free fishing in area; inquire locally.
Trout season 15 Feb.–12 Oct.; sea-trout, 17 Jan.–12 Oct.; salmon, 17 Jan.–31 Aug.
South-Western Region.

Mattock

Joins the River Boyne between Slane and Drogheda.
A good run of sea-trout; trout fishing fair. Mostly preserved.

Trout season 15 Feb.–15 Sept; sea-trout, 1 Feb.–15 Sept.; salmon, 1 Feb.–31 Aug.
Eastern Region.

Mealagh

An 11-mile water flowing into Bantry Bay 1 m north of Bantry.
Small trout; occasional summer salmon and sea-trout. Inquire locally.
Trout and sea-trout season 17 Mar.–12 Oct.; salmon, 17 Mar.–31 Aug.
South-Western Region.

Morning Star

A fair limestone stream joining the River Maigue between Bruree and Croom.
Trout. Inquire locally.
Trout season 15 Feb.–30 Sept.
Shannon Region.

Mountrath (White Horse River)

A stream joining the River Nore below Castletown.
Fair wet and dry fly water for trout. Information from Kilkenny tackle shops.
Trout season 1 Mar.–30 Sept.
Southern Region.

Moy

Runs a rocky, swift course with excellent salmon fishing to Swinford. Sea-trout in lower reaches. Good trout stream. Most of salmon fishing preserved. Free trout and sea-trout fishing in estuary with permission from the Moy Company Manager, Ballina. Fishing also through hotels in area.
Tributary: Deel.
Trout season 15 Feb.–10 Oct.; sea-trout, 1 Feb.–10 Oct.; salmon, 1 Feb.–31 Aug.
North-Western Region.

Mulcair

A 15-mile spate river running into the Shannon estuary above Limerick.
A fair run of spring salmon, with good grilse fishing from June onwards. Some trout.
Limerick, Co. Limerick. Stretch in area.
T, S (D T, W T Electricity Supply Board Office, 41 O'Connell Street, Limerick).

Trout season 15 Feb.–30 Sept.; salmon, 1 Mar.–31 Aug.
Shannon Region.

Multeen
Flows to the River Suir from the west above Golden.

Fair trout fishing. Inquire from tackle shops in Thurles, Cashel, Cahir, Clonmel and Carrick. In recent years some clubs have withdrawn visitors' tickets because of pollution on the Suir.

Trout season 1 Mar.–30 Sept.
Southern Region.

Munhin
A tributary of the Owenmore system running from L. Carrowmore.

Some sea-trout and salmon; small brown trout. Preserved.
North-Western Region.

Nanny
Enters the sea at Laytown, flowing through Duleek and Julianstown.

Fair trout fishing, with sea-trout in lower reaches. Some ticket fishing; inquire locally.

Trout season 15 Feb.–15 Sept.; sea-trout, 12 Feb.–15 Sept.
Eastern Region.

Neir
A rocky stream joining the River Suir above Clonmel.

Some good trout pools. Inquire locally.

Trout season 1 Mar.–30 Sept.
Southern Region.

Newport
A 7-mile water draining L. Beltra into Clew Bay at Newport.

Salmon good May to Aug., sea-trout July to Sept. Trout mainly small. Inquire from Newport House Hotel, Newport.

Trout and sea-trout season 20 Mar.–30 Sept.; salmon, 20 Mar.–31 Aug.
North-Western Region.

Nore
Rises in the Slieve Bloom foothills and runs 87 m past Abbeyleix, Kilkenny and

Inistiogue, where the sea-trout fishing is excellent, to join the River Barrow above New Ross.

Trout are small in the upper river but better in lower reaches, some to 6 lb. Spring salmon and a grilse run. Information on association water from Kilkenny tackle shops.

Tributaries: Mountrath, Gully, Erkina, Dinin, King's River.

Trout season 1 Mar.–30 Sept.; sea trout, 1 Feb.–30 Sept.; salmon, 1 Feb.–31 Aug.
Southern Region.

North Bride (Bride)
Flows through Rathcormac and Tallow to the Blackwater estuary below Cappoquin.

Trout mainly small in upper river but better in lower reaches. Sea trout, some grilse (summer). Dace and rudd. Information from Barbers, tackle, Fermoy.

Trout season 15 Feb.–30 Sept.; sea trout, 1 Feb.–30 Sept.; salmon, 1 Feb.–31 Aug.
Southern Region.

Oily
A 13-mile water entering McSwyne's Bay at Carrick.

Salmon best in August, sea-trout July and August. Inquire locally.

Sea-trout season 1 Mar.–9 Oct; salmon, 1 Mar.–31 Aug.
Northern Region.

Owenass
A headwater of the River Barrow.

Fair trout fishing; inquire locally.

Trout season 1 Mar.–30 Sept.
Southern Region.

Owenavorragh
A rocky stream flowing to the sea at Courtown Harbour.

Fair sea-trout; occasional summer salmon. Bayview and Courtown hotels offer water for guests.

Gorey, Wexford. Water in area.

T, ST (By arrangement with Gorey AC, E. Lacey, 22 Main Street, Gorey)

Sea-trout season 15 Mar.–30 Sept.; salmon, 15 Mar.–31 Aug.
Eastern Region.

Owenboliska
Drains L. Boliska, with a short run to the sea at Spiddal.

Summer salmon; good sea-trout fishing. Some free fishing in area; inquire locally.

Trout season 17 Mar.–15 Sept.; sea-trout, 1 Feb.–12 Oct.; salmon, 1 Feb.–31 Aug.
Western Region.

Owenduff (Ballycroy)
An 18-mile water entering Tullaghan Bay north of Ballycroy.

Good salmon and sea-trout fishing; brown trout small. Details from Rock House, Ballycroy, Co. Mayo. Occasional day lettings in area.

Trout season 15 Feb.–12 Oct.; sea-trout, 1 Feb.–12 Oct.; salmon, 1 Feb.–31 Aug.
North-Western Region.

Owenduff
A fair trout stream running to the south-east of New Ross.

Free fishing, with permission from owners.

Trout season 1 Mar.–30 Sept.
Southern Region.

Owenea
Runs through Glenties to Loughrosmore Bay.

Salmon, sea-trout; mostly preserved.
Northern Region.

Owengarve
A stream entering Clew Bay at Rosturk. Some grilse, sea-trout. Best late in season.

Westport, Mayo. Water in area.

ST, S (DT, WT Adv. R. G. Browne, Shop Street, Westport).

Sea-trout season 1 May–12 Oct.; salmon, 1 May–31 Aug.
North-Western Region.

Owenglin
An 11-mile water offering some summer

salmon and good sea-trout fishing. Trout mostly small. Inquire locally.

Trout season 15 Feb.–12 Oct.; sea-trout, 1 Feb.–12 Oct.; salmon, 1 Feb.–31 Aug.
Western Region.

Owengowla
A short river joining a complex of lakes to Bertraghboy Bay.

One of Ireland's best sea-trout waters, with good summer and autumn salmon fishing. Boats available through Zetland Hotel, Cashel Bay.

Season as Owenglin, above.
Western Region.

Oweniny
A tributary of the Owenmore system, flowing by Bellacorick.

Trout, small on the whole. Inquire locally. Some sea-trout and salmon.

Trout season 15 Feb.–30 Sept.; sea-trout, 1 Feb.–12 Oct.; salmon, 1 Feb.–31 Aug.
North-Western Region.

Owenmore
A 30-mile water running into the north-east corner of Tullaghan Bay.

Salmon and sea-trout lower reaches; mostly preserved.
North-Western Region.

Owenmore (Cloghane)
A short river running into Brandon Bay at Cloghane.

Salmon after summer spates; good sea-trout June to Oct. Inquire locally.

Trout and sea-trout season 1 Apr.–30 Sept.; salmon, 1 Apr.–30 Sept.
South-Western Region.

Owenruff
Tributary of the Corrib system.

Grilse in late season; salmon good in lower reaches April to July. Mostly preserved; inquire from Oughterard hotels.

Sea-trout season 1 Mar.–30 Sept.; salmon, 1 Feb.–31 Aug.
Western Region.

Owentaraglin
A headwater of the River Blackwater.
Trout mainly small. Inquire locally.
Trout season 15 Feb.–30 Sept.
Southern Region.

Owentocker
A 12-mile water entering Loughrosmore Bay at Ardera.
Fair trout fishing, with occasional salmon and sea-trout. Ticket fishing in area; inquire locally.
Trout and sea-trout season 1 Apr.–30 Sept.; salmon, 1 Apr.–31 Aug.
Northern Region.

Owenvane (Owvane)
Runs 13 m to Bantry Bay at Ballylickey.
Small trout; some salmon on summer floods; good sea-trout fishing, given water. Inquire locally.
Trout and sea-trout season 17 Mar.–12 Oct.; salmon, 17 Mar.–31 Aug.
South-Western Region.

Owenwee (Belclare River)
Flows to Clew Bay west of Westport, draining mountain lakes, including L. Nacorra and L. Moher.
Occasional salmon; good sea-trout. Brown trout small. Fishing through Slieve League Hotel, Carrick.
Trout season 15 Feb.–12 Oct.; sea-trout, 1 Feb.–12 Oct.; salmon, 1 Feb.–31 Aug.
Western Region.

Owvane (White River)
Enters the Shannon at Loghill between Glin and Foynes.
Trout small but numerous. Inquire locally.
Trout season 15 Feb.–30 Sept.
Shannon Region.

Raford
A tributary of the Kilcolgan.
Fair trout fishing, with occasional good fish. Inquire locally.
Trout season 17 Mar.–15 Sept.
Western Region.

Rea
Another Kilcolgan tributary.

Dry fly stream, with occasional good fish. Inquire locally.
Trout season 17 Mar.–15 Sept.
Western Region.

Robe
Passes to the south of Claremorris and runs through Hollymount and Ballinrobe to L. Mask.
Limestone water, with good trout, but weed can be a problem. Inquire locally.
Trout season 1 Mar.–30 Sept.
Western Region.

Roughty
A fast-flowing 19-mile water running to the head of the Kenmare river 2 m east of Kenmare.
Best sea-trout fishing May to Sept., with salmon from May to Aug. Spates help. Much water is preserved but worth inquiry to Kenmare Estate Office, Kenmare. Also day ticket through Kenmare AC, local tackle dealers.
Trout and sea-trout season 15 Mar.–12 Oct.; salmon, 15 Mar.–31 Aug.
South-Western Region.

Roury
A small stream, with a few fishable pools in the lower reaches, entering the sea at Mill Cove.
Some sea-trout, occasional salmon. Inquire locally.
Sea-trout season 1 Feb.–12 Oct.; salmon, 1 Feb.–31 Aug.
South-Western Region.

Royal Canal
Runs a more northerly route from Dublin to the Shannon system than the Grand Canal, and has not been navigable for the past 20 years. Some parts dry, and most of open water suffers from weed. The tench fishing can be excellent. Good coarse stretches at Enfield, Hill of Down and Mullingar. Free fishing.

Rye Water
A limestone stream entering the River Liffey at Leixlip.
Trout can be bigger than in main river. Inquiries to Dublin tackle shops.

Trout season 1 Mar.–30 Sept.
Eastern Region.

Shannon

Ireland's largest river, it drains a fifth of the country. Salmon run to the middle reaches, few progressing beyond L. Derg. Big trout. Perhaps the river is more famous for its excellent coarse fishing, especially huge shoals of bream and big pike.

It should not be forgotten that hire cruisers are a method of approaching coarse fishing. Fishing is available through the Central Fisheries Board (see the introduction to this section) and the Electricity Supply Board, 27 Lower Fitzwilliam Street, Dublin (local office 41 O'Connell Street, Limerick). Most of the coarse fishing is free.

Tributaries: Boyle, Inny, Suck, Brosna, Little Brosna, Mulcair.

Trout season above Portumna 1 Mar.–30 Sept.; below Portumna 15 Feb.–30 Sept.; salmon, 1 Mar.–31 Aug.
Shannon Region.

Silver

Tributary of the Brosna system. Fair trout fishing. Central Fisheries Board water (see the introduction to this section).

Trout season 15 Feb.–30 Sept.
Shannon Region.

Slaney

Rises in the Wicklow Mountains and flows 73 m to Wexford Harbour, draining a large area through many small tributaries.

Some spring fish. Salmon best at Enniscorthy and Tullow; fishing Tullow to sea mostly preserved. Good sea-trout fishing in lower reaches.

Enniscorthy, Wexford. 2 m stretch.

S, T (DT Adv. Enniscorthy and Dist. AA, P. Courtney, 5 Weafer Street, Enniscorthy).

Tullow, Carlow, 12 m water in area.

T, S (DT Adv. Tullow AA, W. Ward, The Square, Tullow).

Tributaries: Derreen, Derry, Urrin.

Trout season, source to Bann junction 26 Feb.–30 Sept.; below Bann junction 26 Feb.–15 Sept.; seatrout, above Bann junction, 26 Feb.–31 Aug.; below, 26 Feb.–15 Sept.; salmon, 26 Feb.–31 Aug.
Eastern Region.

Smerlagh

A tributary of the Feale system.

Fair trout fishing, with summer runs of salmon, sea-trout. Inquire locally.

Trout season 15 Feb.–30 Sept.; seatrout, 1 Mar.–30 Sept.; salmon, 1 Mar.–31 Aug.
Shannon Region.

South Bride

Runs to join River Lee near Ovens.

Mostly trout. Some free fishing; inquire locally.

Trout season 15 Feb.–12 Oct.
South-Western Region.

Suck

Flows from L. O'Flynn through Castlerea, Ballymoe, Athleague, Mount Talbot, Ballyforan and Ballinasloe to the Shannon at Shannonbridge.

Excellent coarse fishing, especially for bream, free. Trout can be big. Some salmon in lower reaches. Central Fisheries Board water (see the introduction to this section). Salmon fishing needs Electricity Board licence.

Tributaries: Francis, Island, Bunowen, Killeglan.

Trout season 1 Mar.–30 Sept.; salmon, 1 Mar.–31 Aug.
Shannon Region.

Suir

Rises on Devil's Bit Mountain and runs through Templemore, Thurles, Holycross, west of Cashel, through Golden, Cahir, Clonmel and Carrick-on-Suir to Waterford Harbour.

Best salmon fishing in lower reaches, with spring fish and grilse from June. Trout can be big, and there is some good dry fly water. Up-to-date local information is essential, because local clubs have withdrawn visitors' permits in recent years because of pollution on the Suir; ask tacklists in Thurles, Cashel, Cahir, Clonmel and Carrick for details.

Tributaries: Drish, Clodiagh, Multeen, Bansha, Aherglow, Neir, Anner.
Trout season 1 Mar.–30 Sept.; sea-trout, 1 Feb.–30 Sept.; salmon, 1 Feb.–31 Aug.
Southern Region.

Sullance
Runs south-west to the River Lee at Macroom.
Good trout fishing to wet or dry fly. Late fish run to 5 lb or more. Some fishing through Macroom AA, B. Baker, South Square, Macroom.
Trout season 15 Feb.–12 Oct.
South-Western Region.

Swilly
Flows 25 m to L. Swilly at Letterkenny.
Some sea-trout and salmon; fair trout fishing. Inquire locally.
Trout season 1 Mar.–12 Oct.; sea-trout, 2 Feb.–12 Oct.; salmon, 2 Feb.–31 Aug.
Northern Region.

Tay (Waterford)
A stream entering the sea at Stradbally.
Trout, with a sea-trout run June to Aug. Inquiries to John Casey, tackle, Dungarvan, Co. Waterford.
Trout season 1 Mar.–30 Sept.; sea-trout, 1 Feb.–30 Sept.
Southern Region.

Toon
Runs west of Macroom.
Holds mainly small trout, with bigger fish from River Lee late in season. Some free fishing; inquire locally.
Trout season 15 Feb.–12 Oct.
South-Western Region.

Tourig
Stream entering the Blackwater estuary above Youghal.
Trout, some sea-trout. Best July to Aug. Inquire locally.
Trout season 15 Feb.–30 Sept.; sea-trout, 1 Feb.–30 Sept.
Southern Region.

Trimblestown
A Boyne tributary flowing through Athboy to join the main river above Trim.
Good fly stream. Inquire locally.
Trout season 15 Feb.–15 Sept.
Eastern Region.

Triogue
A headwater of the River Barrow.
Fair numbers of trout. Inquire locally.
Trout season 1 Mar.–30 Sept.
Southern Region.

Tullaghobegley
Runs from L. Altan to the sea at Falcarragh.
Trout; some summer salmon and sea-trout. Inquire locally.
Trout season 15 Feb.–12 Oct.; sea-trout, 2 Feb.–12 Oct.; salmon, 2 Feb.–31 Aug.
Northern Region.

Urrin
Enters the River Slaney near Enniscorthy.
Fair trout fishing; inquire locally.
Trout season 26 Feb.–15 Sept.
Eastern Region.

Vartry
Small acid stream rising near Roundwood to flow to the sea at Wicklow.
Small trout. Inquire locally.
Trout season 1 Mar.–30 Sept.
Eastern Region.

Ward
Small stream running into Malahide Inlet.
Small trout; some sea-trout lower reaches.
Trout season 1 Mar.–30 Sept.; sea-trout, 1 Feb.–12 Oct.
Eastern Region.

Waterville
Short river draining L. Currange to Ballinskelligs Bay at Waterville.

Trout, sea-trout and salmon. Lake Hotel, Waterville, has fishing on famous Butler's Pool, available if not taken by guests.

Sea-trout season 17 Jan.–12 Oct.; salmon, 17 Jan.–31 Aug.

South-Western Region.

Yellow River

A tributary of the River Glen.

Fair trout fishing. Sea-trout fishing can be good late in season. Inquire locally.

Trout and sea-trout season 1 Mar.–9 Oct.

Northern Region.

Twelve

Irish Republic Still Waters

Like Northern Ireland, the South has such an extensive range of lake fishing that it would take a much larger catalogue than this to do it all justice. Instead, the waters below are those which are well known and which have proved themselves good fisheries.

Thousands of small lakes abound in many areas. One could, say, base oneself on Feakle in County Clare and spend a fortnight fishing a different lake every day, perhaps never seeing another angler. In such a situation there is wisdom in taking local advice about the best prospects, for one water may yield very little while another is bursting with fish.

The entries, then, serve as an introduction to Irish waters. Among them are superb coarse fisheries, offering bream as the mainstay, large pike, perch and rudd. Tench are now present in many waters in the Republic, often introduced, because the species has never been widespread. Likewise the roach is something of a rarity, although it is turning up in many places.

For the trout angler, the prospects can only be described as phenomenal; true, there are waters where the native trout are numerous but small, but most of the larger waters, particularly those in limestone areas, hold great trout in abundance. Some have hatches of mayfly and, later, daddy-longlegs, giving rise to the productive method of dapping a natural fly or imitative resemblance while the fish are madly set on clearing these insects off the water. At other times trolling a small spoon from a rowing boat will bring fish. The latter method will also take salmon and sea-trout in those waters where runs are maintained.

The greater part of these lake fisheries are free, although it should be added that parts may be reserved by fishing clubs or hotels, and a local inquiry is advisable prior to fishing. This is a land where inquiries are always welcomed with hospitality, and friendly advice is abundant.

Some waters, too, are maintained by the Central Fisheries Board, which offers day tickets and which anglers may join for a modest annual subscription. The address is given in the introduction to 'Irish Republic Rivers' above.

Co. Cavan

Annagh Lake, Butlersbridge.
● T (Central Fisheries Board water; see p. 229. Fly only).
Lough Gowna, Bellananagh.
T, C (Free. Parts of this big water lie in Co. Longford. A good trout water).
Lough Oughter, Cavan.
T, C (Free. In effect this is a chain of loughs fed by the Erne system. Excellent trout and coarse fishing. B available).
Lough Ramor, Virginia.
T, C (Inquire locally. The lough holds trout to a good size, with bream and rudd).
Lough Sheelin, Kilnaleck.
T (Central Fisheries Board water; see p. 229. Some of the trout run big in this water).
Moyduff Lake, Cootehill.
● T (Central Fisheries Board Water; see p. 229). Fly only).

Co. Clare

Kilbarron Lake, Feakle.
C mainly (Free. There are numerous lakes in this region, some, including Lough Bridget, holding tench in addition to bream, rudd, hybrids and pike).
Loughs Inchiquinn, Dromore, Atedaun and Corofin, Corofin.
T, C (Inquire locally. Much free coarse fishing for bream, pike, perch and rudd).

Connemara

Gowla Fishery, Cashel Bay.
T, ST, S (DT inquiries to Zetland Hotel, Cashel Bay. A lough chain offering some of the best sea-trout fishing in Ireland. B and ghillie available).

Co. Cork

Glenbower Lake, Killeagh.
T (Central Fisheries Board water; see p. 229).
Inchigeela Lakes, Inchigeela.
C (Free. Some good pike from these narrow lakes).
Lee Reservoir, Macroom.
● T (DT inquiries tackle shop, Macroom. Fair trout fishing).
Lough Avavl, Glengariff.
T (Central Fisheries Board water; see p. 229).

Donegal

Lough Fern, Millford.
T, S (Free).
Lough Gartan, Church Hill.
T (Inquire locally. Excellent trout fishing in this lake at the head of the Lennon river).
Lough Inch, Inch.
T, ST (Free).
Rosses Fishery, Dungloe.
T, ST (Inquiries to Sweeney's Hotel, Dungloe, or the Lodge, Doochary.

Good fishing in this loch chain. B available).

Galway

Boliska Lough, Spiddal.
T mainly (Free).
Castlegrove Lake, Tuam.
C (Inquire locally. Good fishing for pike, perch, bream and rudd).
Crumlin Fishery, Inverin.
T, ST, S (DT Adv. The Caretaker, Crumlin Fishery, Crumlin, Inverin. Excellent game fishing in this chain, which includes loughs Fadda, Ugga Beg and Ugga Mhor. B available).
Lough Corrib, Oughterrard.
T, S, C (Free. The largest lake in the republic, Corrib is famed for its big brown trout, especially in the mayfly season (usually the last week in May), when dapping produces large catches. Big pike also inhabit the water. B available).
Lough Nafooey, near Leenane.
C (Free. A good coarse water connected to Lough Mask).

Co. Kerry

Killarney Lakes, Killarney.
T, S (Free. The lakeland consists of Upper Lake, Muckross Lake and Lough Lein. Salmon enter Lough Lein from Feb. to July and Upper and Muckross lakes from Jan. to May. There are numerous smaller mountain waters offering free trout fishing).
Lough Caragh, Glenbeigh.
T, ST, S (DT inquiries to Glenbeigh and Towers hotels, Glenbeigh).
Lough Currane, Waterville.
T, S (Inquire locally).

Co. Leitrim

Lough Melvin, Bundoran, Donegal.
T, ST, S and char (Some free water, some held by hotels).

Co. Leix

Ballyfin Lake, Mountrath.
C (Mountrath and Dist. AA control water; inquire locally for permission. Holds pike, perch, tench and roach).

Co. Longford

Lough Gowna, near Granard.
T, C (Inquire locally. B available).
Lough Kinale, Granard.
C mainly (Central Fisheries Board water; see p. 229).
Lough Ree, Lanesborough.
T, C (Inquire locally. Another of the famous mayfly waters of Ireland, with the rise between late May and late June. The fish run to 10 lb, and in addition there are perch, pike, roach and bream. The shore borders counties Westmeath and Roscommon. B available).

Co. Louth

Drogheda Reservoirs, Drogheda.
T (DT Adv. from Drogheda Corporation. Fair trout fishing).

Co. Mayo

Castlebar Lakes, Castlebar.
● T (Free. Fly only).
Lough Carra, Ballygarries.
T mainly (Free. Good trout fishing).
Lough Conn, Castlebar.
T, S (Free).
Lough Cullen, Castlebar.
T, S (Free. B available).
Loughs Furnace and Feagh, Newport.
T, ST (Inquire hotels in area. L. Furnace is tidal and fishes well for sea-trout and some salmon. L. Feagh is a good sea-trout water).
Lough Mask, Ballinrobe.
T, C (Free. Another excellent dapping water. Trolling is also useful. The water also holds pike, perch and char).
Rooneth Lake, Louisburgh.
S, ST (Inquire locally).

Co. Monaghan

Emy Lake, Emyvale.
● T (Central Fisheries Board water; see p. 229. Fly only).
Lough Eagish, Castleblaney.
C (Free. Mostly pike and perch).
Lough Muckno, Castleblaney.
T, C (Free fishing. Both trout and pike can run big. B available. There are numerous free coarse lakes in the area, some holding carp in addition to pike, perch and rudd).
Lough Ross, Castleblaney.
T, C (Free. Pike in addition to fair trout fishing).

Co. Offaly

Pallas Lake, Birr.
● T (Central Fisheries Board water; see p. 229. The water has been stocked with rainbow trout).

Co. Roscommon

Lough Glinn, Castlerae.
C mainly (Free).
Lough Key, Boyle.
T, C (Inquire locally).
Lough O'Flynn, Castlerae.
T, C (Central Fisheries Board water; see p. 229).

Sligo

Lough Arrow, Ballinafad.
T (Free fishing. Stocked with rainbows and brown trout).
Lough Gara, Monasteraden.
T, C (Inquire locally).
Lough Gill, Sligo.
T, C (Some free. Inquire locally. Holds trout, bream, perch and pike).

Tipperary

Coumshinham and Crott's loughs, Carrick-on-Suir.

T (Inquire locally. Good trout fishing).

Lough Derg, Dromineer.

T, C (Free. A good dapping water, also spinning, trolling, with trout running to 10 lb. The mayfly rise is usually in the first week in May. B and ghillie available).

Co. Waterford

Belle Lake, Waterford.

C (Inquire locally. Holds pike, tench and rudd).

Clonmel Hill Lochs, Clonmel.

T (Inquire locally).

Knockaderry Reservoir, Waterford.

T (Inquire tackle shops, Waterford).

Co. Westmeath

Lough Derravaragh, Crookedwood.

T, C (Central Fisheries Board water; see p. 229. A good trout water with a mayfly hatch, also holding perch and pike).

Lough Ennel, Mullingar.

T, C (Central Fisheries Board water; see p. 229. Restocking promised at time of going to press. Trout to around 2 lb, perch, pike and rudd. B available. Fishing poor at present).

Lough Iron, Westmeath.

C mainly (Central Fisheries Board water; see p. 229. Holds tench in addition to rudd, bream and perch).

Lough Owell, Mullingar.

T (Central Fisheries Board water; see p. 229. B available).

White Lake, Castlepollard.

T (Central Fisheries Board water; see p. 229).

Co. Wexford

Wexford Reservoir, Wexford.

T (Inquire locally. Open 10 Mar.– 15 Sept.).

Co. Wicklow

Poulaphouca Reservoir, Leixlip Reservoir, Ballymore Eustace.

T (D T Adv. tackle shops, Dublin).

Roundwood Reservoirs, Roundwood.

T (D T Adv. tackle shops, Dublin).

Vartry Reservoir, Roundwood.

T (D T Adv. from Superintendent).

Angling Clubs and Associations

When approaching angling clubs for information, please remember that most secretaries do their work (and it can often be hard work) voluntarily, with no pay whatsoever. Please enclose a stamped, self-addressed envelope when you write.

Where information about the clubs' principal waters has been volunteered, it is given in the entries, and so are details of day tickets (DT), weekly tickets (WT) and annual or seasonal membership (ST). It should also be appreciated that club committees hold regular elections, and posts are likely from time to time to be passed into other hands. The entries in this guide were correct at the time it went to press.

England

Abingdon and Oxford Anglers' Alliance. M. J. Ponting, 4 Holyoare Road, Headington, Oxford. WT, ST. Member clubs are Clifton Hampden PS, Oxford APS and Oxford Alliance. Water on Thames, Evenlode, Ray and still waters.

Accrington and Dist. FC. Alan Balderstone, 42 Townley Avenue, Huncoat, Accrington, Lancs. DT.

Andover AA. C. M. Elms, 60 Gallaghers Mead, Andover, Hants. Temporary visitors' membership available.

Appletreewick, Barden and Burnsall AC. J. Mackrell, Mouldgreave, Oxenhope, near Keighley, W. Yorks. DT, WT, ST.

Asfordby SA. H. Birch, Riverside Cottage, Mill Lane, Asfordby, Melton Mowbray, Leics. Holds organized matches on R. Weaver.

Avon FA. J. E. Coombes, 19 Stella Road, Preston, Paignton, South Devon. WT, fortnightly, monthly.

Bath AA. A. J. Smith, 14 Hampton House, Grosvenor Road, London Road, Bath. Water on Avon, Cam Brook.

Bathampton AA. Dave Crookes, 25 Otago Terrace, Larkhall, Bath. R. Avon, Kennet and Avon Canal, Hunstrete Lake.

Bedford AC. Mrs M. E. Appleton, 18 Moriston Road, Bedford. DT, ST.

Bedlington and Blagdon AA. S. Symons, 8 Moorland Drive, Bedlington, Northumberland. DT to holiday residents only.

Belper AC. H. Fitton, 9 Holbrook Road, Belper, Derbyshire. Water on R. Derwent.

Bingley AC. P. Exley, 5 Highfield Road, Frizinghall, Bradford, W. Yorks. DT, ST.

Birmingham AA Ltd. 100 Icknield Port Road, Rotton Park, Birmingham B16 0AP. Extensive waters. ST.

Bodmin AA. Lt-Col. H. M. Ervine-Andrews, V. C., The Old Barn, St Neot, Liskeard, Cornwall. DT, WT, ST.

Border Anglers and Naturalists. H. Garside, 60 Queensway, Greenfield, near Oldham, Lancs.

Boston and Dist. AA. J. D. Maguire, 6 Churchill Drive, Boston, Lincs. DT, ST.

Bradford City AA. See Leeds and Liverpool Canal AA.

Bradford No. 1 AA. See Leeds and Liverpool Canal AA.

Bradford-on-Avon AA. B. Webster, 6 Lyneham Way, Trowbridge, Wilts. Water on Avon, Frome, Kennet and Avon Canal.

Braintree and Bocking AS. P. Thompson, 80 Kynaston Road, Panfield, near Braintree, Essex. S T.

Bristol Amalgamated AS. J. S. Parker, 16 Lansdown View, Kingswood, Bristol. Member clubs: Omnibus A C, City of Bristol, King William IV, Ridgeway, Portcullis, Flowerpot, Stapleton, Golden Carp, Silver Dace, Melksham, Adults. S T.

Bristol and West of England AF. B. J. Williams, 157 Whiteway Road, Bristol B S5 7R W.

Bungay Cherry Tree A C. I. Gosling, 37 St Mary's Terrace, Flixton Road, Bungay, Suffolk. WT, S T.

Calne AA. R. J. Reeves, 16 Wessex Close, Calne, Wilts. R. Avon, R. Marden.

Calpac (Central Association of London and Provincial A Cs). J. C. Watts, 9 Kemble Road, Croydon, Surrey. D T, WT, S T.

Cambridge Albion AS. R. Turpin, 79 King's Hedges Road, Cambridge. D T, S T.

Cammell Laird Sports Club (Angling Section). A. Webster, 3 Glenburn Avenue, Eastham, Wirral, Merseyside. D T, WT, S T.

Canterbury and Dist. AA. N. Stringer, Riverdale, Mill Road, Sturry, Canterbury, Kent. D T, S T.

Cheltenham A C. F. Selley, 2 Hollis Gardens, Hatherley, Cheltenham, Glos. D T, WT. Water on Avon.

Cheshire AA. F. R. James, 34 Sweetbriar Crescent, Crewe, Cheshire.

Chichester Canal AA. B. Minelbrook, 13 Grosvenor Gardens, Aldwick, Bognor Regis, West Sussex. D T, WT, S T.

Chichester and Dist. AS. Mrs Hilary Terry, 1 New Cottages, Coach Road, Shopwhyke, Chichester, Sussex. WT, S T.

Clifton Hampden PS. See under Abingdon.

Colchester APS. D. K. Upsher, 36 Winsley Road, Colchester, Essex. S T only for members within 30 m radius of Colchester.

Colnes AS. K. N. Murrells, 1 Aillie Bunnies, Earls Colne, Colchester, Essex. D T, S T.

Compleat Angler F C. J. M. Honeyball, The Cottage, Parkland School, Brassey Avenue, Eastbourne, Sussex.

Coventry and Dist. AA. Patrick O'Connor, 48 Loxley Close, Wood End, Coventry, Warwicks. D T, S T.

Dartford and Dist. APS. Club Secretary, Lake House, 2 Walnut Tree Avenue, Wilmington, Kent. D T for water at Brooklands, Dartford and Horton Kirby only; S T.

Derby AA. T. Hickton, 7 Crecy Close, Derby. D T, S T.

Derby AF. P. Fox, 16 Ecclesbourne Avenue, Duffield, Derbyshire. D T, S T.

Derby Railway Institute F C. K. Otterwell, 65 Leytonstone Drive, Mackworth Estate, Derby. Limited S T.

Devizes AA. B. K. Nisbeck, 20 Blackberry Lane, Potterne, Devizes, Wilts. D T, S T.

Diss and Dist. A C. M. Howard, 7 Marefield Road, Diss, Norfolk. S T.

Doncaster and Dist. AA. A. Slater, 45 Hindburn Close, Bissacarr, Doncaster, S. Yorks. D T, S T.

Dorchester AA. D. A. J. Pride, 47 Mellstock Avenue, Dorchester, Dorset. Rivers Stour, Frome and lakes. D T, S T.

Durweston AS. J. H. Thatchell, Methody, Durweston, Blandford, Dorset. Water on Avon. D T.

Earl of Harrington A C. J. Callaghan, 3 Calvin Close, Alveston, Derby. D T, S T.

Exeter and Dist. AA. D. L. Beaven, 46 Hatherleigh Road, Exeter, Devon. D T, WT, S T.

Furness FA. M. Beadle, 46 Newton Road, Dalton-in-Furness, Cumbria.

Gerrards Cross and Dist, AS. D. J. Turton, 11 Athol Way, off Ashdown Road, Hillingdon, Middx. S T.

Goole and Dist. AA. D. Whitaker, 39 Westbourne Grove, Goole, North Humberside. S T.

Guildford A S. G. J. Pank, 72 St Philips Avenue, Worcester Park, Surrey. D T for some water.

Harleston, Wortwell and Dist. A C. C. Smith, 23 Pilgrims Way, Harleston, Norfolk. D T, W T Weybread pits; S T Waveney.

Hawes and High Abbotside A A. A. H. Barnes, Maridene Gayle, Hawes, North Yorks. W T, S T. R. Ure and becks.

Hazeldine A A. J. W. Hazeldine, 8 Dudley Road, Sedgley, West Midlands. S T.

Hereford and Dist. A A. Ian Astley, The Lindens, Bishopstone, Hereford. D T, W T, S T.

Howden and Dist. A C. M. Redman, 46 Marshfield Avenue, Goole, North Humberside. D T, S T. R. Derwent.

Hull and Dist. A A. K. Bone, 44 Barrington Avenue, Cottingham Road, Hull, Humberside. S T.

Ilchester and Dist. A A. R. M. Hughes, 32 St Cleers Orchard, Somerton, Somerset. D T, S T. R. Yeo, brooks.

Ingleton A C. Mr Cresswell, 4 Ingleborough Park Drive, Ingleton, Yorks.

Isle of Wight Freshwater A A. S. Rolf, 22 Hillside Road, Newport, IoW. D T, W T, S T.

Izaak Walton (Staffs) A A. A. W. R. Alderson, 13 Lister Road, Cotonfields, Stafford.

Jenks and Cattell A C. T. C. Gilson, 25 Reedley Road, Sneyd Park, Essington, Wolverhampton. S T.

Kelvedon and Dist. A A. M. Frost, 1 Francis Road, Braintree, Essex.

Kent Westmorland A A. Hon. Sec., 11a Blae Tarn Road, Kendal, Cumbria. Limited D T, W T, S T. Kent, Mint, Sprint.

Keynsham A A. G. D. Bingham, 7 Cedar Drive, Keynsham, Bristol. Avon and Chew.

King's Arms and Cheshunt A S. J. Connor, 21 Salisbury Road, Enfield, Middx. D T, W T, S T.

King's Lynn A A. G. T. Bear, 1 Cock Drive, Downham Market, Norfolk. D T, W T, S T.

Lavington A C. M. D. Gilbert, Gable Cottage, 24 High Street, Erlestone, Devizes, Wilts. S T; restricted membership 225.

Leeds and Dist. A S A. Anglers Club, 75 Stoney Rock Lane, Beckett Street, Leeds. See Leeds and Liverpool Canal A A.

Leeds and Liverpool Canal A A. W. M. Troman, 7 Hall Road, Shipley, West Yorks. D T, W T. Combines these clubs: Leeds and Dist. A S A; Bradford City A A; Bradford No. 1 A A; Northern Anglers A A; Saltaire A A; Bingley A A; Keighley A A; Idle and Thackley A A and Halifax A A. All members of these clubs entitled to fish canal waters.

Leek and Moorlands W M C A C. D. White, 20 Campbell Avenue, Leek, Staffs. S T.

Leicester A S. P. A. Jayes, 6 Alston Road, Aylestone, Leicester.

Leicester and Dist. A S A. R. Green, 52 Skampton Road, Leicester.

Lincoln A A. T. McCarthy, 33 Chiltern Road, Brant Road, Lincoln. Match bookings F. E. Butler, 47 Nelthorpe Street, Lincoln.

Liskeard and Dist. A C. B. G. Wilson, The Bruff, Rilla Mill, Callington, Cornwall. D T, W T, S T.

Liverpool and Dist. A A. J. Johnson, 97 Liverpool Road North, Maghull, Liverpool. D T, S T. Canal waters, Leeds and Liverpool and Shropshire Union.

London A A. Mrs P. Ellis, 183 Hoe Street, Walthamstow, London E17. Extensive waters; some D T, S T.

Lower Teign F A. J. Michelmore, 19 Market Street, Newton Abbot, Devon. D T, S T.

Luton A C. D. W. Rayner, 35 Stratton Gardens, Luton, Beds. D T some water; S T.

Lyttleton A A. Mr Wilkes, 31 Mostyn Road, Stourport-on-Severn, Worcs. D T, W T, S T. Water on Severn includes 100-peg match stretch.

Maldon A S. P. Revill, Langford Limes, 94 Crescent Road, Heybridge, Maldon, Essex. Blackwater, Chelmer and Blackwater Canal, pits.

Middlewich AA. G. Stanier, 43 Elm Road, Middlewich, Cheshire. D T for R. Dane. S T Dane, Petty Pool, R. Weaver.

Milton Keynes AA. M. Sando, 6 Kipling Drive, Newport Pagnell, Bucks. D T, S T.

Newport Pagnell FA. F. J. Read, 19 Chicheley Street, Newport Pagnell, Bucks. S T.

Newton Abbot FA. D. J. Horder, c/o 3 Bradley Lane, Newton Abbot, Devon. D T, W T, S T.

Northern AA. G. Wilson, 11 Guildford Avenue, Chorley, Lancs. D T, W T, S T.

North Staffs Association of Anglers. F. Barrett, 177 Hartshill Road, Stoke-on-Trent, Staffs.

Northumbrian AF. P. A. Hall, 25 Ridley Place, Newcastle upon Tyne. R. Coquet, R. Tyne. Special visitors' permit.

Nottingham AA. E. Collin, 224 Radford Boulevard, Radford, Nottingham. D T, S T.

Oxford APS and Oxford Alliance. See under Abingdon.

Penrith AA. T. Cousin, 28 Mayburgh Avenue, Penrith, Cumbria. D T, W T, S T.

Peterborough AA. W. Yates, 75 Lawn Avenue, Peterborough, Cambs. D T, W T, S T.

Petworth AC. D. A. Pugh, 3 Cherry Tree Walk, Petworth, Sussex. S T.

Preston Centre Federated Anglers. G. Jones, 1 Camarron Road, Preston, Lancs. D T, S T.

Radcot A and PC. G. R. Neville, Clanville House, Bampton Road, Clanfield, Oxon. D T, W T, S T.

Retford AA. H. Oxby, 104 Moorgate, Retford, Notts. S T limited membership.

Richmond and Dist. AS. J. Legge, 9 St John's Road, Hipswell, Catterick Garrison, North Yorks. D T, S T, W T.

Ringwood and Dist. AA. J. Steel, 30 Monsal Avenue, Ferndown, Dorset. D T and W T some waters; S T.

Royal Leamington Spa AA. E. Archer, 9 Southway, Leamington, Warwicks. D T, S T.

Rugby FA. M. P. Wagstaff, 4 Crick Road, Hillmorton, Rugby, Warwicks. D T, S T.

Rye and Dist. AS. A. V. Curd, 34 The Maltings, Peasmarsh, near Rye, East Sussex. D T, W T, S T.

St George AC. R. Rudd, 29 Kingsdown Road, Trowbridge, Wilts.

St Helens AA. J. Corkish, 65 Laffak Road, Carr Mill, St Helens, Merseyside. S T.

Salisbury and Dist. AC. R. W. Hillier, 29 New Zealand Avenue, Salisbury, Wilts. D T, S T. Waters on Hants Avon, Bristol Avon, and others; also lakes.

Sheffield Amalgamated AS. A. Baynes, c/o Lansdowne Hotel, London Road, Sheffield. D T, S T.

Sheffield and Dist. AA. J. W. Taylor, 12 West Lane, Aughton, Sheffield. D T, S T.

Shiplake and Binfield Heath FC. George Harris, 16 Green Lane, Sonning Common, near Reading, Berks. S T.

Shropshire Union Canal AA. R. Brown, 10 Dale Road, Golbourne, Warrington, Lancs.

Skipton AA. J. W. Preston, 18 Beech Hill Road, Carleton, Skipton, North Yorks. D T, W T, S T. R. Aire and reservoirs.

Slaithwaite and Dist. AC. A. Bamforth, 43 Binn Road, Marsden, Huddersfield, W. Yorks. D T, S T.

Sommerfields AC. Stan Harris, 73 Burnside, Brookside, Telford, Salop. D T, S T.

Stamford AC. C. Howard, Stamford Angling and Sports Centre Ltd, 13A Foundry Road, Stamford, Lincs. S T.

Stinchcombe and Cooper AC. The Secretary, Stinchcombe and Cooper Ltd, Northgate, Aldrige, West Midlands. S T.

Stoke City and Dist. AA. P. Johansen, 31 East Crescent, Sneyd Green, Stoke-on-Trent, Staffs. S T.

Stone and Dist. AS. J. Harrison, 20 Gower Road, Stone, Staffs. D T, W T, S T.

Suffolk County Amalgamated AA. G. W. Howard, 4 Morrifield Road, Lowestoft, Suffolk. D T, W T, S T. R. Waveney.

The Swindon Isis AC. J. A. Mc-

Donald, 35 Hawkswood, Covingham, Swindon, Wilts. S T.

Thornaby A A. D. Speight, 10 Stainsby Gate, Thornaby, Cleveland. S T. Access to R. Tees, R. Swale, R. Wear by written application with donation to club.

Todmorden A S. D. Howorth, 42 Hallroyd Crescent, Todmorden, Lancs. S T.

Ulverston A A. H. B. Whittam, 29 Lyndhurst Road, Ulverston, Cumbria. D T, S T Ulverston Canal, but let most weekends for matches.

Upper Culm F A. T. A. Blackmore, Sunset, Clayhidon, Cullompton, Devon. D T, W T, S T.

Wallingford Jolly Anglers F C. W. Biggs, 16 Radnor Road, Wallingford, Oxon. D T, W T, S T. Thames.

Warrington A A. J. S. Jackson, 23 Nora Street, Warrington, Lancs.

Wath Brow and Ennerdale A A. D. Edwards, 65 Trumpet Road, Wath Brow, Cleator, Cumbria.

Wellingborough Nene and Dist. A C. G. W. Barker, 139 Knox Road, Wellingborough, Northants. D T, S T.

Wellington and Dist. A A. H. Hayes, 1 Tonegate, Wellington, Somerset. D T, W T.

Whitmore Reans Constitutional A A. R. Harold Hughes, F C A, Star Chambers, Princes Square, Wolverhampton. D T, S T.

Wigan and Dist. A A. W. Gratton, 66 Balcarres Road, Aspull, Wigan, Greater Manchester.

Windermere, Ambleside and Dist. A C. John Cooper, Rylstone, Limethwaite Road, Windermere, Cumbria. D T, W T, S T. Rivers Rothay, Brathay, Troutbeck, also Rydal Water and tarns.

Winsford A A. J. S. Bailey, 22 Plover Avenue, Winsford, Cheshire. D T, S T.

Witham and Dist. Joint A F. R. Hobley, 30 Gunby Avenue, Hartsholme Estate, Lincoln. Extensive waters, including Witham. D T, S T.

York A A. J. Horsley, 20 Burnholme Grove, York. D T, S T.

York and Dist. Amalgamated A S. E. Woodward, 204 Salisbury Terrace, York.

Wales

Caergwrle A C. R. Mathers, 29 Hawarden Road, Hope, Wrexham, Clwyd. S T. R. Alyn.

Chirk A A. L. Davis, 76 Longfield, Chirk, near Wrexham, Clwyd. D T, W T, S T fly only; rivers Ceiriog and Dee.

Clwyd A C. B. J. B. Roberts, 4 Bryn Goodman, Ruthin, Clwyd. S T.

Dee A A. E. E. Owen, 2 Snowdon Crescent, Lache Lane, Chester. S T. R. Dee.

Denbeigh and Dist. A C. J. D. Gambles, 38 Crwd-y-Castell, Denbeigh, Clwyd. S T with waiting list; 2 D Ts per day available.

Dolgarrog F C. F. A. Corrie, 3 Taylor Avenue, Dolgarrog, Conwy, Gwynedd. D T, W T, S T, limited. R. Conwy and 2 lakes.

Glynneath and Dist. A A. R. W. Cole, 24 Woodlands Park Drive, Caddoxton, Neath, West Glamorgan. D T, W T, S T.

Llandeilo A A. D. Richards, Llysnewydd, Ffairfach, Llandeilo, Dyfed. D T, W T, and S T with waiting list.

Llay Hall A A. M. Tilley, Daisy Bank, Kellows Lane, Caergwrle, near Wrexham, Clwyd. W T, S T.

Montgomeryshire A A. Reg Thomas, 128 Oldford Rise, Welshpool, Powys. D T, W T, S T. Severn and tributaries; also 3 m canal match stretch, tel. Simon Pugh, 0938 4408.

Rossett and Gresford Flyfishers Club. P. H. Leng, 17 Greenfield Road, Little Sutton, South Wirral, Cheshire. S T only. R. Alyn.

Scotland

Berwick and Dist. A A. J. Moody, 12 Hillcrest, East Ord, Berwick-on-Tweed. D T, W T, S T. R. Whiteadder.

Drongan Youth Group A C. John Hunter, 52 Bonnyton Avenue, Drongan, Ayrshire. S T only. R. Coyle; trout only.

Eden A A. James Fyffe, 67 Braehead, Cupar, Fife. D T, S T.

Gala A A. R. H. Watson, 41 Balmoral

Avenue, Galashiels, Selkirks. DT, WT, ST.

Glasgow and West of Scotland CFA. J. Frackleton, Flat 14/5, 140 Charles Street, Glasgow.

Greenlaw AA. A. Lamb, Waterford, Greenlaw, Berwicks. DT, ST.

Greenock and Dist. AA. Brian Peterson, 22 Murdieston Street, Greenock. DT, WT, ST. L. Thom, L. Compensation and reservoirs.

Gretna Green AA. J. Mills, Kirtleside Farm, Rigg, Gretna, near Carlisle, Cumbria. DT, WT, ST.

Inverurie AA. James E. Duncan, 6 West High Street, Inverurie, Aberdeenshire. DT, WT, ST.

Kilmaurs AC. J. Watson, 7 Four Acres Drive, Kilmaurs, Ayrs. DT, ST. R. Anwick, Glazert Water.

Kilsyth Fish Protection Association. W. Claris, 34 John Wilson Drive, Kilsyth. DT, ST.

Kilwinning Eglinton AC. M. S. Tudhope, 15 Viaduct Circle, Kilwinning, Ayrs. DT, ST.

Kintyre Fish Protection and AC. J. Tunnah, Ceolmara, Peninver, Campbeltown, Argylls. DT, WT, ST.

Kirriemuir AC. H. F. Burnen, 13 Clora Road, Kirriemuir, Angus. DT, ST. No Sunday fishing. ST restricted to Kirriemuir. South Esk.

Larbert and Stenhousemuir AC. A. M. Arthur, Lynwood, 11 Old Bellsdyke Road, Larbert, Stirlings. DT, ST.

Lauderdale AA. D. M. Milligan, 2 Sidegate Mews, Haddington, East Lothian. DT, ST.

Loch Lomond AIA. R. A. Clerment & Co., Bank of Scotland Building, 224 Ingram Street, Glasgow. DT, WT L. Leven; ST waters feeding L. Leven.

Montrose AC. G. S. Taylor, Brago, Russell Street, Montrose, Angus. DT, WT, ST, limited.

Newton Stewart and Dist. AA. J. Stuart Loy, Park Cottage, Creetown, Newton Stewart, Wigtownshire. DT, WT, ST.

North Berwick AC. G. B. Woodburn, 29 Craigleith Avenue, North Berwick, East Lothian.

Rannoch and Dist. AC. J. Brown, The Square, Kinloch Rannoch, Perths. DT, WT, ST.

St Boswells AA. R. Black, Kilgraden, Springfield Terrace, St Boswells, Roxburgh. DT, WT, ST.

St Mary's AC. J. Miller, 6 Greenbank Loan, Edinburgh. DT, WT, ST. St Mary's Loch, Loch o'the Lowes.

Shetland AA. A. Miller, 3 Gladstone Terrace, Lerwick, Shetland Islands.

Stranraer and Dist. AA. J. Johnstone, 13 Dalrymple Court, Stranraer, Wigtowns. DT, WT, ST.

United Clyde Angling Protective Association. J. Quigley, 15 Auchter Road, Cambus Court, Wishaw ML2 8PJ.

Northern Ireland

Banbridge AC. Mrs William Martin, Lenaderg, or Anglers Rest, Corbet, Katesbridge. DT. Upper Bann.

Belfast AC. R. Buik, 7 Knockvale Grove, Belfast 5.

Belfast Pikers. L. Nixon, 7 Sharmon Park, Stranmillis, Belfast 9.

Castlewellan and Annesborough AC. P. Garland, 8 Annesborough Park, Annesborough, Castlewellan. DT. Ballylough Lake.

Clady and Dist. AC. Tickets from McErlean's Bar or Weir's Bar, Clady. Clady River.

Enniskillen, Erne Anglers. Ken Stewart, 114 Windmill Heights, Enniskillen, Co. Fermanagh.

Glebe AA. F. Elliott, 111 Lower Main Street, Strabane, Co. Tyrone. DT, ST. River Finn.

Gracehill, Galgorm and Dist. AC. Tickets from T. McCord's shop, Bridge End, Galgorm. River Maine.

Iveagh AC. Tickets through Sidney Beckett, sports outfitter, 54 High Street, Lurgan. Lagan River.

Lisnaskea, Sir Richard Arkwright AC. Bob Maher, Derryharney, Enniskillen.

Newry and Dist. AA. Tickets from P. McCourt, Church Street, Newry. Clanrye River, Grinan Lake.

Omagh AA. Tickets from Tyrone Angling

Supplies, Bridge Street, Omagh. D T. Rivers Strule, Camowen, Owenkillew and Drumragh.

Randalstown A C. C. Spence, Toome Road, Randalstown. D T. River Maine.

Rathfriland A C. Tickets from The House of David Crory Ltd, Main Street, Rathfriland. Upper Bann.

Shimna A C. Tickets from Mackies, jewellers, 125 Main Street, Newcastle. Shimna River.

Warrenpoint, Rostrevor and Dist. A C. Tickets from P. J. Murtagh, sports shop, The Square, Warrenpoint. Mill Dam, Waterworks.

Irish Republic contacts, by district

Athlone, Midland A C. Barry Brill, 31 Battery Heights, Athlone, Co. Westmeath.

Athlone, Athlone A A. Aidan Gallagher, Ardkeenan, Drum, Athlone, Co. Westmeath.

Athy. Mrs Jo Ann Snell, 25 Avondale Drive, Athy, Co. Kildare.

Ballinakill. Denis Bergin, The Square, Ballinakill, Co. Laois.

Ballinamore. P. J. Martin, Ballinamore, Co. Leitrim.

Ballinasloe. Patrick Lawless, 4 Hillcrest Park, Ballinasloe, Co. Galway.

Ballyforan. Michael Donohue or Frank Grogan, Ballyforan, Co. Roscommon.

Ballygar. Patsy Scanlon, Ballygar, Co. Galway.

Ballymote. Michael Wilcox, Ballymote, Co. Sligo.

Cappoquin. William Deavy, Richmond House, Cappoquin, Co. Waterford.

Carrickmacross. Tom Ward, Coolfore, Carrickmacross, Co. Monaghan.

Castlepollard. Vincent Baker, Castlepollard, Co. Westmeath.

Cavan. Mrs B. O'Hanlon, St Martin's Creegham, Cavan.

Drumconrath. Jim Meade, Drumconrath, Co. Meath.

Dublin. Nicholas Bolger, 36 Farney Park, Dublin 14.

Enfield. Bill Carey, Enfield, Co. Meath.

Fermoy. Jack O'Sullivan, 4 Patrick Street, Fermoy, Co. Cork.

Lanesborough. Tony Dalton, 24 The Green, Lanesborough, Co. Longford.

Loch Gowna. Jimmy Sloan, Loch Gowna, Co. Cavan.

Lough Allen A C. B. McGourty, Carrick Road, Drumshambo, Co. Leitrim.

Mallow. David Willis, 7 Dromore Drive, Mallow, Co. Cork.

Mohill. Willie Burns, Mohill, Co. Leitrim.

Monaghan. Thomas McEntee, 46 Dublin Street, Monaghan.

Newmarket-on-Fergus. R. G. V. Boelens, Carrowmere, Newmarket-on-Fergus, Co. Clare.

Plassey. John Morrison, 42 Rossa Avenue, Limerick.

Prosperous. Oliver Reilly, Prosperous, Co. Kildare.

Rooskey, Rooskey and Dist. Anglers. Mrs Bride Duffy, Rooskey, Co. Roscommon.

Scarriff, Mount Shannon and Whitegate A C. P. Cahill, Mountshannon, Co. Clare.

Scarriff, Chipboard A C. Joe Murphy, Mountshannon Road, Scarriff, Co. Clare.

Shannonbridge. Dermot Kileen, Shannonbridge, Co. Offaly.

Shannon Town. Mrs Mary Byrne, Shannon Town Centre, Co. Clare.

Tulla. Brian Culloo, N. T. Tulla, Co. Clare.

MAPS

14

NORTHERN
IRELAND

DONEGAL

BELFAST

SLIGO

13

GALWAY

DUBLIN

IRELAND

LIMERICK

KILLARNEY
CORK

12